# AK-47

## SURVIVAL AND EVOLUTION OF THE WORLD'S MOST PROLIFIC GUN

## MARCO VOROBIEV

Published by

Gun Digest® Books, an imprint of Caribou Media
Gun Digest Media, P.O. Box 12219, Zephyr Cove, NV 89448
www.gundigest.com

To order books or other products call 1-920-471-4522
or visit us online at **www.gundigeststore.com**

CAUTION: Technical data presented here, particularly technical data on handloading and on firearms adjustment and alteration, inevitably reflects individual experience with particular equipment and components under specific circumstances the reader cannot duplicate exactly. Such data presentations therefore should be used for guidance only and with caution. Caribou Media accepts no responsibility for results obtained using these data.

ISBN-13: 978-1-946267-10-8
ISBN-10: 1-946267-10-4

Cover Design by Al West
Designed by Dave Hauser
Edited by Corrina Peterson and Corey Graff

Printed in the United States of America

10 9 8 7 6 5 4 3 2 1

# RELATED BOOKS

Available at Gundigest.com

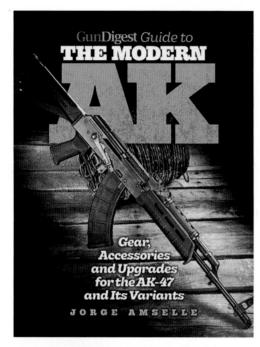

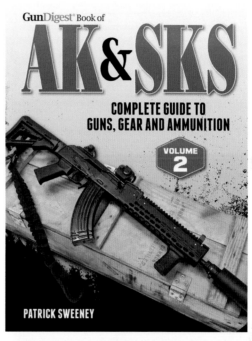

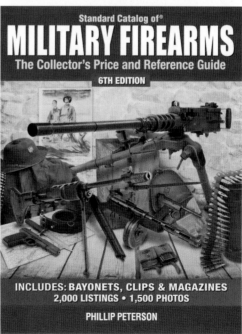

# DEDICATION

## To my family.

Family. It encompasses many things, is represented by a variety of situations and characters, and ultimately defines who we are. To each, it has different meaning. It often includes real and abstract objects, places, people, etc., like the happiest place or the warmest place in the universe and such. It represents our base, the foundation from where we really come from, the roots, something to lean on, something that has your back no matter what. It includes those who came before you, those who are around you and those who will be there after you are gone. It's the unit that instills values into you, the launching pad, the safe cove and a support base.

At least that's what you want your family to be. I understand that not all of us have families that are as solid, as reliable, as supportive as we want them to be. Nevertheless, families are families, with a full range of complicated relationships and dynamics. I am one of those lucky individuals who has the solid base, the unwavering support, the shoulder to lean on, the oasis of love and understanding—my family.

I always thought that my family was ordinary. My ancestors can be traced to the 1500s from the northern Baltic region called Svear. Most of the men in my line were involved in blacksmithing and manufacturing. All male ancestors, at least the ones I know about, served in the military. Many died fighting wars. Most of the women were strong-willed and independent, and ruled their households with an iron fist, typical of the northern Russians. One of my great-grandfathers served in the Tsar's own Loeb Guard Engineering Battalion in St. Petersburg and fought in World War I before returning and settling as an office worker for a silverware manufacturing plant. The other was an NCO and fought during the Great War, receiving a St. George Cross for bravery and distinction. After discharge, he also worked as bookkeeper at the same factory. His brother, a Cavalry Lieutenant, perished during one of the cavalry charges.

My grandfathers were both killed in World War II. One, a Winter War veteran, squad leader, and sergeant, died in December of 1941 in a desperate attempt to break through the Nazi's siege of Leningrad to resupply the city with much needed provisions. The other was a scout, and died in 1943 near Kaluga from sniper fire during a raid behind enemy lines in an attempt to secure a prisoner. All of their brothers and cousins, 12 men in total, perished on the fields of WWII.

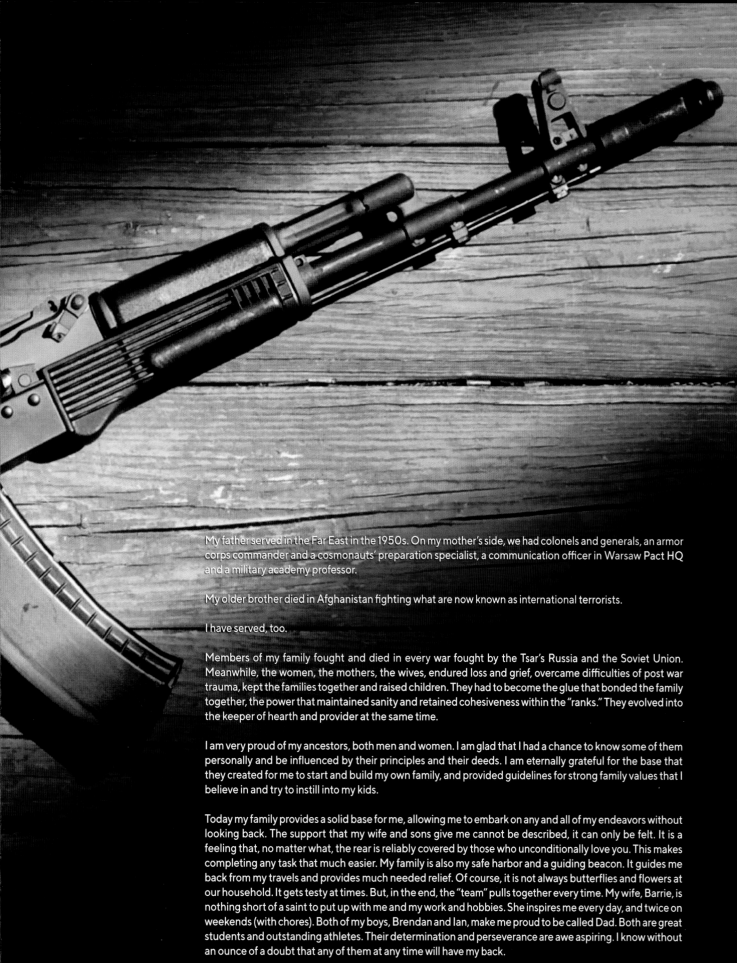

My father served in the Far East in the 1950s. On my mother's side, we had colonels and generals, an armor corps commander and a cosmonauts' preparation specialist, a communication officer in Warsaw Pact HQ and a military academy professor.

My older brother died in Afghanistan fighting what are now known as international terrorists.

I have served, too.

Members of my family fought and died in every war fought by the Tsar's Russia and the Soviet Union. Meanwhile, the women, the mothers, the wives, endured loss and grief, overcame difficulties of post war trauma, kept the families together and raised children. They had to become the glue that bonded the family together, the power that maintained sanity and retained cohesiveness within the "ranks." They evolved into the keeper of hearth and provider at the same time.

I am very proud of my ancestors, both men and women. I am glad that I had a chance to know some of them personally and be influenced by their principles and their deeds. I am eternally grateful for the base that they created for me to start and build my own family, and provided guidelines for strong family values that I believe in and try to instill into my kids.

Today my family provides a solid base for me, allowing me to embark on any and all of my endeavors without looking back. The support that my wife and sons give me cannot be described, it can only be felt. It is a feeling that, no matter what, the rear is reliably covered by those who unconditionally love you. This makes completing any task that much easier. My family is also my safe harbor and a guiding beacon. It guides me back from my travels and provides much needed relief. Of course, it is not always butterflies and flowers at our household. It gets testy at times. But, in the end, the "team" pulls together every time. My wife, Barrie, is nothing short of a saint to put up with me and my work and hobbies. She inspires me every day, and twice on weekends (with chores). Both of my boys, Brendan and Ian, make me proud to be called Dad. Both are great students and outstanding athletes. Their determination and perseverance are awe aspiring. I know without an ounce of a doubt that any of them at any time will have my back.

Thank you, my family.

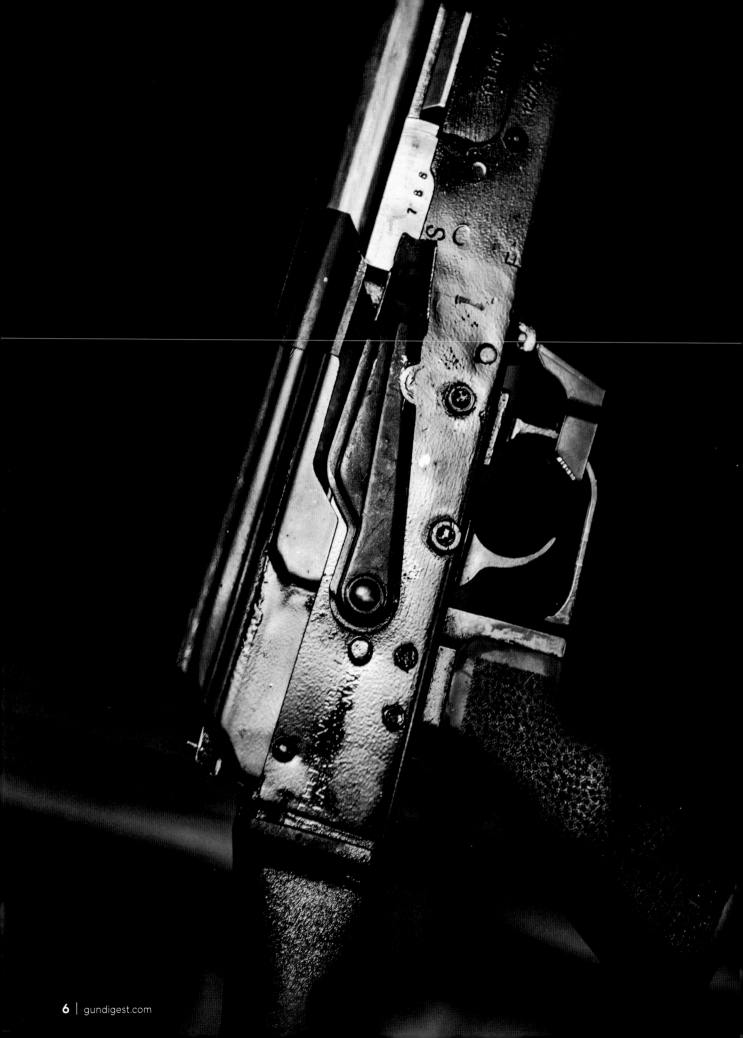

# CONTENTS

# FOREWORD

Students of Mikhail Kalashnikov and his iconic weapons will find this book as refreshing as it is informative. Marco Vorobiev pulls the murky mystery away from a world-class (and world-changing) story of technical and personal triumph. The broad brushstrokes are well known: While a humble tinkerer convalesces from combat wounds he reveals a genius for design. Fast forward over many difficulties and suddenly the distinctive silhouette of the Kalashnikov is more recognized than the Coke bottle. Seven decades later, the AK-47 is still the most popular military weapon on the planet. How did it survive to become so?

Vorobiev writes from a wonderful perspective—that of the combat veteran who has come to admire his rifle to the point of reverence. As a young Soviet, Vorobiev scrambled over the hillsides of Afghanistan, a Spetsnaz commando with a Kalashnikov. When the wall went down, he was among the first to emigrate. He became completely devoted to the "American dream" and today has an American family and business. But he remains in close contact with Russian friends, many of whom are the sources of the intricate details of the peaks-and-valleys story of the most manufactured rifle in the world.

Tech junkies can wade into all sorts of manufacturing details, while first-time readers on the subject will delight in a fast-paced, fact-filled narrative. Vorobiev started learning English in his late 20s, about the same time as Josef Conrad. Like Conrad, his prose sometimes still has a certain Slavic lilt to it. I found it high-spirited and friendly, as if I'd just met a new friend. But I'm honored to have been a friend, peer and student of Marco for more than a decade.

When you finish this fascinating journey, you the reader will likely become the authority on all things Kalashnikov within your club or group of shooting friends. In future decades, this piece of outstanding research will become a primary source material for historians, as well as inspiration for inventers and engineers. How Mikhail Kalashnikov, the optimistic tank sergeant from Siberia, overcame mountains of disappointment and a political deck stacked against him is an impressive human story, and Vorobiev is the man to tell it.

Richard Venola
Beatty, Nevada
2018

# ACKNOWLEDGMENTS

It's not easy to be a writer. It's even harder to be a gun writer. Not everyone can tell a good story. Even fewer people can tell a correct gun story. Novelists can look forward to the possibility of their books making it on the New York Times best seller list, or even Oprah's Book Club, with promises of financial rewards often associated with worldwide recognition. The fate of common gun writer is less prosperous. In fact, we need a day job to support the ability to write about the things we love. Unlike a novelist, who usually is a decent researcher and sometimes a good storyteller, an average gun writer has to be a researcher, historian, layman gunsmith, somewhat of a marksman, technically savvy, firearm trained and at the end hopefully not a boring storyteller. Gun writers' work depends on many people and companies. Often times your relationship with those people and companies determines what and how you write an article or a book. Luckily for me I was able to build strong professional relationships with many companies in the firearm industry and, more so, great personal relationships with people who work and/or run these companies. Their continuous support makes my job much easier.

When I embarked on the adventure that this book represents, I knew that writing it would take me not only to the historical archives literal and virtual, but also to the current situation surrounding the AK rifle. It was quickly evident that I'd need help, not only with information, but also with more tangible items like the rifles themselves and the accessories.

There are many companies that I want to thank for providing me with valuable help in completing this book: one of the leaders in the accessories business, always innovating Midwest Industries, Inc. out of Waukesha, WI (midwestindustriesinc.com); no introduction needed, always exciting, firearm accessories powerhouse MagPul (magpul.com); one of the largest U.S. AK rifles manufacturer I.O., Inc., out of Palm Bay, FL (ioinc.us); firearm everything, U.S. firearm importer and manufacturer, the company responsible for millions of smiles on the faces of happy American AK shooters Century Arms (centuryarms.biz); the innovator, the inventor, the gunsmithing god and creator of infamous "Assneck" rifle, Krebs Custom (krebscustom.com); the leader in affordable quality ammunition, always ready to help, Wolf Performance Ammunition (wolfammo.com); optics innovator, maker of the first AK-designated scopes and a friend, Hi-Lux, Inc.(hi-luxoptics.com); the most pleasant and helpful, world leader in squid jigs manufacturing Armament Technology, Inc., Tangent Theta, Inc., and ELCAN Optical Technologies (armament.com); no substitute, no compromise, no replacement in sight, must-have precision Black Hills Ammunition (black-hills.com); AK accessories supplier and trend influencer FAB Defense (themakogroup.com); importer of exotic, hard-to-find AK parts and accessories Legion USA (legionusa.com); source for outstanding modern AK optics, Primary Arms (primaryarms.com); soon becoming a leader in everything optics, Vortex (vortexoptics.com); my neighbor and just good bunch of folks, EOTech (eotechinc.com); world-renowned trigger magicians Geissele Automatics and its sister AGL Defense (geissele.com, algdefense.com). Also smaller guys who, though small, continue to innovate and produce outstanding product that I used writing this book: the maker of excellent AK side mounts RS Regulate in Michigan (rsregulate.com); the maker of unique LINCH (left-hand charging handle for AKs) Davis Tactical Solutions (davistacticalsolution.com); the gunsmith extraordinaire Erie Ordnance Depot in Portage, OH.

I would also be hard pressed to write without help and inspiration from gun industry friends and colleagues, consummate firearms professionals: David Fortier, Marc Krebs, Dillard "CJ" Johnson, Patrick Sweeney, Timothy Yan, Bill Alexander, Richard Parker, James Tarr, Troy Storch, Jeff Hoffman, Bill Geissele, Uli Wiegand, Bill Filbert, SGM Kyle Lamb USA (ret.), Scot Hoskisson, John Wu and Alex Sergeyev. And my personal friends Eric Mustafin, Anton Vatniskiy, Jim Weishuhn, Charlie McMahon, Fadil Issa and Scott Shmunk.

I also would like to thank all the World War II veterans on both sides of the "pond," those who are still with us, those who gave all and those who have passed away since. Every year the veterans' ranks shrink dramatically. Without their sacrifice, I would be writing this in German if at all. Also, those who recently answered the call and put on a uniform to face other threats, the other plague – international terrorism. I salute you all.

And last but not least, I want to express my gratitude to all the service men and women who stand on the wall today. Who through their service, dedication and sacrifice provide the freedom allowing someone like me to exercise my liberty, express myself and write articles and books. Thank you and godspeed.

*Images in this book are by Peter Draugalis (www.draugalisphotography.com), Richard King (Richard King Photography), Vitally Kuzmin, Marco, Brendan and Ian Vorobiev and/or came from Vorobiev's personal archives and other open public sources.*

# ABOUT THE AUTHOR

Marco was born in the foothills of the Southern Ural Mountains in the city of Orsk in the Soviet Union to Evgeniy and Tatiana Vorobiev. In 1973, his family relocated to a regional center city of Orenburg. Marco's father, an avid fisherman and hunter, would take Marco and his brother to an air rifle range every weekend to teach them the basics of Marcosmanship. At school, Marco and all of the children were introduced to .22 competition rifles and the basics of proper firearm handling. This was coupled with bi-annual trips to the school's 50-meter gun range. At age 12, as part of scout games, Marco was introduced to the AK rifle. At 15, as a future conscript, he started the mandatory beginner's military preparation class at the high school.

By his graduation, he could disassemble an AK in 12 seconds flat and had shot his future service rifle twice.

At the same time, like many Soviet boys, Marco played ice hockey, but at age 12, he became interested in SAMBO wrestling and joined one of the premier clubs. At age 15, he had won a junior national championship. One year later, he placed third in the USSR senior nationals.

After graduating from high school, he was accepted on an athletic scholarship to Orenburg Polytechnic Institute School of Mechanical Engineering, where he studied mechanical engineering and continued to wrestle, placing high at junior and senior nationals for both Sambo and Judo, and earning him the rank of Master of Sports of USSR in Sambo and Black Belt in Judo. At the end of his sophomore year at Orenburg Polytechnic Institute, Marco transferred to Leningrad Institute of Railway Engineers in today's Saint Petersburg, where he continued to pursue a mechanical engineering degree.

Vorobiev's interrupted relationship with firearms continued when, in the summer of 1985, he was drafted into military service. At the end of basic training at the airborne training center, Marco was selected and transferred to SpetsNaz mountain training center where he commenced three months of training before being deployed to Afghanistan as a sniper and assaulter. There, he spent the next 16 months fighting insurgents, interdicting enemy's re-supply convoys and caravans. In February of 1987, Marco was air lifted out of Afghanistan after sustaining injuries in combat.

After discharge from the military service, Marco continued his studies at the School of Mechanical Engineering at Railway Institute in Leningrad. In 1989, he moved to the United States and settled in Long Island, New York, where he got married and eventually started a long and successful career in the railroad industry. His 16-year-long railroad career took him to Alabama, back to Russia, Arizona and Michigan, where he finally settled with his family.

In 1994, Marco's affinity with firearms led him to start collecting. It started with gathering rifles and handguns that were issued to him in the service and grew to a sizable collection of many variations of Kalashnikov rifles and other guns. At about the same time, Marco started to consult several writers and AK gunsmiths. In 2001, he organized and led a trip to Russia's arsenal city of Izhevsk to visit the infamous Izhmash plant, the premier AK manufacturer in Russia. During that visit, he met the AK creator Mikhail Timofeyevich Kalashnikov.

After retiring form railroad work, Vorobiev started his own consulting company that helped American companies to expand their business abroad. It wasn't too long before the company's activities spilled over to firearms. In 2005, his company launched a firearm and tactics training division that focused on Warsaw Pact doctrine for small arms application. In 2009, answering calls from his firearms industry friends, he started writing. Since then he has written extensively about firearms and tactics. His articles appeared in the *Guns & Ammo, Shotgun News, The Book of the AK, The Book of the AR* and *Be Ready* magazines among others. Marco has hosted and appeared in many segments of G&A TV. He appeared in the NBC Discovery Production's "Foreign Special Ops" show on AHC (Military Channel) and award-winning documentary the "Maidan Massacre."

Today, he continues to write for several publications, and consults for firearms, firearm accessories and tactical gear manufacturers.

Vorobiev lives in Ann Arbor, Michigan, with his wife and two sons.

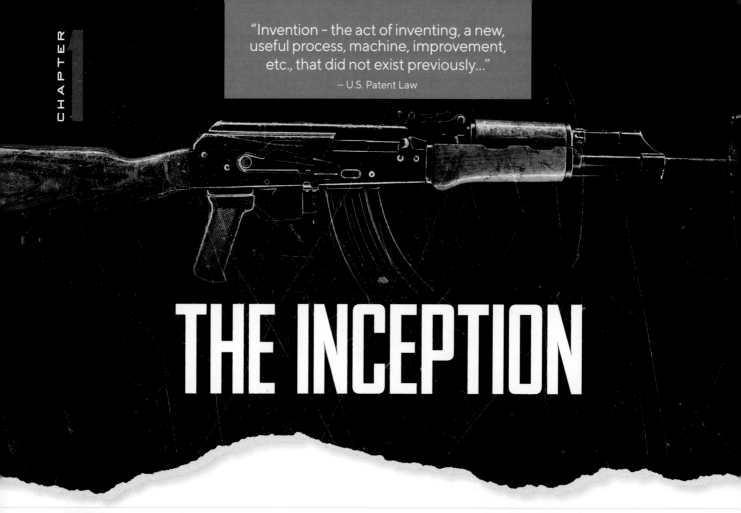

> "Invention – the act of inventing, a new, useful process, machine, improvement, etc., that did not exist previously..."
> – U.S. Patent Law

CHAPTER 1

# THE INCEPTION

The story of the rifle we know today as AK did not start in 1946 when the first models of the gun were submitted for testing, not in 1944 when the infamous Sturmgewehr Stg. 44 was a common trophy among German guns captured by the advancing Soviet soldiers, not in 1943 when the intermediate cartridge M43 was developed by the Soviets, not even in 1942 when the first German MP-43 prototypes were captured on battlefields, and certainly not in 1947 when the new Avtomat got its designation.

Its story goes further back, to pre-war 1939 when famous Russian/Soviet firearms designer Professor Lieutenant-General Vladimir Fyodorov wrote, "The evolution of individual firearms will be toward the merger of two types of guns—an automatic rifle and a machine pistol based on the design of a new cartridge. The creation of a single cartridge with a reduced effective range for rifles and an extended range for machine pistols would allow creation of the future weapon—powerful due to adoption of automation, with a selector for single and automatic fire, light and compact due to the adoption of a new cartridge that has smaller overall dimensions, a smaller caliber (6 – 6.25mm) and with a casing without a rim."

*AK-47 Avtomat Kalashnikov is the most prolific individual battle weapon in the world. Its story is full of surprises, downfalls and triumphs.*

**14** | gundigest.com

*World's first Avtomat (automatic rifle). The Fyodorov Avtomat was firing a smaller, more manageable round compared to the full rifle rounds used by the army at that time.*

Or, should we say that the story of the AK as an automatic rifle concept goes even further back, to 1916 and beyond when the same Vladimir Fyodorov, who at that time was a Captain in the Russian Imperial Army, created his "Avtomat Fyodorova." In fact, Fyodorov started his work on the automatic rifle in 1906 and on the intermediate 6.5mm rimless cartridge in 1913. The Tsar's government even ordered a limited run of the new Fyodorov rifle.

However, no funds were provided for any further development of a new cartridge and the Avtomat had to be adapted to fire the 6.5 Arisaka cartridge, due to the abundance of the Japanese ammunition. The real mass production of the Fyodorov automatic rifle never commenced as intended due to the Tsar's Russia bogging down in the mire of WWI. Only after the Bolshevik Revolution did first mass production of the rifle begin at Kovrov Arsenal.

In total, only 9,000–15,000 rifles were produced during 1920–1924 before production ended due to lack of a reliable ammunition supplier. At the end, the Fyodorov Avtomat was truly the first automatic rifle, or what we now call an assault rifle. Fyodorov himself said that his rifle was not designed to arm any infantry detachment, but rather to be issued to special purpose troops such as motorcycle commands, cavalry scouts and designated infantry riflemen.

Actually, the term "assault rifle" does not apply to the AK. In fact, the term itself is a contradiction. The German term "Sturmgewehr" (assault rifle—Eng.) paints the gun into a corner and puts it into pretty strict criteria, like the rifle is only good for an assault, for storming fortified positions or a building, and probably is not an ideal weapon for mounting a defense, etc. Therefore, it does not apply to Fyodorov's gun and certainly not to Kalashnikov's rifle. The AK is not and never was an "assault rifle," no matter what Hitler liked to call his rifles or how much today's gun opponents misuse the term. The AK was thought out, designed

*Colonel of the Russian Tsar's army Vladimir Fyodorov, designer of world's first automatic rifle, the Avtomat Fyodorova.*

and built as an Avtomat (automatic rifle)—the Avtomat Kalashnikova. As such, it was capable of all tasks required of any battlefield rifle.

Having cleared the confusion with terminology, let's get back to the subject at hand, the AK rifles. As I mentioned before, the history of the AK as a concept started long before WWII, but history of the AK as a firearm started with adoption of the intermediate cartridge M43.

## THE M43 CARTRIDGE

Until recently, there was much confusion and contradiction pertaining to the history of the Soviet cartridge Model 1943, the M43. It should not be a big surprise, especially when talking about Soviet firearm development. Though the information about the M43 cartridge was not a state secret, the amount of information offered by so many "experts" added to the confusion.

On July 15 of 1943, the meeting of the Technical Committee of the Commissariat of Armament took place in Moscow. All of the firearm designers, heads and leading specialists of the Ammunition Designers Bureau (OKB-44) and military experts were invited to attend. The topic of discussion was a review of

*According to Fyodorov's concept of using a less powerful cartridge in automatic rifles, the smaller 6.5 Arisaka round was selected due to lack of interest from the Tsar's government in developing a completely new cartridge.*

*(top) A Tsar's Army Officer fires his Fyodorov Avtomat somewhere in the battlefields of the Great War in Europe.*

*(above) Soviet soldiers use their Fyodorov Avtomats during the Soviet Winter War against Finland. Interestingly, both sides used these guns.*

the foreign weapons chambered in a reduced-power cartridge and their effectiveness in battle.

At that time, the Soviet Armed Forces were armed with the old-school infantry Mosin Rifle Model 91/30 and its carbine modifications, limited numbers of Tokarev semi-automatic rifles (SVTs), and three types of Avtomats or machine pistols: model PPSh (Shpagin), PPD (Degtyarev) and PPS (Sudayev). Although chambered in the awesome, high velocity Tokarev TT 7.62X25mm cartridge, the latter could hardly be considered automatic rifles and were designated to the storm troops, reconnaissance units, officers and NCOs. They had proven their effectiveness during assaults on the fortified German strongholds and inner city fighting.

Large detachments of storm troops, called "Avtomatchiki," armed with machine pistols or sub-guns, were part of every infantry regiment and a smaller part of every battalion. The high velocity of the 7.62X25mm Tokarev round and high rate of fire made Soviet machine pistols a formidable weapon in any situation. However, the Avtomats suffered from lack of effective range. They were limited to about 200 meters.

On the other end of the spectrum of Soviet infantry guns were the full-size

*The Soviet 7.62X39mm cartridge Model 1943 (M43) in comparison with 7.92 Kurtz and .30 M1 rounds.*

rifles firing the powerful 7.62X54 rimmed rifle cartridge. Born on the battlements of the Russo-Turkish War and refined in the trenches of WWI, the Mosin Model 91/30 rifle was the main battle rifle of the Soviets during the Great Patriotic War. Extremely accurate and easy to master, it may have served exceptionally well during position warfare when the distance between warring parties was close to 1,000 meters. Its effectiveness would be reduced drastically at closer ranges, especially in close-quarter city fighting. The same can be said about the SVT rifle.

During the meeting, the representative of the Head Artillery Commissariat (GAU) demonstrated a captured German automatic carbine MP-43 chambered for the reduced-power, intermediate 7.92mm cartridge (the 7.92mm Kurtz) and an American 7.62mm M1 self-loading carbine firing a pistol cartridge of increased power. Despite the new-ish guns presented, the main focus of the committee was on the German cartridge that appeared to have the same projectile as the 8mm Mauser ammo that was pressed into a reduced-size Mauser casing. It was also noted that this new German ammunition was expected to perform at 800-meter ranges.

At the end of the meeting, the committee came to the conclusion that was captured in the minutes: "Modern warfare demonstrated that effective fire on the enemy is conducted at ranges of up to 400 meters. Therefore, there is no need to have an uneconomical (rifle) cartridge. It is necessary to switch to a smaller cartridge and, as a result, to have a smaller and lighter weapon. The best caliber can be a 6.5mm-caliber cartridge, which is able to match a straight shot at the range of 400 meters to that of the rifle Model 91/30.

"It is decided: Instruct OKB-44 to calculate the optimal speed of the bullet and its optimal mass for 5.6mm, 6.5mm and 7.62mm calibers as most common, with length of the barrel 520mm and the average pressure at 3,000 kg/cm$^2$. The bullet must have sufficient lethal force to disable a human at a distance of 1,000 m. Calculation tables for bullets must be presented in 10 days."

The task was urgent and not entirely clear. The Designers Bureau OKB-44 note dated 1947 says: "At the time of the new cartridge development we had nothing to go by. Consultations in Head Artillery Commissariat, Academy of Science and in Commissariat of Armaments did not lead to anything. NOBODY KNEW WHAT IS REQUIRED FROM THE NEW CARTRIDGE." By the way, a 6.5mm cartridge was being pushed, and based on subsequent events, it is safe to assume that Vladimir Fyodorov was present at the meetings.

It was a light bullet with transverse load of 18-20 g/cm$^2$ recommended for the new cartridge. The recommended barrel length was 520 mm. In addition, Fyodorov proposed to develop a light machine gun for the proposed cartridge. In fact, many of Fyodorov's pre-war proposals were used to create the new 7.62X39mm Model 1943 or M43 cartridge.

## ENTER KALASHNIKOV

While the Soviet scientists were hard at work developing an intermediate cartridge, in Matay, Kazakhstan, young tank mechanic Sergeant Mikhail Kalashnikov was creating his first firearm. In fact, the first of Kalashnikov's firearm creations were machine pistols and had nothing to do with an "assault rifle," or the intermediate cartridge.

While Kalashnikov recovered from severe chest wounds received near Bryansk in 1942, he had plenty of time to talk to the wounded infantry soldiers and listen to numerous stories of how standard infantry small arms lacked much needed battlefield efficiency. Tales abounded of how the Soviet infantry units could not match the fire intensity of the German units and needed more automatic weapons. Specifically, the young and aspiring mechanic was inspired by an Airborne Lieutenant who had a degree in weapons design and was recovering from wounds in the same hospital. They spent hours exchanging ideas. And, the junior officer guided Kalashnikov on the right path by explaining the main principles of weapons design. Mikhail also read anything weapons-related he could get his hands on in the hospital library. As a result, armed with ideas, inspiration and knowledge,

*Senior Sergeant of Soviet Armor Corps Mikhail Timofeyevich Kalashnikov.*

he started to work on his first gun—the Machine Pistol chambered in the standard Tokarev 7.62X25mm cartridge.

After recovery, Senior Sergeant Kalashnikov was granted leave to his hometown to continue his full recovery. Instead of going home to his parents, he went to Matay where he worked at Railroad Depot. He went there so that he could build his gun.

The man had an incredible memory. During our meeting at his house in 2001, Kalashnikov reminisced about his time at the Railroad Depot in Kazakhstan. With a smile, he remembered the women who were assigned to help him. Kalashnikov was assigned women helpers as machinists, welders and fitters not because his project was not important and therefore "lesser" workforce was given, but because women were the only quali-

*Meeting Kalashnikov (left) at the legendary firearm designer's home, the author (right) found him to be a good storyteller. Kalashnikov obviously enjoyed taking a stroll down memory lane.*

fied workforce available. Just like the iconic "Rosie the Riveter" in the U.S., women stepped up and replaced their fathers, brothers and husbands who went to the front lines. In the Soviet Union, women replaced men at milling machines, at smelting ovens, at tractor and truck controls, at any job that was traditionally done by the men, in order to aid the war effort. The deeds of these women are nothing short of battlefield heroism. Their dedication and sacrifice helped to bring an end to that terrible war.

Here he was at the Railroad Depot with a small army of Russian Rosie the Riveters helping him to build his first gun. Kalashnikov remembered that most of the women did not have mechanical education and lacked proper terminology and lingo used by the metalworkers. Instead, they brought their own softer, "female" touch to the project by calling certain gun components a "little rabbit" or "birdy," etc. At a time of war and hardship, this was very much welcomed as something humane, something "normal," a much-needed distraction.

In three months' time, the first working prototype of Kalashnikov's machine pistol was ready. It would be in extremely

*Just like in the U.S. with men gone to war, women picked up the slack and filled a void in the workforce. In the Soviet Union, women and children took most of the load of the war effort.*

bad taste to compare Kalashnikov's first gun to the AK. They have nothing in common, not in design, not in concept and not in the intended use and purpose. In fact, designing his machine pistol, Mikhail Kalashnikov did not know that, at the same time, work was being done on the intermediate cartridge and seeds were being planted for a whole new type of weapon.

*Looking at Kalashnikov's machine pistol, one cannot help but notice striking similarities with the American Thomson submachine gun, or "Tommy Gun." Several components were also borrowed from other already existing firearms.*

The prototype, though fully functioning, needed to be refined. It needed a better shop, better instruments, better machines and more qualified help. From Matay, Kalashnikov was sent to Alma-Ata, where he refined his design and built a better sample at the Moscow Aviation Institute workshop. In the face of German advance, the Institute (among other entities) was evacuated to the capital of Kazakhstan. The sample was submitted for evaluation to the then-head of the Dzerzhinsky Military Engineering Academy, Anatoli Arkadievich Blagonravov, an outstanding scientist in the field of small arms, who was in Samarkand, Uzbekistan, at that time.

Head of the Dzerzhinsky Artillery Academy, General Blagonravov was the first to evaluate the new gun. He discovered several flaws and shortcomings in Kalashnikov's design. In June of 1942, Kalashnikov's submachine gun was tested at the proving grounds of Moscow Military District. The gun was rejected for mass production due to excessive expense of the manufacturing process.

The final official conclusion was: "The Kalashnikov's machine pistol gun is more complicated and expensive to manufacture than the PPSh-41 and PPS, and requires the application of complicated and slow milling operations. Therefore, despite many attractive features (light weight, small length, the single shot regime of fire, the successful combination of a fire selector and a safety, a compact cleaning rod, etc.), it is of no industrial interest in its present form."

Despite overall negative reports and overall test results, General Blagonravov understood the young designer's potential and recommended that Mikhail Kalashnikov be sent to further his technical education and gain practical experience. As a result, at the end of 1942, Kalashnikov was sent to the Central Research and Testing Facility for Firearms and Mortar Ordnance (NIPSMVO) that belonged to the State Military Academy of the Red Army.

Here, in 1944, he created a prototype of a self-loading carbine, which, although never adopted for service, in part served as a prototype for the creation of his Avtomat. And, that is where in 1945 Mikhail Kalashnikov began developing automatic weapons for an intermediate 7.62X39mm Model 1943 cartridge. Even more importantly, he met his future wife Ekaterina, who worked as a draftsman in Degtyarev Designers Bureau. It was there that the Kalashnikov automatic rifle was born, modified and perfected. As a result, it won the 1947 competition and was accepted for service.

*The first "official" Kalashnikov rifle was the self-loading carbine Model 1944.*

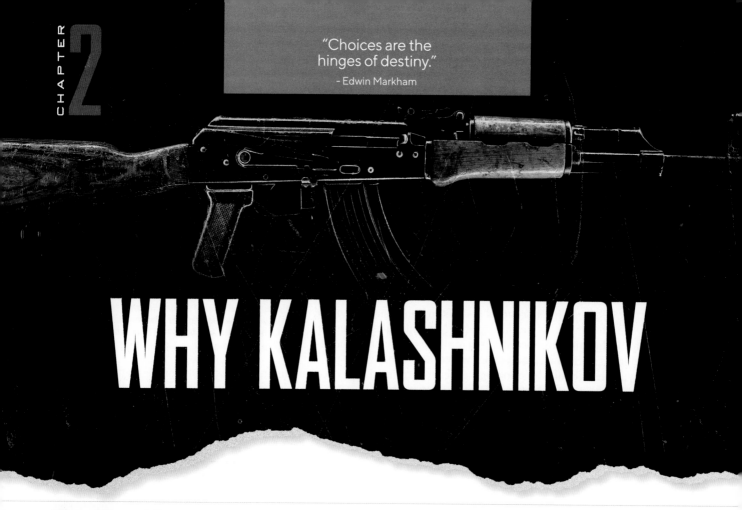

## CHAPTER 2

"Choices are the hinges of destiny."
– Edwin Markham

# WHY KALASHNIKOV

**M**eanwhile in Moscow...

The roots of the AK rifle as a functioning infantry weapon can be traced to the end of 1942, when Soviet troops on the Volkhov Front captured the first samples of German MP-43 automatic carbines that were chambered for the new intermediate 7.92X33mm or 7.92mm Kurtz cartridge. Note that, at that time, the new German rifle was not called an assault rifle. It was classified as "Maschinenpistole," or machine pistol. In fact, the first new rifle had been supplied to German troops in secret, or rather without Hitler's knowledge. German designers and military brass had to convince the Fuhrer that the new gun was an effective infantry weapon and had several advantages over Hitler's beloved K98 Mauser. In the summer of 1943, at the same meeting in the Commissariat of Armament where urgent development of the new intermediate cartridge was sprung, it was also decided that, apart of from the new ammunition, the whole new firearm complex or family of weapons would be developed. The new guns were supposed to provide the troops with ability to effectively engage the enemy at the ranges up to 400 meters, which exceeded the capability of the machine pistols that were in service with Soviet infantry.

In November of 1943, the new cartridge design drawings and specifications were distributed to all firearm development organizations. Cartridges developed by ammunition designers Semin and Elizarov, with a rimless 41mm long "bottle"-shaped casing and pointed lead core bullet 8 grams (123.5 grain) in weight, were to become the standard cartridge for the new family of small arms for the Red Army. This spurred the development of an automatic rifle (carbine) or Avtomat, self-loading (semi-automatic) carbine and manual-action carbine.

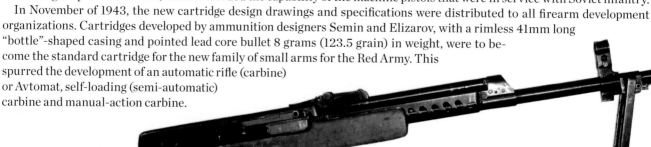

**Sudayev's AS-44 Avtomat almost made it as the main battle rifle of the Soviet Armed Forces. However, the sudden death of its creator stopped any further development.**

*Aleksey Sudayev, the creator of legendary PPS-43, arguably the best machine pistol of WWII.*

Six months later, in the middle of 1944, the Armament Directorate started to receive submissions. The first submission was the Sudayev Avtomat AS-44, developed by Aleksey Ivanovich Sudayev, the creator of the already famous PPS-43 machine pistol subgun. Universally recognized as the best submachine gun of WWII, the Sudayev's PPS was "born" and built in Leningrad during the brutal siege by the Nazis. It encompassed the best features required of this type of gun. It was light, compact, simple and reliable. Even after the war, several countries continued to build (under license and without) the PPS-43 for service in their respective militaries. Moreover, Poland still builds this iconic weapon today, and I.O., Inc., out of Palm Bay, Florida, imports its pistol version to the U.S.

After initial testing, the selection committee recommended the AS-44 for further development. As a result, after Sudayev's revisions, a limited production run of AS-44 Avtomat was ordered for military testing in the field. In spring and summer of 1945, the tests were conducted by Soviet troops in Germany and back in the Soviet Union. Although the tests were mostly positive, troops complained about AS's excessive weight and the short life span of the firing pin and extractor. A new set of tests of the revised (lighter) version of the gun was scheduled for early 1946. After the final refinement of the original design, Sudayev's Avtomat AS-44 could very well have become the new main battle rifle of the Soviet Armed Forces, and I would be hard at work writing a book about it right now. However, the untimely death of Aleksey Sudayev after a short battle with sickness brought a halt to further development of the promising rifle. As a result, the AS-44 was never adopted for service, sharing a fate of other Avtomats designed by Korobov, Rukovishnikov, Dementyev and Bulkin.

Here is where the young Sergeant Kalashnikov enters the scene. After recovering from battle wounds and a short stint in Kazakhstan where he built his original-design machine pistol, Kalashnikov was already working at the Central Research and Testing Facility for Firearms and Mortar Ordnance (NIPSMVO) in Shurovo, near Moscow. Here, in 1944, he developed a self-loading carbine. In its design, he used several systems inspired by the American M1 Garand rifle, features that Kalashnikov later incorporated into his design of the AK. Spurred by several officers working with him at the test grounds, he entered the second round of the competition for design of the new family of guns, this time for the automatic rifle.

Even though Mikhail Kalashnikov did not take part in the first round of competition, he was always very interested in the test results and closely watched all the developments around the project. At that time, the clear frontrunner was Sudayev's AS-44, which needed some serious revisions. However, since the death of Sudayev, any further development work was effectively stopped. Nevertheless, numerous tests, including military field-testing, allowed Soviet specialists to accumulate a significant amount of data. The new set of specifications for the automatic rifle encompassing the new data was issued. And, in 1946, the main armament office announced a new competition with a new set of specifications. This time the Avtomat had to be designed to eliminate a live target at 500 meters, have a sighting range of 800 meters and weigh no more than 4.5 kg (9.9 lbs.).

At the first stage of the new contest, sixteen draft designs were submitted to the Department of Small Arms of the State Automobile Inspection. Among them was the project of M.T. Kalashnikov, developed with help from officers of the Shchurovsky testing range. The commission selected four designs for prototype sample production and subsequent testing. The four designs were that of Colonel-Engineer Rukovishnikov, Senior Sergeant Kalashnikov and test engineer Baryshev, Tula Designers Bureau engineer Korobov and Bulkin and Kovrov Arsenal Plant №2 engineer Dementyev. All other entries were rejected.

The officers who were assigned to the tests developed an interest in Kalashnikov's design. Perhaps they were drawn to the originality of some of his solutions. But, it was also evident that the young tank mechanic lacked essential design skills, especially in the area of structural calculations. Again, they were eager to help the promising designer by proofing and correcting his drawings and calculations.

In November 1946, after approval of his design, Kalashnikov was sent to Kovrov Plant №2, where he was supposed to start

*SSgt Mikhail Kalashnikov with the group of officers who mentored the promising designer while working at GAU Proving Grounds.*

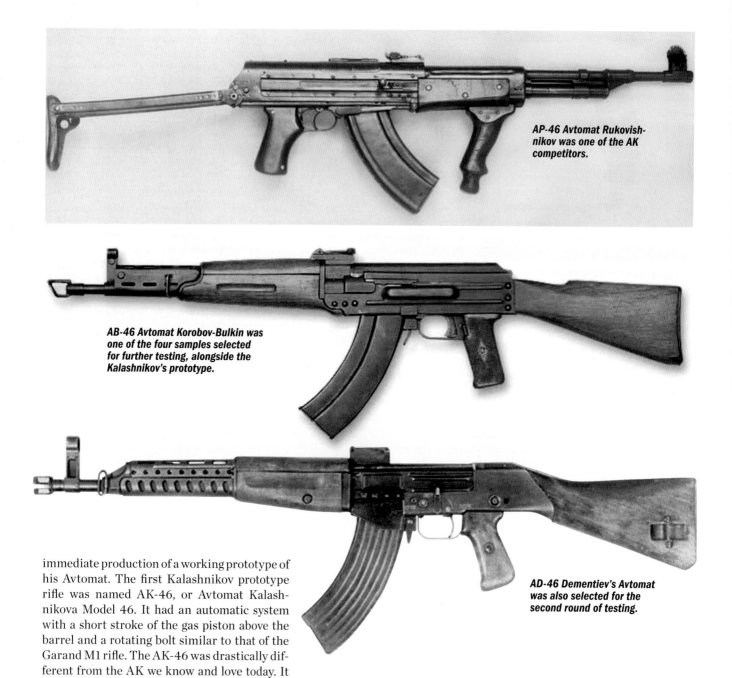

AP-46 Avtomat Rukovish-nikov was one of the AK competitors.

AB-46 Avtomat Korobov-Bulkin was one of the four samples selected for further testing, alongside the Kalashnikov's prototype.

AD-46 Dementiev's Avtomat was also selected for the second round of testing.

immediate production of a working prototype of his Avtomat. The first Kalashnikov prototype rifle was named AK-46, or Avtomat Kalashnikova Model 46. It had an automatic system with a short stroke of the gas piston above the barrel and a rotating bolt similar to that of the Garand M1 rifle. The AK-46 was drastically different from the AK we know and love today. It had a two-part receiver, with upper completely detaching from the lower receiver, and separate safety and fire control levers both located on the left side of the gun.

In December of the same year, the AK-46 underwent first evaluation and testing. Kalashnikov's two main competitors were Tula's Bulkin AB-46 and the Dementyev AD-46 rifles. Bulkin jealously watched every step of the testers, meticulously checked to see if his rifle was properly cleaned, and was always present at the evaluations of targets. It seemed he was suspicious that other competitors may sabotage his project. As it turned out, that was not unwarranted. However, later Mikhail Kalashnikov himself would describe Alexander Dementyev as his main and strongest competitor through the entire competition.

The second round of tests revealed several shortcomings of the AK-46 and, as a result, the commission found it not suitable for further development. Yet again, history could have taken a slightly different turn and I would be telling you about the firing characteristics of Bulkin's or Dementiev's rifle. However, the young and ambitious designer was not giving up and, with help from several officers Kalashnikov served with since 1943, he was able to get the commission to reverse its decision and to allow him to further refine his Avtomat design.

Upon return to the Kovrov Plant, Kalashnikov went to work. He decided to radically rework his earlier design. To expedite the process, he was assigned experienced designer and drafter Alexander Zaitsev. As a result, a totally new Avtomat was actually submitted for the next round of tests. The new gun had little if any similarity with the AK-46, but it received a significant face lift, closely resembling the rifle of one Kalashnikov's main competitors—the Bulkin AB-46. This caused some friction initially, but later gave way to a peaceful resolution. After all, this was for the benefit of the Motherland.

Here I should clarify a certain point in reference to a Soviet firearm design of that time. This may give fuel to conspiracy mongers, but may also answer a few legitimate questions. Copying or "borrowing" someone's designs (including those of direct competitors) was not only allowed, but was encouraged and welcomed by the testing personal, selection committee and higher-ups. After all, intellectual property (in today's sense) was then considered property of the State and belonged to the people of the USSR. As such, it would be used to benefit the Motherland and its people. It should also be noted that use of some of the proven components alone does not guarantee the success of the final prototype. It is innovative use of the components and their optimal interaction and work as one machine or mechanism that leads to successful operation of the unit. This requires considerable engineering and design work, which was done by Kalashnikov and Zaitsev in the shortest possible time.

## HUGO SCHMEISSER AND GERMAN INPUT

I suppose here is where I also should address the common misperception of the possible involvement of Hugo Schmeisser and/or any other German "specialists" in the design of the AK or any other automatic rifle under this tender.

Hugo Schmeisser was "captured" by the Soviets and brought along with other German designers and arms specialists to work in the Soviet Union as part of reparations after the war. Was he used for a slave labor? He certainly was not allowed to leave the USSR, but he was allowed to bring his family, live in an apartment complex much better than those of the Soviet workers, and he was paid, which was not the same for millions of Soviets who were forced into slave labor in Germany by the Nazis. He often complained to the authorities about a small pay not allowing him to take his family on holidays! Slave

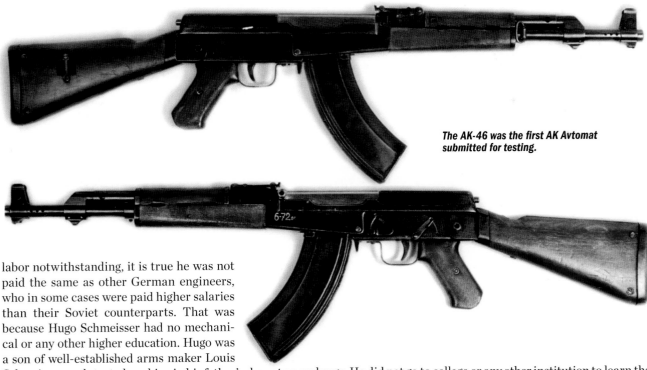

*The AK-46 was the first AK Avtomat submitted for testing.*

labor notwithstanding, it is true he was not paid the same as other German engineers, who in some cases were paid higher salaries than their Soviet counterparts. That was because Hugo Schmeisser had no mechanical or any other higher education. Hugo was a son of well-established arms maker Louis Schmeisser, and started working in his father's shop at an early age. He did not go to college or any other institution to learn the craft. He learned it on the job. At that time, as has continued in the Soviet Union and later in Russia and quite honestly, in the whole civilized world, there were pay scales that were different for degreed specialists compared to mere skilled labor personnel. However, Schmeisser had a chance to better his financial situation by taking a more active role at his job. Instead, he was a reluctant worker who complained a lot and rarely completed a task. As such, he was assigned minor projects and was described by his German colleagues as a *prima donna*.

However, all of the above is hearsay. Facts are what are important when we talk history. After shoveling through copious amounts of gossip, rumors, insinuations, after all the smoke clears, what remains are the facts. Here are some hard historical facts: Hugo Schmeisser was brought to the then-closed industrial city of Izhevsk, home of the Izhevsk Machine Building Plant, aka Izhmash, in 1946, along with fifteen other Germans to form Designers Bureau №58. Neither Izhmash nor its designers

were anywhere near the ongoing Avtomat competition. It was only after all the tests were conducted, and selection made, that the decision to build Kalashnikov's AK-47 rifle on an industrial scale at the Izhmash plant was passed in 1949.

At that time, the Soviets were struggling with the stamped portion of the AK receiver and discarded the idea in favor of the expensive milled one. Hugo Schmeisser, based on his design of the Stg. 44 gun, was viewed as a stamped metal specialist. But, did he assist the Russians in making a switch to the stamped receiver? As we know, the AKM (or Avtomat Kalashnikova Modernized) with its stamped receiver was adopted in 1959, seven years after Hugo Schmeisser was allowed to leave the Soviet Union and go back to Germany in 1952. If Schmeisser was a good stamping metal "specialist," then why did it take the Russians seven years after his departure to concur on the subject? Wasn't the three years while he worked in the facility where the AKs were being built enough to solve the puzzle?

The fact is that Hugo Schmeisser had nothing to do with design and development of the AK Avtomat itself. He also had very little if anything at all to do with the later modernized AKM version. Even later in life when asked if he assisted in the development of the AK, Hugo Schmeisser said, "I gave them couple of pointers."

These are the facts and they are undisputed. Use these facts with applied logic and the picture becomes much clearer. The Stg. 44 and AK cannot be more different. They operate differently and employ different solutions in their respective designs. However, there are similarities not between the guns *per se*, but between the designers. Both lacked formal education, both were driven by thirst for knowledge and ability to create something functional. Both designers started out by building a machine pistol,

After complete AK redesign (bottom), it was clearly a new gun and had more similarities with Bulkin's AB-46 (center) than with the AK-46 (top).

both worked on machine guns and eventually both created an iconic weapon, only separately and with one being more of an "icon" than the other.

## 1947 TEST RESULTS

Back to our AK story. The next round of tests, at the end of 1946 and beginning of 1947 (January), produced three clear leaders—slightly improved Dementiev AD-46 and Bulkin AB-46 rifles, and totally redesigned Kalashnikov and Zaitsev Avtomat. Test results showed that none of the rifles fully satisfied the accuracy requirements. Dementiev's AD was plagued with the same reliability issues as before. Bulkin's AB-46, though being the most accurate, had numerous reliability issues and problems with the longevity of a slew of critical components. Kalashnikov's Avtomat, though the least accurate of the three, was the most reliable and, even better, the most production-ready. This fact alone played a major role in why I now write this AK book.

The decision was made to recommend Kalashnikov's Avtomat, with its official designation the AK-47, to military field-testing due to its inherent reliability and simplicity of operation. The original requirements for accuracy were postponed indefinitely and later discarded. One can consider this decision as justified based on the situation at the time. The Soviet Armed Forces could use a reliable and inaccurate rifle now, or wait for development of a reliable and accurate one God knows when.

The decision was a hard one to make. None of the tested guns complied with accuracy requirements for automatic or burst fire. However, the last word was for the end user, the Soviet Military represented by their Main Armament Office (GAU). And, the end user preferred the reduced weight and size to accuracy, at the same time highlighting the reliability, survivability and ease of handling of the AK. Based on the sum of these features, Mikhail Kalashnikov, with his creation—the legendary AK-47

№1—emerged victorious.

Serial production of new Avtomats would be launched at the Izhmash Plant, where the first run of the new AK rifle was completed by the end of 1949. Based on the results of the military field tests, the new automatic rifle was adopted by the Soviet Armed Forces in two versions, designated "7.62mm Avtomat Kalashnikova AK" and "7.62mm Avtomat Kalashnikova with folding stock AKS" (for the Airborne troops).

That was it. The rational, prudent and reasonable decision was based on reliability, simplicity, ease of handling and most of all on ability to start mass production of the gun immediately. Its relative ease of manufacture and low cost also played a role in confirming the decision.

Was the AK's emergence as the ultimate victor and eventual legend a result of incredible luck, or sinister play behind the curtains? Well, luck certainly had its hand in this story more than once. But, at the end, there was no conspiracy or sinister plot. It was reason that prevailed.

*Hugo Schmeisser with another German colleague enjoying a day off in the Izhevsk Kirov Park in 1950.*

*The AK-47 Kalashnikov Avtomat was adopted for service in 1947.*

## A TEAM EFFORT

Another question still persists. Could Kalashnikov, having no formal education, compete and win against more experienced competitors? Yes, he could! God awarded him with huge engineering talent that was noticed by the well-respected among firearms professionals and widely recognized arms specialist General Anatoly Blagonravov in 1942. The question, "Can a regular guy create an iconic weapon?" had been answered by history many times over. Kalashnikov and his Avtomat is only one example. Hugo Schmeisser had never received a formal education, but his Sturmgewehr 44 receives worldwide recognition. Eugene Stoner, the creator of the American M16 rifle, also had no special education. Like Kalashnikov, he was a regular grunt during WWII. Another American—Ronnie Barrett, photographer and amateur shooter—created a 50-caliber Barrett M82 sniper rifle that is used today by the military.

Was it Mikhail Kalashnikov alone who created the AK? Of course not. He had help from a number of people every step of the way.

It was Zaitsev who convinced Kalashnikov to completely redesign the AK-46 before submitting it for the final round of testing. Major Deykin, a GAU representative and Kalashnikov's mentor, supported the idea and solicited the help of the head of the testing department at the proving grounds, Major Lyuty, who himself suggested eighteen drastic revisions to the original design. This lead to the "re-birth" of the AK rifle and paved the way to the current AK configuration that we all know and love.

Of course, the birth of a new Avtomat became possible due to the realization of personal dreams, thoughts and desires of Mikhail Kalashnikov. However, without the help and support of a number of real people, mentors, colleagues, assistants, scores of drafters and detailers, the realization of the dream that was an AK would have been impossible.

It truly was an ultimate team effort for the benefit of the Motherland.

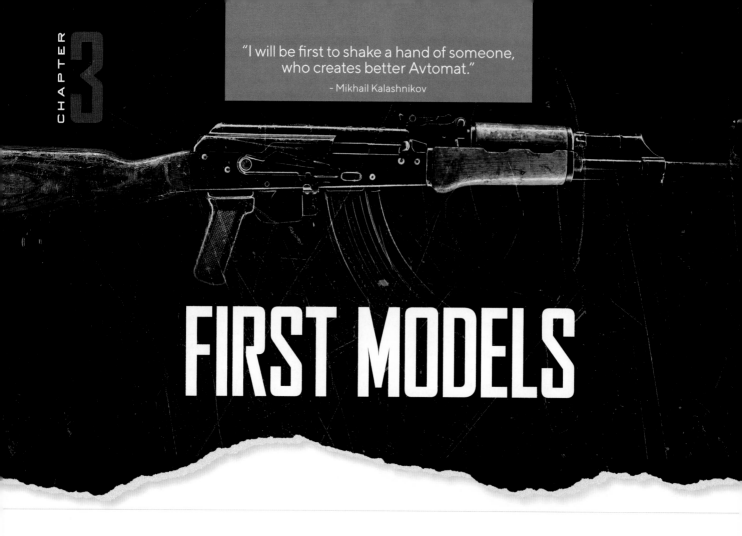

## CHAPTER 3

> "I will be first to shake a hand of someone,
> who creates better Avtomat."
>
> – Mikhail Kalashnikov

# FIRST MODELS

Let's go back, now, to the final version of Kalashnikov's rifle. After the first round of field tests, the young designer had doubts about drastically changing the design of the AK-46, due to the lack of time between tests. He literally had to be talked into a complete redesign. But, as they say, he who does not take risks, does not drink champagne. The design team took a risk and managed to simplify the gun design and improve its reliability for use in the most adverse conditions. These were truly revolutionary changes. Particular importance was placed on the reliability of the automatics, ease of manufacture, improvement of performance and appearance. As Alexander Zaitsev later remembered, "Everyone worked with inspiration, with the soul. All those who could help us with anything, did it. Only when the work was done and the documentation was submitted, we could relax with a sigh of relief." The new sample was christened the AK-47, and the Model No. 1 was born.

The amount of work that was done in a very short time was staggering. The bolt carrier was now jointed with a gas piston rod. The trigger group was redesigned. The receiver's top cover now completely enclosed the moving internal parts. The fire selector lever became multifunctional. It now not only switched the fire mode from single shot to full automatic, it also became a safety and closed the slot for the charging handle, protecting the receiver from dust and dirt. Finally, the barrel was shortened by 80 mm—from 500 to 420. This directly violated the original specifications and could possibly disqualify the rifle from the competition altogether. Kalashnikov later wrote, "What we did was a real breakthrough in technical thought, innovative approaches. We, in essence, broke the established ideas about the design of weapons, broke those stereotypes that were even laid out in the competition specifications."

Time was not the only thing the Kalashnikov team lacked. It also lacked the funds necessary to complete the project. Money was always in short supply. When work on the second sample came to a screeching halt because of that, Kalashnikov decided to take a trip to Moscow. Help came from the Chief Marshal of Artillery, N. N. Voronov. The Marshal was an avid hunter with an office full of taxidermy. Standing in the office of the highly ranked officer, the young sergeant for the first time realized that military brass not only trusted him, but also expected results. With Kalashnikov in his office, Voronov placed a call to accounting and screamed, "You are pushing companies with no clear results, I however, have a specific model and specific designer." Then he hung up the phone and wished Mikhail good luck. The necessary funds were made available the same day.

In total, five models of the AK-47 were manufactured. The main differences from the 1946 model were the charging handle moved from the left to the right side of the receiver, and separate safety and selector levers became one and were also placed on the same side as the handle, eliminating the possibility of confusion between the two levers—the safety and the fire control. The magazine was moved closer to the trigger guard, with the mag release lever in-between. The internal mechanism's main change was the piston rod, now directly attached to the bolt carrier with a thread and pinned in place. The new gun had a stamped receiver.

Model No. 2 saw changes to the design of the gas chamber and the shape of the gas rod and piston. A double-chamber muzzle brake-compensator was added. Model No. 3's muzzle compensator had two oval 10x7 mm ports at the top. Experimental models No. 4 and No. 5 had metal folding stocks. One of them had a muzzle brake and the other did not.

The second round of tests revealed the complete dominance of the AK-47 rifle over other submitted samples. With competitors out of the way, it was time to test the new gun against the firearms currently used by the Red Army and demonstrate its superiority. This time the new AK-47 rifle was pinned against the infamous PPSh Shpagin machine pistol, or more correctly submachine gun. The PPSh at that time was in service as the main infantry weapon, or the Avtomat. Here the dominance of the Kalashnikov was even more dramatic. While having similar size and weight, and the same rate of automatic fire, the AK had double the effective range and, due to better ballistics, much better penetration in comparison with the PPSh. The new rifle expanded the Avtomat's capabilities. Now soldiers could fight in urban settings and wooded areas, and they could successfully engage enemy personnel protected by helmets and body armor. The new gun could easily take down targets at 500 meters, whereas the PPSh would reliably deliver hits on the target at only 200 meters.

The design of the AK-47's trigger group provided for more accurate single-shot fire. Most of the machine pistol subguns of the era fired from an open bolt, where a massive bolt had to travel forward after the trigger was pulled and slam into battery, negatively affecting the sight/target picture. In Kalashnikov's Avtomat, only a small part—the hammer—had to rotate at the time of shot. Tests against the PPSh were the proverbial "nail in the coffin" of the way the Red Army fought before the AK.

The AK-47 was born. In the end, the Soviet firearm designers achieved the impossible. From the ashes of WWII, they created the modern weapon, the firearm that took the Soviet Armed Forces light-years ahead of the "competition." A quantum leap.

# THE DESIGN OF THE AK-47'S TRIGGER GROUP PROVIDED FOR MORE ACCURATE SINGLE-SHOT FIRE.

*The final version of Kalashnikov's Avtomat, designated AK-47, was accepted as the winner of the contest. However, it was not the version of the AK that would be issued en masse. There was still work to be done.*

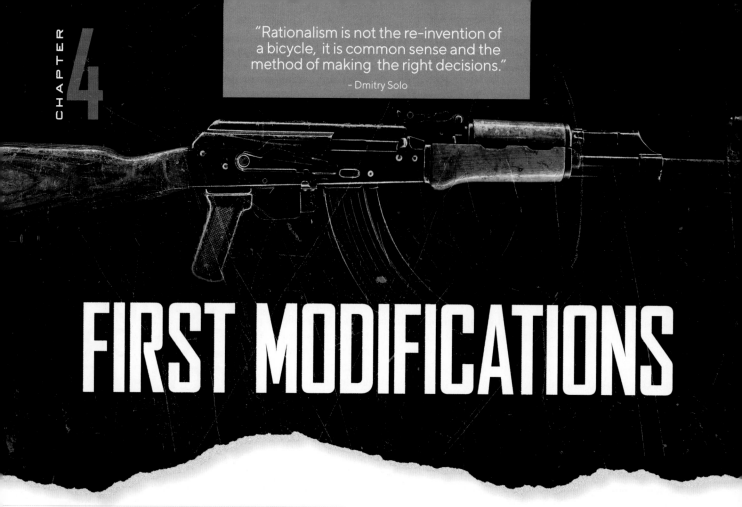

## CHAPTER 4

> "Rationalism is not the re-invention of a bicycle, it is common sense and the method of making the right decisions."
> – Dmitry Solo

# FIRST MODIFICATIONS

**M**odern military is not an abstract concept. It is a real term referring to the evolving nature of armed forces and the doctrines they espouse in order to stay ahead of potential adversaries. As militaries evolve, doctrines and weapons evolve. It falls on the shoulders of arms designers to create weapons that correspond to all the requirements of the modern military and combat.

The Soviets were not an exception. As soon as they made the best automatic battle rifle in the world, they started to tinker with it, to make it more reliable, lighter, easier to manufacture, and to increase its production to shorten the complete rearmament program.

*AK-47 Type 1 with combination stamped-milled receiver.*

*At the same time with its fixed-stock sibling, the AK-47S underfolder was released for service with airborne troops.*

As they rolled off the Izhmash production line, the first models of the AK-47 Avtomat had a combination receiver. The main part of the receiver was made of stamped steel, and the front trunnion was machined. The AKs were made this way initially and until 1951. However, almost immediately the manufacturer encountered a major problem, with a high percentage of rejection during the stamping process. The cause of the problem was a lack of modern and more efficient sheet steel stamping technology. Considering that, the gun's receiver had numerous forged, machined parts installed into a stamped shell that also included a number of stamped parts. This was a major issue, initially with cost effectiveness and production complexity, and later with reliability in the field.

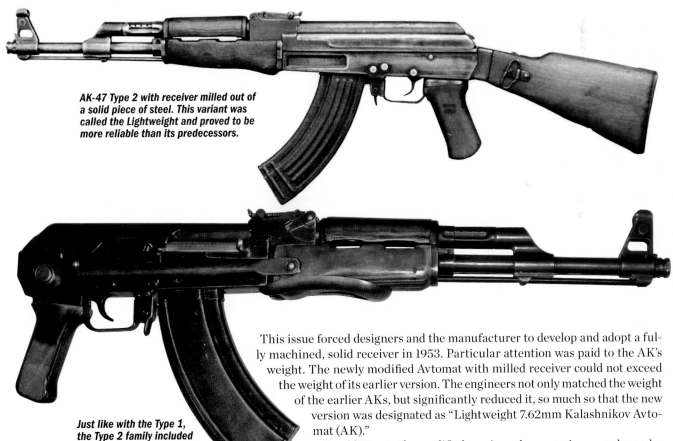

*AK-47 Type 2 with receiver milled out of a solid piece of steel. This variant was called the Lightweight and proved to be more reliable than its predecessors.*

*Just like with the Type 1, the Type 2 family included the underfolder, with metal tubular stock that folded under the gun.*

This issue forced designers and the manufacturer to develop and adopt a fully machined, solid receiver in 1953. Particular attention was paid to the AK's weight. The newly modified Avtomat with milled receiver could not exceed the weight of its earlier version. The engineers not only matched the weight of the earlier AKs, but significantly reduced it, so much so that the new version was designated as "Lightweight 7.62mm Kalashnikov Avtomat (AK)."

In addition to the modified receiver, the magazine was also redesigned. The newly redesigned magazines were made of stamped steel with strengthening ribs. Prior to this, AK magazines were made from thicker, smooth sheet steel and had flat sides. Though it could not be confirmed, the introduction of the strengthening ribs would suggest that the sheet metal used in production of the new magazine could have been thinner to reduce the overall weight of the Avtomat. Inadvertently, this magazine became the iconic AK mag that we all know and love. This model is probably the AK magazine that is in wide use today in every conflict throughout the world.

Here is where I will throw a bone to the Schmeisser's AK conspiracy theory fans. Strictly based on my personal opinion and using known facts and logic, I can speculate that if Hugo Schmeisser was involved in anything AK, it can possibly be seen in the similarities between the modified ribbed AK magazine and the mag from the Stg. 44. Add the time frame of the

*One can see similarities between German Stg. 44 magazines (top) and newly modified Soviet AK-47 mags (bottom). Be that as it may, at closer look these magazines are very different, from the type of insertion and retention, to the stamped ribs.*

modification—1951–1953—and the fact that Hugo Schmeisser left the Soviet Union in 1952. Also, we must remember that Schmeisser was not assigned to major projects, and what he himself told the West German journalist, "I gave them a few pointers." All of this makes Schmeisser's involvement in the new magazine improvement questionable at best. Although, based on undisputed historical fact, I am of the opinion that the reluctant and undereducated Schmeisser had absolutely nothing to do with the design and creation of the AK-47 rifle at any stage of its development. However, when it comes down to the modified ribbed magazine, I cannot, in good conscience, categorically deny the German's involvement. But, that's as far as I'll go.

In the years that followed, the design of the AK was improved continuously. Based on a constant flow of complaints and suggestions coming from the field to the manufacturing plant pertaining to the shortcomings of the first serial models of the AK-47, the overall design review was initiated and the idea of design refinement of the gun's system became widespread. After a review of the use of the earlier serial models of the gun, the team of developers identified several areas where the AK could be improved, such as low overall reliability, failures when used in extreme climatic and adverse conditions, inaccuracy and unexceptional performance characteristics.

Troops in the field who actually used the rifles did not just send in complaints, but also suggestions about how to further refine the gun's system. Particularly close attention was paid to the AK by all branches and echelons of the Soviet military structure, as it was the most widely issued individual weapon system. As such, no effort was spared to make sure that the new gun was as close to the perfect infantry weapon as possible. All the feedback that

*Apart from numerous smaller parts and components, one other major modification, or rather addition, was the ability to accept a bayonet. The original AK-47 rifle was adopted for service without one. Shown here, the Type 2 milled receiver AK-47 with Type 1 Bayonet.*

came from outside was passed on to and sorted through by the gun's creator and his team, so that necessary improvements could be incorporated into the design changes.

Kalashnikov and his team of designers were the lead on the AK improvement project. However, to do design work that was tied into current production required help from numerous Izhmash designers, technologists, engineers and other plant specialists.

The main directions of the design development were determined by the Main Armament Department through its representatives at the plant. They not only monitored progress, but also organized practical implementation of the plans. In many cases, these were leading management specialists capable of solving complex technical issues. They were also involved in the process of analyzing all the feedback that was coming from the troops in the field, creating plans of the modifications and evaluating the final product. In turn, the military made their specialists available as a conduit from the field.

Throughout the process, the leading officer for Avtomats, Vladimir Sergeevich Deikin, who had great testing experience from participating in the development of various weapons, was the most frequent "guest" at the plant. Possessing extensive information on the experimental development of new guns from various design bureaus and showing personal interest in the design, Deikin provided constant assistance to the plant and designers with further, more radical improvement of the AK-47 rifle than was required during the initial launch of it in mass production. Together with the Main Armament Department (GAU) within the DoD, the Weapons Production Ministry also participated in the development and practical implementation of long-term plans for the further improvement of weapons technology. The main attention was paid to the design im-

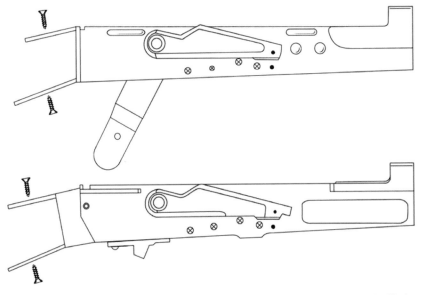

provement of the AK-47 Avtomat. Only a weapon of improved and proven design could serve as a base for the successful solution of all other problematic issues tied to setting up and successful launch of mass production for any other weapon.

Increasing the survivability of components and improving their performance, stabilizing the reliability of the automatics, and enhancing the combat capabilities of the AK-47 were the main directions for design and technological improvement of the weapon system. The first stage of the design development work was to be completed by the end of the first year of serial production, but encountered technical difficulties in connection with the implementation of the system, requiring further postponement of the completion date. The main obstacle to ensuring the normal course of production and processing of the documen-

*This outline drawing clearly shows the differences between the combination stamped-milled receiver of the AK-47 Type 1 (top) and the first milled receiver of the Type 2 (bottom).*

tation in the plant's view was the stamp-riveted construction of the receiver. The practical use in the field experience of the new AK-47 rifle, despite the overall positive results, showed that without more drastic modernization geared toward replacing the stamped-riveted construction of the receiver, which lacked the rigidity of a more solid milled one, the work to eliminate a large percentage of rejects and return rifles would be difficult.

A set of drawings was produced and work commenced on a modified version of the Kalashnikov. This "modernized" sample was presented for tests at the end of 1949. The Deputy Chief Designer of Izhmash at that time wrote the following in his letter

*The new one-piece pistol grip replaced the much more complicated version of the Type 1. This design has carried over to today's AK Avtomats.*

to the testing team:

"The milled receiver improves the quality of the whole Avtomat. It eliminates the change in its dimensions during operation, and greatly simplifies the assembly operations due to the preservation of dimensional stability throughout the manufacturing process. From the point of view of economics, the introduction of a milled receiver dramatically reduces the cost per unit, since the time required to manufacture the front trunnion, the rear trunnion, the stamping of the receiver and most importantly the assembly of all these elements by riveting in complex devices is much greater than for manufacturing of the entire solid milled receiver."

Apart from the milled receiver, the new gun also had:

• A safety lever that was removable during disassembly. The old one was not detachable, and was installed by riveting, which made a very tight fit and affected receiver dimensions.

• An ejector that was strengthened by changing its shape and rounding its base.

• A new one-piece pistol grip with new attachment by nut and bolt that eliminated possibility of splitting wooden parts at the time of assembly and simplified any repairs.

The modified Avtomats had many other changes that were previously approved by the Proving Grounds and GAU. The new rifles were issued with interchangeable magazines. The plant had already organized mass production of the magazines. The Test Team as well as the Office of Small Arms Weaponry had approved all of the changes including the milled receiver.

Though the new milled receiver was universally accepted and praised, the order went out to the Research Technological Institute to develop a stamped version of the AK receiver that would be easy to produce. The reason for that order was that it would simplify production of the Avtomats during wartime.

With all the positives come the negatives. The most negative effect from production of the AK using a milled receiver was excessive use of metal. Total metal waste was around 1.5 kg (3.3 lbs.) per receiver. That was deemed unacceptable. After taking a closer look at the manufacturing process, the Izhevsk plant found a way to minimize the waste and get within the parameters of metal use per rifle that was set by the government. This included realizing economy from other metal components. However, even with taking steps to reduce waste, the metal overuse continued to be very high well into the mid-1950s. The total consumption of metal per rifle was approximately 15 kg (33 lbs.), with a total weight of finished product of about 3.5 kg (7.7 lbs.) This made workers at the Izhmash plant continue a persistent search for ways to reduce metal consumption.

By the end of 1950, the first test batch of milled receiver AK rifles was manufactured. The first factory tests of two milled AKs produced expected, positive results. Mass production of the newly modernized Avtomat commenced. However, the name

*The Type 3 milled receiver AK-47 (Lightened) was approved as the final variant for the Soviet Armed Forces.*

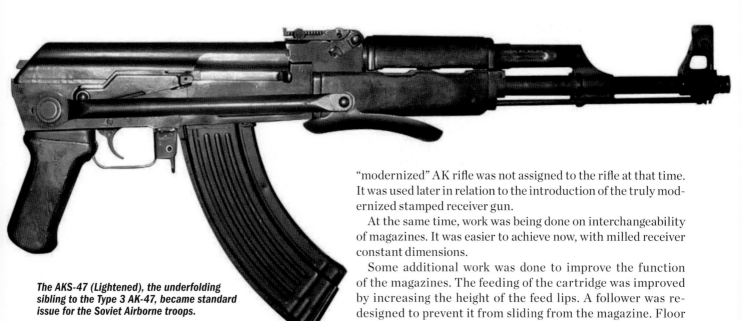

*The AKS-47 (Lightened), the underfolding sibling to the Type 3 AK-47, became standard issue for the Soviet Airborne troops.*

"modernized" AK rifle was not assigned to the rifle at that time. It was used later in relation to the introduction of the truly modernized stamped receiver gun.

At the same time, work was being done on interchangeability of magazines. It was easier to achieve now, with milled receiver constant dimensions.

Some additional work was done to improve the function of the magazines. The feeding of the cartridge was improved by increasing the height of the feed lips. A follower was redesigned to prevent it from sliding from the magazine. Floor plate retention was improved by adding a locking detent. All of the improvements to the magazine were done in response to the complaints that came from the field.

After several tests to ensure the interchangeability of magazines, mass production commenced by the end of the first year of serial production of the rifles themselves. The magazine stopped being an integral part of each individual rifle, with that firearm's serial number stamped or engraved on it. Instead, any new magazine would now fully comply with specifications that said, "Any magazine must be attached and detached to and from any rifle."

Interchangeability of the magazines was a very important issue. Achieving this would allow the manufacturer to take the magazines out of the rifle's manufacturing process and launch a separate mass production of the mags, independent from the rifles. The newly produced magazines would "meet" their rifles only in the packing shop, where they could be put in the box with any rifle before shipping to the end user.

The final AK documentation was accepted by the Ministry Commission in December of 1950. In addition to the milled receiver and the above-mentioned small modifications, the final version of the Avtomat included the following improvements.

- Strengthened return spring.
- Hammer and extractor springs made of triple wire coil.
- Strengthened receiver cover.
- The rotation of the safety lever limited to the vertical position.
- Redesign and location of the rear sling attachment.

All the changes were approved and, most importantly, documented, a very important matter that would simplify serial production of the AK-47. The newer version of the Avtomat had a huge usage reserve that provided the AK with plenty of potential for further development. At last, the final highly functioning version of the AK-47 with milled receiver was completed. Rifles started to arrive in the hands of Soviet soldiers *en masse*. Looking back, one can easily see that the AK-47 was a product of the relentless effort of hundreds of military personnel, from privates in the field to officials in plush Moscow offices; some whose names and deeds are well documented in the annals of history and some simply forgotten. It would be safe to say that the AK-47, the Avtomat Kalashnikova, was a product of true team effort.

In the end, two models were approved for mass production: the AK-47 (Lightened) with fixed buttstock and AKS-47 (Lightened) with underfolding metal stock for mobile troops. By the early 1950s, both models were being supplied to the Soviet troops in great numbers, launching the greatest re-armament program and making Soviet Armed Forces the best-armed force in the world.

## FIRST COMBAT APPLICATION

The first combat use of the AK-47 in the world arena occurred on November 1, 1956, during the suppression of the uprising in Hungary. Until then, every effort was made to conceal the new rifles from prying eyes. The soldiers carried them in special cases, concealing the overall shape of the gun. After shooting, all empty cases were carefully picked up. In Hungary, the AK proved itself in real battle, especially within an urban environment.

It was time to spread the wealth.

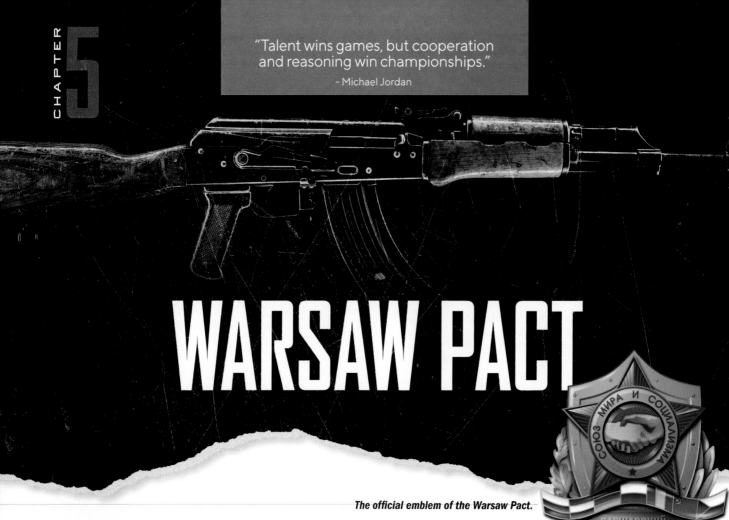

## CHAPTER 5

"Talent wins games, but cooperation and reasoning win championships."
— Michael Jordan

# WARSAW PACT

*The official emblem of the Warsaw Pact.*

**W**hile World War II was still raging, the Soviet Union was actively engaged in the formation of a circle of its future allies. Since the second half of 1943, when the fate of Nazi Germany was already determined and its defeat was only a matter of time, the Soviet leadership began signing bilateral treaties with its allies.

Unlike Britain and the U.S., which were military allies of the USSR, relationships with the new East European countries were built not only in the military arena, but on a broader basis. The Soviet side tried to transfer all of its sociopolitical and socioeconomic systems to the countries of Eastern Europe. And, I must say, it was quite successful. By the end of the 1940s, pro-Soviet regimes were established in Poland, Czechoslovakia, Hungary, Bulgaria, Romania and Albania, as well as the Soviet occupation zone of Germany. They were dominated by the political system of the communist-style parties (under different names, for example, the "Polish United Workers' Party" or the "Socialist Unified Party of Germany," which did not change their essence). This time also brought the establishment of a state monopoly in the economy (albeit with preservation, in many cases, of peasant farming and small business). The exception was Yugoslavia, which also was trying to build socialism, but with its own specifics and its charismatic leader, Josip Broz Tito, who did not want to recognize Stalin's "guiding and supervision role."

On May 11, 1955, representatives of the Soviet Union, the Polish People's Republic, the Czechoslovak Socialist Republic, the Hungarian People's Republic, the German Democratic Republic, the Socialist Republic of Romania, the People's Republic of Bulgaria and the People's Republic of Albania met in the capital of Poland. The delegation of the People's Republic of China was also present as an observer. The participants of the meeting stated the need to take retaliatory measures for the establishment of the North Atlantic Treaty Organization (NATO) and the inclusion of West Germany in this bloc, as well as its remilitarization.

It was recognized that joint measures of security and defense outlined in the bilateral treaties were no longer sufficient. As a result, on May 14, 1955, the Treaty of Friendship, Cooperation and Mutual Assistance was signed in Warsaw.

The aim of the Warsaw Pact was to ensure the security of the members and to maintain peace in Europe. The Warsaw Pact also stated that the parties to the treaty would respect the independence and integrity of the allied states, and not interfere in their internal affairs. The purely defensive nature of the agreement was declared. In complete compliance with the Charter of the United Nations, the Treaty member states promised to refrain from the threat or use of force, to resolve disputes by peaceful means, and to consult among themselves on all-important international issues affecting their common interests. They declared their readiness to take part in all international actions aimed at ensuring international peace and security, to achieve effective measures for the general reduction of armaments and the prohibition of weapons of mass destruction. They would also provide immediate assistance by all means, including the use of armed force, in the event of an armed attack in Europe on one or more of the Treaty member states.

To implement the goals and objectives of the Warsaw Pact, it created appropriate political and military bodies, including the Political Consultative Committee and the Joint Command of the Armed Forces. The Committee of Ministers of Defense was the supreme military organ. It dealt with the organization of joint military actions: exercises, maneuvers, command-staff games, as well as interaction in the field of training and training troops, standardizing charters and instructions, introducing new types of weapons, logistical support for troops, etc. Narrower and more specific issues were placed on the Technical Committee. It dealt with issues pertaining to weapons and military equipment improvement, as well as standardization, facilitating interaction on the battlefield and technical support. Another task of the Technical Committee was to determine the specialization in production of weapons for individual Warsaw Pact countries.

The overall command of Warsaw Pact troops was carried out by the Joint Command of the Armed Forces. Its head was the commander of the United Armed Forces. This post was always occupied by the representative of the USSR.

The composition of contingents allocated by each country to the Joint Armed Forces was determined, as a rule, by bilateral agreements with the USSR, revised every five years. The composition of the Joint Armed Forces highlighted the most prepared units and formations of constant combat readiness. By 1990, they included the following Soviet units:

• Western Group of Forces (on the territory of East Germany): 1st and 2nd Tank Armies, 3rd, 8th and 20th Conventional Land Forces Armies (three or four divisions each).

• The Central Group of Forces (in Czechoslovakia): two tank and three motorized infantry divisions.

• The Northern Group of Forces (in Poland): one tank and one motorized infantry division.

• The Southern Group of Forces (in Hungary): two tank and two motorized infantry divisions.

The Polish army was represented by the 1st, 2nd and 4th Conventional Land Forces Armies (the first two with five divisions, the last with three) and two Reserve Divisions—a total of 15 divisions, including five tank divisions.

Czechoslovakia allocated the 1st and 4th Conventional Land Forces Armies (four or five divisions) and the 2nd Reserve Army (six divisions)—a total of 15 divisions, including six tank divisions.

The National People's Army of the GDR provided the 3rd and 5th Conventional Land Forces Armies (three divisions each) and five Reserve Divisions to the United Armed Forces, a total of 11 divisions, of which two were tank divisions.

Bulgaria was represented by the 1st, 2nd and 3rd Conventional Land Forces Armies (three divisions each), totaling nine divisions.

Romania, with the 2nd and 3rd Conventional Land Forces Armies (four divisions each), had a total of eight divisions, including two tank divisions.

Hungary dedicated a total of six divisions.

All of these forces had to be equipped and trained according to the new global doctrine of the treaty. Standardization was essential.

To develop joint operations and cement cohesiveness of the joint forces, multiple joint command and staff exercises and military maneuvers were conducted within the framework of the Warsaw Pact. The exercises were conducted on the territory of all member countries. Among the largest military exercises were war games with code names "Quartet" (1963), "October Assault" (1965), "Rhodopes" (1967), "Dnepr" (1967), "North" (1968), "Brotherhood in Arms" (1970), "West-81" (1981) and "Shield-82" (1982).

In particular, the "Rhodope" operation was

*Overall command of the Warsaw Pact Forces was placed on Joint Command of the Armed Forces, led by the USSR.*

carried out in May 1967. Its objective was a demonstration of the military presence of the Warsaw Pact countries in the border regions of Greece in Bulgaria. Though framed as a military exercise, this action was in the time of the military coup in Greece. Armed forces of the USSR, Bulgaria and Romania took part in the war games at that time. The only real military operation conducted by the Joint Armed Forces was Operation "Danube," the deployment of troops into the territory of Czechoslovakia to suppress the Prague Spring uprising in 1968. Along with the Soviet troops, the 2nd Army of the Polish Army and the Hungarian 8th Motorized Rifle Division participated, as well as a small group of soldiers from East Germany.

Success of any joint force operation lies not only in standard tactics and centralized command, but also in logistics, supply and other resources available to the troops in the way of standard equipment and weapons. By equipping Warsaw Pact troops with new AK rifles, Soviets ensured that their own and allied forces would be far superior to anything NATO could muster with its kaleidoscope of post–WWII weapons and calibers.

However formidable a force it may have been in Europe, the Warsaw Pact could not withstand the test of time and ceased to exist with the fall of the Soviet Union in 1991.

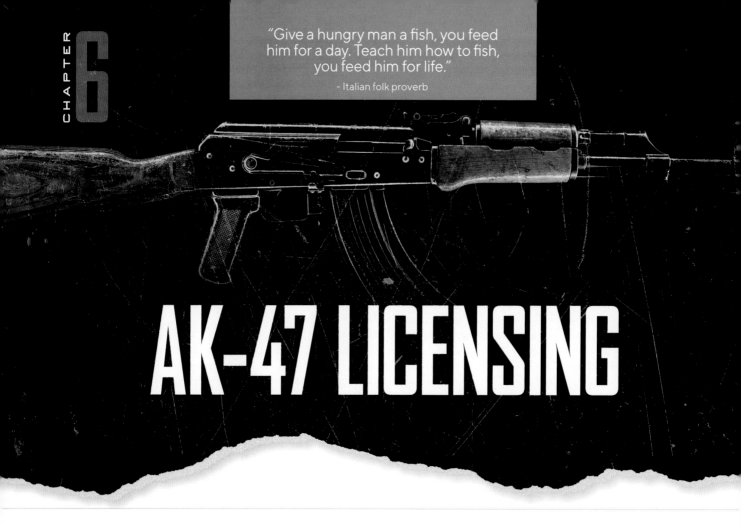

CHAPTER **6**

> "Give a hungry man a fish, you feed
> him for a day. Teach him how to fish,
> you feed him for life."
>
> – Italian folk proverb

# AK-47 LICENSING

In the years following WWII, similar to West European NATO countries, there was complete and utter confusion with small arms in the East. A similar or worse situation was with pro-Soviet Asian countries. The troops were armed with weapons of different quality, safety, performance and caliber. These included obsolete Soviet models and captured German rifles, machine guns and submachine guns. There was an urgent need to come up with a common weapon system.

After some discussions, Warsaw Pact military leaders agreed to keep the Soviet rifle cartridge 7.62x54R as the ammunition for machine guns and sniper rifles, and as the main ammo to accept the intermediate 7.62x39mm cartridge. Almost immediately, limited shipments of AK rifles commenced to the allied troops. However, it was clear from the

*East German troops armed with PPSh-41 machine pistols.*

beginning that Soviet arsenals could not satisfy the Avtomat vacuum in the Soviet Union and in all other friendly countries. Before too long, the Soviets started to give out free licenses for production of the AK Avtomats to friendly countries.

Hungary was the first country to receive a license, technical documentation, training for its staff, plus new equipment for the production of weapons and ammunition. On January 1, 1955, the FEG plant started production of the AK-55 rifle, which was an exact copy of the Soviet AK. Subsequently, military and technical cooperation between the USSR and the Hungarian People's Republic continued, and a number of Soviet-designed weapons were produced in Hungary.

The next country that began to produce Kalashnikov's Avtomat was China. Their version of the gun was named Type-56; it

*Numerous Joint Force exercises were staged to instill cohesion within Warsaw Pact armed forces.*

*Hungary's AK-55 was produced under Soviet license. It was an identical copy of the Soviet Type 3 AK-47.*

is generally similar to the AK, except for an integral needle bayonet in a stowed position folding down and back. This addition was "borrowed" from another Soviet gun that was licensed to China earlier—the SKS. The shape of the blade was copied from the even earlier licensed Soviet Mosin Model 91/30 rifle. Also, early models of the Type-56 Avtomat did not have chrome-lined bores and chrome-plated gas piston and bolt groups, which significantly reduced the survivability of these components. Nevertheless, the Type-56 enjoyed almost 30 years as the main battle rifle of the People's Liberation Army of China. China continues to produce these Type-56 rifles for export. We here in the U.S. know these Chinese Kalashnikovs better than anyone. I am, of course, talking about the PolyTech Legend. The stamped-receiver versions of the Type-56 rifle do not fit into this chapter as guns licensed by the Soviets. They are a different story for a different chapter.

Shortly after China, with a minimum time gap, production of the infamous Soviet weapons was established in East Germany, Poland, Bulgaria, Romania, North Korea and Yugoslavia. In addition, a program consisting of "screwdriver" assembly from Soviet components was established in Egypt, Syria, Libya, Cuba, Lebanon and India.

Since all of the licensed copies of the Type 3 AK-47 Avtomat were almost exact copies of the original, and their production was established under close supervision of the Soviet specialists, their tactical-technical characteristics were also identical.

All in all, the Soviet Union, as one of the world's full-fledged arms exporters, legally transferred (sold) licenses for the production of Kalashnikov Avtomats to 18 countries. Most of the countries that received the license were Soviet Warsaw Pact allies.

Another 11 countries started production of AK clones and/or AK-based rifles without any license.

*The Chinese Type 56 Avtomat was a licensed copy of the Soviet milled receiver AK-47.*

*This later version of the Type 56 sported underfolding spike bayonet.*

*The Bulgarian AKK and AKKS (pictured), just like the Chinese Type 56 and Hungarian AK-55, are an exact copy of the Soviet AK-47 and AKS-47.*

*(top) Polish kbk AK (pmK) and kbk AKS (pictured) are not an exception, and followed AK-47 and AKS-47 design.*

*(above) Polish kbk AK can be equipped with special removable buttstock pad and muzzle device for launching rifle grenades.*

One example is of this Finland. In the 1950s, when the question of re-armament of the Finnish Armed Forces arose, it was decided to not waste time developing weapons of their own design, but rather to adapt the already well-known foreign system. Due to efforts from Finnish government officials who supported normalization of relations with the USSR, the Finnish military was largely focused on Soviet models. This led to the choice favoring the Soviet Kalashnikov Avtomat as a main battle rifle; a license for its production was soon acquired from Poland. Finns turned the AK into the Valmet Rk 60. The Valmet Rk 60 was an exact copy of the original Kalashnikov rifle internally, but it was drastically different in its external appearance. It sported a tubular pistol grip and crutch-like stock. The front sight and gas block were combined. The dioptric rear sight was placed on the top cover. The barrel was tipped with a three-pronged flash suppressor-compensator with bayonet lug. The Valmet's milled receiver was slightly modified. It was machined with a slight slant from the magazine well up. Most likely this receiver modification was done out of weight consideration. A new modernized version of the Valmet Rk 62 Avtomat is still in service with Finnish Armed Forces.

A similar situation occurred with Israel. Development of the new Israeli rifle was spurred by the Arab-Israeli conflict of 1968, which resulted in the capture of several thousand brand new Soviet AK-47 and AKM rifles that were supplied to the Arab countries by the Soviet Union. These guns were highly praised by the soldiers on the front lines. The leadership of the Israeli Armed Forces decided to develop a rifle "the same as the Russian AK, only better." Since diplomatic relations with the USSR were non-existent, the Israelis approached the Finnish company Valmet. Valmet sold the necessary equipment, tools and drawings to the Israelis, and provided the specialists to establish production of the new rifles in Israel.

Like the Valmet, the Israeli Galil rifle looks different from the original AK. It was based on the already un-AK appearance of Finnish Valmet gun. In addition, the Galil was adopted for the needs of the Israeli Defense Forces. The rifle received a metal tubular folding stock, original front handguard an upward-bent charging handle. Unlike the Finnish Valmet Rk 62, which was chambered for the standard AK 7.62X39mm M43 cartridge, the Israeli Galil fired the 5.56X45mm NATO round. Additionally, the Galil rifle turned out heavier than the Valmet and its Soviet counterpart, weighing 3.95 kg (8.7 lbs.).

In 1973, the Israeli Armed Forces received the first 10,000 of the new domestically built Galil AR rifles. The Galil carbine variant SAR was kept in service by the Knesset Guard and the Armored Corps until the late 2000s. Its civilian semi-auto version has been and still is imported into the U.S.

The next beneficiary of the free-for-all AK-47 proliferation was the South African Republic.

The 1970s and 1980s saw close cooperation between Israel and South Africa in general relationship and in the military arena especially. One of the results of such cooperation was the new South African 5.56mm Vector R4 rifle that was a modernized version of Israel's Galil AR. The R4 entered into service with the South African Defense Force in 1982, replacing the Belgian FN FALs. All modifications to the Israeli rifle were made to address more rigid requirements to conduct combat actions in the most adverse conditions of the sub-Saharan Africa war theater. Initially, the R4 had a fixed stock, which was replaced by a folding metal one. Each rifle was equipped with a removable bipod.

There have been plenty more unlicensed AK models built throughout the world over the years. However, the rifles in this chapter were based on the original AK-47 milled-receiver models. I will talk about the other "pirated" Kalashnikov clones later. But now, back to the AK evolution...

*The Finnish Valmet Rk 62 Avtomat looks drastically different from the original AK-47.*

*The Israeli Galil rifle is visually very different from the standard AK and unique in its features.*

*Despite the cosmetic differences, the Valmet Rk 62 internally is unmistakably AK.*

*The South African Vector R4 rifle is unmistakably an Israeli Galil variant, and as such, another AK.*

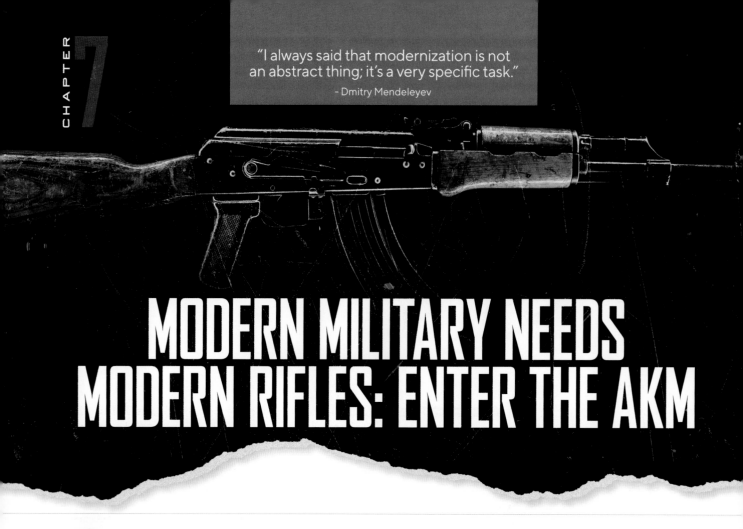

## CHAPTER 7

"I always said that modernization is not an abstract thing; it's a very specific task."

- Dmitry Mendeleyev

# MODERN MILITARY NEEDS MODERN RIFLES: ENTER THE AKM

A new rifle was not the only weapon system that was being introduced to the Soviet Armed Forces after the war. New armored troop transport/assault vehicles were developed that made troops very mobile in the battlefield. The mass frontal infantry advance with heavy armor support gave way to the highly mobile and lightning-fast armored vehicle-borne assault troops. Though the new AK-47 Avtomat fit well within the new doctrine, the soldier's combat load was far from perfection, especially considering the weight of the gun and ammo in the total load. Modern, mobile forces needed lighter rifles. And so, the evolution of the "perfect" infantry rifle continued.

Since 1949, AKs, specifically AK-47s, had been supplied to the Soviet troops *en masse*. After adopting the milled receiver, most of the new Avtomat's shortcomings were eliminated. However, the considerable weight of the gun remained. This inspired other designers to look elsewhere for the solution. One would think that Kalashnikov's position as a premier rifle designer was solidified with such wide adoption of his Avtomat, but something else happened that put the fate of the AK in jeopardy and launched the next stage in its evolution.

In the early 1950s, German Korobov (from the Degtyarev Design Bureau) introduced his TKB-517 rifle. It was significantly lighter, had better accuracy, and was also cheaper to produce. This event caused a stir and spurred the development of tactical and technical specifications for a new Avtomat (automatic carbine) and light machine gun that had to be standardized to the new rifle as much as possible. Once again, competitive tests for several rifles were conducted in 1957–1958. Mikhail Kalashnikov presented a modernized sample of his Avtomat and, based on it, a light machine gun for these tests.

Once more, the preference was given to Kalashnikov's Avtomat as the most reliable of all tested rifles. The sufficient familiarity of troops and industry with Kalashnikov's rifle also played a considerable role in issuing the final decision.

As a result, in 1959 the 7.62mm Avtomat Kalashnikov Modernized, or simply AKM, was adopted for service with the Soviet armed forces.

*The Korobov Avtomat TKB-517 was one of the guns in the long line of potential AK competitors.*

*The AKM Modernized Kalashnikov Avtomat (top) and its paratrooper version AKMS (bottom) were adopted for service in 1959.*

The AKM (Kalashnikov Avtomat Modernized, GRAU Index 6P1) is a deep modernization of the AK, adopted in service in 1959. The aim of this modernization was to increase the gun's effectiveness by improving the range (from 800 to 1,000 meters), reliability and ease of operation while significantly reducing its weight. To achieve this, designers made several external and internal changes to the overall design and system as a whole.

The AKM's receiver was now made of stamped sheet steel, which allowed makers to greatly reduce the weight. The buttstock was raised upward to bring it closer to the rifle's line of aim. Changes were made to the trigger group. A hammer delay was added. Because of that, the hammer is released a few milliseconds later when the rifle is fired in full-auto mode. This delay practically does not affect the rate of fire; it only allows the bolt carrier to stabilize in the extreme forward position before the next shot.

Improvements positively impacted accuracy. Especially evident was the decrease of vertical dispersion. It improved by almost 30 percent. Additionally, the gas block and gas tube were redesigned to eliminate a row of vent ports on the top of the gas tube. Those vented propellant gases from the gas chamber and contributed to the rising haze when the rifle got hot during firing. The front sight also got a makeover. It was now shorter at its base as a result of the AK weight watchers program. The muzzle of the barrel on the AKM now had a thread. A detachable petal-type muzzle compensator (the so-called "tray compensator") could be attached to the rifle. It was designed to compensate for drift of the Avtomat's point of aim up and to the right when firing in full-auto mode. When shooting bursts, the pressure of propellant gases escaping from the barrel pushed on the lower shoulder of the compensator, thus aiding the shooter in bringing the rifle back within the original line of aim. Having the thread on the muzzle of the new Avtomat allowed users to install suppressors, PBS or PBS-1, that are used with newly developed sub-sonic 7.61 mm U.S. cartridges (reduced power and not to be mistaken with the U.S.-made). In addition, a newly designed under-barrel grenade launcher, the GP-25 Kostyor, could be installed on the AK.

At the same time, in an effort to further reduce the weight of the rifle, Izhmash Arsenal engineers explored using Bakelite material as a substitute for laminate wood. However, due to unfavorable heat transfer characteristics, most of the Bakelite gun furniture was abandoned in favor of birch laminate. Only the iconic AKM pistol grip has survived.

Alongside the fixed-stock AKM, the folding stock AKMS (GRAU index 6P4) variant for airborne troops was also adopted. The main differences from the original AKS underfolder rifle were the stamped metal used in fabrication of the folding stock and changes to the folding mechanism that brought the stock up in line with the gun's bore plane. To utilize advances in night vision technology, two more variants were introduced at the same time, the AKMN (GRAU index 6P1N) with fixed stock and the AKMSN (GRAU index 6P4N) with underfolding metal stock. These variants sported a side-mounting rail for mounting night sights. The reason for locating the rail on the lower rear left side of the receiver was the rigidity of that particular spot. During my meeting with Mikhail Kalashnikov in 2001, the man himself was saying how important it was for the AKM stamped receiver to "dance" or flex during firing. Placing the accessory rail in the lower left of the receiver also placed it out of the way of the receiver "dancing," thus eliminating chances for the optical sight to get out of whack.

A a side note, for those who love to talk about AR modularity, the AK rifles had an accessory rail in 1959, way before the AR was even born as a weapon system.

This moment began the triumphant march of Kalashnikov's Avtomat around the world. In fact, it is an AKM variant of some kind that most the Americans call the AK-47. The AKM rifle is most widely spread throughout the world. It is most likely the AKM and not any other rifle that is on our TV screen every day, no matter what conflict is being covered in any part of the world.

## CHAPTER 8

"Keep what you have and take
what you want..."
– Harvard University School of Business,
Strategic Business Planning Manual

# AKM LICENSING AND "ILLEGAL" COPIES

**K**alashnikov's Avtomat was quickly becoming the most popular battle rifle in the world, gaining popularity year after year. By the time the AKM rolled out, several countries had established their own production of the AK rifle under the Soviet license. During my research for this book, I could not find any references to distinct AKM licensing to any foreign entity. Most likely, the Soviets transferred AKM documentation and technology via amendment to the existing license, or without any licenses at all. What we know is that Bulgaria, Poland, East Germany, Romania and Egypt have been building essentially an exact copy of the Soviet AKM for years, and all but Germany continue to build them today.

Essentially, all of the licensed AKM

*The Bulgarian AKKM and its underfolding AKKMS sibling (shown here in the hands of Bulgarian soldiers) is one of the closest licensed copies of the original Soviet AKM.*

Avtomats were the same internally and kept close to the original design. However, unlike the milled-receiver AK-47, where all licensed guns were identical, AKM copies started to show cosmetic differences attributed to the particular country's military traditions and armament. Several countries, like Bulgaria, Poland and Egypt, chose to keep the original design throughout. The rifles from these countries are considered to be most similar to the original Soviet AKM.

Others, like East Germany and Romania, chose to replace elements of the AKM furniture. The East German MPi-KM sported a plastic stock, a pistol grip, and a wooden upper handguard, which was later also replaced with a plastic one. The Romanian AIM Avtomat kept the Bakelite grip and laminate wood stock and upper handguard close to the original Soviet AKM design. However, the laminate wood lower handguard had a vertical front grip. Both countries produced underfolding models, the East German MPi-KMS72 and Romanian AIMS. They also both used a wire side-folding stock as a replacement for a fixed one.

*Poland's Kbk-AKM (PMK-M) is another representative of the closest licensed copies of the AKM. Shown here with drum magazine, PBS-1 suppressor and Wz. 1974 Palad under-barrel grenade launcher.*

*East German MPi-KM (shown here is the earlier version with wooden lower hand-guard) and MPi-KMS72 underfolder are AKM copies dressed in plastic furniture. These AKs are known for their quality.*

*Romanian AIM and AIMS folder are close copies of the Soviet AKM Avtomat. The front vertical grip incorporated into the lower handguard is the distinct feature of all Romanian AKs.*

## HUNGARIAN CLONES

The most drastic departure from the norm were the Hungarian AKM clones. The FEG AKM-63 and its underfolder sibling were pretty close copies of their Soviet samples, with the only difference being the blond solid wood furniture and original-design pistol grip. The AKM-based AMD-65 and AMP-69 Avtomats were something entirely different, configuration-wise. The AMD-65 sported the single wire, crutch-type folding stock; a pistol grip that was typical to Hungarian design; a metal lower handguard and a front grip that was identical and symmetrically opposite to the pistol grip. Other distinctive features included a reduced-capacity 20-round magazine, lack of upper handguard and location of the front sight, which now was seated right against the gas block. The barrel was tipped with a two-chamber muzzle brake unique to the AMD.

The AMP Avtomat was a shortened and compact version of the AMD. It had a similar crutch-type folding stock with the addition of a spring-loaded buffer, a plastic lower handguard without front grip and a shorter barrel. It was supplied with even smaller-capacity magazines for better concealment. It was also equipped with a side accessory rail for mounting a rifle grenade launching sight.

All in all, no matter what modifications the Warsaw Pact and other "friendly" countries made to the guns to adapt them to their armed forces, these guns remained essentially AKMs. Non-select-fire, commercial versions of most licensed AKM copies, with the exception of the East German MPi-KM, have been or are still imported into the U.S.

However, there are those countries that, for some geopolitical reason, Soviets did not "shower" with their knowledge and advances in weapons technology. China and Yugoslavia are examples of such countries, and had to develop their own versions of stamped-receiver AKs.

Considering that, the relations of the Soviet Union with the world patent system were extremely tense, and the Soviet For-

The Hungarian FEG AKM-63 (top) is a close copy of the AKM. However, the AMD-65 (middle) and AMP-69 (bottom) represent a departure from the traditional AK configuration.

eign Ministry chose to ignore some liberties taken by the fraternal socialist states with respect to the intellectual property of the Soviet citizens. As such, the popularity of the AK did not bring financial or any other material dividends to the rifle's designer. After all, this was an achievement of not just an individual, but of all Soviet people. Therefore, the AK-47 and AKM designs belonged to the Union of Soviet Socialist Republics. Obviously, Mikhail Kalashnikov was recognized and awarded by the Soviet government, along with others who participated in the development of the Avtomat. However, it was not widely advertised and rather kept quiet as it dealt with the security of the Motherland.

It was much later, after the fall of the Soviet Union, when worldwide fame finally found Kalashnikov. He was able to realize some indirect monetary rewards attached one way or the other to his infamous gun, before he passed away. But, I am sure that it paled in comparison to what he would have received had he owned the rights to his de-

sign in the free market economy. Unfortunately for Kalashnikov, it was left to the Soviet Motherland to distribute the design and know-how and the rest of the intellectual property as it saw fit.

Numerous modifications of the Kalashnikov rifle were popping up. Alongside the Romanian and Chinese industrially designed variant, there were scores of versions "built on the knee" of Middle Eastern or Central Asian craftsmen, who created homemade "Kalukov" (mispronunciation of the Russian word "Kalashnikov" by the Afghan Muj) guns. This was thanks to the AK's simple design and use of less sophisticated manufacturing technologies.

All the old Soviet license agreements have been expired for some time now. However, the "Rosoboronexport," as official distributer of Russian military hardware, says that eight countries continue to produce Kalashnikov system firearms illegally. I am pretty sure that Rosoboronexport would be glad to sell an AK manufacturing license to any entity that wants to build these guns. They claim that Russia today loses approximately $2 billion per year from sales of unlicensed AKs.

The Egyptian Maadi MISR Avtomat (shown here in the hands of Egyptian soldiers) is considered to be the closest copy to the original AK design due to close Soviet supervision during early production. Later, the quality of the Maadi declined drastically.

## CHINESE AKS

The most mass-produced unlicensed variant of the AKM is without a doubt the Chinese Type-56S and its later modifications, Type-81 and Type-86. It is estimated that roughly 15 million copies of these rifles have been produced. Large-scale production was stopped when the People's Liberation Army switched to the Type-85. However, limited production for the commercial export market continues to this day.

Overall, Chinese engineers had to modernize the AK rifle on their own, as the Chino-Soviet relationship degraded drastically during the mid-1950s. Constant border disputes and Mao's belief that Khrushchev's policies betrayed the Communist ideals were the fuel of bickering that ultimately led to the cool down in relations. My personal opinion is that the rift happened when the not-totally-insane Khrushchev refused to share hydrogen bomb technology with the very "motivated" and ambitious Mao.

*The Chinese effort to build a modernized version of the Type 56 outside of the Soviet license resulted in Type 56S. This modernized AK featured a thicker stamped receiver. The rest of the gun remained unchanged.*

Nevertheless, the Chinese engineers had done a good job with their modernized version of the Type 56S. By examining the Chinese variant, it is obvious that there was no direct Soviet influence in developing it, though one can also see that Chinese firearm designers had some "guidelines" to go on. It is especially evident when looking at the stamped receiver. My guess is that some of the first Soviet-built AKM rifles (supplied to and deployed by the NVA and VC in Vietnam during the Vietnam War) somehow made it to China even before the 1975 conflict. To be honest, the stamped receiver of the modernized Chinese rifle is well done and projects an appearance of robust structure, weight consideration notwithstanding. However, the rest of the gun is simply borrowed from its milled predecessor, including vented gas tube, fully hooded front sight and thicker smooth top cover. The geometry of the gun was left intact. The new gun retained the 800-meter rear sight. And as previous models, the new Type 56S lacked chrome plating in the gas chamber, piston and trigger group.

The modernized Type-56 have been produced in three main configurations, distinguishable by type of folding stock and folding attached bayonets, hence the term double folder. Just like the Soviets, the Chinese also played with their version of Bakelite material for gun furniture and magazines, with a certain degree of success.

But perhaps the most distinguishable feature of all Chinese AKs and other Soviet clones is their lack of birch laminate furniture. Instead, the Chinese guns sport soft, solid wood stock, grip and handguards. The reason is simple—there are no birch forests in China that can produce suitable hardwood for the laminate. This one is for the proponents of the so-called Chinese "Dragunov" theory.

In general, the Chinese managed not only to copy the Kalashnikov Avtomat, but also to preserve the good quality of the materials used in its construction. Decent reliability and cheapness are the main features of the Chinese AK variant. China can safely be called the master of copying Soviet weapons, since no other country in the world has so far succeeded in producing Kalashnikov rifles without losing quality.

The main beneficiary of the success of the Chinese AK development (or, more accurately, copying) was Iran.

During the Iran–Iraq war of 1980–1988, the Iranian government purchased large quantities of Chinese Type 56 AK rifles to arm the Iranian Army. Eventually, the Iranian Defense Industries Organization (DIO) conglomerate established its own production of Type 56 Avtomats under the designation KL-7.62. Basically, the KL-7.62 is an unlicensed version of the Chinese Type 56 rifle, and in its original form was virtually identical to it. However, later the gun was upgraded with plastic parts replacing wooden ones. This slightly improved the rifle's dimensions and weight. By design, the KL-7.62, just like the Type 56, is a copy of the Soviet AK.

*An Iranian Defense Factory worker assembles the KL-7.62 Avtomat, which is a licensed copy of Chinese Type 56S, evident by the front sight block and Bakelite furniture.*

## YUGOSLAVIA

The complicated geopolitical situation in central and southern Europe that developed in the 1950s drove dissent into the Socialist camp. Yugoslavia was among the "unhappy campers." The iron fist ruler of Yugoslavia, Marshal Josip Bros Tito, had a different view of the Socialist paradise than what the Soviets were "suggesting." As a result of the bickering, the Soviets drastically reduced their economic cooperation and assistance to Yugoslavia. This included the military cooperation and inadvertently affected assistance with arms manufacturing.

Many think that, post-war, the Yugoslav Army was armed just like the militaries of other Socialist countries, with licensed copies of the Kalashnikov Avtomat. In fact, Yugoslavia established production of its own AK-based infantry firearm system outside of the Soviet sphere of influence.

In 1959, the factory "Crvena Zastava" in Kragujevac began work on its own system of automatic weapons based on the Soviet AK. Due to the foreign policy situation at the time, when Yugoslavia was not in warm and cozy relations with the USSR, it was impossible to get the license for production of the AK, and therefore the development of its own version began without the agreement of the Soviets. Factory managers were able to enlist the support of the Department of Infantry Weapons and

Tactics. However, they failed to secure any support from the General Staff of the Yugoslav People's Army for copying of the Kalashnikov.

The event that spurred the beginning of the development of the Yugoslavian AK was the defection of two Albanian soldiers in 1959. Both servicemen crossed the Yugoslav border with their personal weapons in hand—Soviet-issue milled-receiver AK-47 rifles. Immediately these Avtomats were sent to the Crvena Zastava factory. At the plant, engineers came up with the idea to create a whole series of small arms, based on the AK design, with the designation FAZ (Familija Automatskog Oruzja Zastava). The emphasis, of course, was heavily placed on developing an automatic carbine. Samples of the "Albanian" rifles were thoroughly studied, and all their components were accurately copied by sulfur sulfate casting.

Soon the designers realized that two full-scale copies were not enough to fulfill the task before them. Shortly, the Yugoslav government solved this problem. During a visit to one "friendly" Third World country that received Soviet military assistance, Tito managed to secure the purchase of two-thousand AKs, some of which went directly to the Crvena Zastava plant.

In the end, the Yugoslav designers created two prototypes with milled receivers. A sample with a fixed wood stock was designated "A," and one with a metal (folding) stock was designated "B," while the whole system received the common name M-64.

The designers tried to adapt the M-64 carbine to shoot rifle grenades. Similar to the French design, the barrel was fitted with a special nozzle that served as a grenade seat/guide and played the role of a flash hider. This design found its place on a new modification of the M-59 carbine (a Yugoslav copy of the Soviet SKS carbine). But, for use with the M-64 Avtomats, engineers had to design an improved attachment that also included a new type of sight for rifle grenades. This new sight was installed on the gas tube and simultaneously played the role of a gas regulator. When raised and deployed for use with grenades, it blocked the gas port.

Although the Department of Infantry Weapons and Tactics fully supported the adoption of the FAZ series of rifles, the high command of the Yugoslav People's Army (JNA) rejected it. In their opinion, equipping all of the Yugoslav Army with automatic rifles would result in excessive consumption of ammunition. However, time showed the advantage of automatic infantry weapons on the battlefield when the Soviets, along with Warsaw Pact allies, rolled into Czechoslovakia in 1968. Shortly after, the Yugoslav government started negotiations with the Soviets to purchase AK and AKM Avtomats for the Special Forces of the JNA.

Hearing about the negotiations with the Soviets, the management of the Crvena Zastava factory immediately notified the Yugoslav leadership that such weapons had already been developed. The government then decided to use the FAZ automatic weapon system as the basis for development of the new domestic small arms program. The Belgrade Military Technical Institute had prepared a set of technical documentation for the new weapons that included a number of additional requirements. In 1970, a new M-70 automatic rifle was introduced, which was put into serial production and adopted by the JNA. Its prototype M-64 has remained an experimental model only and, at present, it can only be found in museums.

The Yugoslavian M-70 Avtomat was developed by the Yugoslavs internally, without any help from the Soviets. Though following AK configuration in its appearance, it is very different from the original Soviet Avtomats.

The M-70 Avtomat had a milled receiver, a rear sight mounted on the sight block just like the Soviet AKM, a fixed wood stock and a plastic pistol grip. At the same time, the M-70A version with a folding metal stock was released.

Ultimately, it was decided to change the design of the trigger group by adding a trigger retarder, similar to that of the Soviet AKM. These newly modified Avtomats still had a milled receiver and received the new designation of M-70B, due to modification to the stock and addition of muzzle brake–compensator, the same as on AKM rifles. The folding metal stock version received a designation of M-70AB.

The next step in modernization of the M-70 was the introduction of the stamped receiver. The new M-70B1 and M-70AB1 folder rifles had receivers made of 0.9mm-thick sheet metal and used an RPK-type, more robust front trunnion. Somewhere between the Albanian defectors, the purchase of AKs from the third party or direct negotiations with the Soviets in 1968, the Yugoslav engineers acquired an RPK design that they employed in creation of the M-70B1 Avtomat that we all know and love here in the U.S.

In addition, in the 1970s, the factory Crvena Zastava engineer Bozhidar Blagojevic used the M-70 carbine as a base to develop an M-76 sniper rifle chambered in 8mm Mauser (7.9x57mm) caliber. Yugoslavian gun makers also developed and produced short versions of their Avtomats, similar to the Soviet AKSU. The M-92 fired the standard AK 7.62x39mm cartridge and M-85 chambered in 5.56mm NATO.

Eventually, the modern M-21 version was developed to fire 5.56mm NATO ammunition. It was adopted in 2008 by the Serbian Army. This variant represented a new weapon system that showed accuracy comparable to that of the M4 carbine during testing at the Special Purpose Unit SAJ (CAJ) of the Ministry of Internal Affairs of Serbia proving grounds. At the same time, it displayed significantly higher reliability characteristics.

Besides the M-21 variant, today Serbia produces a modernized version of the M-70AB2 Avtomat, the M-70ABZ, which is now supplied to Iraq and Afghanistan through orders approved by the U.S. Department of Defense. These rifles no longer sport the cleaning rod and rifle grenade sight/gas regulator. Instead, provisions were made for attachment of the Soviet-designed GP-25 under-barrel grenade launcher.

Iraq, just like Iran with Chinese Type 56 rifles, is also a beneficiary of "free for all" unlicensed AK dumbassery.

After importing thousands of AK-47 rifles from many countries, in the late 1970s Saddam Hussein ordered the Iraqi Ministry of Defense to develop a domestically produced copy of the Soviet AKM rifle. These guns were supposed to replace worn out rifles for Iraqi troops after years in the continuing Iran–Iraq war. Capitalizing on the favorable relationship with Yugoslavia, Iraqi technicians secured cooperation with the Crvena Zastava arms factory. By 1980, Iraq purchased tooling and machinery to establish its own factory near Baghdad under license from Zastava with aid from Yugoslav engineers and technicians. The result was the introduction of AK-type rifles of excellent quality in a country not previously known for superior domestically produced weapons. The Iraqis produced AKM copies of the Yugoslavian M-70B1 and M-70AB2 rifles that became known as the "Tabuk." The first Tabuks were supplied to Iraqi troops by the end of 1980, and since then these rifles have seen action in all conflicts that Iraq was involved in. Today the Tabuk carbines are used by all branches of the new Iraqi Defense Forces and continue to be among the most serviceable and robust weapons among Saddam-era arsenals.

The Tabuk carbine is the Iraqi version of the Kalashnikov Avtomat firing the 7.62x39mm cartridge and was produced in Al-Qadisiya, Iraq. It is based on the Yugoslav M-70B2 rifle and was produced under license from Crvena Zastava. Just like the M-70B2, it has an RPK-style stamped receiver, wood furniture, a rubber back plate buffer, a sight for a rifle grenade launcher and a beveled muzzle brake compensator. I'm not sure if the Tabuks are still being made today. Methinks that the U.S. is pretty

The Iraqi Tabuk AK is an identical copy of Yugoslavian M-70 Avtomat.

generous with our taxpayer money and supplies Iraqis with plenty of cheap AKM-style guns from every corner of central and eastern Europe at no cost to our new "allies."

The fact remains that the AKM basic design became a base for the most of the AK rifles built around the world, licensed and unlicensed. Most of the AK rifles built in the U.S. are based on AKM design. Though most of the U.S. AK builders claim that their rifles are all American-made and based on "original" Romanian or Polish drawings, the guns they build are unlicensed AKM copies.

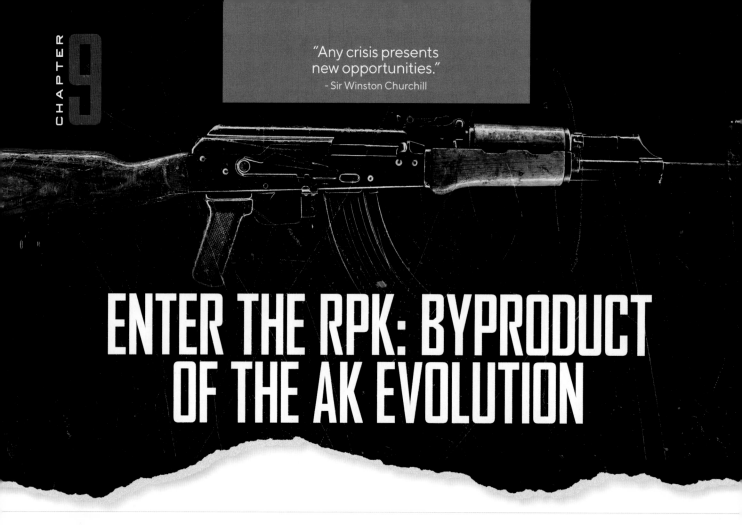

## CHAPTER 9

> "Any crisis presents
> new opportunities."
> - Sir Winston Churchill

# ENTER THE RPK: BYPRODUCT OF THE AK EVOLUTION

**A**s we continue to examine AK evolution and the effect it had on firearms development in the USSR and Russia, we cannot ignore another momentous event that produced a byproduct that became a prominent weapon still used today: the RPK—Kalashnikov's light machine gun.

Before we dive into the history of RPK development, let's talk about the light machine gun situation in the Soviet Army leading to its introduction.

The idea of unifying automatic small arms on the basis of one cartridge and one system was evolving in the USSR since the 1920s. Once the intermediate 7.62x39mm cartridge was adopted, the Soviets started work on a family of infantry weapons. Three guns had to be developed for the new ammo: the Avtomat, a semiautomatic carbine and a light machine gun.

*The RPK—Kalashnikov's light machine gun—is unmistakably AK.*

*The RPD-44 light machine gun, designed by legendary Soviet firearm designer Vasily Degtyarev, fired the M43 cartridge.*

The RPD light machine gun was the first weapon using the new intermediate 7.62x39mm M43 adopted by the Soviets. The Degtyarev light (handheld) machine gun was developed by the legendary Soviet gun designer Vasily Degtyarev in 1944, hence its designation RPD-44. At the time of the RPD creation, Degtyarev was the chief weapon designer responsible for developing many iconic weapons used by the Red Army, such as Degtyarev Pehotny (Infantry) DP machine gun, Degtyarev Tankovy (Tank) DT machine gun, .50 Cal. DShK machine gun that is still built and used today, anti-tank 14.5mm PTRD rifle and PPD machine pistol.

Before arrival of the Kalashnikov RPK, the RPD-44 was the squad automatic weapon for Soviet Infantry.

When Degtyarev was working on the RPD prototype, he suggested using a disk magazine similar to that of the DP-27 machine gun. However, experiments showed that the best option would be belt fed. The choice of belt feeding was also due to the fact that the new machine gun would be used on armored vehicles and fortified machine gun nests, where 500-round or more capacity machine gun belts could be used, which increased the effective rate of fire.

The RPD light machine gun became the main infantry squad machine gun and infantry support weapon, replacing the disc-fed DP-27. The RPD was also more convenient to use than the RP-46 with universal disc/belt-feed, since it could be serviced by one soldier and thus was more mobile. Degtyarev's RPD was supplied to many USSR-friendly countries and saw use in many military conflicts. It is still used today by warring factions around the world. In addition to the Soviet Union, the RPD was produced in China under license and designated the Type-56.

The RPD saw service with the Soviet Armed Forces from the early 1950s to the mid-1960s, when it was replaced by the Kalashnikov RPK. The Soviet military began to send the RPDs to warehouses for storage, which many called a bad decision, citing the RPD's advantages in weight and accuracy. However, there are other factors that played into the demise of one and rise of the other.

That is where another Kalashnikov takes center stage.

What happened in the early 1950s that led to the disturbance in the Soviet small arms universe? One would think the Soviet troops had their awesome AK-47 Avtomat and pretty solid RPD machine gun and were all set. What caused the "ripple" in the firearms development time continuum? Korobov happened, or his TKB-517 rifle to be precise. Not only was Korobov's lighter and cheaper rifle responsible for the creation of a better AK (the AKM), but inadvertently it spurred an event that led to the creation of the light (handheld) machine gun from Kalashnikov, the RPK. As described earlier, the introduction of a lighter and easier-to-produce TKB-517 rifle as a potential competitor to the AK-47 Avtomat caught the So-

After testing, the decision was made to replace the belt-fed RPD (top) with magazine-fed RPK light machine gun (bottom).

*The RPK light machine gun was based on the Kalashnikov system and had a high degree of similarity with the AKM Avtomat.*

viet military top brass by surprise. In line with its best traditions, Soviet officials reacted in their own way by trying to "kill two birds with one stone."

In March 1953, when it was clear that the current AK design had to be modernized to react to modern Soviet military requirements and to address the "attack" from other designs, the Small Arms Division of the Main Armament Office developed tactical and technical requirements for not only the new automatic rifle, but also for a unified new light machine gun. In 1956, several light machine gun prototypes were tested. The designers who submitted samples included Kalashnikov, Korobov, Konstantinov, V.V. Degtyarev (son of Vasily Degtyarev) and Garanin. The new light (handheld) machine gun was to replace the RPD-44 chambered for the same intermediate M43 cartridge, in service with motorized infantry, airborne and marine units. Apart from retaining the combat effectiveness of the existing light machine guns, the tactical and technical requirements included a significant reduction in the gun's weight and the complexity of its manufacturing.

After a series of tests, in 1961, Kalashnikov's light machine gun—the Ruchnoy (handheld) Pulemyot (machine gun) Ka-

lashnikov (RPK), index 6P2—was adopted and entered service with the Soviet Armed Forces. The new gun was closely unified with the AKM Avtomat that was adopted two years earlier. The RPK was a motorized infantry squad automatic weapon, designed to destroy the enemy's manpower and suppress its firepower capabilities. With the replacement of SKS carbines with the modernized AKM rifle, and the RPD light machine gun with the RPK, the automatic weapons in the squad-platoon unit became fully unified in use of ammo and the firearm system.

The deep unification of the components and assemblies of the machine gun with the already mastered AKM greatly simplified production of the RPK. Quick mastering of it by the troops (especially since the AK system is one of the easiest to learn and master) provided for good reliability of the new machine gun.

Another important factor was the ease of disassembly, care and repair. The RPK operating system is very similar (if not identical) to that of the AKM. So much so that most of their parts and assemblies are interchangeable. The interchangeability of the components between the AKM and RPK boosted the already high repairability of weapons in the units' armory workshops and military district arsenals.

*The RPK quickly gained popularity among troops around the world. Shown here the RPK is in hands of a Mongolian soldier.*

However, for production, the unification of the Avtomat with a light machine gun also had a downside—the requirements for survivability of the components of the entire family of Kalashnikov guns were determined by the survivability requirements for a machine gun. The Vyatsko-Polyansky Machine-Building Plant "Molot" was chosen as manufacturer of the RPK.

Though the RPK by design was very similar to the AKM, it also had several distinct features that distinguished it from the Avtomat. The difference between the RPK and AKM was seen in the introduction of the following design changes:

• Increased length of the barrel to boost the muzzle velocity from 715 m/s (2,346 fps) to 745 m/s (2,444 fps).
• Strengthened front trunnion.
• Increased barrel weight/thickness to provide a greater rate of fire compared to AKM.
• Equipped with lightweight folding bipod to ensure stability during firing.
• Increased capacity of the magazine (box-type, up to 40 rounds; drum, up to 75 rounds) to increase the combat rate of fire.
• Buttstock made to mimic that of the Degtyarev's RPD for convenience during shooting (the thinner neck of the stock allowed machine gunners to hold it with their left hand).
• Equipped rear sight with windage adjustment turret.

As mentioned earlier, one of the main reasons for adoption of the RPK for service with the Soviet Armed Forces was standardization. Although by design it was basically identical to the AKM, its differences were important.

The barrel length, increased to 590 mm (23.2 in.), allowed an increase in the effective range of fire to 800 meters (875 yards). Increasing the capacity of the magazine and increasing the thickness of the walls of the barrel allowed for more rapid fire. When firing from a stationary position, the bipod improved accuracy. All of these elements made the RPK a viable squad fire support gun that no unit would want to be without.

The experimental machine guns had a slightly modified AKM buttstock, but for the production model, the shape of the RPD stock was chosen. The RPK's accuracy when firing from its bipod allowed designers to do away with the compensator. The magazine feeding system inherited from the Avtomat forced them to develop mags of greater capacity. The result was two models, the box-type and a drum. All RPK and AKM magazines now were interchangeable. This is a very important factor in a unit's combat effectiveness.

Another important feature of the RPK is its versatility. It can be fired from the bipod or resting on any surface, and it can also be shot as a regular rifle with its stock against your shoulder. Compared to the RPD, the RPK is light enough where it can also be deployed "from the hip" on the move during an advance or assault, with or without a sling. Not very effective fire in terms of accuracy, but at certain moments in a fight it can have a psychological effect on enemy troops, which explains the use of this tactic from the First World War to the present.

The RPKS model was developed with a folding stock, with the same shape as the RPK, specifically for service with airborne troops. The RPKS was 0.3 kg (0.67 lb.) heavier than the standard RPK with a fixed stock. In addition, the RPKN with fixed

**For service with airborne troops, the folding version of the RPK, the RPKS (shown here) was adopted.**

stock and RPKSN folder versions have been issued with ability to accept night vision optics by means of a side-mounted accessory rail. In some conflicts, Afghanistan in particular, the RPKN equipped with an optical sight was used as a substitute for a sniper rifle. This was possible because the RPK inherited a semi-auto capability from its close relative the Avtomat, one more useful feature that played in the RPK's favor during the selection process.

Many consider the RPK's mag-fed design a disadvantage, preferring a belt-fed system. Critics continue to claim that it was a mistake to abandon the belt-fed RPD light machine gun in favor of the RPK.

## MAGAZINE VS. BELT

The choice of feeding systems for light machine guns is a long-standing subject

*After landing, the RPKS stock is quickly deployed for rapid enemy engagement.*

of discussion. The metal link belt has a comparatively low weight (which allows for more ammo in loadout), it can be compactly packed into boxes of various shapes and sizes. Users can increase the belt capacity by simply connecting the belts together. Additionally, the belt feeding mechanism is directly synchronized with the movement of the automatic parts. However, the gun must be equipped with a special receiver with a feed mechanism driven by the energy of the moving components. A metal belt (it has not yet been possible to replace the metal with plastic in production prototypes) is relatively expensive in production, is susceptible to corrosion and can carry mud, sand and other contaminants into the gun.

The RPD machine gun uses a non-disintegrating metal belt, for convenience placed in a round metal box (can or drum) that attaches to the bottom of the gun. In early versions during the development stage, it was proposed to use 100- and 200-round capacity belts fitted in round and rectangular belt cans respectively. Later it was decided to abandon the 200-round belt and

*There was no magazine interchangeability between the belt-fed RPD and AKs.*

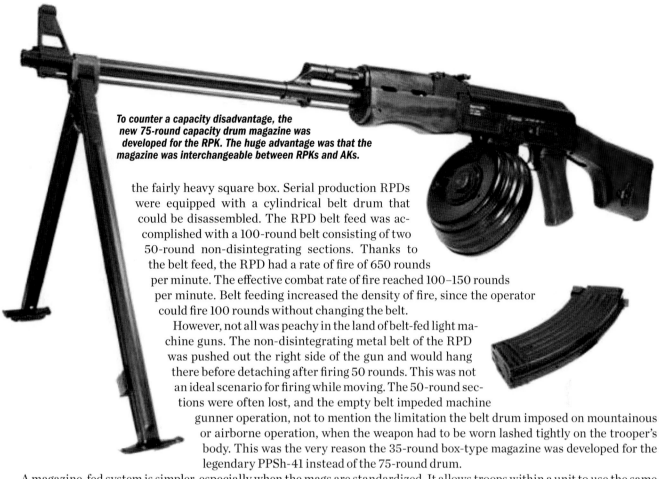

*To counter a capacity disadvantage, the new 75-round capacity drum magazine was developed for the RPK. The huge advantage was that the magazine was interchangeable between RPKs and AKs.*

the fairly heavy square box. Serial production RPDs were equipped with a cylindrical belt drum that could be disassembled. The RPD belt feed was accomplished with a 100-round belt consisting of two 50-round non-disintegrating sections. Thanks to the belt feed, the RPD had a rate of fire of 650 rounds per minute. The effective combat rate of fire reached 100–150 rounds per minute. Belt feeding increased the density of fire, since the operator could fire 100 rounds without changing the belt.

However, not all was peachy in the land of belt-fed light machine guns. The non-disintegrating metal belt of the RPD was pushed out the right side of the gun and would hang there before detaching after firing 50 rounds. This was not an ideal scenario for firing while moving. The 50-round sections were often lost, and the empty belt impeded machine gunner operation, not to mention the limitation the belt drum imposed on mountainous or airborne operation, when the weapon had to be worn lashed tightly on the trooper's body. This was the very reason the 35-round box-type magazine was developed for the legendary PPSh-41 instead of the 75-round drum.

A magazine-fed system is simpler, especially when the mags are standardized. It allows troops within a unit to use the same magazines and change the magazines faster. However, as a rule the magazine's capacity is limited. Though the capacity of the standard AK box magazine was increased to 40 rounds for use with the RPK, it still fell short of the RPD's 100-round belt. Also, the weight of steel magazines left much to be desired. Later, the Bakelite material used in construction of RPK mags addressed the weight issue. However, the lesser capacity was still a problem.

That problem was solved with the introduction of the 75-round capacity drum magazine designed by Krupin. The new magazine had a diameter of 163mm (6.4 inches) and weight of 0.9 kg (~2 lbs.) when empty and 2.12 kg (4.7 lbs.) fully loaded. All in all, it was a reliable mag and provided flawless feed when properly used. The one negative characteristic of the drum was reloading. The drum mag was reloaded in a rather tricky way, by using a ratchet lever to advance the internal mechanism to free up space for cartridges. It is inconvenient in field conditions, but only slightly so when compared to reloading a metal belt without a machine. Also, the large capacity partially negates the reloading inconvenience. However, one of the main and undisputed advantages of the magazine-fed RPK over the belt-fed RPD is weight.

How much lighter is the RPK compared to the same caliber predecessor? The RPD with the fully loaded 100-round belt weighs 9.8 kg (21.6 lbs.), while the RPK with loaded 75-round drum magazine is 6.8 kg (15 lbs.). The difference of more than 6 pounds is huge. Ask anyone who has to hump it up the mountains. However, it gets better. The weight of two RPD belts loaded with 200 rounds of ammo is 4.8 kg (10.6 lbs.), five RPK 40-round magazines loaded with the same number of cartridges weigh 4.26 kg (9.4 lbs.), and two drum mags with 75 cartridges each weigh only 4.4 kg.

Perhaps the most compelling advantage is that the RPK mags are interchangeable with the other squad weapons, the AK Avtomats. In my personal experience, this RPK mag advantage is also its curse, especially in a combat zone like Afghanistan, where the higher capacity magazines were popular among other troops carrying regular AKMs. If machine gunner was not paying attention, he could find himself down one or two 40-rounders, or even one day find that he is missing a drum magazine.

## RPK EVOLUTION

Being a direct result of the AK evolution, the RPK light machine gun went through several stages of evolution itself, just like its close relative the Kalashnikov Avtomat. And, it continues to evolve today.

Perhaps the most significant evolution of the RPK happened at the same time as the AK's family of weapons received the most monumental boost in development, when the infantry small arms went the sub-caliber route in 1974. I will talk about the AK transition into the more modern AK-74 fighting platform later in this book and in greater detail. However, I'll go ahead and put the RPK story to bed now.

The first significant step in RPK evolution, apart from on-going additions of folding stocks and side accessory rails, was the adoption of the RPK-74 as part of the AK-74 family of guns.

In early 1974, a new unified 5.45mm firearm complex was adopted, including the new 5.45x39mm cartridge and four models

*The RPK-74 light machine gun was adopted for service in 1974 as part of the AK-74 family.*

of 5.45mm-chambered Avtomats and light machine guns. The reduced recoil impulse 5.45x39mm cartridge, with signifi-cantly greater muzzle velocity and thus a shorter flight time to the target, improved accuracy by about a half as compared to the RPK chambered for the 7.62x39mm round.

The 5.45x39mm family of small arms included two versions of light machine guns, the RPK-74 (GAU index 6P18) with a fixed stock, and RPKS-74 (GAU index 6P19) with a side folder, for use with mobile and airborne troops. The differences in their design compared to the AK-74 are the same as in the PPK compared to the AKM. Though, like the earlier AK-74 rifles, the new RPK-74s had laminate wood furniture, later models received a set of plum-colored poly-amide composite parts like the Avtomats.

In addition, the new cage-type flash suppressor was added, along with a newly designed magazine. This time, only the box-type Bakelite magazine with 45-round capacity was issued with the RPK-74. The weight of the fixed stock RPK-74 with the loaded magazine is 5.46 kg (~12 lbs.) and the RPKS-74 folder is 5.61 kg (12.4 lbs.). As with .30 caliber RPK, two more versions of the 74 gun were released, the RPK-74N and RPKS-74N, with an accessory rail on the left side of the receiver for use with night optics, hence the addition of the letter "N" in model designation.

The next step in RPK evolution coincided with the AK-74 upgrade to AK-74M as a universal platform for all troops. After the creation of the AK-74M, observing the unification principle, the RPK-74 was upgraded to the

level of the RPK-74M (GAU index 6P39). It was a universal version of a squad light machine gun designed for use by troops no matter what branch of military they were in. The new M versions could also be deployed with a variety of collimator or optical sights.

The RPK-74 has gotten bad rap. Some people have tried to directly compare this weapon to the PKM light machine gun, which is absurd. In my opinion, the bad rap is undeserved, and comparison is a mistake. I think both come simply from ignorance. The fact is, an RPK-74 is an excellent weapon when used properly. It is essentially an AK on steroids. That makes it a great addition to an infantry squad. No need to retrain the operator, and it takes the same magazines, which is very important in a gunfight.

Nevertheless, as I have mentioned, what makes this gun special are the longer and heavier barrel and 50 percent larger capacity magazine. The heavier barrel allows longer bursts, and the larger-capacity

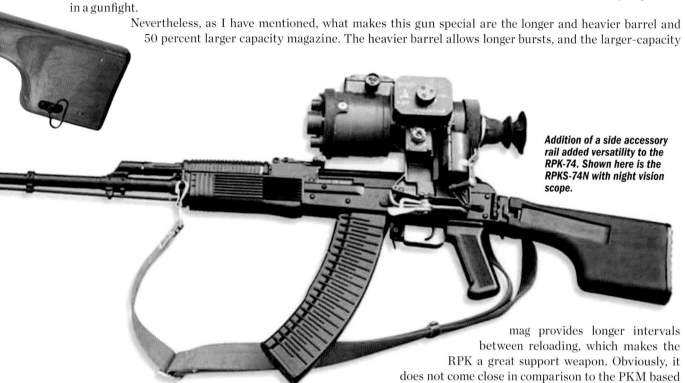

Addition of a side accessory rail added versatility to the RPK-74. Shown here is the RPKS-74N with night vision scope.

mag provides longer intervals between reloading, which makes the RPK a great support weapon. Obviously, it does not come close in comparison to the PKM based on firepower. However, the ability to fire it as a conventional rifle, with lesser weight that allows the gun to be easily maneuvered, makes the RPK-74 a very valuable addition to any dynamic close contact fire fight. The attached bipod and virtually no recoil make the RPK a formidable weapon at distance as well. It would be extremely incorrect to directly compare the "knock down" power of the 5.45x39 cartridge to the standard PKM round. However, lack of recoil and controllability on full auto allow the RPK-74 to deliver a great number of rounds on the designated target down range.

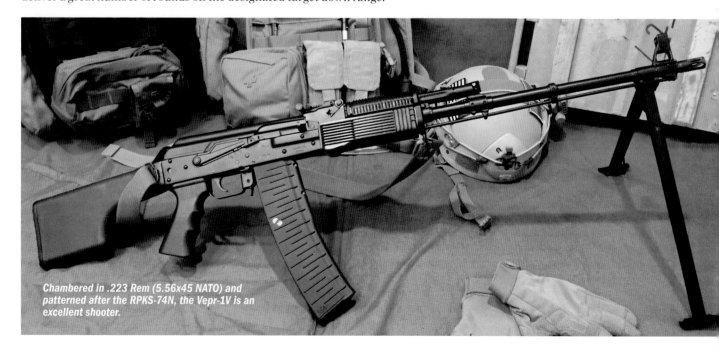

Chambered in .223 Rem (5.56x45 NATO) and patterned after the RPKS-74N, the Vepr-1V is an excellent shooter.

While in service, my unit utilized these guns to great effect. The RPK-74 was ever-present on any and all of our combat missions. The gun's 45-round magazines were very popular with troops. So just like the RPK, if you were the guy who carried it, you had to be especially vigilant when it came to your magazines. If you were not paying attention you might find your mag pouch one or two magazines short.

All in all, the RPK-74 is one of my favorite guns at the range. It shoots like a dream, with no recoil, smooth operation, etc. It's almost unfair to the guy resetting targets that get knocked down with no effort. If you have not fired the RPK-74 and you get a chance, fire one. And if you are lucky enough to shoot one in full-auto mode, it will shatter your entire universe.

The RPK-74 and its versions are still operational in Russia, former Soviet republics and a number of other countries.

After the collapse of the Soviet Union, when defense orders abruptly dried up, the RPK manufacturer at Molot was forced to look elsewhere for revenue. The plant's engineers developed several models of "Vepr" hunting carbines, based on the RPK

*In 2017, the Vyatsko-Polyansky machinebuilding plant Molot presented its new modular light machine gun.*

*At the same time Molot released its new machine gun, Kalashnikov Concern presented its version of the Squad Automatic gun, the RPK-16.*

design, for the civilian commercial market. The Vepr inherited the quality that was built into the military version, and thus received a well-deserved warm reception from hunters and recreational shooters alike. Up until recently, the Vepr rifles were a popular AK variant in the U.S. However, in the summer of 2017, the Molot plant made the U.S. Anti-Russian Sanctions list, effectively ending any import of Molot products stateside, which of course included the Vepr.

## MEANWHILE IN RUSSIA

I do not know what U.S. politicians were thinking when they imposed the anti-Russian sanctions as a tool of political pressure. I am not a politician and do not much care for any of them, no matter the nationality. Therefore, you will not hear me discussing rights and wrongs of the decisions made by those in power. However, the anti-Russian sanctions had a directly opposite effect from what was intended. Once again, Russia rose to the challenge and revitalized its domestic industries, from agriculture to its military industrial complex. Kalashnikov Concern, with its subsidiary the Izhmash, made the list of sanctioned companies early on, and Molot being the most recent addition. Losing access to the largest commercial market in the world, these companies were supposed to shrivel up and die. Instead, with financial backing from the Russian government, these arsenals introduced not one but two new RPKs.

## MODERN, STYLISH, FASHIONABLE

Modularity and multi-caliber capabilities are perhaps the most fashionable trends of "western" firearms development in recent years. Almost all the rifles positioned as "XXI century weapons," such as the FN SCAR, Beretta ARX or Bushmaster ACR, are modular in design. Some weapons systems allow caliber change, say, from a reduced-impulse intermediate 5.56x45mm NATO (.223 Rem.) to .300 Blackout or 6.5 Grendel or the widely used 7.62x51mm NATO (.308 Win.), all the way to .338 Lapua if you really have to reach out and touch someone. The AK platform, on the other hand, was repeatedly chastised for being too "monolithic," considering it a sign of the backwardness of its manufacturers and obsolescence as a modern weapons system. Now, the two largest Russian arms manufacturers released two modular platforms based on Kalashnikov's RPK light machine gun, and one of them is also slotted for the civilian market.

Recently, Russian television showed photos and general descriptions of the latest firearm from the Vyatsko-Polansky machine-building plant Molot. It was a prototype of a light fire support machine gun with replaceable barrels of different lengths. The gun is designed for use with infantry squads and special purpose units, and as such is chambered for the 5.45x39 cartridge. Its civilian version, however, would be a multi-caliber semi-automatic carbine with three replaceable barrels to accommodate calibers 7.62x39mm, 6.5 Grendel and .366 TCM. Both military and civilian versions are of modern design and equipped with a folding telescopic stock, an adjustable gas system and a hinged top cover with integrated Picatinny rail. Another of the improved ergonomic features is a bent up charging handle similar to that of the Israeli Galil. Apparently, this was made to facilitate a reload of the weapon with the shooter's left hand. I personally don't see an advantage. This becomes a huge

The new Kalashnikov RPK-16, chambered in 5.45x39mm, can be fed from the newly designed high-capacity drum or standard RPK or AK magazines.

pain when any type of optic is installed.

There is no information on the prospects of the military version of the gun yet. Judging by the available photographs, this sample will be equipped with two barrels, short and long, which, based on conditions or mission, will turn it into a light machine gun or an Avtomat. This is very similar to the concept of the RPK-16 from the Kalashnikov Concern, which was first introduced at the "Army-2016" exhibition in Russia. In fact, the RPK-16 was the first true modular Kalashnikov.

The RPK-16 is a development initiated solely by the Kalashnikov Concern on its own accord, which, based on the designers' intent, should combine a light fire-support weapon with the dimensions of the Avtomat for urban combat. This follows closely another western trend in combat firearms development. In the early 2000s, the U.S. Marine Corps initiated the IAR program (Infantry Automatic Rifle), in which it planned to make a light machine gun in reality an automatic rifle with heavy barrel. Based on the results of the competition, a Heckler & Koch machine gun was adopted in 2009 under the M27 IAR index. Basically, the new weapon is a slightly modified H&K 416 rifle. Years ago, the same U.S. Marine Corps deployed AR15A2 H-Bar as a DMR. Funny how history has a tendency to repeat itself.

The new RPK-16's design incorporates modern ergonomics, such as folding telescopic stock and ergonomic pistol grip. Perhaps the main feature of the new machine gun is that its essential components, such as locking mechanism, gas system and receiver, are basically the

*(above) The new Molot modular machine gun can be reconfigured for several missions and/or calibers. The gun's barrel has a "quick-change" capability.*

*The Romanian AES-10 is a licensed copy of the Soviet RPK light machine gun with the addition of carrying handle.*

*The Chinese "RPK," the NHM-91, is not a licensed copy of an RPK; it is not an RPK copy at all. The NHM-91 is another version of the Type 56S rifle.*

same as those of the RPK-74. The most important difference is the replaceable barrels of 370mm (14.6 inches) and 550mm (21.7 inches) in length. Because of this feature, the functionality of the weapon can be changed.

Another feature of the new RPK is a removable top cover with a full-length Picatinny rail, which is rigidly attached to the receiver. It is fixed in place in front by a sliding lock, and in the rear by the spring-loaded latch, to take out any play. This scheme, according to the developers, allows you to reliably mount modern sighting systems and maintain an absolute zero after removing the cover. New rigidly affixed handguards with accessory rails in line with the one on the top cover allow the new gun to use tandem optics and modern battle accessories. The RPK-16 is a magazine-fed gun and, as such, it uses standard AK-74 and RPK-74 30- and 40-round magazines, as well as a Unicorn or a Laxness Monster or Sasquatch, also known as the newly developed 5.45 drum magazine with 95-round capacity.

There are a couple of differences between Kalashnikov's RPK-16 and Molot's modular fire-support machine gun. The Molot barrels are attached to the receiver by use of a barrel nut, similar to the AR barrel attachment system. Some people see it as a potential problem. On the AR platform, the bolt locks into the slots in the barrel stem. If the nut is loose and there is play in the barrel, the bolt still rigidly holds the cartridge in the chamber. In the AK systems, the bolt locks into the front trunnion. If the nut is loose and the barrel is not seated properly, which increases the headspace, it may lead to out-of- battery fire causing damage to the gun or, even worse, injury to the shooter.

The RPK-16 barrels are fixed not with a nut, but with a transverse slider block similar to that of the PK and PKM machine guns. This design, according to the manufacturer, should guarantee the same barrel seating during replacement every time. Experts familiar with Molot's design think that there should not be a concern with the barrel nut backing out. If necessary, this issue is solved using a thread lock. However, the question remains, how can an average user at home adjust the headspace when swapping out barrels? One can assume this problem is solved by precision manufacturing of the barrels.

## WHO NEEDS A MACHINE GUN TRANSFORMER?

Before we all get excited, let's remember that the RPK-16, as well as the new modular machine gun from Molot, was developed purely on the initiative of the manufacturers themselves to show off the arsenals' capability to adapt to modern trends in firearm design and produce a "modern" weapon. However, it is not certain that the newly introduced guns will spark any interest from the Russian military.

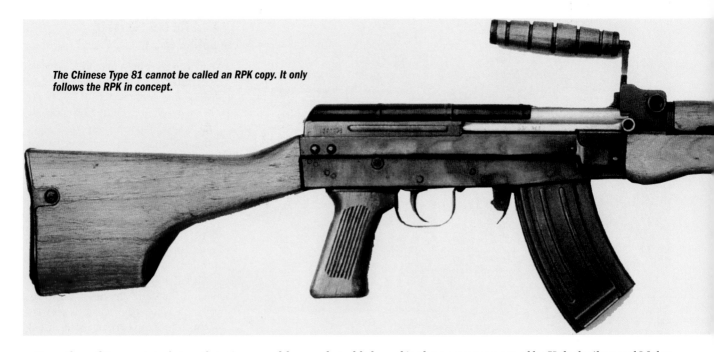

The Chinese Type 81 cannot be called an RPK copy. It only follows the RPK in concept.

From the military point of view, there is no need for a replaceable barrel in the manner proposed by Kalashnikov and Molot manufacturers. Surely the quick barrel change has a military application, but it is a limited one. For example, in a fortified defensive position designed for prolonged defense when rapid and intense machine gun fire is required. There are and have been a number of machine guns made with such capability throughout history, including the PK and PKM Kalashnikov machine guns. Personally, I can tell you that our machine gunners never carried spare barrels outside of wire. A properly trained machine gun operator should be able to run his gun without need for a replacement barrel. This may not apply to the 900-round-per-minute German MG-42, where barrel replacement was a necessity. It's certainly not needed for the PK or PKM. After all, modern combat tactics have change drastically in recent years. There are no more frontal assaults by wave after wave of enemy infantry. Therefore, there's no need to use a machine gun with 250–500-round belts as a mower. However, if there is a need to replace a machine gun's barrel, the facilities for it are provided on proper models, but for an entirely different reason. And, if a need arises for a quick barrel change, it should be done in the field by the operator without use of any tools. Neither the RPK-16 nor Molot's new gun offer such a feature. To replace the barrels on the modular light machine gun and its brother the hunting carbine released by Molot, one would need a special wrench and several minutes of labor in the armorer's workshop. The RPK-16 barrel is changed with the tools that are included in its kit (punch and screwdriver). However, one would have to check the gun's point of impact. At both arsenals, engineers understood that there is no need for quick barrel replacement in such a type of weapon.

The current status of the RPK-16 is that design and development work is complete, and all preliminary tests are done and were successful. At present, Kalashnikov is manufacturing a test batch of the new RPKs for military field-testing. It was also recently reported that Russia's Ministry of Defense intends to order an experimental batch of new machine guns.

The status of the Molot's initiative is still unknown. At the same time, methinks that the modular gun in its civilian version under the Vepr brand will be very interesting to the civilian market. Russian firearms laws permit only one gun per firearm purchasing license. Therefore, a multi-caliber, modular carbine would be an attractive proposition to Russian shooters, be it for hunting various game, or for practical or recreational shooting. It's like buying several guns on one license. The modular modern Vepr carbine may attract practical shooters, who can use inexpensive 5.45x39 or 7.62x39 ammo for training and compete with the more precise 6.5 Grendel.

There is also a third caliber version. It is a smooth bore .336 TKM caliber. Again, it would most likely be overlooked by experienced shooters, but considering the Russian firearms law, it will also find popularity with novices and beginners in Russia. The law dictates that a new firearm purchaser must go through a five-year grace period when he or she is only allowed to own smooth bore firearms. After the grace period, they may apply for rifles. Now, with the .336 TKM available, they can purchase a new modular Vepr carbine with smooth bore .336 barrel right away, and after the grace period, simply purchase additional barrels.

Regardless of whether the Russian armed forces adopt any or both of the RPKs, it is obvious that these guns will find use in civilian form. What is important is that the RPK, as a representative of the Kalashnikov family of weapons, continues to evolve despite critics who claim that the entire platform is outdated.

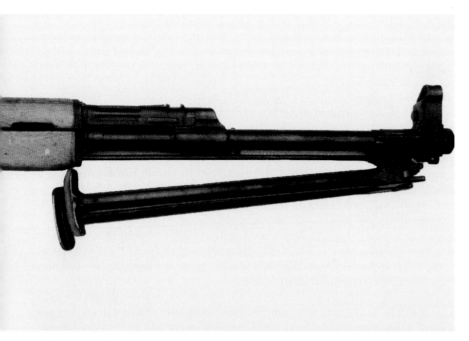

## RPK LICENSED AND UNLICENSED COPIES

In fact, the RPK light machine gun was a very popular weapon from its inception in 1961. It was adopted for service with the militaries of more than 20 countries. Obviously, several countries produce the RPK themselves. And just like with the AK Avtomat, some were making RPKs under license and some weren't.

Perhaps the closest copy of the RPK was produced by the Romanians.

The defense industry enterprises of Romania under the Soviet license, in addition to the versions of AKM Avtomats, also produced a light machine gun, which is a modified version of the RPK Kalashnikov machine gun. The design, operating principles and technical characteristics of the Romanian variant are identical to those of the original weapon. The only differences are the adjustable-by-height bipod and addition of a carrying handle. Its civilian semi-auto variant, designated AES-10, is well known to U.S. shooters. It has been imported into the U.S. and sold by several distributors. For a while, the AES-10 was the closest thing we could buy to the original military spec RPK.

Romania also produced a copy of the Krupin-designed drum magazine.

The makers of unlicensed copies are the usual suspects: China and Yugoslavia.

When someone here in the U.S. shooting community says Chinese RPK or clone or variant thereof, one may think that they are talking about the Norinco NHM-91 rifle.

However, the Norinco NHM-91 imported into the U.S. looks only slightly like an RPK because of the longer barrel and bipod. In reality, it is something else. In fact, China did produce a proper RPK clone, the Type 81, where Chinese gun designers did not copy the RPK *per se*, but rather copied an RPK concept and several external features of the Kalashnikov gun.

A civilian semi-auto variant (based on the Soviet AKM-design clone, the Chinese-made Type 56), the NHM-91 rifle was built to imitate the appearance of the Russian RPK light machine gun. First

*The Chinese drum magazine is different visually and by design. Compare the Soviet RPK drum magazine (left) to the Chinese design (right).*

imported into the States in 1991 by China Sports, Inc., these rifles have been modified to meet the requirements of a 1989 Executive Order by President George H. W. Bush prohibiting importation of certain "assault rifle" configurations of military-style semi-automatic rifles. These modifications included a one-piece U.S.-made thumbhole stock and the inclusion of a rivet on the receiver to prevent the use of standard AK/RPK magazines. In 1994, all Chinese rifles, including the NHM-91, were banned from import to the U.S. under Clinton's Assault Weapons Ban.

As I've stated, one cannot say the design of the NHM-91 rifle is based on the Soviet RPK. Maybe with a stretch one can make an argument that the NHM-91 was based on Type 56, Type 56 was based on AKM, and in turn the RPK was based on the AKM, therefore proving that NHM-91 is an RPK clone. In my opinion, all it proves is that the Chinese NHM-91 rifle had Kalashnikov heritage. It had a typical Chinese AK 1.5mm-thick stamped receiver, and a longer and thicker chrome-lined barrel measuring 508mm (20 inches) compared to the 590mm (23.2 inches) of the original RPK. The NHM-91 was equipped with a forward-mounted steel bipod, giving it the appearance of an RPK, and it came from the factory with two 30-round stamped steel magazines and a 75-round drum mag of Chinese manufacture. I will talk about this more later in this chapter.

However, as I mentioned earlier, the Chinese did make an "RPK" of their own, the light machine gun Type 81.

The development of a new unified firearm system for the Peoples Liberation Army of China, to replace the obsolete Type 56 and Type 68 Avtomats, was launched in the early 1970s. As a result, in 1981, a new family of weapons under the designation Type 81 and chambered for the 7.62x39mm cartridge was adopted, consisting of a light machine gun Type 81 and an Avtomat Type 81 (Type 81-1). Just like the Soviet RPK, the light machine gun was designed as a fire support weapon for the infantry squad and, also like the RPK/AKM, is standardized with the Type 81 automatic carbine.

In fact, the machine gun is a heavily modified carbine. The main differences between the Type 81 machine gun and the Type 81 Avtomat are the longer and heavier barrel, folding bipods and carrying handles, which obviously resulted in an increase in weight and dimensions. Again, the Type 81 is not a direct copy of the Soviet RPK, but rather an RPK or light fire support weapon concept. One cannot deny obvious cosmetic similarities to the RPK, but that is where the similarities end. Also, one cannot deny that the Chinese arms designers borrowed from the AK design. God knows they had plenty of experience building Kalashnikov-based weapons. However, the Type 81 gun encompassed many original solutions borrowed from other weapons systems. Its automatic system is short stroke gas piston driven with bolt locking by rotation. The gas system is equipped with a two-position gas regulator and additionally a valve that completely closes the gas port for launching rifle grenades.

The safety/selector lever is located on the left side of the receiver, above the trigger guard, and is conveniently controlled by the thumb of the right hand. On later versions, including the Type 81S that were sold for export, the safety/selector lever was located inside the trigger guard behind the trigger. The front and rear sights are identical to those of the Type 56 AKs. The front is an adjustable post with full guard and the rear is the "U" slot leaf that is adjustable for elevation. The Type 81 machine

*Chinese drum magazine loading procedure 75-round (left) drum and 100-round (right).*

gun is magazine fed and accepts standard AK magazines and 75-round drum mags of Chinese design.

The gun is built on a stamped receiver of original design. Its furniture is made of wood and, unlike its Avtomat brother, its fixed stock is shaped more like the machine gun stock.

The main advantage of the Type 81 machine gun is its high degree of unification with the Type 81 Avtomat, and somewhat greater range and accuracy due to longer and heavier barrel and bipod. In addition to the People's Liberation Army, the Type 81 firearm system was supplied to Algeria, Bangladesh, Burma, Nepal, Pakistan, Sudan and Sri Lanka. For export, the light machine gun Type 81 was supplied under the designation Type 81MGS.

Here in the U.S., AK enthusiasts are familiar with the AK/RPK drum magazine. There are two basic types (not counting recently developed U.S.-made .223 magazines). One is the Soviet 75-round drum designed by Krupin, described earlier. The other is the Chinese design that uses a completely different feeding system.

There were two versions of the drum magazine made by the Chinese Norinco company, with 75 and 100 rounds capacity. The 75-rounder has the same weight and dimensions as the Soviet 75-round drum magazine for the RPK, but, as I've mentioned, has a completely different design. The design is largely based on the Thompson submachine gun drum magazine.

The cartridges are loaded into individual feeders by ones and twos in three rows inside the drum. This ensures a very high feeding reliability. To load the drum magazine one must remove the back panel, release the coil spring tension by pressing a button, then rotate the feeder assembly clockwise three times, bringing the drum mechanism to safe and ready-to-load position. Next, the shooter simply loads cartridges into their individual slots (feeders) until the mag is full and closes the back panel. The mag is now loaded. To make it ready for operation one must wind a spiral spring.

Advantages of this system are the fast and convenient loading, the possibility of long-term storage without winding the spring, and reliable feeding. Disadvantages include a possible delay in firing if the spring is not wound, it would not run partially loaded, oand pening the drum cover in field conditions for loading could cause dirt and other contaminants to enter the magazine.

The 100-round drum is identical to the 75-rounder by design. To increase the mag capacity, the fourth row was added. The 75-round mag is slightly more reliable due to less stress on the spring.

Another example of a successful unlicensed RPK copy was the Yugoslavian M72 light machine gun variant. Once more, this gun is very familiar to U.S. shooters. It has been imported to the States in various forms as whole and as parts kits. Nevertheless, it has secured a well-deserved place in the American AK scene.

The Zastava M72/M72A is a gas-operated, air-cooled, magazine-fed, selective fire, shoulder-fired weapon with a bipod. It is designated as a squad automatic weapon to deploy in a fire-support role, just like the Soviet RPK light machine gun.

The Zastava M72 was developed and manufactured by the then-Yugoslav Zastava Arms Company. Generally, the M72 is almost a direct copy of the RPK. And, just like the RPK, it is chambered to fire the 7.62x39mm M43 round. The only visual

*The Yugoslavian Zastava M72 light machine gun follows the RPK pattern closely, with few visual differences: the standard AK (M70) Avtomat stock and ribbed barrel.*

differences are the barrel with cooling fins, wooden stock of regular AK shape, and wooden handguards of slightly different design. There were several versions of the M72 produced over the years:

• M72—Standard version with a milled receiver and fixed wooden stock.
• M72B1—Same as the M72, but with an updated stamped receiver and barrel cooling fins.
• M72AB1—Same as the M72B1, but with an underfolding stock.

Later, the M77B1 chambered for the 7.62 NATO cartridge was released. Distinct external features of this version were the box-type magazine of different shape and carrying handle. This RPK clone was shortly followed by the M82 and M82A folder, both chambered for the 5.56 NATO round. Both of these guns also had carrying handles. Iraq has also produced the M72 copy under licenses from Zastava and under the "Tabuk" name. I should also mention the Finnish-built Valmet M78 light machine gun that was loosely based on the Kalashnikov. However, upon closer examination it doubtlessly betrays its AK pedigree.

I've managed to get ahead of our AK evolution story while talking about the RPK. I just wanted to put the RPK story to rest so I don't have to return to it again later. Now that it is done, we move on with the AK's transformation.

## CHAPTER 10

> "Copying successful samples and
> catching up with someone is the
> unpromising chore. To move ahead is
> the inspiring and meaningful work."
>
> – Valeriy V. Lobanovskyi

# THEIR BULLETS ARE FLYING FASTER

Perhaps nothing affected the design of the AK or made such a dramatic and profound mark on it as the introduction of the sub-caliber Kalashnikov. I can only compare it to such a "cosmic" event as when, according to Darwin's Theory of Evolution, our ancestors got up on two feet. After that, everything else was a mere modification.

We pick up our AK evolution story in the cool and turbulent 1960s. Along with rock-n-roll, a sexual revolution and experimental drugs, the '60s mark an era of modern firearms. This was the time when .30-caliber military rifles gave way to the more modern, manageable, accurate, adaptable and lighter weapon platforms that continue to be used today.

The idea of reduced-caliber ammunition for military infantry arms has been around for a long time. It has been implemented each time weapon development technology leaped forward, resulting in the reduction of the standard calibers. We saw the main military arms caliber reduced from the .45 and .50 that were widely used throughout the 1800s to .30 caliber as the primary infantry weapon caliber in the early to mid-1900s. The idea of further reduction of caliber down to 6.5 or 5.6mm (.240 or .220 respectively) was also considered by several countries since the beginning of the 20th century. However, it was not until the 1960s that the low impulse, sub-caliber, high-velocity round was introduced as viable military ammunition for the main battle rifle.

The U.S. Army adopted the M16 rifle in the mid-1960s, and the Soviets were watching. Soon the idea of small calibers for the main battle rifle was found viable. The positive experience with M16 rifles wielded by American GIs in Vietnam added legitimacy to sub-caliber ammunition. The Soviet military started development of its own small-caliber ammo in the early 1960s. As a result, by the mid-1970s, the USSR started a massive rearmament program, going away from the 7.62mm M43 round as its main small arm cartridge and moving toward the new reduced-impulse and high-velocity ammunition with sub-caliber projectiles. The benefits of the reduced-impulse ammo were immediately evident, starting with considerable reduction in ammo combat load (1.4 kg or 3.1 lbs. for eight fully loaded magazines) compared to its 7.62 counterpart and ending with round performance. Flatter trajectory and high velocity provided for significantly improved accuracy and range.

In 1974, the Soviet Armed Forces adopted a completely new weapons system for the 5.45x39mm cartridge. It consisted of AK-74 and AKS-74 (side folder) Avtomats and an RPK-74 light machine gun. In 1979, the AK-74 family of guns was expanded by adoption of the shortened version of the Avtomat, designated the AKS-74U, designed for use as a personal defense weapon (PDW) for tank and armor vehicle (APC) crews and artillery personnel, a niche that was occupied by submachine guns in Western militaries and by the APS Stechkin automatic pistol in the USSR. The production of the AKM in the Soviet Union was curtailed by the early 1980s, but a limited number of 7.62-caliber rifles remain in service today. I will talk about the AK-74 family of guns more later. But first, let me tell about the wonderful ammo it shot.

After some years of development, a new 5.45x39mm round was created. This round featured a bottlenecked, tapered case, 39mm long, made of steel, loaded with slim, relatively long 5.45mm nominal caliber bullet (actual bullet diameter is 5.62 mm). The bullet itself featured a combined steel and lead core with a hollow nose. The new round produced a muzzle velocity of about 900 m/s (2,953 fps) from the 415mm (16.3-inch) barrel. The new 5.45mm round casing had a smaller diameter compared to its 7.62x39mm predecessor, which significantly reduced the weight of the round.

## 5.45X39MM 7N6 CARTRIDGE

The introduction of the AK-74 rifle by the Soviets in 1974 coincided with arrival of the totally new high-velocity, low-impulse 5.45x39mm cartridge.

The high-energy and low-impulse sub-caliber round improved the accuracy and combat effectiveness of the AK, and offered a 30 percent reduction in weight for a soldier's loadout.

The round the AK-74 fires is drastically different from the original 1943 7.62x39 intermediate round and had a designation of 7N6. The flatter trajectory of the 5.45mm round had increased the range of direct fire against a running target from 526m to 625m; however, the range of terminal effect decreased from 1,500m to 1,350m. The decrease in diameter and size of the bullet delivered the inevitable increase in muzzle velocity accompanied by decreased recoil impulse. It was different not only in the bullet diameter and muzzle velocity, but also in construction of the bullet itself.

## THE "POISONED" BULLET

The most drastic departure from the original 7.62x39mm round lies with the 7N6's bullet. Due to a hollow space and core shift, the trajectory of the round radically changes once it strikes the target, causing significant trauma.

The 7N6 cartridge's bullet had a full metal jacket and steel core surrounded by lead. It also had an "air pocket" at the very tip, causing its jacket to deform on impact. Higher bullet speed flattened the trajectory and decreased wind deflection. Ammunition load was lightened. All this addressed the problem of enhancing combat efficiency of the "cartridge-weapon" complex.

However, due to its light weight compared to its 7.62mm predecessor, it got a bum rap for its lack of stopping power. In my opinion, it stopped everything and everyone just fine. On impact, the 5.54mm projectile is deformed and loses its stability when the steel core, encased in softer lead, moves forward, thus offsetting the round's center of gravity. It then starts to

*The appearance of the M16 rifle firing a low-impulse 5.56x45mm round triggered development of Soviet sub-caliber AK ammunition.*

**5.56x45mm NATO cartridge (left) next to standard AK 7.62x39mm M43 round (right).**

tumble and changes its original trajectory. A bullet with such impact characteristics causes extensive damage to soft tissue, internal organs and bones. Another characteristic of the 7N6 bullet is its penetration ability. When it strikes a hard surface such as body armor at high velocity, the initial impact energy is absorbed by the steel jacket of the projectile. The soft lead and front air pocket allow the steel core to move forward through the jacket and through light armor. I have personally seen a military issue body armor vest with two 7N6 jackets stuck in the aramid textile layer with holes made by the bullets' cores, to the great misfortune of the vest owner.

Many would like to argue that some Soviet soldiers in Afghanistan preferred the 7.62mm-chambered AKM to the 5.45mm AK-74 due to its better stopping power. As valid as this argument may be, the other reasons may have carried more weight. As noted earlier, the fact that the main rifle of the Afghan opposition was a Chinese clone of the AK-47, chambered in 7.62x39 caliber and with the ability to refill magazines with captured ammo on long-range patrols, was far more valid reasoning.

The other reason for wide use of older AKM rifles was a lack of silencing devices for AK-74 guns. However, the proven PBS-1 silencer designed for 7.62x39 AKM rifles was widely utilized with high effect when engaging sentries or point guards. Nevertheless, the new high-velocity and low-impulse 5.45X39mm 7N6 cartridge offered far superior controllability on full auto and, more importantly, 30 percent reduction in weight (considering full ammo load).

There are many anecdotal stories about the 5.45x39mm cartridge and its bullet. One was the bullet with offset center of gravity causing horrible wounds. That one is partially true, unlike the one that suggests its lightweight 5.45mm bullet was easily deflected and did not penetrate as well as its heavier .30-caliber sibling, which is totally opposite of reality. My favorite came from the Afghan Mujahedeen who called it a "wasp" and "poisoned bullet." That has some merit because of the drastic and unpredictable fly pattern of the 7N6 bullet. Once it enters soft tissue it leaves a nasty wound channel and two cavitation voids, making it hard to treat wounds in the field.

Nevertheless, nothing speaks to the capability of a weapon or ammo like the designer himself. In 2001 when I met Kalashnikov, he told me that he was against the adoption of

*The new low-impulse, high-velocity 5.45x39mm 7N6 round (right) next to the standard AK 7.62x39mm M43.*

**I, too, have an anecdote** pertaining to the 7N6 high deflection probability and "poor" penetration performance.

Early on in my service, when I was still going through basic training, we had our first outing to the regimental range, where we were to get familiar with the AK-74 Avtomat. We were resting in the prairie grass field by the ammo shed while waiting for our relay's turn at the firing line. Watching our comrades shooting their AK-74 rifles, the rest of the platoon of greenhorns was involved in heated discussion about the gun and the ammo it fired. Some of us were seeing the AK-74 and "needle-like" ammo for the first time. While spewing a bunch of nonsense, we did not notice when a junior sergeant appeared before us. Eventually seeing what looked to us like a seasoned veteran, the chatter stopped.

Spirited by the effect he had on the pathetic looking draftees, the sergeant started to tell us how the bullet of the new 7N6 round had an offset center of gravity and was way too light. He continued to say with the confidence of a professional that if it was fired at his feet (which were covered by thick prairie grass) from the distance of 3 meters (~10 feet) he would be totally safe. The bullets would just be deflected and ricochet away without so much as a scratch to his feet.

We were shocked by what we just heard. The question lingered, why would the Motherland give us such useless guns and send us to fight a war? I am pretty sure everyone in my relay was thinking and pondering the futility of their miserable lives while staring into the far beyond with unblinking eyes and mouths agape. I know I was. We would remain in this state for quite some time and would see an onset of full-blown depression if it weren't for a Warrant Officer who was in charge of the ammo dump, and who was standing and listening to the wonderful presentation on the stupidity of Soviet ammo designers. The 'brave" sergeant's asinine confidence was about to be tested in a most unexpected way.

The WO decided to challenge the sergeant's competence by having some soldiers fetch several glass soda bottles and place them in the grass at the distance of roughly 3 meters. Without hesitation, he grabbed the nearest soldier's rifle, inserted a magazine loaded with six live rounds and rocked the charging handle. Next was a burst of automatic fire in the direction of the obscured bottles. I remember it like it was yesterday. The pieces of colored glass flew everywhere like brown, green and crystal shards of water from an exploded water balloon. After the second it took to process what just happen, we burst out laughing. I'm not sure if we were laughing at the embarrassed and disgraced sergeant who tried to impress the greenhorns with some bullshit story and wound up eating his own crap, or if we were laughing with the relief that the guns we were supposed to fight with actually worked, and newly found confidence that the Motherland's weapons provided a proverbial light at the end of the tunnel toward making it home safe.

Though late, I have found out that the range clown wasn't far off the mark pertaining to the center of gravity of the 7N6 projectile. In fact, the design of the bullet itself was different from the standard rifle round and surely had different behavior characteristics.

*A new family of AKs firing low-impulse 5.45x39mm ammunition was adopted for service in 1974.*

the 5.45-caliber cartridge. He though that the 7.62x39mm had more unexplored potential. However, later in our discussion, Kalashnikov mentioned that he was a huge fan of the AKS-74U rifle. The shortened version of the AK-74, and as all AK-74 family guns, it was also chambered in 5.45x39mm. He then described how the gun and cartridge exceeded expectations during tests on year-old hogs at 350 meters. Personally, I love the 5.45x39mm round. I think that it is pretty close to being the perfect carbine cartridge, with its low recoil impulse and how it carries its energy way past any other modern carbine round.

AK ammunition, like the gun it was fired from, has evolved. Soviet ammunition engineers developed several cartridges for the AK-74 family of guns:

• 7N6 (released in 1974, bullet with steel-core, lead "pusher" and bi-metal jacket).

• 7N10 (released in 1992, increased penetration, bullet with a tempered core). Armor penetration is 16mm (a little over 5/8 inch) from a distance of 100 meters (about 107 yards).

• 7U1 (subsonic round for use with suppressor).

• 7N22 (released in 1998, armor piercing bullet with a core made of high-carbon steel). Penetration of 5mm (3/16 inch) steel armor plate from a distance of 250m (~274 yards), almost two times better than the original 7N6.

• 7N24 (increased precision, bullet made with tempered tungsten-carbide core).

A bullet with a steel core of a standard 5.45mm cartridge fired from an AK-74 provides the following penetration characteristics:

• Penetration with a probability of 50 percent of steel plates with a thickness of 2mm (little less than 1/16 inch) at a distance of 950m (~1040 yards), 3mm (2/16 inch) at a distance of 670m (~738 yards) and 5mm (3/16 inch) at a distance of 350m (~383 yards).

• Penetration with a probability of 80–90 percent of a steel helmet at a distance of 800m (~875 yards).

• Penetration with a probability of 75–100 percent bulletproof vest at a distance of 550m (~602 yards).

• Penetration of 50–60cm (20-24 inches) into a parapet of compacted snow at a distance of 400m (438 yards).

• Penetration of 20–25cm (8–10 inches) into the earth barrier from the compacted loam soil at a distance of 400 meters.

• Penetration with a probability of 50 percent of a wall of dry pine beams cross-section 20x20cm (8x8 inches) at a distance of 650m (~711 yards).

• Penetration of 10–12cm (~4–5 inches) into the brickwork at a distance of 100m (~109 yards).

The Soviets saw the armor piercing potential of the high-velocity 5.45mm cartridge and started to work on it right away.

In 1986, new bullets with a heat-treated core of increased hardness were developed, providing a significant increase in the penetration effect; the new bullet goes through a steel helmet at a distance of 960 meters, and through a flak jacket with titanium plates at a distance of 200 meters.

*The 7N6 bullet construction was unconventional. The air pocket in the front caused this projectile to behave erratically on impact.*

The next improvement of the bullet in 1992 again increased the armor penetration. The newly improved AP round could now penetrate the army bulletproof vest at a range of 200 meters (~218 yards), and the heavy level 3 vest at a range of 50 meters (~54.5 yards) with the same initial speed.

In the end, I think the 5.45x39mm 7N6 AK cartridge is the best fighting carbine round available today. Is it perfect? Probably not. But, still it outperforms anything on the battlefield today. I can hear the haters rise up in defense of the .223 cartridge, saying how much more accurate it is sitting at the bench at their local ranges, shooting high-quality brass-cased expensive ammo out of their custom-built ARs. There is no argument from me. Of course the $1,000+ semi-automatic sporting AR shooting store-bought ammunition at 100 yards would prove to be more accurate, but only marginally. However, with all things equal, the standard M4 firing bulk ball ammo does not stand a chance against accuracy (especially on full-auto) and range of the typical AK-74 firing the 7N6 round.

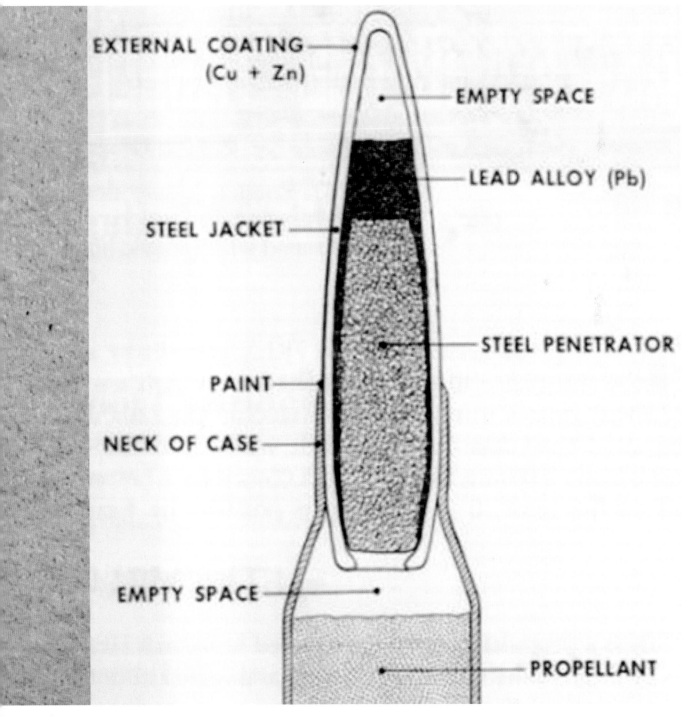

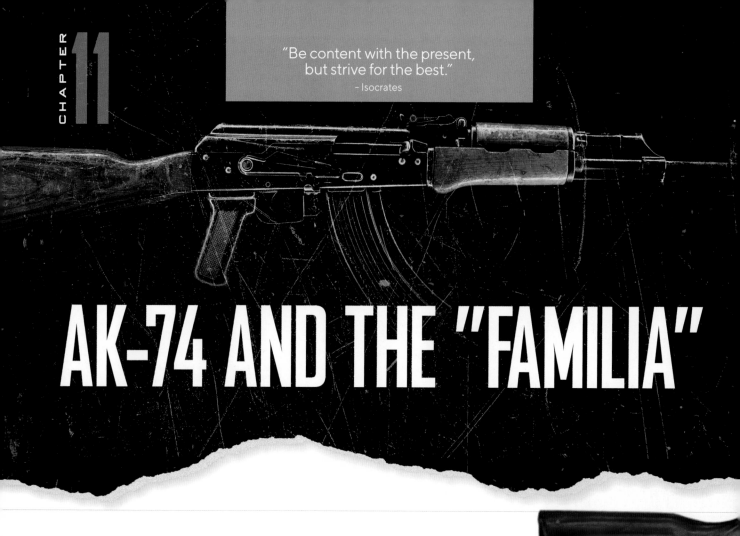

## CHAPTER 11

"Be content with the present,
but strive for the best."
- Isocrates

# AK-74 AND THE "FAMILIA"

Though the Russians may claim that they were working on the low-impulse, sub-caliber, ultimately it was an American designer that spurred the next and perhaps most dramatic stage of AK evolution.

The AK-74, Kalashnikov Avtomat, caliber 5.45mm (GRAU index 6P20) was developed in 1970 by Mikhail Kalashnikov himself and adopted by the Soviet armed forces in 1974. It is the further development of the AKM. The development of the AK-74 is associated with the transition to a new low-pulse cartridge, the 5.45x39mm. The new guns were first used in Afghanistan during the Soviet–Afghan campaign, then in all conflicts in post-Soviet territory. Currently, the AK-74 Avtomat is in service with the Armed Forces of most countries of the former Soviet Union. It's a legendary gun with an incredible history full of doubts and intrigues when even its creator was against it. That is its story.

Despite the fact that the AK had very good tactical and technical characteristics, there was a constant feeling of the need to reduce the caliber of the main combat weapons for the modern motorized infantry. There has been a tendency among Soviet firearms designers and engineers to search for an optimal caliber for modern small arms. By the mid-1950s, the advantages of sub-caliber ammunition were clearly evident. Reduction in powder positively impacted the recoil impulse, which in turn lead to better accuracy, especially in the full-auto rate of fire.

The overall positive test results laid the ground for creation and release of tactical/technical requirements for new types of automatic infantry weapons of smaller caliber. Soviet designers were faced with the task of designing and developing an Avtomat or automatic carbine for the new low-impulse cartridge. The "bump" to accelerate work in this direction was the appearance of the 5.56mm-caliber M16 rifle in the U.S. Army. The positive experience of using a small caliber cartridge by the Americans in Vietnam forced the Soviets to begin work on development of a similar cartridge for their automatic infantry guns. As soon as the new ammunition was available and accepted by the Soviet military, it was decided to develop a new family of small arms for the new cartridge. In 1964, the engineers compiled a draft of tactical and technical requirements for a new Avtomat project. The official requirements for the new family of small arms were issued to all firearms designer's bureaus and organizations in 1966. Work began in earnest in 1967 to develop a weapon for the new low-impulse, sub-caliber cartridge. By early 1968, ten Avtomats were offered for competitive testing, from which two were selected for the final military tests: yet again, the Kalashnikov Avtomat and Konstantinov CA-006 rifle.

As a side note, though we know Konstantinov's gun did not make the cut, it did not go away and get lost in the annals of firearms history. It is still very much alive. I will talk more about that a little later in the book.

It must be noted that most rifles submitted for trials were of highly advanced designs. The main goal of the new weapon was to significantly improve performance of the existing 7.62mm AKM Avtomat, with emphasis placed on accuracy. Most rifles that were submitted for evaluation featured so-called "balanced automatic action." This meant additional weight would travel in the opposite direction to the bolt carrier to counterbalance the recoil and reduce its effect on the gun's stability. This type of counterbalance is very complicated, negatively affecting the reliability of the gun and making the gun more expensive to produce. The only weapon of the conventional design was the A-3 entry by Kalashnikov's team. The sample they presented for testing was more or less the old AKM Avtomat, adapted for the new 5.45mm ammunition.

During testing, the main battle unfolded between the Konstantinov CA-006 and the Kalashnikov A-3 Avtomats. As I mentioned before, the product of Kalashnikov's team A-3 was a deep modification of the AKM, the main battle rifle of the Soviet armed forces. In the automatic system of the gun, a traditional scheme, only the bolt and barrel were re-designed to accommodate the new 5.45mm ammunition.

The Izhevsk Avtomat did not demonstrate overwhelming superiority over its rival during the tests. However, the Kalashnikov gun had one important advantage: it had an established and proven production base. The design of the AKM was simple and completely integrated into the production cycle of not one but two arsenals (Izhevsk and Tula). It was familiar to the troops in great detail. The cost of development and the ability to quickly establish mass production at the height of the Cold War played a decisive role in choosing an A-3 Avtomat. In addition, the new Kalashnikov sub-caliber gun was lighter than its competitor.

Based on the results of the competition, once again it was decided to adopt the rifle of Kalashnikov design. By decree of the Council of Ministers of January 19, 1974, and the Order of the Minister of Defense of the USSR, the Soviet Army adopted a

IN 1974 THE SOVIET ARMED FORCES ADOPTED THE NEW SUB-CALIBER AK-74 AVTOMAT (TOP) AND ITS FOLDING SIBLING AKS-74 (BOTTOM) FOR THE AIRBORNE TROOPS.

unified automatic caliber firearm complex of 5.45mm caliber, which received the AK-74 designation for the year of its acceptance. Ultimately, apart from the 5.45mm Kalashnikov Avtomat (with designation AK-74 and GRAU index of 6P20), the entire family of infantry weapons was adopted for service with the Soviet armed forces. The new armament complex included the AK-74 and AKS-74 (folder) Avtomats and the RPK-74/RPKS-74 (folder) light machine guns. A little later, in 1979, a shortened AK-74U (Avtomat Kalashnikov sample 1974 Shortened) was also adopted. I have covered the RPK-74 in the RPK section of this book, but the AKSU deserves a separate mention below.

The two main versions that began to be supplied to the troops were the AK-74 with fixed laminate wood stock, and the AKS-74 with stamped-steel skeletonized folding stock. It is worth mentioning that the new folding stock on the AKS-74 folded to the left side instead of under the gun. This allowed the stock to be shortened to fall in line with the fixed-stock dimensions. This was impossible with underfolders, which had to clear the magazine and nestle around the lower handguard.

The AK-74 design, just as with its AK predecessors, was subject to tweaking and small alterations, even during mass production. In a way, the AK-74 was going through an evolution of its own. When first released in 1974, the new gun was "dressed" in a slightly modified set of AKM laminate wood furniture. By the late 1970s, the original AK-74 Avtomat laminate furniture was very different from the first models. The handguards were "scalloped" and the "skinnier" buttstock had a more defined cone and two lightning grooves.

At the same time, to keep up with modern times, the Soviets were working on a plastic substitute. In the early 1980s, the first models appeared dressed in plum-color composite furniture. Attempts were made early on to replace expensive and technologically heavy laminate components with composite. Bakelite was rejected due to poor heat diffusion in the handguards and for being too brittle. The only Bakelite component that survived was the iconic AK pistol grip. In 1986, the new plum set of

*Later models of the AK-74 sported glass-filled polyamide composite furniture of dark plum color.*

furniture was made of an impact-resistant glass-filled thermoset AG-4B polyamide composite.

The plum color of the AK-74 is often discussed by AK pundits. Many say that the Soviets did not have the technology to color the composites. That is as stupid a theory as the recently revived theory of the Earth being flat. One needs to remember that by the time the updated plastic-clad AK-74 rolled around, the Soviet Union was already on its second space station the size of three football fields. The notion that a country that can put something like that into orbit cannot figure out how to color plastic is ridiculous. In fact, the decision was deliberate, and perhaps the last one that the Russians made out of practical thought instead of what "modern trends" dictated. All one has to do is leave the plum-dressed rifle in the woods or bushes and walk away to a distance of 30–40 feet. The same is true with the Soviet red laminate furniture and orange Bakelite magazines. I know it may shatter someone's entire universe when it comes to the concept of camouflage. It definitely goes against everything that "armchair commandos" may know about concealment and camouflage. But the truth is that true black does not occur naturally, and black objects in the daytime draw attention. Whereas orange, red, and combinations of the color spectrum are present in almost any environment,

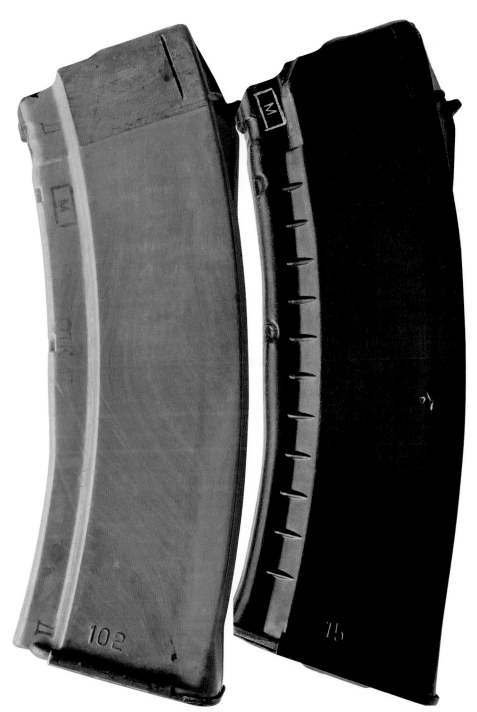

*AK-74 upgrades included a switch from Bakelite material to glass-filled polyamide plum-color plastic in production of the magazines. Here are Bakelite (left) and plum plastic (right) AK-74 magazines.*

especially wooded areas, with winter desert (tundra) being an exception.

The gun's furniture is not the only component that went through the mini-evolution. The 45-degree gas block inherited from the AKM Avtomat was replaced with the 90-degree one on later models. The infamous AK-74 muzzle brake's construction changed to make it cheaper to produce. Instead of one-piece construction with laser-cut zigzag front gas ports, the newer model was constructed of two pieces where the baffle was welded in to the main body of the brake to block the expansion chamber, leaving two radial slits on both sides. To reduce the probability of mechanical damage to the top cover of the receiver, its mounting was reinforced. The design of the return spring guide rod was changed with the addition of the locking "lip." This would allow users to retain the top cover on the gun when shooting grenades from the GP-25 or GP-30 under-barrel grenade launchers. The AK-74's orange Bakelite 30-round magazines were replaced by the plum-colored polyamide ones. Here I want to add that there

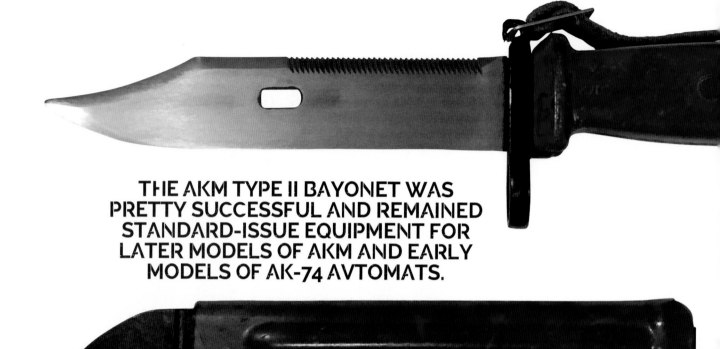

**THE AKM TYPE II BAYONET WAS PRETTY SUCCESSFUL AND REMAINED STANDARD-ISSUE EQUIPMENT FOR LATER MODELS OF AKM AND EARLY MODELS OF AK-74 AVTOMATS.**

was a wide color spectrum of magazines, from milky brown to outright dark red.

One more important component that evolved was the AK-74 bayonet. Although, I'm not sure if I would call what happened to the bayonet an evolution. In my opinion, it was changed for the worse. The original AK-74 bayonet was issued with later models of AKM rifles, especially the ones that were made by the Tula arsenal. The new model had a rigid Bakelite scabbard that was lighter and did not require a rubber insulation sleeve. The bayonet's Bakelite handle was redesigned and had two additional features.

Besides being a wire cutter, the bayonet could now also be used as a hammer and a pick. To do so, one needed to press the muzzle ring/handguard into the opening of the scabbard; the steel butt of the bayonet's handle became a hammer and the blade a pick, with the scabbard being the handle.

Final bayonet design modification was made when the plum-colored AK-74 was adopted for service. The new bayonet had a spear-type double-edged dagger-like blade, with the handle and scabbard made from the same dark plum-color glass-filled polyamide as the new rifle's furniture. This version of the AK bayonet lost its hammer and saw functions, but retained wire-cutting ability. In the 1990s, the same model bayonet was produced, dressed in black plastic to match AK-100-series rifles, and still is the current model for all new Russian AK-74Ms that are issued to Russian soldiers today.

Now, a bit about why I think it was a bad idea and how it came to be. The late AKM/early AK-74 Bakelite bayonet was not a perfect bayonet in the least—because it wasn't a bayonet. The Soviets realized that the time of the bayonet charge across no-man's land was over. Although the bayonet charge may still occur, it was becoming a rarity on the modern battlefield. What the soldiers needed was a multi-functional tool. What designers made was a bayonet, fighting knife, camp knife, saw, hammer, wire-cutter and pick, all in one. It had a Bowie-like blade, good balance for throwing, heavy handle to knock out a sentry and hand strap for fighting. What the later-model AK-74s were issued with is simply a pig sticker, especially if you had been instructed under penalty of incarceration not to sharpen it.

Why would the Soviets discard a good thing and make a turd instead? I will try to answer this question with my own theory solely predicated on observation. The reason for the shape of the new AK-74 bayonet is the same as the reason the U.S. military did away with the M7 bayonet and switched to the M9. The grass is always greener on the neighbor's yard, they say. Once Soviet firearms designers got their hands on the first examples of the M16 rifles and bayonets captured in Vietnam, they thought that the Americans knew something they didn't, and decided to change the blade of a perfectly good bayonet to a double-edged dagger, rendering it useless. The Americans, in turn, were "inspired" by the captured Soviet AKM bayos and came up with a dras-

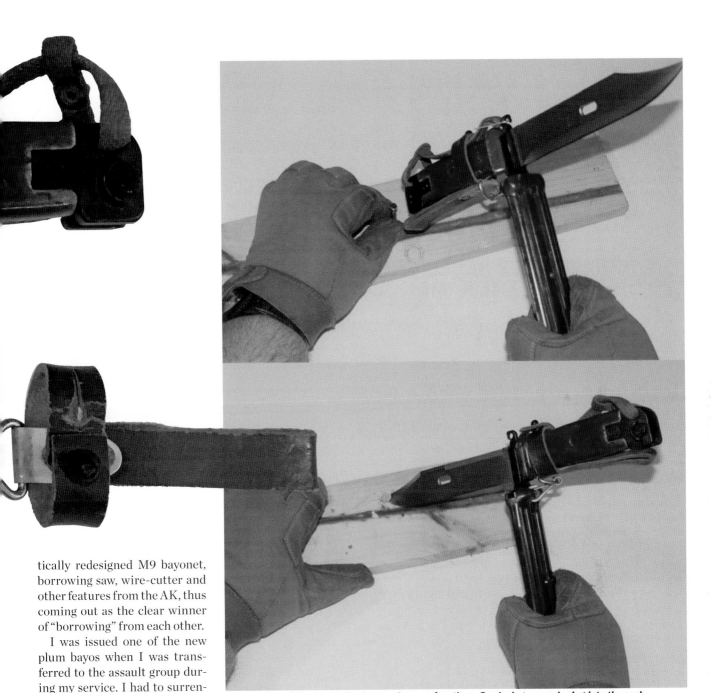

The new Type II bayonet gained a couple more functions. By placing a muzzle ring into the scabbard's neck, it could be used as a hammer. If you turned the bayonet around, it became a pick.

tically redesigned M9 bayonet, borrowing saw, wire-cutter and other features from the AK, thus coming out as the clear winner of "borrowing" from each other.

I was issued one of the new plum bayos when I was transferred to the assault group during my service. I had to surrender the AKM-style bayonet that came with my SVD rifle earlier. I took it as a travesty. The new bayonet was outright useless. We couldn't even open our C-ration cans properly with the damn things. And, since we were not expected to execute a bayonet charge anytime soon, after a while we stopped carrying them all together. Luckily our personnel were also issued NR-40 fighting knives.

After that short trip down memory lane, lets get back to my favorite gun, the AK-74.

The design of the new Avtomat included the following components and assemblies:
• Barreled action (receiver, front trunnion and barrel)
• Top receiver cover
• Front and rear sights
• Bolt and bolt carrier
• Muzzle brake
• Gas tube with upper handguard
• Trigger group
• Lower handguard and buttstock
• Magazine

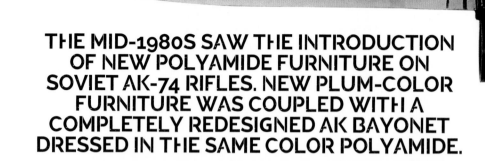

**THE MID-1980S SAW THE INTRODUCTION OF NEW POLYAMIDE FURNITURE ON SOVIET AK-74 RIFLES. NEW PLUM-COLOR FURNITURE WAS COUPLED WITH A COMPLETELY REDESIGNED AK BAYONET DRESSED IN THE SAME COLOR POLYAMIDE.**

## MAIN DIFFERENCES IN DESIGN AND INNOVATION

The main difference between the new Avtomat and its predecessor is the long and massive muzzle brake. This innovation, together with the reduction in caliber, allowed engineers to significantly reduce the recoil and improve the gun's accuracy, especially when shooting in full-auto. Although the compensator contributed to a significant decrease in recoil and thus increased accuracy, at the same time it significantly worsened the sound characteristics of the rifle. The powder gas now escaped not straight out of the muzzle, but out the sides, amplifying the sound of the shot.

The AK-74 design has basic components, assemblies and mechanisms identical to those of the original Kalashnikov design. The new rifle has nine assemblies unified with the AKM. Throughout the AK-74, 52 parts are identical to those on the AKM. The total volume of parts unification of the new Avtomat with the AKM was more than 70 percent. This is clearly evident during the assembly and disassembly of the AK-74. All metal parts are protected from corrosion with a special paint-like coating. The main design changes were more external, with some minor inner-working elements. The fire controls of the new Kalashnikov remained unchanged. Many components of the AK-74 are made from casting blanks. The barrel of the Avtomat is manufactured by means of rotary forging, during which the barrel and chamber are formed to a smaller caliber. All production was aimed at adapting a new model of the AK-74 to the production facilities of arsenals that had previously produced AKs and RPK machine guns of older modifications.

The new gun inherited the front and rear sighting system, consisting of the front post sight that can be adjusted for elevation and windage for sighting purposes, and the range-adjustable rear sight. Some models of the Avtomat are equipped with side rails for use with optical and night sights. The GP-25 or GP-30 underbarrel grenade launcher can be installed on all versions of the AK-74. As before, the AK-74 is issued with the standard bayonet.

The AK-74's accuracy of automatic fire was improved in comparison with the AKM by almost two times; the accuracy of single fire by approximately 50 percent.

Ranges of fire are:
- At single ground and air targets—500 meters (~547 yards)
- At group ground targets—1,000 meters (~1,094 yards)

Range of direct (flat) shot:
- At chest size target—440 meters (~481 yards)
- At full size humanoid silhouette—625 meters (~684 yards)

Accuracy requirements for the AK-74:
- All four bullet impacts must fit into a circle with a diameter of 15cm (~6 inches) at a distance of 100 meters (~110 yards).
- The average POI (Point of Impact) must deviate from the POA (Point of Aim) by no more than 5cm (~2 inches) in any direction.

Note, again, that these were the parameters for accuracy for automatic rate of fire.

AK accuracy is checked by firing a single shot at a test target or a black rectangle 35cm (~18 inches) high and 25cm (~10 inches) wide affixed on a 0.5x1-meter (20x24-inch) white board. The accuracy check is done at the range of 100m, from the prone position with a rest, with no bayonet and with regular bulk 7N6 cartridges. The rear sight is set at "3." The method used takes into account the average deviation of impacts from the centerline of grouping and must consist of at least 50 percent of all impacts. The total includes the deviations of the bullets and the average impact points.

In general, there was a significant improvement in the accuracy relative to the AKM and even more so in comparison with the AK-47. As an example, here are the AK-74 accuracy results when looking at the total median deviation at a distance of 800m (vertical and horizontal respectively) compared to other rifles:

- AK-47—76cm and 89cm (30 and 35 inches)
- SKS—47cm and 34cm (18 1/2 and 13 1/2 inches)
- AKM—64cm and 90cm (25 and 35 1/2 inches)
- AK-74—48cm and 64cm (19 and 25 inches)

## AK-74 VARIANTS

As mentioned earlier, from the very beginning the AK-74 Avtomat was produced in two versions:

- AK-74—the main and base model with fixed stock
- AKS-74 (GRAU Index 6P21)—the version with side-folding skeletonized metal stock for service with airborne troops

Shortly, the main basic models were followed by:

- AK-74N—"N" is for "night vision." This fixed stock version was equipped with side accessory rail for mounting the NSPU night vision scope.
- AKS-74N—As with its fixed-stock sibling, this "night" version had a rail for mounting optics and side-folding stock.

With development of the AK-specific collimator and optical sights, the AK-74N and AKS-74N gained popularity, the latter of those especially with special operations troops, who would often use night or day optics on their guns. This feature lead the way to the creation of one universal version and current-issue Russian service Avtomat, the AK-74M.

*The AK-74N with USP-1 "Tulip" (1P29) universal optical sight.*

*An AK-74N with 1PN51 night vision sight.*

The AK-74 family of guns also included four automatics or light machine guns—the RPK-74, er model with folding stock, as well as both variants designated RPK-74N and RPKS 74N2 respectively. I have told the RPK story earlier. variations of squad the RPKS 74 paratroop-equipped with optics rail and

However, the other prolific gun from the same family that is worth a separate mention is the famed AK-74 short version, AKS-74U. Here in the States, for some reason, it's called the "Krinkov." As a Russian speaker, I do not recognize this word and do not know how it came to be. The Russian word "Krinka" refers to a clay pitcher. How it would come to be the American identification of the Soviet gun is beyond my comprehension. If we dig deep into the gun's history, we can find 19th-century Bohemian firearms designer Karel Krnka (pronounced Krynka), whose weapons were supplied to Russian troops during the Russo-Turkish war of 1876-1877. But, one can see that attaching Krnka's name to the Soviet gun that was made in 1970 makes no sense. Most likely, the name came from the Afghan Mujahedeen or a *Soldier of Fortune* magazine reporter who visited the Muj and had a chance to see this exotic Soviet AK. It is a known fact the Afghans are unable to pronounce the Russian name of Kalashnikov, and call the AKs "Kulakof." It may be that the Afghan "Kulakof" got somehow transcribed by the reporter as "Krinkov." Or, maybe feeling creative, the reporter came up with it on his own, like the James Bond girl Anna Top or Car Talk's fake limo driver Boris Droppoff. Trust me when I say that not all reporters are firearms specialists and sometimes revert to their creative side, for better or for worse. In this case, the name stuck. However, do not refer to the AKSU as "Krink" or "Krinkov" when talking to a Russian. He simply would not understand what you are talking about.

Designed as a personal defense weapon for tankers, APC drivers, artillery crews and helicopter pilots, the AKSU was to replace the APS, a Stechkin automatic pistol. It packed by far more serious firepower than a handgun, even an automatic pistol. However, it did not get the intended respect among the troops, especially among the Spetsnaz. It did not offer any advantages over regular AKS rifles and was always discarded in favor of its full-length siblings. Nevertheless, the AKSU—or "Suchka" or "Ksyuha" or "Okurok" (little bitch, women's name Kseniya, and cigarette butt, respectively)—had a "cool" appearance and was often used as a prop for taking pictures. Just look at Ossama's selfies. However, the compact AKSU's real popularity came from Russian police and anti-terrorism units. Its compactness and firepower made it conducive to operating in the close quarters of the urban concrete jungle. To this day, this short Kalashnikov is in service with police and can often be seen on the city streets in Russia.

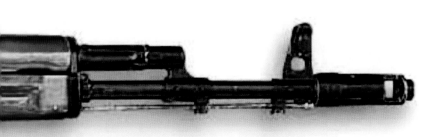

Advantages of the AK-74 include:
- High reliability of operation under difficult conditions
- Ease of maintenance in the field conditions
- Simplicity and reduced production costs
- Less recoil
- Greater accuracy
- Extended range
- Increased hit probability
- Reduced weight of the gun and ammo
- More ammunition in the loadout

Shortcomings include the lower single-shot accuracy of fire by 1.28 times compared to the M16A2 (mainly due to the better inherent quality of the SS109 cartridge). At the same time, the AK-74 has 1.34–1.43 times better accuracy in full-auto compared to the same rifle. In comparison with the American M4A1 carbine, the AK-74 still has a lower accuracy in firing by single fire, but only marginally, yet the AK-74's automatic fire accuracy is significantly better. The AK-74 has arguably inferior ergonomics compared to Western guns of the same type. There is no push-button mag release. The selector/safety lever cannot be operated without removing the control hand from the pistol grip.

Some may complain about the AK's weight distribution, with the majority of it placed toward the front of the gun. Personally, I like the AK's balance, it contributes to stability during rapid firing.

*Replacing the automatic Stechking pistol that was in service with tank, APC and artillery crews, the AKS-74U shorty was a logical choice due its commonality with the main battle rifle, the AK-74, with coolness factor to boot.*

## USE AND COMBAT APPLICATION OF THE AK-74 AND PERSONAL EXPERIENCES

Since the first days of its arrival in combat units on the front lines, the new Avtomat proved to be a reliable and effective personal battlefield weapon. New fixed-stock models were supplied to motorized infantry combat units, and AKS-74s equipped with side-folding stocks were shipped to airborne, marine infantry and border guard detachments. The new Avtomat immediately outperformed the old AKM in fire efficiency by almost 1.5 times. The accuracy of the new low-impulse, high-velocity cartridge and the gun itself allowed users to conduct very effective automatic bursts and single-shot fire.

It just so happened that the release of the new Avtomat coincided with the beginning of the Soviet–Afghan campaign. The majority of

*The AK-74 and AKS-74 were the main combat weapons of the Soviet troops in Afghanistan.*

Soviet troops in Afghanistan, from truck drivers to the highly trained Spetsnaz soldiers, were armed with the AK-74 family of guns. The 5.45-caliber AK-74 Avtomat and its folding model AKS-74 were the most widely issued main battle rifle of the Soviet armed forces in Afghanistan. It was issued with bayonet, belt magazine pouch (later in the war, use of belt pouches was all but abandoned in favor of captured or handmade chest pouches and, since 1985, Soviet-made chest pouches called "Lifchik"), cleaning kit, oil bottle, four 30-round Bakelite magazines, four stripper clips with a loading spoon and a drop case that no one ever used. It was an outstanding rifle for what it had to do and for the environment in which it operated. It retained the AK reliability and gained accuracy and additional improvements. In my opinion, it offered far superior controllability on full auto and, more importantly, 30 percent reduction in weight (considering full ammo load).

Although, the standard non-folding AK-74 was prevalent with the infantry, the AKS-74 with skeletonized side-folding stock saw use with assault, reconnaissance and special operations troops. A good number of the folding AKS-74 Avtomats used by the Spetsnaz units were the AKS-74Ns; these variants had a side rail installed for use with optics and had a designation "N" for night vision.

My military experience also included time with the AK-74 Avtomat, or, rather, with its folding stock version the AKS-74. I started my service with the AKS-74 in hand and ended it with an AKS-74N. I carried an SVD sniper rifle in between, but that is a different story for a different book.

The first time I laid my eyes on the AK-74 rifle was when I, along with a bunch of brand new recruits, passed through the gates of the training base in Fergana. As we huddled around the army troop transport trucks that brought us from the train station, a company-sized unit returning from the range passed by. The first thing that stood out was that they were all shouldering weird-looking AKs. Though very familiar with AK platform, we had never seen this "new" gun. There was something very different about our new rifles. All rifles, though familiar in shape and size, had muzzle devices attached to them. Not having encountered the AK-74 before, all the greenhorns started to chatter with nonsense theories as to what that device was. By the end of the heated discussion, we came to the conclusion that the strange muzzle device attached to the otherwise normal-looking AK was the "silencer." Before long, I was shouldering my very own newly issued AKS-74 Avtomat with the "silencer."

Mine was a well-used unit, which is to say not new, but in excellent working order. It was clad in laminate wood and had the standard triangular skeletonized stock. It did not have a side rail for mounting optics. It was just a plain ol' workhorse.

We were instructed on cleaning these rifles using solvent, oil and oil-absorbent paper. The vast majority of recruits in my company knew how to strip an AK.

Every male in the Soviet Union had the "honor" to spend 2-3 years in the Soviet military doing the bidding of the Motherland. To get a leg up on the process, Soviets instituted a Beginners Military Preparation Course for junior and senior classes of high school. The twice-weekly class was designed to introduce young men to everything military—marching in formation, digging a foxhole, putting on a gas mask and such—but the main goal of the class was to make us proficient with an AK. As a rule, every school would have a couple of demilled old service rifles, usually AKMs. As a final test for the course, we had to complete two exercises: the field tactical exercise and, behold, a trip to a real military range. There, we were given an AK (the real full-auto military gun) and had to shoot three rounds on semi-auto into a 100-meter static target, and six rounds on full-auto at resetting metal silhouette targets that were set at 200–400 meters. To summarize the above, every 16-year-old punk or otherwise in the Soviet Union had training on the AK-type rifle and could field strip it with eyes closed.

I had no trouble taking my rifle apart, cleaning it and putting it back together.

Back, now, to the training base in Fergana. Soon there was the first trip to the range. We were once again issued our rifles, this time with mag pouches and three empty magazines. Note that throughout our basic training we were issued the same gun every time, with the same pouch and usually the same mags. To ensure that we had our own stuff, the gun's serial number was written onto our military ID and the pouch identified by a wooden tag with our name on it, which we had to make.

At the range, after a lengthy safety briefing, we moved into the operational instruction and were taught how to load a magazine. That is when I first saw a 5.45x39mm round. It was completely different from its infamous 7.62mm predecessor.

Our first drills had us lying in prone position, firing in semi-auto at chest-sized silhouette paper targets set at 100 yards. Having fired an AK rifle before and expecting it to kick, I was pleasantly surprised when I squeezed off my first round. There was almost no recoil. I finished the exercise and to my amazement scored 27 out of a possible 30 without even trying. My gun shot true.

Next came the full-auto drill. We were still firing from the prone position at the standard Soviet military resetting silhouette targets, set at 200–400 meters in checkered formation. Once again, I was pleasantly surprised, expecting much stronger kick.

A Soviet Spetsnaz unit waits in ambush early in the Soviet–Afghan campaign. The unit commander is armed with an AKS-74 Avtomat.

*A Spetsnaz officer poses with his AKS-74N equipped with NSPU night scope.*

There was very little recoil, which made it really easy to knock down targets. The targets we were engaging were of two types: a full-height standard humanoid silhouette (a.k.a. standing or running silhouette) and a machine gun crew. We were also taught to fire short bursts on a count of 22, depressing the trigger on the word twenty and releasing it on the word two. This way, only 2–3 rounds would discharge from the rifle. The instructions dictated that we aim at a right knee or right-side taper of the full height target; this way the first round would strike a target in the abdominal/chest area and the second would sail over the target's left shoulder, striking the following target in the chest. It works! Later, I was able to achieve this on a regular basis.

The rifles we used during basic training were sighted in by the armorers. We were supposed to identify our point of impact (POI) in relation to our point of aim (POA) and adjust our POA accordingly. For the most part, our guns were shooting true. Some had minor deviations. If the deviation was minor, the trooper would make his POA adjustment. In the case of major problems, that particular gun would be sent back to the armory for sighting.

Our training progressed with the addition of actual weapons applications, i.e. firing from a vehicle, mountain firing and firing on the move.

The AK-74 performed exceptionally well throughout the Soviet–Afghan campaign. For my part, I have to say that not once did any rifle in my group malfunction. Between operations and during idle time, we constantly practiced with our rifles at the range, engaging targets from 50–400 meters. In the right hands, these rifles were extremely accurate. Coupled with legendary reliability, this makes the AK-74 an irreplaceable instrument of war for harsh environments.

The old principle "take care of your rifle and it will take care of you" was very much employed by the Soviet soldiers in Afghanistan. Despite the outside appearance, our guns were always in great mechanical shape. The internals were always well cared for. We cleaned our Avtomats every chance we got, but the ever-present fine abrasive Afghan "moon" dust was a formidable opponent. It would wear the coating off our guns and polish them to a shine.

Never did I hear a single complaint about the accuracy of AK-74 rifle. If you complained, then you were just a poor shot. A couple of training sessions or shooting classes could fix that.

In the beginning of this book, I promised to throw in a couple of anecdotes, maybe an interesting story, and dispel a myth or two. I don't want to disappoint, so here goes.

Back in 2001, fellow writer David Fortier, renowned AK smith Marc Krebs and I visited my friends from the Moscow Quick Reaction Unit, or as it is called Moscow SOBR. It's something like the U.S. SWAT only more badass. I only say that because they were armed as an Army special forces unit and had to deal with terrorists on a weekly basis. Nevertheless, this unit was on duty the first time after coming back from the region of Chechnya, where at that time Russia was battling the radical Wahhabi–Islamic terrorists.

We were politely conversing with these guys (who, by the way, were fully armed with their duty weapons, machine guns and such), stopping only for the next shot of vodka, when the question of AK-74 accuracy came up. After a pause caused by what they thought was a dumb question, one operator picked up his standard-issue AK-74M and, while patting it gently, told us that he used to pass the time at the block-post by shooting wires off the telephone pole at distance. If the rifle is capable of that and one calls it inaccurate, it's time to take a basic marksman course.

I loved my AKS-74. Everything about the gun was easy: shooting, cleaning, handling. I was getting pretty proficient with it. I was getting good, too good. In fact, due to my above average shooting ability, which I have never claimed then nor would I claim now, the commanders had something different in mind for me. They pried

*The AK-74 (bottom), though retaining overall standard AK appearance, was drastically different looking compared to the AKM (top).*

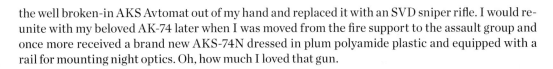

the well broken-in AKS Avtomat out of my hand and replaced it with an SVD sniper rifle. I would re-unite with my beloved AK-74 later when I was moved from the fire support to the assault group and once more received a brand new AKS-74N dressed in plum polyamide plastic and equipped with a rail for mounting night optics. Oh, how much I loved that gun.

## WHAT WOULD MTK THINK?

It turns out that not everyone was a fan of the new sub-caliber AK. In fact, the creator of the AK Avtomat, Mikhail Kalashnikov himself, was categorically against modifying the AKM for the 5.45x39mm cartridge. Some people think Kalashnikov was absolutely right, especially when his point of view was supported by the country's leading weapons experts. His argument was that the 7.62mm M43 cartridge was not fully developed and still had developmental potential. He told me the same thing during our dinner at his summer home in 2001. However, no matter how valid his argument may have been, it did not in any way affect the Soviet military top brass' move to adopt the AK-74 family of weapons chambered for the low-impulse and high-velocity cartridge and start the mass production of these guns to replace old and "outdated" AKMs.

It is worth mentioning that Kalashnikov's opposition on this issue was strictly his individual decision, one of the few made during the evolution of the AK, and could potentially have positive effect on the future development of the AK weapons platform. Most of Kalashnikov's ideas and objections during the late stages of the AK evolution were deemed to be absurd by some experts. Fortunately for the Soviet military, or unfortunately for the fans and followers of the great designer, at that time Kalashnikov already did not have strong influence on the production of military small arms.

An illustration of the growing discontent between the designer and manufacturers was the proposal to raise the angle of the AK's stock to bring it in line with the bore and, ultimately, with the sighting line, which Kalashnikov categorically rejected. Such an elementary modification could improve the accuracy of the AK's automatic fire almost twofold. However, Kalashnikov argued that raising the stock would expose soldiers to enemy fire, because the shooter would have to raise his head higher to aim. This argument had no foundation for most of the people who actually shot AKs. Even if the stock was slightly higher, the sight line remained at the same position in relation to the shooter's eye. The difference is the positioning of the head (slight forward) and cheek weld to the buttstock. Consider, too, that the AK's magazine protrudes down, forcing the shooter to rise from ground-level anyway. Even if the argument was valid, the practical effectiveness of properly aimed accurate fire and ability to reliably hit targets outweighs marginal exposure increase if it even exists. Exposing the top of one's helmet from the foxhole for 2–3 seconds to deliver two precisely aimed short bursts is not critical, compared to the impossibility of accurately firing a larger-caliber AK.

No matter how much it pains me, as a former and current user of the AK-74, I have to disagree with Kalashnikov on this point. I think that he later realized the errors in his earlier arguments and became a fan of the 5.45mm cartridge and AKSU Avtomat. During our meeting, he told me what a great weapon it was and what it did to the hogs at the test range. Go figure.

*There is a myth that Soviet Spetsnaz units preferred the 7.62mm AKM Avtomats to the standard issue AKS-74s. It is completely untrue. Every Spetsnaz unit had several AKMLs (AKMN and AKMN-1) as unit standard-issue weapons, with the ability to accept the PBS-1 suppressor and NV optics.*

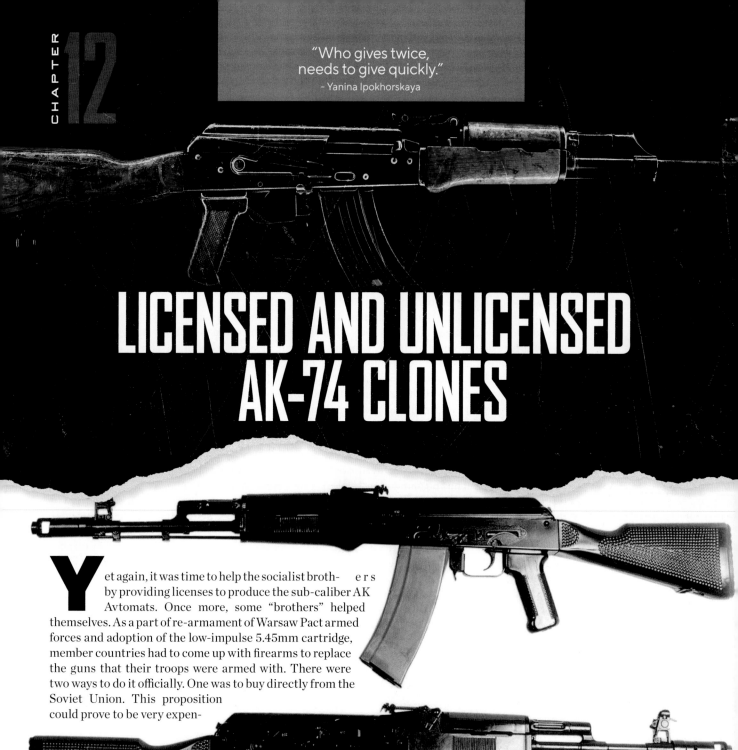

## CHAPTER 12

> "Who gives twice,
> needs to give quickly."
> - Yanina Ipokhorskaya

# LICENSED AND UNLICENSED AK-74 CLONES

**Y**et again, it was time to help the socialist broth-    e r s by providing licenses to produce the sub-caliber AK Avtomats. Once more, some "brothers" helped themselves. As a part of re-armament of Warsaw Pact armed forces and adoption of the low-impulse 5.45mm cartridge, member countries had to come up with firearms to replace the guns that their troops were armed with. There were two ways to do it officially. One was to buy directly from the Soviet Union. This proposition could prove to be very expen-

*The East German MPi-AK-74N clone of the AK-74 is perhaps one of the closest copies, with some details typical for East German AKs, like plastic furniture. It was also considered to have exceptional quality.*

sive for the buyer and problematic for the seller, which was trying to re-arm its own military. The second way was to buy a license from the Soviets and build their own. Since the majority of the Warsaw Pact countries already produced Kalashnikov system-based rifles, the transition would be quick and painless. There was, of course, a third way: try to develop their own rifles for the new cartridge. We start with the licensees.

## EAST GERMAN AVTOMATS

East Germany (DDR) was one of the first Warsaw Pact member countries that produced AK Avtomats chambered for the

5.45x39mm cartridge. These were the MPi AK-74N with fixed stock, the MPi-AKS-74N folder and MPi-AKS-74NK with a folding stock and a shortened 317mm (~12.5-inch) barrel.

In 1981, East Germany purchased a license from the USSR to manufacture the AK-74 Avtomats and almost immediately started to produce the rifles with minor modifications.

Some if not most of the components used in making the 7.62mm guns were used in production of the new 5.45x39mm Avtomats, such as a plastic or wire folding stock, plastic handguards of a modified shape and pistol grip. In addition, the side rail for attachment of optical and night sights was installed on all East German AK-74 variants, which was reflected in the model designations. One important detail is worth mentioning. Although there were two versions, the fixed stock and a folder for air mobile troops, both variants were based on the same license, which only covered a standard fixed-stock AK-74 Avtomat. The wire stock that the East Germans were using to make their folding gun did not require a rear trunnion block replacement with folding mechanism, and the folding stock was simply installed in place of the fixed one.

The new Avtomats were adopted for service with the armed forces of the DDR with the following designations:

• MPi-AK-74N (Mashinenpistole-Avtomat Kalaschnikow fur Nachtsichtgerat und ZF Modell 1974)—a copy of the fixed sock AK-74N rifle with a side accessory rail

• MPi-AKS-74N (Mashinenpistole-Avtomat Kalaschnikow mit Stutze fur Nachtsichtgerat und ZF)—identical to the MPi-AK-74N except the addition of the wire folding stock

*Apart from the fixed-stock Avtomat, the East Germans also produced the MPi-AKS-74N folder and MPi-AKS-74NK shorty.*

Additionally, based on the MPi-AKS-74N, the East Germans released a shortened variant for tank and APC crews, with designation MPi-AKS-74NK (Mashinenpistole-Automat Kalaschnikow mit Stutze fur Nachtsichtgerat und ZF Kleine).

Another detail begs attention. The East German gun makers were the first to go with a side rail for mounting optics and night sights across the entire AK model line. This was something the Soviets did not do until the release of the last Soviet-built AK, the AK-74M, as the standard battlefield weapon for all branches of the military.

The 5.45x39mm Avtomats were produced at two weapons factories, in the cities of Suhl and Visa, until 1989, until the DDR joined the FRG (Federal Republic of Germany). The tactical and technical characteristics of the East German Avtomats of the MPi family are very similar if not identical to those of the Soviet guns. By design, the East German-made Kalashnikovs did not differ from the Soviet AKs. As a matter of fact, they are almost exact copies of their Soviet-built siblings judging by the main components, assemblies, operation, gas system and magazines.

After the reunification of Germany, the MPi family of Avtomats of the former National People's Army of the DDR was adopted by the Bundeswehr as a weapon of a limited standard. Here in the U.S., there are several copies of the East German AK-74 variants in the hands of AK owners. These came into the country mainly in the form of parts kits, then were assembled into fully functioning guns. Occasionally one will pop up for sale and some lucky individual has a chance to add one more remarkable rifle to his or her AK collection.

## BULGARIAN AKK-74

The Bulgarian Arsenal AKK-74 is considered to be the closest copy to the original Soviet AK-74. It was produced by the Bulgarians under Soviet license and under direct supervision by the Izhmash engineers and other specialists.

*The Bulgarian AKK-74 is the closest copy of the Soviet AK-74, often distinguished by the solid wood furniture that was at one point painted. Later models even came in the Soviet plum-color composite furniture.*

In the early 1970s, the Bulgarian "Arsenal" plant began production of the Kalashnikov Automatic Carbine (AKKM), which essentially was an exact copy of the Soviet AKM. Based on successful experiences with the production of high quality Kalashnikov rifles, production of the new family of weapons chambered for the 5.45mm cartridge started in the mid-1980s.

Three main variants were adopted for service with Bulgarian armed forces: the fixed-stock infantry model AKK-74, which was an identical copy of the AK-74; the AKKS-74 with side-folding skeletonized stock for use with air mobile troops; and also a copy of the Soviet AKS-74 folder, the AKK-74(N), equipped with a side rail for mounting night optics like its Soviet twin the AK-74N.

Up until the mid-1990s, the Bulgarian AK was almost identical to its Soviet sibling. It was later the Bulgarians started to deviate from the norm and introduced their own AK-based models. However, until then the Bulgarian Avtomats could only be distinguished from the Soviets' by the factory stamps, and by the markings of the selector lever: the letters "ЕД" instead of

*Though very different from the AK-74, the Bulgarian AR rifles, with a milled receiver and underfolding stock, employed many AK-74 internal components. Top to bottom: Arsenal AR (5.56x45mm), Arsenal AR-F (7.62x39mm) and Arsenal AR-F (5.56x45mm).*

Russian "ОД." The quality of manufacturing was also quite high and remains so today.

I'm not sure why, but one could sense and trace evidence of particularly close attention that the Soviets paid pertaining to the manufacturing of the Bulgarian AKs and their quality.

When I visited the Izhmash plant in 2001, the then Commercial Development Director of the company, Mr. Konstantinov, asked me, "What should I do with Bulgarian Arsenal?" Confused by the question, I asked, "Why?" He replied that the Arsenal owed a lot of money to Izhmash. Since I was a big fan of the Bulgarian rifles we could buy in the U.S., I said nothing, stating that it was not my business and secretly hoping that the Russians would not do anything to screw up further shipments of high-quality AKs to U.S. shooters.

Further development of the AKK-74 Avtomat went the way of improving the design, but actually adopting it to the Soviet/Russian AK-74M. Arsenal's last AK-74 Avtomats looked very similar to the AK-74M and AK-100 series, with little or no difference. Here in the U.S. we know them as SLR series rifles that are finished in the States by the Arsenal USA in Las Vegas, NV, and sold through its subsidiary K-Var Corp.

Mass production of military weapons for the 5.45x39mm cartridge is currently stopped due to lack of demand. It is also worth pointing out that the Bulgarians produced several modifications of the Soviet AKSU shorty, such as the Arsenal AR-SF, M4-SF, AR-M8F and AR-M9F, with a variety of stock options. One can tell the later models of the Bulgarian 74-series rifles by the safety/selector lever markings on the receiver: "S" for Safe, "A" for full auto and "J" for semi-auto fire.

These days, Bulgaria offers a large number of Kalashnikov Avtomats of various modifications and chambered in a variety of calibers. If the field of cheaper AKs is firmly occupied by Romania, then in a market where AK buyers demand AKs that are as close as possible to the original Soviet or Russian variants, Bulgarian gun makers have carved and firmly occupied a niche. One success of the Bulgarian Arsenal is a recent award to supply the Iraqi Army, Police and Security Services with AK Avtomats in 7.62x39mm and 5.56 NATO calibers. These guns were different from the AK-74 family of guns, leaning more toward the AKM design. However, they retained several features from the 5.45mm sibling, such as gas block and skeletonized side-folding stock.

With entrance into the world firearms market, the Arsenal AK acquired its own unmistakable style: black plastic AK-100-series furniture and a "waffle" magazine in combination with an old-school milled receiver. The throwback to the AK-47 design was most likely due to licensing problems. Since all conceivable periods of limitation on the AK-47 as an industrial model had already expired, and the Russians did not want to extend the license for the production of modern weapons to a NATO country, the result produced an interesting hybrid of the AK-47 and AK-74.

It has been reported that about 7,000 Arsenal AR and Arsenal AR-F (underfolder) Avtomats were sold to the illegal armed group the Autodesfensas Unidas de Colombia (AUC). Looking at the reports coming from Syria, one can also recognize Bulgarian-built rifles in the hands of Kurdish fighters (most likely courtesy of the U.S.). However, the largest buyer of Arsenal products is the United States, which buys Bulgarian Kalashnikovs for the needs of the Iraqi army.

We here in the U.S. are familiar with Bulgarian Avtomats thanks to the efforts of Arsenal USA. They have a reputation of high-quality Kalashnikovs. However, the Bulgarian Arsenal's recent commercial success in the world gun trade puts in jeopardy a steady supply of these rifles to the U.S. commercial market. I really wish that all the wars stopped, so that we could have our guns.

## HUNGARIAN NGM-81

Hungary also produced its own fully licensed copy of the AK-74 Avtomat. The NGM-81 is a licensed copy of the Soviet AK-74 rifle, the production of which was set up by the Hungarian company Fegyver e Gazkeszulekgyar (FEG) in Budapest in a very short time.

*The Hungarian NGM-81 was produced in two configurations, with fixed and underfolding stocks. In their appearance, the NGM-81 Avtomats closely resembled the AKM and not the AK-74.*

By design and from the point of view of all main components, assemblies and mechanisms, the NGM-81 is a copy of the AK-74 Kalashnikov Avtomat, but Hungarian designers made several small changes.

Looking at the NGM rifle, it is readily apparent that the Hungarian gun makers used their experience building the 7.62mm AKM-type rifles. It appears that they went for the components unification in order to reduce the cost of tooling and ultimately production of the new 5.45mm Avtomats. Main deviations from the Soviet AK-74 design in the Hungarian NGM-81 rifle were the use of solid blonde wood furniture, with a pistol grip that is typical for all Hungarian AKs, the 45-degree AKM gas block and an elongated flash hider similar to the one that was issued with the Soviet NSPU night scope. Additionally, the NGM-81 Avtomat was issued with stamped steel ribbed magazine designed for the 5.45x39mm cartridge and similar in appearance to its 7.62mm counterpart.

The underfolding stock variant of the NGM-81 was released at the same time for service with air mobile troops. However, the underfolding stock mechanism was "borrowed" from the AKM, or rather AKMS design. The barrel on the NGM gun was cold forged and chrome lined to increase its survivability.

New Avtomats began to come into service for motorized infantry troops of the Hungarian army. However, the withdrawal of Hungary from the Warsaw Treaty organization and its further orientation to the North Atlantic Bloc necessitated the unification of the armaments and equipment of its army with NATO standards.

As a result, in 1990 new models of the NGM-81 with fixed and underfolding stocks and chambered for 5.56mm NATO cartridge were released and adopted for service with the Hungarian armed forces. The magazine feed was also modified to accommodate use of the standard AR magazine.

Production of the Hungarian copy of the AK-74 was discontinued shortly after its launch. As a result, a small number of NGM-81 Avtomats chambered in 5.45x39mm caliber were produced. However, the 74-series rifles served as the base for production of the 5.56mm NATO NGM-81 variant.

## POLISH TANTAL

In 1991, one of the most original variants of the 5.45mm Kalashnikov Avtomats, the Kbk wz.88 Tantal, entered service with airborne troops and special forces of the Polish armed forces.

The first work to develop arms for the new low-impulse ammunition in Poland started at the Research and Development Center in Radom back in 1980. By the end of 1985, the first prototype of a 5.45mm wz.81 Avtomat appeared. This weapon was designed by a team of engineers under the leadership of a head designer Shpadersky. In 1986, the first batch of the new Avtomats was presented for field-testing. The design of the new gun, originally designated as wz.81, was modeled after the Soviet 5.45mm AK-74 rifle, and just like their colleagues in other countries, the Polish designers logically tried to maximize use of components and assemblies from the AKM.

Before the end of 1987, the experimental Avtomat was redesigned. Several components and assemblies were improved. The improvements included use of bolt carrier, bolt and magazines that were interchangeable with the AK-74, and introduction of a short-burst mode. In January 1988, the new gun was subjected to extended military tests and in 1989, based on the results, a recommendation was issued to compile all the necessary documentation for production of the initial batch of the new 5.45mm Avtomat. The first serial production batch was manufac-

THE POLISH 5.45MM KALASHNIKOV AVTOMAT, KBK WZ.88 TANTAL, IS A TRUE AK-74, WITH SEVERAL UNIQUE FEATURES. THE ELONGATED MUZZLE DEVICE ADAPTED FOR LAUNCHING RIFLE GRENADES IS STILL A VERY EFFECTIVE MUZZLE BRAKE.

tured in the same year.

In 1990 the new rifle was handed over for field testing, and the following year it entered service with the Polish Army under the name 5.45mm Karabinek kbk wz.88 (5.45mm Avtomat Model 1988). Along with the Tantal Avtomats, the Polish armed forces also received a Soviet 5.45mm Kalashnikov light machine gun, the RPK-74.

Unlike the East German or Hungarian variants, which were close copies of the AK-74 and AKM rifles, bearing unmistakable resemblance to their Soviet siblings, the Kbk wz.88 Tantal trigger group allowed not only firing in semi- and full-auto modes, but also fixed three-round bursts. Corresponding changes were made to the design of the safety/selector lever that could also be operated by the shooter's thumb.

The barrel of the new Avtomat was cold forged and chrome lined. One of the new and distinctly different features of the Tantal Avtomat was its multifunctional two-chamber muzzle brake/compensator, which performed not only as a flash hider, but also allowed firing of rifle grenades.

The use of a new 5.45mm cartridge with flat trajectory allowed increased range of a direct shot at a human size target from 525m (574 yards) for AKM to 625m (684.5 yards). The main modes of fire from the Tantal are automatic, firing short bursts of up to five shots; long bursts, up to 10 shots; and continuous fire. The range of effective fire at ground targets increased to 500m (547 yards); effective range to airplanes, helicopters and parachutists also increased to 500m. However, the Tantal's lethal velocity range, in comparison with AKM, dropped from 1,500m (1,640 yards) to 1,350m (1476 yards) due to bullet mass.

After the dissolution of the Warsaw Treaty organization, the Poles began to look elsewhere and, in 1989, began work to upgrade 5.45mm Kalashnikov Avtomats for the new standard 5.56mm NATO cartridge. It was decided to adopt the standard weapons of the Polish armed forces with minimal changes to the design of the Kbk wz.88 Tantal rifles. The designers of the Military Institute of Technology and Armament tried to fulfill this requirement as precisely as possible, and unavoidable changes would be carried out within the capabilities of the existing manufacturing base. As a result of these efforts, a new 5.56mm automatic carbine, the Kbk wz.90 Tantal, was released in 1990.

The Polish armed forces were preparing to join the North Atlantic bloc not empty-handed. The use of a new cartridge demanded the following design changes: the barrel diameter and rifling, size and shape of the chamber and bolt face. Changes were made to the rear sight, taking into consideration the different ballistics of the 5.56mm SS109 round.

The rest of the design of the Kbk wz.90 rifle was completely identical to the 5.45mm wz.88 Avtomat. However, in many respects the new 5.56mm Kbk wz. 90 carbine did not fit NATO standards. The Poles had a long way to go to adapt their Kalashnikovs to NATO requirements.

Along with the Tantal full-length rifle, a 5.45mm wz.89 Onyks shortened and lightened Avtomat was developed based on the 5.45mm Soviet AKS-74U and Kbk wz.88 Tantal guns. The new shorty was intended for use by the air mobile and special operations troops, as well as the crew members of combat vehicles.

In comparison with the Tantal Avtomat, the Onyks had a shortened 216mm (8 1/2-inch) barrel and a new muzzle device, which, considering the short length of the barrel, played the main role of flame arrester while allowing the shooting of rifle grenades.

The trigger group was identical to that of the 5.45mm Kbk wz.88 Tantal Avtomat, with three modes of fire. Like the Soviet AKSU shorty, the Onyks had a flash hider/booster and an L-shaped flippable rear sight for a range of 100, 200 and 400 meters. However, unlike the Soviet relative, where the rear sight was mounted on the hinged top cover, the Onyks' sight was mounted on a bar that protruded above the receiver cover, because the top cover itself was not hinged nor attached to anything on the gun. Just like the AKSU and other AK shorties, the

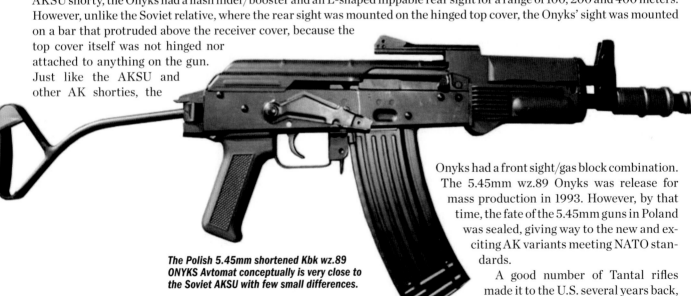

The Polish 5.45mm shortened Kbk wz.89 ONYKS Avtomat conceptually is very close to the Soviet AKSU with few small differences.

Onyks had a front sight/gas block combination. The 5.45mm wz.89 Onyks was release for mass production in 1993. However, by that time, the fate of the 5.45mm guns in Poland was sealed, giving way to the new and exciting AK variants meeting NATO standards.

A good number of Tantal rifles made it to the U.S. several years back, mostly as parts kits. Several suppliers

*The Polish 5.56mm carbine, KbS wz.96 Beryl, is the only AK-74 derivative that fully meets NATO standards for small arms. It is the main battle rifle of today's Polish armed forces.*

offered them for sale as kits and as complete rifles built on U.S.-made receivers. I had a chance to test one, from Century Arms, with a folding wire stock. I remember many Tantal owners complaining about the key-holing problem with these rifles, attributed to the "wrong" barrel diameter making the bullet tumble. One minor detail that these shooters fail to notice is that the grouping these guns produced is rather acceptable by Western standards, even with a tumbling bullet fired from a bore that is larger than the projectile's caliber. Don't take my word for it. This is basic ballistics.

In the case of Tantal rifles, with very few exceptions, the groups were nice and tight, well within the parameters of the rifle's specifications. I've shot mine many times at different locations and at a variety of ranges, always with the same result: tight groups with one or two key-hole impacts, similar to all three types of ammo I shot with the original Soviet-made 7N6, producing almost no side impacts, and with Wolf very slightly edging Hornady V-Max rounds.

The true reason for side impacts is the less-than-desired stability of the 5.45mm bullet in flight, caused by the effects of wrong rifling on the projectile brought on by the slightly larger diameter of the bore. Some people in the industry have expressed opinions on this matter, saying that Century installed 5.56mm-diameter barrels on their Tantals. Why would a manufacturer use other caliber barrels with right caliber chamber profiles? They didn't, at least not on purpose. Their barrel supplier made a mistake. It lies with the way the bore is measured. Instead of measuring the diameter of the bore by the bottoms of the rifling grooves, the barrel maker drilled a right diameter (5.45mm) hole through the barrel blank, then cut the grooves, making the barrel a larger caliber. You may ask, was it his first time making a rifle barrel? Perhaps not. The problem is in the way American (Western) gunsmiths and Russian (Soviet) gun makers used to measure the diameter of the bore, determining the caliber of the gun. Russians always measured the bore diameter by the tops of the rifling grooves, whereas the Western method of bore measurement entails measuring the bottoms of the grooves to determine the caliber.

A good example of this is the creation of 9mm Makarov cartridge. We know three widely used 9mm calibers: the 9mm Luger/Parabellum (9x19mm), 9mm Kurtz (9x17mm or .380 Auto) and 9mm Makarov (9x18mm). Except the Makarov ammo bullet is 9.2mm in diameter. Did the barrel maker know about this Soviet/Russian method of measuring and made a wrong assumption, instead of trusting the drawing or doing his own measuring? I don't know. Nevertheless, the mistake was made. The actual diameter of projectile in the 7N6 5.45x39mm cartridge is 5.6mm. I bet the initial hole was drilled with that diameter, where it should have been 5.45mm. The difference between the bullet and the bore diameter measured by the tops of the groove is necessary for the rifling to "grab" the bullet and make it spin. Instead, the U.S.-built Tantal rifles had 5.6mm bores, which provided minimal spin of the projectile.

The elongated hole is produced on impact when the tip of the bullet impacts the target surface, causing the already unstable bullet to deviate and "swing" its rear. The problem is more evident at short ranges where the bullet is less stable. The longer the range, the fewer keyhole impacts I found. However, it renders the defective Tantal rifle useless at any distance past 200–300 yards, as the bullet simply runs out of steam and gravity takes over. A problem? Of course! However, Century Arms has corrected the issue on later guns. In addition, in 2011–2012 they issued a recall for the older models. By the way, the same diameter trick is often used by gun makers in Europe when making hunting rifles to meet some of the local laws and regulations. Several countries in Europe require the projectile fired from the hunting rifle to lose its terminal velocity past 300 meters.

Nevertheless, I found the Polish Tantal rifle to be an excellent shooter. I really liked the Tantal's recoil, or rather lack thereof. Of course there was a recoil, but it's negligible at best even in comparison to my beloved AK-74. Probably the best shooter in my opinion.

*The Polish 5.56mm shortened carbine KbS wz.96 Mini-Beryl is simply the Onyks Avtomat chambered in 5.56x45mm NATO caliber with modern handguards and stock.*

## POLISH BERYL

Meanwhile, work on the new model of the Avtomat (in standard and shortened versions), chambered for 5.56mm NATO ammunition, began in 1995. In December of the same year, the first trial batch of new Beryl Avtomats was released. In 1997, after several changes to its design, it was adopted by the Polish Armed Forces and received the index of "Assault Carbine KbS wz.96 Beryl."

The design and operating principles of the Beryl Avtomat are exactly the same as those of the Tantal. Obviously, the main differences were dictated by the different ammunition the Beryl fired. Differences included the design of the barrel, bolt, muzzle device and magazine. But, Polish designers went further and modified or completely changed the designs of receiver, stock, handguards and sights. The longer 457mm (18-inch) barrel had six 228mm-pitch right-handed rifling grooves. The muzzle device acting as flash hider was also adapted for firing rifle grenades. The receiver was slightly different from the receiver of the Kbk wz.88 Avtomat. The composite handguards received diagonal ribs for better grip.

The metal stock (folding to the right) was more robust. The inspiration for its shape came from the Belgian FNC rifle. The stock was also equipped with a rubber butt plate to soften recoil produced by the under-barrel grenade launcher. The trigger and trigger group with two-sided safety/selector lever remained the same. The new Beryl rifle also inherited the Tantal's ability to fire a single shot, fixed 3-round burst and continuous full-auto fire. To stabilize the weapon when firing in full auto, a light metal removable bipod was issued with the gun. The same bipod was issued with earlier Tantal rifles. A removable Picatinny rail section can be installed over the top cover of the Beryl, allowing use of a variety of sights.

Since the late 1990s, the Radom Weapons Factory has produced these guns for the Polish armed forces.

Along with the development of the full-length 5.56mm Beryl rifles, a new short Avtomat was developed, which also had to meet NATO standards. The new 5.56mm shorty was called the Kbk wz.96 Mini-Beryl.

This shortened Mini-Beryl was based on the earlier 5.45mm Onyks wz.89 and its full-length sibling the Beryl wz.96. Main differences were in the design of the barrel, front trunnion, handguards, muzzle device and shortened magazine. Its operation was similar to the Beryl rifle.

Externally the Mini-Beryl is similar to the earlier Polish shorty, the Onyks. However, a number of changes were made to its design. The barrel was lengthened to 235mm (9 1/4 inches). The muzzle device, though similar to the muzzle device of the Onyks, has a deeper thread for screwing onto the gas chamber, which somewhat reduced the expansion chamber. The gas chamber is slightly longer than that of the Onyks.

In addition, a new metal skeletonized folding stock was introduced. Instead of the fixed accessory rail on the left side of the receiver, standard for all Kalashnikov Avtomats, the quick-detachable bar from the wz.96 Beryl rifle was installed on top of the receiver. It made possible the use of a variety of night and optical sights. Adopted for service with the Polish armed forces in 1997, the 5.56mm Kbk wz.96 Mini-Beryl Avtomat is mass-produced in Radom.

Today, the Beryl and Mini-Beryl are fully compliant with NATO standards and are in service with the Polish armed forces, which are an integral part of the North Atlantic alliance. A true descendant of the Soviet AK-74 is being fielded by NATO troops.

## AZERBAIJANI AVTOMAT KHAZRI

Our next licensed entry is the Azerbaijani Avtomat Khazri.

Khazri is an Avtomat designed for Azerbaijan by the Izhmash Plant and based on the AK-74M. It has been manufactured since 2011 under the Russian license in Azerbaijan.

The Azerbaijani AK is a very close copy of the Russian gun, but has several changes. Compared to its Russian version, the designers changed the way accessories, such as night vision devices, laser designator, flashlight, etc., are attached to the gun. This slightly changed its appearance, basically due to new quad rail handguards and a more ergonomic pistol grip. However, the weight of the weapon did not change. Assembly in Azerbaijan is done with parts and main assemblies supplied from Izhmash in Russia. As the next step in licensed production, the Defense Industry of Azerbaijan will produce some AK-74M parts domestically. A total of 26 components, including the barrel, are planned for production in Azerbaijan.

In compliance with the state defense order, the Defense Industry of Azerbaijan produced and shipped 5,000 AK-74M Khazri Avtomats to the Ministry of Defense the first year. The Russian-Azerbaijani contract is signed for ten years, during which time it is planned to deliver to the armed forces 12,000 AK-74Ms annually. According to the terms of the contract, all AKs manufactured in Azerbaijan will be supplied only to its Ministry of Defense and other law enforcement agencies. No exports are permitted under this contract.

In recent years, only two contracts for licensed production of Kalashnikov Avtomats have been signed. Both contracts en-

*The Azerbaijani Khazri Avtomat is an exact licensed copy of the Russian AK-74M with addition of a Picatinny rail section on the top cover.*

compass production of 100-series AKs: a factory for production of AK-103 Avtomats for a 7.62mm cartridge is being built in Venezuela, and an assembler of AK-74M guns is licensed in Azerbaijan.

## CZECHOSLOVAKIA

I could not find any reference to a licensing agreement between the Soviet Union and Czechoslovakia pertaining to the production of AKs firing the new low-impulse 5.45mm cartridge in Czechoslovakia. Considering the fact that during the Cold War Czechoslovakia opted to develop their own Avtomat, the Sa vz. 58 (Samopal vzor 1958), chambered for the 7.62x39mm M43 cartridge, it would be illogical to assume that the Czechoslovakian government turned around and bought the license to build AK-74s.

However, the Czechs did build their own family of guns based on the AK-74 design. The series of weapons for the new low-impulse 5.45mm cartridge was called LADA, and included the Avtomat, shortened Avtomat and light machine gun.

After the creation of the 5.45x39mm ammunition and its proliferation throughout the Warsaw Pact camp in the mid-1970s, Czechoslovakian firearm designers started to work on the new SRAZ (System of Small Automatic Weapons) small arms system. As a result, in January 1986 the company Ceská Zbrojovka started developing a new weapons system, with the designation LADA.

In consideration of the unification of firearms and out of concern for savings, the Czechs decided not to develop the original system like the CZ Sa vz. 58, but to modify the Soviet AK-74 design to include their wishes and preferences.

In 1989, after a series of testing, the Ceská Zbrojovka introduced a 5.45x39mm family of small arms, LADA. The shortened Avtomat had a combination gas block/front sight and a short 185mm (7.3-inch) barrel that was different from the full-length sibling. The machine gun, however, had a longer and heavier barrel with an attached lightweight folding bipod.

The operating system of the Czechoslovakian LADA Avtomat was identical to the Soviet AK. Following the Poles, Czech designers wanted to significantly improve the accuracy of automatic fire. They introduced an additional feature into the trigger group, allowing a fixed three-round burst besides semi and automatic fire.

The safety/selector lever is located on the left side of the receiver above the pistol grip. Unlike on the Polish Tantal, the AK signature safety lever was removed out of redundancy. However, the absence in the design of the LADA AK-style safety,

*The Czechoslovakian little-known LADA Avtomat was in fact a departure from the traditional VZ. 58 design. The LADA falls closely in line with original AK-74 design.*

which also served as cover for the charging handle slot, definitely reduced the service capabilities and reliability of Czech guns, especially when used in adverse conditions. Some improvements were also made to the construction of the gas tube and the handguards, with a system of attachment that is more convenient. The design of LADA's stamped receiver was simplified compared to the Soviet AK-74.

A standard Avtomat and a machine gun were equipped with a cage-type muzzle brake/compensator, and a shorty with a flame hider/booster.

The rear adjustable sight was designed for a maximum range of 800 meters (875 yards) for both the short and regular length Avtomats, and for the machine gun 1,000 meters (1,094 yards). The rear sight was relocated from the rear sight block (as on the AK) to the top of the receiver cover. This increased the length of the sighting line. An accessory rail was attached to the left side of the receiver for mounting optical, collimator and night sights. The LADAs are fed from 30- or 45-round box-type magazines identical to the rest of the AK-74 family guns. The plastic handguards are made of impact-resistant polyamide composite and the pistol grip is of cast rubber. The skeletonized metal stock folds to the right and does not obstruct the charging handle when folded.

As a result of the cessation of activity of the Warsaw Treaty Organization (Warsaw Pact) in the early 1990s and the subsequent reorientation of Czechoslovakia to NATO, the Czechs decided to rework the LADA weapon system for the standard 5.56 mm NATO cartridge, with hopes of export sales and possible orders from the Czech Army after joining NATO.

At the end of 1991, Ceská Zbrojovka introduced a modernized small arms system chambered for the NATO 5.56x45mm cartridge and with a new designation—the CZ 2000 (Ceská Zbrojovka model year 2000).

The new CZ 2000 guns differed from their 5.45mm predecessors with a barrel of 5.56mm caliber and different twist rate of rifling (from 195mm to 178mm), as well as transparent plastic magazines that allow the shooter to clearly see the ammuni-

**The Czech CZ 2000 family of guns chambered in 5.56x45mm NATO caliber was to become the Czech armed forces small arms. From the top: short Avtomat, carbine and light machine gun.**

tion. In addition, the new magazines had an innovative feature. The sides of the magazines were equipped with sliding, lockable slots that permitted magazines to be attached to each other to simplify and speed up reloading.

Military tests of the 5.56mm CZ 2000 showed that all the samples of this family of guns met the requirements, in terms of the probability of hitting the target when fired in fixed three-round bursts, which provided an increase in the accuracy of firing from unstable and unsupported positions.

The innovation introduced into the design of the trigger group allowing the three-round bursts made it possible to increase the efficiency of shooting from the LADA/CZ 2000 Avtomat by a factor of 1.2 compared to the American M16A2 rifle.

In addition, Czech designers succeeded in increasing the range of effective fire on the full-size humanoid silhouette target to 650 meters (711 yards) using the standard 5.56mm NATO cartridge. As such, the LADA/CZ 2000 Avtomats were characterized by high service and operational qualities, practically matching those of the Soviet AK-74 and American M16A2 assault rifle in reliability and efficiency in various operating conditions.

However, due to budgetary constraints, the Czech Army has not purchased CZ 2000 guns, and there are no data pertaining to any export sales, as the international AK market was already flooded with other Kalashnikov system variants modified for the 5.56x45mm cartridge produced in Russia, Romania, Yugoslavia, Bulgaria and others.

As a result, the LADA/CZ 2000 project was closed in 2007. Too bad, because it sure seems like a worthy AK variant to add to a collection. And, I bet it would shoot great, too.

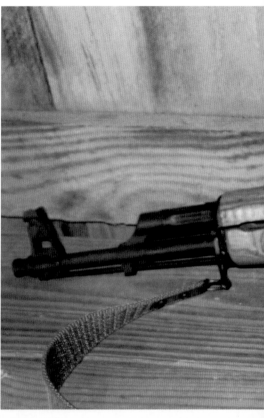

*(above) The PM Md.86's civilian semi-automatic version, the SAR-2, was imported into the U.S. in great numbers.*

*(left) The Romanian PM Md.86 Avtomat, other than a muzzle device and caliber itself, closely resembles AKM rather than the AK-74.*

## ROMANIAN PM Md.86 AVTOMAT

The Romanian PM Md. 86 Avtomat that was an unlicensed copy of the Soviet AK-74 appeared after Romania refused to purchase a license for the production of Kalashnikov Avtomats chambered for the new 5.45x39mm cartridge. Romanian gun makers decided to independently modify the designs of the two rifles that were in service with the Romanian armed forces, the PM Md.63 and PM Md.65, for new ammunition. As a result, automatic rifles appeared, one with a fixed stock and one with a folding stock, both receiving the designation of RM Md.86. The reason for one designation for a rifle with both a fixed and folding stock is that any of the PP Md.86 guns could be fitted with either stock. The weight of the rifle was 3.1 kg (6.8 lbs.). The box-type magazine's capacity was 30 rounds. The initial muzzle velocity was 880 m/s (2,625 fps) and effective sighting range was 1,000 meters (1,094 yards).

Structurally and operationally, the PM Md.86 is an exact copy of the Soviet Avtomat (most likely AKM or its Romanian variant PM Md.63) with some changes: a metal wire stock folding to the right, a muzzle brake, and a trigger mechanism with ratchet lever that allows not only automatic or single-shot fire but also fixed three-round bursts.

Romanian designers borrowed the lower handguard with an additional grip directly from the PM Md.63 gun. Similar to other AK-74 variants, the accessory rail was installed on the left side of the receiver for attaching night and optical sights. The under-barrel grenade launcher could also be attached to the new Avtomat. For special forces and crews of combat vehicles, a shortened version was also developed.

From the original Kalashnikov Avtomats, these Romanian variants were distinguished by a very unusual shape and size of almost all external components—the size and shape of the stock, the handguards, the charging handle that was enlarged and bent upward and front sight block that seemed unnecessarily large. It should be es-

*Apart from its fixed-stock version, the PM Md.86 was also configured as a folder. It retained the front grip typical for a Romanian AK.*

pecially noted that the Romanian gun designers "love" the front grips on their AKs. This feature appeared on the very first Romanian-built AKs and continues to appear on all subsequent models. Such a feature cannot be explained by anything other than personal preference.

The RM Md.86 was actively exported under the name AIM-74 with a fixed stock and AIMS-74 with the folder. For the civilian market, a semi-automatic version was released. For the U.S. market, it was designated as SAR-2.

Just like with its other East European siblings, in addition to the full-length version, there was also a shortened variant for service with armored vehicle crews and those servicemen for whom the smaller-dimension Avtomat was a personal defense weapon. The shortened version of the RM Md.86 differed from the full-length only by the length of the barrel, which was reduced to 302mm (~12 inches), and gas block/front sight combination.

It's hard not to notice that even the Romanian adaptation for the 5.45mm cartridge cannot be called purely Romanian. It is quite difficult to gather all the most interesting ideas and features in one model and make it work without your own experience in developing such guns. However, the Romanians managed to do just that. They succeeded to copy those and incorporate them into a gun of their own, and were able not only to supply them to the Romanian armed forces, but also offer them for export, saturating the civilian market with semi-automatic AKs.

One more distinguishing feature of Romanian post-Soviet-era AKs is less than perfect quality, especially compared to other variants. The majority of poor quality claims pertain to the fit and finish. Except for tilted gas blocks and front sights, the internal component quality was okay. Despite this, the Romanian AKs were very popular and actively exported, bringing in huge profits. Recently the volume of import into the U.S. declined drastically because the Romanians placed the emphasis on supplying numerous U.S. "allies" in the Middle East.

## RECONFIGURED VARIANTS—BULLPUPS

Apart from the licensed and unlicensed AK-74 copies, there were a couple of variants that were simply made out of existing rifles. These were reconfigured externally by the engineers to comply with requirements of their respective militaries and were re-issued as locally made rifles with local designations.

The K-3 is an Armenian Avtomat of the bullpup configuration. It was developed by the Defense Industry Department of the Ministry of Defense of Armenia in 1996. The K-3 bullpup is based on the standard AK-74 rifle and entered service with the Armenian Defense Force in 1999. Today the K-3 sees limited service with special operations troops in Armenia, and was never intended or supplied for export.

- Weight: 2.7 kg
- Length: 700mm
- Barrel length: 415mm
- Caliber: 5.45X39mm
- Rate of fire: shots/min: 600-650 rounds/second
- Muzzle velocity: 900 m/s (2,953 fps)
- Aim range: 400 meters (437 yards)
- Feed: standard AK-74 30- or 45-round magazines

Very little is known about this variant, only that for the first time the K-3 5.45mm Avtomat was introduced to a wide audience in 1996. Despite the fact that the principle of operation is practically identical to the standard AK-74, its bullpup configuration is drastically different. Part of the gun's trigger group (hammer to be precise) and the magazine are located behind the pistol grip and the trigger. Typically, the Kalashnikov safety/selector lever is left in the back of the receiver. The ejection of empty casings is to the right, making shooting from the left shoulder difficult. Sights are made on high blocks, diopter rear sight is adjustable in range. The muzzle brake has a modified design to facilitate the launching of 3K-3 fragmentation grenades also developed in Armenia. To fire a rifle grenade, a regular live cartridge is used.

The K-3 Avtomat is similar to the AK-74. However, according to the gun's creators, it is cheaper and more accurate, and has less recoil. The Armenian bullpup is made mostly out of metal. Its design includes an accessory rail for mounting a standard 4X-power PSO-1 optical sight, which is also produced in Armenia.

*One of the distinct features of the PM Md.86 is its bent upward charging handle. I assume it was done to accommodate operation with stock folded.*

*The Armenian-made K-3 Avtomat is based on the Soviet AK-74, but very different in configuration and appearance. It is the first mass produced bullpup AK-74 variant.*

Regardless, it's commendable for any country to develop and produce a firearm of its own design, especially such a small country like Armenia. The fact remains that most of the former Soviet republics have stockpiles of awesome Soviet-built AKMs and AK-74s. Not using free, proven guns that you already have is like pissing against the wind. Why do it? That's why the bulk of the Armenian armed forces are armed with the best variants of Soviet-built 7.62mm and 5.45mm AKs.

One more bullpup comes to us from the Ukraine. We all know about the Vepr rifles here in the U.S., but this one is of a different breed.

After the collapse of the Soviet Union, each of its former republics tried to prove independence in all possible ways and, naturally, without creating firearms of their own design the independence would not be complete. Because providing its armed forces with domestically produced weapons is the best proof of the country's independence, the Ukraine was actively proving its independence in this way. As it turned out, there were a lot of people in the Ukraine who had pretty good and original ideas about firearms, as well as a well-developed scientific and industrial base that could easily be employed in development of such firearms.

The Ukrainian version of the bullpup AK was the Vepr Avtomat. This gun was introduced in 2003, and was developed in association with a rather interesting organization, the Scientific and Technical Center for Precision Engineering of the National Space Agency of Ukraine. At the time of its introduction, there were jokes floating around about the type of weapon the Vepr represented, considering the entity that made it. Most popular was that the Vepr was a gun for the space wars. However, all jokes aside, the new Avtomat turned out to be nothing to laugh at. When the Vepr was released, some specialists compared it to the infamous Russian special purpose weapon complex, the Groza. I would not go as far as agreeing with those specialists, but in many respects such a comparison is valid.

Just like the Groza, the Ukrainian Vepr was based on the AK-74, and also like the Groza, the Vepr was configured as a bullpup Avtomat. However, unlike the Groza, the new Ukrainian Avtomat was not chambered for 9x39mm or 7.62x39mm (calibers used by the Russian Groza), but for the 5.45x39mm cartridge. Even though the Vepr acquired some Groza features that are common in bullpup guns, it did not acquire the Groza's characteristics.

The main feature of the Vepr is that it was possible to maintain the maximum compatibility of parts and assemblies with the AK-74. This was very important for the Ukrainians, since they inherited a huge stockpile of AK-74 Avtomats after the fall of the Soviet Union. The considerable numbers of Soviet AKs provided the barreled actions for the new guns, and an almost infinite source of repair parts and assemblies.

The weight of the new Avtomat is 3.45 kgs (7.6 lbs.) empty; the length is only 702mm (27.64 inches), with a barrel length that is standard for a full-length Avtomat, at 415mm (16.34 inches). That is where the differences from the AK-74 end. The muzzle velocity is 900 m/s (2,953 fps), the automatic rate of fire is 600 rounds per minute, and the gun feeds out of standard 30- to

*The Ukrainian bullpup Vepr Avtomat is based on the Soviet AK-74, or rather built from it.*

40-round AK-74/RPK-74 magazines. Basically, the new Vepr is the AK-74 in bullpup configuration.

However, the new Ukrainian gun had several advantages over its Soviet counterpart. Combined with the fact that the Vepr uses the 5.45x39 cartridge that already has a low impulse, the bullpup configuration produces better accuracy when fired in full-auto mode. The gun became more manageable at that rate. The Vepr kept the performance characteristics of its full-length cousins, but offered a far more compact package. One may ask, why isn't everybody converting their AKs to bullpup configuration? There are actually several reasons.

In the bullpup configuration, the Avtomat lost its balance. This takes getting used to when firing. The ejection of spent casings to the right, with typical AK "gusto," makes it impossible for a lefty to use this gun. Even when a right-handed shooter uses it,

*The Russian Special Purpose Weapon Complex OC-14 Groza is based on the AK-74 and preceded Armenian or Ukrainian variants. However, it is produced in very small runs.*

*Unlike the Armenian or Ukrainian bullpups, the OC-14 Avtomat/ grenade launcher named Groza is a versatile weapon that can be configured for different missions. It fires a special 9x39mm sub-sonic round.*

*The Groza-1 is chambered for the 7.62x39mm cartridge and was designed for use by Russian special operation troops.*

the face is way too close to the ejection port. Inhaling the powder gases caused irritation in the shooter's throat and eyes. Not the most pleasant feeling.

The magazine change is cumbersome to say the least. Unlike AR-style magazine retention, where the mag is simply pushed into the mag-well, the AK mag has to be rocked into retention, not an easy thing to do under one's armpit. The sight line (sight radius) had been shortened, negatively affecting long-range accuracy. However, any modern optical or collimator sight takes care of that. When scrutinizing the Ukrainian Vepr, one must remember that shooters can get used to the new configuration and become proficient with magazine changes, leaving only the one serious shortcoming—the location of the ejection port in relation to the shooter's face.

In addition to the gun's layout, changes were made to the controls. Immediately noticeable is the placement of the charging handle. It has been moved ahead over the barrel and it is no longer reciprocal, i.e., it remains in place when the gun is fired. The charging handle could be placed on either side for right- or left-handed operation. The safety lever on the Vepr is a lateral button that is located above the trigger, which is an improvement compared to the standard AK.

However, a more important design element of the Vepr is the fact that handguards and other components are not affixed to the barrel, making it almost a floating barrel if not for the gas block. This design feature played a significant role in improving the accuracy of the gun.

The early models of Vepr were equipped with sights taken directly from the AK, but as the sighting line was reduced due to a change in the weapon's layout, it was decided to replace standard AK "U"-slot rear sights with a diopter or "peephole" type. Both sights are mounted high and both fold out of the way of reflex, collimator or optical sights. The Vepr Avtomat is configured to accept a wide range of such aiming devices.

Initially, the Vepr was developed to accept the grenade launcher similar to the Russian Groza complex. This way one would designate the Vepr as a complex and not just an Avtomat. Unfortunately, the standard GP-25 grenade launcher was not compatible with the gun in bullpup configuration. A special modification had to be developed. It turns out that, with the grenade launcher installed, the gun is more stable when firing. Its balance becomes more evenly distributed, although the weight of the gun is increased. An interesting detail is that when the grenade launcher is installed, the Avtomat's safety also becomes the grenade launcher safety. This totally makes sense.

In the end, the Ukrainian-built Vepr Avtomat is just another version of the AK-74. I'm sure its creators would argue until red in the face that it is the next step in the AK development, citing how they were able to improve accuracy and reduce the dimensions. But, you don't need to be Samuel Colt or John Browning to see that it's just the same gun dressed in prettier rags. Also, with positives like accuracy and reduced dimensions, the Vepr also inherited all the bullpup configuration shortcomings, like cumbersome magazine changes and rear-heavy balance, among others.

I read somewhere that Vepr creators claimed the Vepr had fewer parts than its AK predecessor. Well, again, no special education required to see that their claim is erroneous. They removed the stock and the lower and upper handguards, and added a massive butt plate, cheek piece, trigger linkages, two-piece lower handguard, gas tube cover and folding sights. Basic mathematics is not in their favor.

Today, Vepr Avtomats see service along with standard-configuration Soviet-built AK-74s in the hands of the Ukrainian armed forces. However, they are not widely used or issued to the regular infantry troops. Use of teh Vepr is reserved to where its compactness is a requirement. The rest of the troops have to be content with Mr. Reliable AK-74 Kalashnikov Avtomat. It

**I crack a smile every time** TsKIB SOO's name is attached to very cool special purpose weapons. The reason for my amusement is in this organization's name. The name TsKIB SOO is an abbreviation for Russian "Central Designer and Research Bureau of Sporting and Hunting Weapons." I suppose one could think of international terrorists as dogs, i.e. game, and hunting these animals down could be called a sport.

was always easier and cheaper to grab a ready and proven gun from the warehouse than to create and mass-produce something new. Today, the Vepr project is suspended.

## RUSSIAN GROZA COMPLEX

Since I mentioned the Russian shooting complex Groza earlier, and since it is a direct derivative of the AK-74, or AKSU to be exact (to the point of having receivers with all the cutouts for the folding stock that is not there), I have to talk about it here. Although it is not a licensed or unlicensed AK variant produced abroad, it is an important piece in the AK evolution.

The OC-14 Avtomat/grenade launcher shooting complex named Groza ("thunderstorm") was developed at the TsKIB SOO in Tula, and produced in small batches at the Tula Arms Factory (TOZ) in the mid-1990s. Abbreviation "OC" in the weapon's official index stands for "Sample TsKIB" and is assigned to all firearms developed by Tula's TsKIB SOO for combat use.

The TsKIB SOO develops both military and civilian firearms. All civilian guns have designation "MC." The development of the Avtomat/grenade launcher complex for close combat was started in 1992 by designer Valery Telesh, who had created the 40mm GP-25 and GP-30 under-barrel grenade launchers with his colleague Yuri Lebedev. In 1994, the first prototypes were ready. The main idea for creating a specialized complex was the modular design of the weapon, it was supposed to be very flexible for a variety of applications.

Initially, the Groza complex was developed for the special forces of the Ministry of Internal Affairs for special 9x39mm SP-5 and SP-6 cartridges. Its variant, the Groza-1 (another designation was TKB-0239), was created for the Army Special Forces for the widely used 7.62x39mm cartridge.

The OC-14 Groza Avtomat was based on and built with the AKS-74U receiver, using other components and mechanisms from the shorty AK. The main changes in the inner workings of the Avtomat were forced by the adaptation of the gun to the 9x39mm SP-5 cartridge and the new gun's bullpup configuration. The design of the bolt, barrel with chamber and trigger group had been changed.

The main advantage of the Groza is its true modularity. With the addition of a muzzle extender and front vertical grip configuration, the Groza can be used as a compact fighting carbine; with the addition of a suppressor it can be used as a special purpose rifle. The same gun turns into a grenade launcher with the addition of a 44mm under-barrel launcher. In this configuration, the standard pistol grip and handguard are replaced with the grenade launcher. The OC-14 Avtomat was tested during a counter-terrorist operation in Chechnya, but it did not find much popularity among front line troops and, as such, did not see mass production.

Just like the Ukrainian Vepr, the Groza is essentially a conversion of conventionally built weapons into the bullpup configuration. As a result, it received all the major drawbacks of the new layout, including the impossibility of shooting from the left shoulder, high powder-gas contamination in the face of the shooter, not the most comfortable balance with weight shifted back, and not the most convenient location of the charging handle and safety/selector lever.

The high position of the sights in combination with a long magazine increases the profile of the shooter when shooting prone. A short sighting line potentially reduces accuracy when shooting at distance. Obviously, the addition of modern aiming devices would help with this drawback. In the grenade launcher configuration, an additional so-called inconvenience was the combination trigger for shooting the Avtomat itself, and the grenade launcher that required an additional switch. I personally do not see it as an inconvenience. It's not as if one would switch between firing a rifle and grenade launcher on the fly. To fire an under-barrel launcher takes preparation and time. I don't think that flipping a switch would contribute to significant delay. In any case, training with the gun would fix any problems with running it.

As mentioned earlier, the OC-14 Groza was not mass-produced and, as such, was not widely used by Russian troops in the field. However, the Groza complex is adopted for service and several special operations units are armed with it. They use the Groza mainly in the numerous anti-terrorism operations in southern Russia. Regardless of its wide use or lack thereof, the OC-14 Groza shooting complex represents another subspecies in the AK lineage.

In reviewing the Russian-built AK-74–based variants, I must also mention that the last Soviet development in this area—the AK-74M and the entire 100-series of the AKs that came in a variety of calibers and configurations—was based on the AK-74. This group of AKs deserves a closer look in this book, as representatives of a major stage in AK evolution. I will tell you more about it later. But first, let me touch on where the Soviet Union finds itself at the time of the next stage of development of its prolific gun.

*The Russian OC-14 Groza shooting complex is produced in very limited numbers and destined for Russia's special operations operatives, who can configure it to the mission at hand.*

# NO MORE SUPERPOWER

**A**ll things come to an end. Empires crumble. Some lie in mere shadows of their former selves, like the British, but most simply disappear. First, it was the Roman Empire, then the Mongol, then the Ming, then the Ottoman, then the Russian, Spanish, Portuguese, etc. In 1991, it was the Soviet Union's turn.

The collapse of the Soviet Union officially happened when in 1991 the leaders of Russia, Ukraine and Belarus signed a document that lead to the dissolution of the Soviet Union as a state. In reality, like cracks in a foundation, the process of collapse began much earlier.

In 1982, I was still in high school, and it seemed nothing could rock the solid Soviet Motherland from its core, even when Leonid Brezhnev, the Soviet leader at the time, died in November of 1982. The shock of that event was stunning. One could read "Now what?" in the faces of the people. The Soviet citizens, who for years made fun of Brezhnev's frailty in the sanctity of their homes or at private parties, were facing uncertainty. However, after the initial shock and disbelieve wore off and the new Premier/Chairman/President Yuri Andropov took up the reins of power, everybody realized that the country was as solid as ever and no plight, flood or famine would come anytime soon.

*Leonid Brezhnev was the leader of the Soviet Union for 18 years. During his time in office, Soviets saw loosening of old laws, Olympic games, industrial boom, achievements in space and the beginning of the Afghan war. He should have retired 5-6 years before his death in 1982.*

Then, in February of 1984, Andropov also passed away, after only one year and three months in office. At that point, the Soviets knew that nothing would disturb their belief in the Soviet state as a counter-imperialism fortress. Sure enough, four days later a new leader was appointed and everyone moved on, or so they thought.

One may never in his or her life experience the death of the head of state while still in office, let alone two of them. I considered myself a very lucky kid, witnessing the events of two leaders departing this world.

*Former KGB Chief Yuri Andropov, after being appointed as Soviet leader, hit the ground running with the introduction of workplace discipline tightening policies. The Soviets dodged a bullet, with Andropov passing after only 15 months in office.*

## ANDROPOV ERA

While in office, Andropov went after the economy by enforcing management efficiency. For the first time, the managers of industries and organizations, including the Communist Party elite, felt their chairs starting to rock. In just over one year in the office, Andropov removed 18 Ministers (Secretaries) and 37 Central and Regional Communist Party leaders.

He also introduced stricter discipline in the work place. There was an army of undercover operatives and volunteers from the Communist Youth Organization that would roam markets, department stores and other public places during work hours. These "operatives" would approach people with the question, "Why aren't you at work?" They would detain a person who did not have a "legitimate" reason for skipping work.

My mom was once approached by such an imbecile during her lunch hour when she went to the nearby grocery store. When it was pointed out to the overzealous idiot that it was lunch hour, he retreated into the grey mass from which he materialized.

I, too, had a personal encounter with the operatives. In the Soviet Union, the educational system was great. I say that without any sarcasm. It turned out awesome specialists in all areas. The higher education was outstanding. Even the grade and high schools were pretty good, providing a solid base of knowledge and skills to set students on the way to pursue their goals in life. I only say this because, as a father of two boys who are going through the educational system here in the U.S., I can directly compare.

Anyway, the Soviets knew that not all high school students have the ambition to pursue higher education or can get in to colleges or universities. Mandatory vocational training for all high school students was established. One day a week, my class had to go to an off-site vocational training center for the whole day to learn a profession; in case our college ambitions fell through we'd have a job right after school. For boys, our center offered training for such trades as auto mechanic/driver (this one was the most popular, as it entailed getting a driver license. Of course that is what I signed up for), pastry chef, stone mason, electronics technician for boys. In addition, girls could sign up for any of the above classes, plus nurse assistant and day care specialist.

Because of the high student count, my classes at the training center took place in the afternoon, or what we referred to as the second shift. A couple of my friends (including a future European middle-weight junior boxing champion) and I would take public transportation and then walk to the training center. And, because our bus stop was near the department store, we would often go in to peruse the musical records section to see what new albums were available. This was a large and very popular department store and, as result, it was always crowded.

One day, my friends and I met up on our journey to our professional training. As usual, we went into the store. We were fighting through the crowd trying to get to the records counter when some kid not much older than us grabbed my boxer friend by the sleeve and pulled him aside. I knew then that it was a mistake on the part of the overzealous young commy. Before he could even finish his question, "Why you are not in school during school hours?", he was spread-eagle unconscious on the floor of the department store from my friend's left hook. It quickly became apparent that this future party "leader" wasn't alone and several of his minions were coming. We didn't want to get tangled with the officials and "good Samaritan" helpers and did the best thing one could do in this situation. We ran. And, because we were all athletes, the pursuit ended before it even began. The activists-volunteers had no chance.

It was December of 1983 and things were about to get even more interesting. Andropov and his policies were dead two months later. I remember my father telling me then that we dodged a bullet with Andropov. If the esteemed leader had continued on his course, the entire Soviet population would wear black pajamas while working for the benefit of the Socialistic Greater Good in exotic labor camps, the Pol Pot's Khmer Rouge Cambodia style.

## NEXT UP: CHERNENKO

For a second time in under two years, after only four days of deliberations, Konstantin Chernenko, the Central Committee and Politburo Member and Chairman of Defense Council, was appointed to the position of the leader of the Soviet Union.

However, as they say in Russia, "The music did not play long." Yet again, only one year and one month later, in March of 1985, Chernenko was also dead. The frequency with which the frail Soviet leaders were dying was staggering. The people started to grow immune and indifferent to their leaders' ultimate demises.

**The day that Konstantin Chernenko's passing was announced,** my friends and I showed up for practice at the Spartak Sports Complex as we had every day for years, only to find that the administrator would not allow us to go into our locker room and would not unlock the gym. So, we stewed around in the lobby waiting for the coach to show up. He finally came in and, seeing us in the lobby, was startled and surprised. He was about to unleash his mighty fury on our behinds when it was pointed out to him that the administration would not let us practice. The coach immediately re-directed his query toward the woman administrator. Shaky from personal grief and sorrow, she replied that Chernenko was dead, to which our coach replied, "So? He is dead, but we are still alive! Give me the damn key."

As it turned out, Chernenko was the last Soviet leader to die while in office. I guess at that time the Soviet leadership got tired of constantly voting for a new Premier on the account of the candidates being too old and feeble. On March 11 of 1985, only hours after Chernenko's death, 54-year-old Mikhail Gorbachev was voted by the Politburo to replace him.

Gorbachev was one of the youngest members of the Politburo, and probably the healthiest, and therefore was not expected to die anytime soon. They were right. At the time of this book 32 years later, Mikhail Gorbachev is alive and well.

There were two other things that the Central Committee members did not expect: that Gorbachev was very progressive, and that he turned out to be the last Soviet leader to ascend to power. One more thing that no one could predict was that Gorbachev's reform policies ultimately lead to collapse of his country and his own removal from power.

*Already very sick at the time of his appointment as the Soviet leader, Konstantin Chernenko ruled the USSR for only 13 months until his death.*

## LIFE UNDER GORBACHEV

Gorbachev's first initiative was Glasnost ("openness"), where the central government drastically reduced state censorship over the media. Articles and investigative reporting TV programs flooded the media sphere, revealing the corruption and other misgivings of the Soviet "Top," especially in the regions.

Heads rolled and arrests were made of numerous Party Chiefs and members of their families. People who just a short while ago could not be touched started to receive lengthy sentences for offenses ranging from corruption to abusing the power of public office. Every day in the papers there was an article or announcement that some regional Party Operative was arrested or had committed suicide. The regular folks loved it. Finally, those who were stealing for years were getting what they deserved.

*Newly appointed as Soviet leader, "young" Mikhail Gorbachev changed the Soviet Union's internal and foreign policies.*

One of my strongest memories from that time is of spontaneous meetings at the Metro (subway) stations, not protest meetings or demonstrations, but some sort of discussion groups. Just a bunch of people on their way home, before boarding their train, arguing about newspaper articles.

*Though guaranteed by the Soviet Constitution, free speech was more "free speech within the confines of the official party guidelines." During Glasnost, Soviets could freely express their opinion anywhere.*

The next reform was the famous Perestroika ("reconstruction"). It was a confusing process. Even Russian historians do not have a clear picture of what it actually entailed. Only those who were in the Soviet government understood what it was. I can only describe what I saw happening and the changes it brought. Basically, decentralization of power happened. The iron fist loosened its grip and more authority was passed to the regions and the Soviet Republics. It almost immediately had a very positive effect on the political and social-economic life of the Soviet citizens. Now anyone could run for an office in free elections, and privately owned enterprises started to pop up like mushrooms after a good rain.

Religion that was embedded into people but swept under the rug or hidden away was having a rebirth. Don't get me wrong. It was not like the Soviet government did not allow religion or closed churches, synagogues or mosques. Of course, the early Bolsheviks, who were rabid atheists and inspired by Lenin's "Religion is poison for the masses" quote, did destroy or expropriate their share of religious objects, and executed tens of thousands of members of clergy. However, that was in the past and was looked upon by the "modern" Soviets as a part of Stalin's terror. As such it was universally condemned. After all, Soviet society was a modern society and was living under the newly adopted "Brezhnev's" Constitution with several basic rights and freedoms.

The Soviet Constitution included civil and political rights. Among these were the rights to freedom of speech, freedom of the press and freedom of assembly, and the right to religious belief and worship. In addition, the Constitution provided for freedom of artistic work, protection of the family, inviolability of the person and home, and the right to privacy. In line with the Marxist-Leninist ideology of the government, the Constitution also granted social and economic rights not provided by constitutions in some capitalist countries. Among these were the rights to work, rest and leisure, health protection, care in old age and sickness, housing, education and cultural benefits.

This all looked pretty good. Except for one detail. The Soviet Constitution also recognized the guiding role of the Communist Party of the USSR as a main guarantor. What did it mean to Soviet youth growing up in those times? The modern Soviets of my youth certainly did not build any churches or other places of worship, buy they did not destroy or seize any either. However, the churches, mosques and synagogues were open.

People were allowed to go and worship, but with one caveat. If you wanted to climb the corporate ladder at work, you could not violate the one of the main principles of Communism, which is denial of God's existence. No one would stop you from going to the church, but you could forget about getting a promotion. But, people did it anyway.

*Most of the Soviets were for Perestroika, like these people during a pro-Perestroika demonstration.*

People also celebrated all main religious holidays. For us that was Easter. The schools would even close earlier on Saturday (yes, we went to school on Saturdays) in preparation for Easter Sunday. We had our own Palm Sunday. Since there are no palms in middle Russia, it was called Pussy Willow Sunday. Our Ash Wednesday was called Parents Day and everyone went to pay respects. I actually grew up close to the church and went to school by its morning Matins bells. When I heard the Vespers (evening) bells, I knew I had to go home for dinner. The eastern orthodox priests were allowed to marry and have kids like the parishioners they served. One of the kids in my clique was a priest's son. A redheaded troublemaker, he was always getting into mischief.

Nevertheless, during Gorbachev rule religion saw resurgence. The number of churchgoers increased 100-fold. Donations from the local gov-

*This Perestroika-era lapel pin says "Perestroika Democracy Glasnost."*

ernment and newly well-to-do private entrepreneurs skyrocketed. Churches were being restored and re-built, and new ones erected.

Though being religious was no longer frowned upon, the guiding hand of the Communist Party was still there trying to discourage the youth from the clutches of competition from organized religion. During the all-night Easter service, disco clubs were open all night. My group of friends would go to the disco for a while, then leave shortly before midnight, hop over to the church, take part in activities and then return to the disco for the rest of the night.

The third and most important reform that Gorbachev introduced was the removal from the Constitution of the Communist Party as overseer, thus passing it on to the people to decide by whom they wanted to be ruled.

I had two different experiences with Gorbachev's reforms. One is weird and suppressed, and I could not realize its full potential. I was drafted into the armed forces almost immediately after the first of the reforms took place, and spent two years away from the inner-Soviet turmoil. Where I served was an isolated place. The letters from home traveled sometimes up to a month to reach us. The freshest newspaper was at least three days old. We had limited access to TV, and our weekly political

*No more Communist Party as ruler of the Soviet people. The poster reads, "We will defend our freedom and democracy. We don't want the communism concentration camp."*

*For the first time, Soviet leaders would just meet with people on the street and engage in conversations. It was done by Gorbachev and has never been repeated since.*

information hour was directly borrowed from the 1970s and was full of praises for the Communist Party and achievements of the Soviet people.

My first shock was when I got a letter from my mom informing me that my father had left the Communist Party. My dad was a head of the regional architect, a construction inspectorate. Without approval from his office, no building would be commissioned. This was a high enough position to warrant a party membership. I don't know how to describe my father with respect to him being a member of the Communist Party. I want to say he was a good Communist, but that would almost be derogatory today. When I say it, I mean he was honest, always truthful, never stole anything, never used his position to enrich himself (unlike his subordinates), never used privilege, he never was afraid to look people in the eyes and tell the truth. Are these the traits of a good Communist, or just good human being?

Basically, my father stood out from the majority of his peers and did not want to be affiliated with them. He later told me that his

*(left) Fist punks.*

*(below) First motorcycle "gangs" on their Jawas.*

decision was purely economic. When he was asked for the monthly party dues, he flipped and surrendered his registration card at the next meeting. He did not feel the party deserved any more of his hard-earned rubles. Nevertheless, I was shocked after receiving the news, with a sense of complete disbelief and despair. I even wrote a letter home expressing my emotions and fears. About a month later, I got a letter from my father calming me down and informing me that he was still gainfully employed and that, since his demarche, several of his colleagues had followed suit. That was my first Perestroika experience. I did not fully feel it, being in the war zone and all, but I knew things were changing.

My second experience with the Gorbachev reforms was when I was discharged from military service and came home. Stepping off the train, I immediately realized how much I had missed. One of the first things I noticed was the advertisements everywhere. Old Soviet slogans like "Hail the Communist Party!" were replaced with Pepsi billboards. The next thing was that the police (Militsia) officers now carried batons, "Like in America," I thought to myself, and took a cab home. I continued to be amazed at the new things around me. Rock concerts everywhere. It seemed that if one wanted to see some live music, all he or she had to do was go to any park or cultural center. Punks with crazy hairstyles, leather jackets and army boots. I was soaking it all in. I remember barely sleeping. The summer of 1987 in Leningrad (today St. Petersburg), with white nights and an unmistakable sense of freedom, was truly a magical time.

*Quality and "image" (picture notwithstanding) of Soviet music has changed. For the first time, Western music gave way to the new Soviet music at disco clubs.*

If someone asks me when was the best time in the Soviet Union, I would say it was then, right before it all came crashing down. It was the uncertainty that made that time special. People knew they had new rights and freedoms and law enforcement was not sure what those were or where the border of lawlessness was. However, they also knew that the old ways were no longer acceptable.

Newly found freedom and liberties spread far and wide through the Soviet Union and abroad. The drastic change in foreign policy by the USSR resulted in the complete collapse of the socialist camp, with its symbol the Berlin Wall. By 1990, all of the East European countries had managed to gain independence from Soviet control and took the course of integration with Europe. The pseudo-independence of the Republics paved the way for the rise of newly found nationalism. Driven by the population's emotions rather than the rational, and sensing the central government weakness, some Soviet republics vowed their complete independence. The first that succeeded were the Baltic republics, followed by the Caucuses. By December of 1991, all but two Soviet republics held referendums and voted for independence. Only Russia and Kazakhstan still held to the starting-to-crumble Soviet state, until on December 8, 1991, the newly democratically elected presidents of Russia, Ukraine and Belarus signed the Belavezha Accord, dissolving the Soviet Union and establishing a Commonwealth of the Independent States.

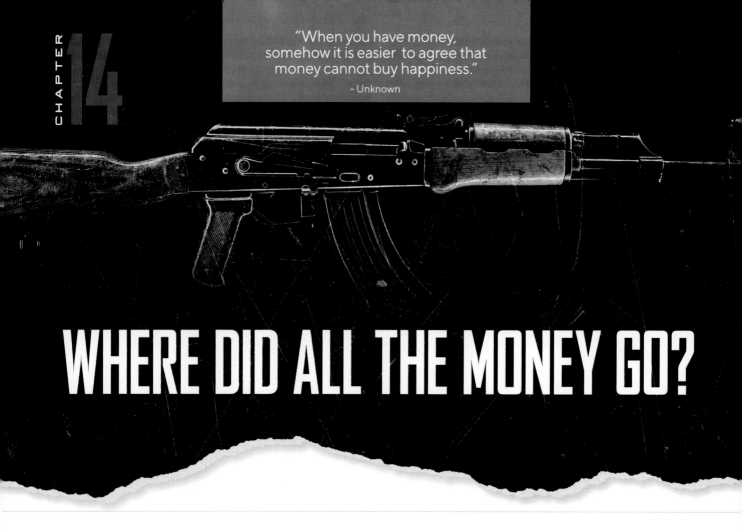

# WHERE DID ALL THE MONEY GO?

**W**hat did the collapse of the USSR have to do with the AK? It had everything to do with the AK and other products of the Soviet military industrial complex. With the fall of the Soviet Union, the State Planning market system collapsed like a Jenga® tower. What is the State Planning system (GosPlan, in Russian)? That is when manufacturers or producers do not need sales or marketing departments. Soviet plants, factories and agricultural entities had sales departments that took and processed orders. However, the State Planning Agency did all the selling. It also took care of product distribution.

Everything in the Soviet Union ran on a five-year planning cycle. Every five years, all entities made plans for the next five years and set goals. The Soviet five-year plan gave workers something to strive for, and if a company or organization achieved its goals everybody who worked there got a bonus.

*The world's biggest marking department, the old GosPlan (state planning) building near the Kremlin in Moscow. Today it is the Gosduma (state parliament).*

In addition, often companies would try to reach their goals sooner than five years and get an even higher bonus. Sounds great, but what happens with all the product that this system generates? It gets sold through even distribution. For example, Plant XYZ produced 2,000 widgets in the second quarter per plan. The State Planning Agency gets notified and per its plan

notifies retail locations or end users, such as other companies, that they need to transfer payments to the plant and accept the delivery of so many widgets this month. Still not bad, right? Everyone is employed, no need to worry about the pipeline or downturn in economy.

What happened with less fortunate entities, like collective farms in bad need of a new tractor? The tractor would be provided to the farm at no cost, based on their request and verified need. It may have taken a while, but they would have their tractor. Huge amounts of Soviet-made products were exported to other countries. Everything was priced well below the normal pricing for that type of product. That was the brilliant Soviet marketing strategy. This is where the Soviets got their hard currency.

*Corporate sales meeting with management of the Soviet State Planning Agency, the best salesmen in the world. The sales volume that these people handled is unimaginable. Note the military personnel.*

If some countries could not pay, the Soviets bartered for something else—fruit and vegetables, pots and pans, etc. All of the bartered goods were then sold to the Soviet citizens at home.

It worked great until the Soviet Union came crumbling down in December of 1991. The Soviets or Russians lost a huge customer base. The friendly countries were looking elsewhere for their shopping needs. The Soviet Republics that were no longer Soviet were looking elsewhere as well. The curtain was lifted, opening a floodgate for other, better, cheaper, more desirable products, bringing in a free market economy. For the first time, the end users would decide which widget they wanted and how many. For the first time, the state-run sales office heard "no." The State Planning Agency be-

*Once huge and fully integrated, the Automotive Lenin Komsomol Plant in Moscow was responsible for the production of millions of Moskvich cars, but could not compete or restructure. This is what it looked like in its heyday (top) and this is what it looks like now (bottom).*

*Millions of Soviet engineers, scientists and qualified workers were laid off and forced into selling things on the impromptu street markets.*

came unneeded, and now Russian companies had to compete on their own. They had to build new sales and marketing departments. Simply picking up a phone and accepting an order no longer worked. No orders meant no cash.

The State Planning or its military division also ran the production and distribution of the Soviet military industrial complex products at home and abroad. Apart from stocking strategic stores, it would distribute armament to the military districts whether they wanted it or not. Of course, a state re-armament program notwithstanding, the Soviet military industrial complex also pushed its wares on its socialist camp brothers quite heavily. With the wall now down, the now fully independent East Europeans looked elsewhere for protection. They could not wait to join NATO with all of its benefits. Just like that, the Russian defense industry lost most of its customers overnight. And, as with all other Russian industries' consumers, the new Russian armed forces could say "no" to the State distributors, effectively shrinking the customer base even further.

In addition, the now softer, more gentle Russian armed forces, having no enemies and only friends, shrunk by half. Fewer soldiers equalled fewer guns needed.

Another factor that contributed to the collapse of the Soviet industrial base (including its defense industry) at the fall of the USSR was the deep industrial integration throughout the Soviet Union. The tanks were built in Russia, but their engines in the Ukraine. It was the same story with helicopters, planes and even some small arms. The Soviet system of mutual bartering was no longer working. Everyone wanted cash.

The new economic conditions affected everyone. It was time to adapt. Military factories had to convert to civilian products to compensate for lost production and revenue. It was a hard and dangerous time when the lack of state funding would force a plant or factory to look for other sources of financing, often getting involved with an ever-growing criminal element.

Arsenals did it the best way they knew how, by adopting military weapons for civilian use as sporting and hunting rifles. This particular program proved to be successful, but could never replace military arms production. It was time to look for other markets and new opportunities.

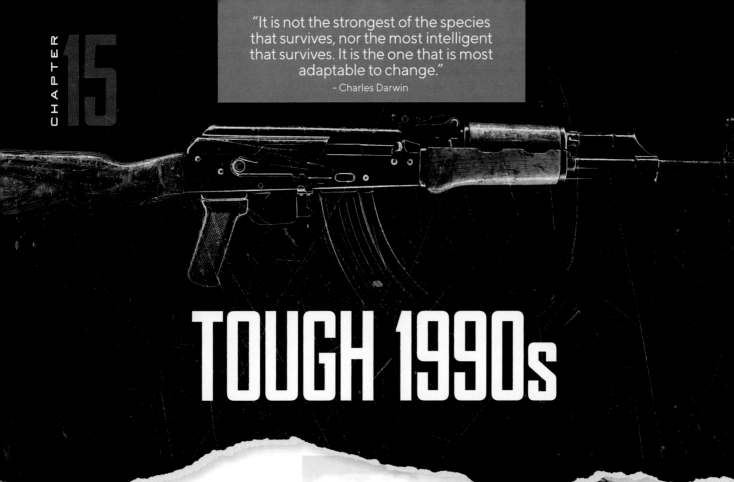

CHAPTER 15

"It is not the strongest of the species that survives, nor the most intelligent that survives. It is the one that is most adaptable to change."
– Charles Darwin

# TOUGH 1990s

*The Vyatsko-Polyansky machinebuilding plant Molot employed the vast majority of the adult population of Vyatskiye Polyany, Russia.*

*Located in the industrial city of Izhevsk, the Izhevskiy machinebuilding plant Izhmash is one of the biggest and oldest Russian arsenals.*

On top of the economic near-collapse and lack of orders, manufacturing companies that solely depended on the state budget, like AK-makers Izhmash and Molot, lost most of their financing. The situation was exacerbated by the number of people these companies employed. Izhevsk was a large industrial city with a developed industrial base and possibly would not get hit as bad, but to find employment for thousands of laid off workers in reasonable time would be problematic. A worse situation was developing with the Vyatsko-Polyansky Mashinostroitel'ny Zavod Molot, which employed close to half of all of the adult population in the city of Vyatskiye Polyany. Other than a few eateries, barbershops and beauty salons, and a couple of stores and shops, there were no other companies or organizations that could pick up the employment slack if thousands of Molot employees had to be laid off. However, out of chaos comes something positive.

The Russian arsenals already produced hunting rifles for the civilian market. Clumsy bolt-action rifles were bought by Soviet hunters for many years, mostly because there was nothing else available on the market. In many cases, the Soviet-built hunting rifles were prized for reliability, but often more for decorative stock and receiver engraving. Besides, most of the hunting in my region was done with smoothbore guns. I remember my dad's friend buying a new IZh over/under shotgun and showing it to my dad. The thing was gaudy, decorated with woodcarving of hunting scenes and receiver engravings of pheasants or ducks. I remember him bragging about what a great gun it was and how much money he had to fork over to get it. I don't believe that guy ever shot a gun.

The "Plain Jane" IZh-27 is plain looking, but a very good shooter. The custom version of this gun won numerous Olympic medals.

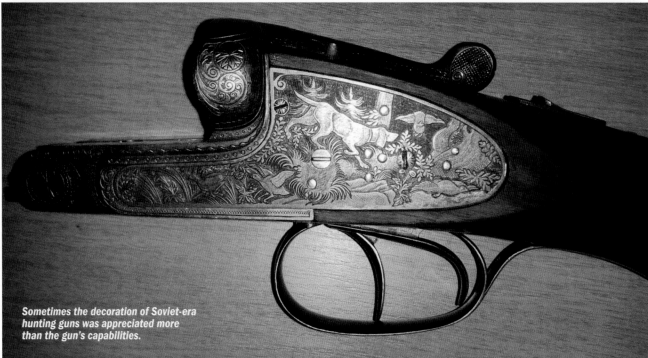

Sometimes the decoration of Soviet-era hunting guns was appreciated more than the gun's capabilities.

Years later while living in Alabama, I picked up a brand new IZh over/under shotgun of my own, just a plain Jane, the most simple-looking one I could find. It shoots true. I even won some money with it at a match in Alabama. However, every time I shoot the damn thing, my right hand middle finger that rests behind the trigger guard is on fire, and after several shots it feels broken. What I'm trying to say is that Soviet hunting guns were not made for normal humans and no amount of gaudy decorations could hide the fact that, to shoot them, you had to be impervious to pain and discomfort. It was time for something else.

The fall of the Soviet Union saw not only the introduction of a market economy, but also the loosening of many laws and restrictions. These new, more liberal laws also affected the firearms regulations. The road was paved for Russian gun makers to take advantage of these and bring new firearms to the market. No one was going to compensate the loss of orders or resulting lost revenue. They were left to fend for themselves. So, want to survive? Start selling! Want to innovate? Sell some more! The financing for development of new models had been slashed or eliminated altogether.

*One of the most popular hunting rifles in the Soviet Union was the Hunting Carbine Los-7, chambered in 7.62mm caliber.*

AK makers Izhmash and Molot had a solid base from which to start with their transition to the potentially prosperous civilian market. The AK and RPK platforms presented that base. New AK variants for the civilian market were released by each arsenal, each carving and occupying their own niche in the firearms market around the world.

Can these rifles be considered a stage in AK evolution? Perhaps not, but a solid subspecies for sure, a subspecies with the heritage and pedigree of its ancestor but defined by its unique purpose. It could and it did go through some form of transformation, either to bring this type of AK variant back to its original state or build it into something else using the available accessories. In either case, these new civilian AKs provided us with plenty of fodder for interesting builds and awarded us with plenty of enjoyment in their regular unmodified state.

*Based on the Mosin 91/30 rifle, the Kochetov carbine was another hunting rifle available to Soviet hunters.*

## AK HUNTING CARBINES

For Izhmash the choice was clear. The AK had legendary reliability and simplicity. The gun that almost everyone in Russia was intimately familiar with was already developed and built. With a few small modifications, the Saiga hunting carbine had arrived.

Named after the Saiga antelope, the Saiga semi-automatic rifles are a family of Russian semi-automatic rifles manufactured by Kalashnikov Concern (formerly Izhmash), which also manufactures the original AK Avtomat and the SVD Dragunov sniper rifle. Saiga rifles are a sporterized version of the AK Avtomat modified for civilian use. Saigas have been imported to the U.S. since the early 1990s by various importers. The number of imported Saigas rose to a staggering 140,000 rifles annually. When I met with the Director General of Izhmash, Maxim Kuzyuk, in 2010, he confided to me that the goal was to bring the export to the U.S. alone up to 300,000 per annum.

The Saiga hunting carbine has its roots in the 1970s. Though not very popular at that time, it laid a foundation for Izhmash to re-introduce it again in the 1990s. Hence, Izhmash did not have to start from ground zero, all it had to do was visit the drawings vault. The Saiga was a hunting carbine designed to take medium-sized game. Back in the 1970s, no sporting calibers other than 7.62x39 and 7.62x54R were available, so the re-introduction of Saiga in the 1990s also saw introduction of several "new" calibers, like the .308 Winchester (7.62x51mm), the more prevalent .223 Remington (5.56x45mm) and the 5.45x39mm, along with the original and 7.62x39mm.

The Saiga rifle takes the majority of its components directly from the AK-74M and AK-100 series Avtomats. It is built on a stamped receiver and has a 90-degree gas block. The sporting Saiga has a modified magazine latch and lacks the bullet ramp, so it cannot accept a standard AK magazine; physically the magazine catch will not allow a magazine to lock in place in the mag well. Even if the AK mag can be "muscled" into place, the gun would not feed properly. A new set of magazines of various capacities was designed to work in the Saigas. As a side note, these mags could be easily modified with a file or Dremel tool to work in the regular AK.

All of the Saiga rifles came with a "Monte Carlo" sporting stock and elongated handguards. The trigger and trigger guard of most of the rifles in the U.S. versions are placed on the receiver farther back than on a typical AK.

*Based on the Russian AK rifle, the sporting semi-automatic Saiga rifle has been imported to the U.S. in significant numbers.*

Another interesting note pertaining to the Saiga hunting rifles is that the guns were offered for sale not only in the U.S., but also in Europe and obviously in Russia itself. They had to comply with the firearm laws in each particular country. Most European countries mandate that the barrel of a hunting gun have special rifling that causes a bullet to lose its terminal velocity past 300 meters. In Russia, all sporting guns must have a groove in the chambers at the neck of the cartridge. When it is fired and the casing expands, the groove mark is clearly visible. This way one can determine if a sporting or hunting gun was used in the commission of a crime. However, we in the U.S. are not subjected to these unnecessary regulations. All of the U.S.-destined Saigas had the same barrel that the Russians used to build their military AK Avtomats.

An abundance of Saiga rifles in the U.S. provided plenty of fodder for conversions back to the original AK configuration. These conversions were done by many gunsmiths and could be as simple as installing the separate stock and a pistol grip, or as complicated as bringing the rifle within parameters of a combat Avtomat (the select-fire capability notwithstanding). Converted Saigas are notable for their "pedigree" among Kalashnikov collectors and enthusiasts, and are considered to be "true" Kalashnikovs. Extra value is given to the converted Saiga because it is made from brand-new parts and the fact that it came off the same assembly line as their full combat-ready Avtomats. These factors allow converted Saigas to command high sales prices relative to other Kalashnikov rifles. Such rifles may be sold at two to four times the value of a stock, non-converted factory Saiga, depending on parts used and the gunsmith who performed the work.

However popular the Saiga rifles are here in the U.S., it seems that further import of these guns has come to an end and will not resume anytime soon. The Kalashnikov Concern is one of the companies on the list of Russian entities sanctioned by the U.S. In 2014, the Obama Administration imposed sanctions on several Russian companies and individuals in response to "Russia's actions in Crimea." Again, I do not care to get involved in the political discussion even if it is clearly a dumb one. However, we have to go on the fact that sanctions on Russia will probably not be removed in the foreseeable future, and will likely last for 50–60 years or longer. Russia will never give in to pressure, they never have. Like one of my acquaintances said, "Russians will eat snow before they give up." It seems the sanctions did not have the desired effect on Russia. Instead, they may have had quite the opposite result. In fact, Russia launched a huge import substitution program that saw rapid and significant growth of its industries. They have managed to re-orient themselves to Asia and the Middle East to compensate for sales shortfalls created by the sanctions. This program also included the Russian gun makers. The only people these sanctions affected were the American companies who had business in Russia, and us—the AK enthusiasts.

## VEPR

Even after the sanctions imposed on Kalashnikov Concern, Russian-built Kalashnikovs continue to arrive on our shores by way of the other hunting/sporting rifle that is based on the Kalashnikov design—Molot Arsenal's Vepr. The Veprs are intended for the civilian market, and are marketed as high-quality hunting rifles. These semi-automatic rifles are based on the RPK machine gun and manufactured by the Molot plant in the small industrial town of Vyatskiye Polyany, located on the Vyatka riverbanks in Kirov Region, Russia.

The RPK descendant Vepr rifle was another Kalashnikov that arrived stateside in considerable numbers.

Just like the Saiga, the Vepr is offered in several popular calibers, including .223 Remington, 7.62x39mm, 5.45x39mm, 7.62x54R, .308 Winchester and 6.5 Grendel. The hallmarks of Vepr rifles are the receiver and heavy barrel inherited from the RPK. The barrel and gas block are chrome lined just like its military brethren. Due to the intended use, Veprs lack features seen on typical AKs. And, just like Saigas, Veprs cannot accept standard AK magazines. Their sporterized buttstock is different from that of the Saiga. It's not the classic "Monte Carlo" style, but rather a thumbhole-type that is a clear advantage over the Saiga. This setup makes it easier to install the traditional stock and pistol grip. One can do that with a screwdriver at home.

Similar to the Izhmash Saigas, the Veprs are often converted to the original military configuration. However, these converted Veprs do not resemble any existing AK variants and stand on their own unless they are converted to the RPK configuration with the use of correct parts and accessories. In this case, the owner of such a converted Vepr would be in a possession of the closest copy to the original Soviet/Russian RPK.

*Molot's ability to produce good quality barrels and overall quality of the Vepr rifle make it easy to convert it to something more "sexy," like this Vepr-1VS (bottom). Chambered in .223 Rem caliber Vepr-1V (top) imported by the I.O., Inc., was converted by them back to the RPK configuration. This rifle was the closest thing to the original Russian RPK.*

As a side note, the Vepr conversion into the military configuration is not as easy as I made it sound. Early generations of the Vepr were manufactured with slant-back receivers, making them incompatible with most AK furniture sets without a special block. The receivers were changed to straight-back on later models.

With the heavy receiver and barrel inherited from the RPK, the Vepr is a bit heavier than the standard AK. Even with the equivalent AK furniture, a Vepr weighs over a pound more than the Saiga. The extra weight contributes to the RPK-based Vepr being a better shooter. The majority of Russian hunters would prefer the Vepr over the Saiga, even though they pay more for the privilege to own one.

The Vepr has clear advantages when compared to other AK-based sporting rifles, especially when it comes to quality. Veprs are assembled with heavier RPK-style trunnions that are machined rather than hot hammer forged. The gun's heavy barrel is cold hammer forged and heat treated for eight hours. It's then annealed and chromed in a vacuum to ensure a high quality chrome lining. The barrels of the Veprs designated for export to the U.S. are military barrels without any Russian or European restrictions.

The gun's rear sight is adjustable for windage and designed for 1,000-meter range. The Vepr has a forged steel bolt with a spring-loaded firing pin and two locking lugs. The .308 Win. and 7.62x54R models have three locking lugs for even more strength and accuracy. Each Vepr rifle is hand-fitted and factory-tuned.

A good number of Veprs, though much smaller than the Saigas, have been imported to the U.S. on a regular basis by SSI and others since the 1990s. In January of 2016, Molot-Oruzhie, a commercial subsidiary of the Molot machinebuilding plant, signed an exclusive import deal with Arsenal USA. Molot's emphasis then was placed on the larger caliber models like the Vepr 308 and the Vepr 54R, which were also made to look like the Soviet SVD sniper rifle (a mistake, in my opinion). Though these rifles did see sales among the Dragunov rifle fans, Molot's bread and butter here in the U.S. was always the 5.45mm, the 7.62mm and .233-chambered rifles. This is all neither here or there, because as of June of 2017 all of the Molot-Oruzhie imports came to a screeching halt. Molot made the U.S. sanctions list.

## AK SHOTGUNS

Hunting rifles were not the only subspecies created by the AK evolution. The transformation transcended to the smoothbore guns. I don't know exactly what drove Izhmash designers to venture outside of their usual realm of rifles, but I suspect it was the same reason the Saiga and Vepr rifles were created—re-orientation of arsenals toward the commercial civilian market. Also consider the Russian firearms law that prohibits a person from owning a rifle without prior possession of a smoothbore gun, the requirement for a novice gun owner in Russia to possess a shotgun for five years before being given a license to purchase a rifle. Weird, but true. Therefore, the smoothbore firearms customer base is much larger than the market for rifles. It was an easy decision for the Russian gun makers.

Because of the AK system's simplicity and its ability to be adapted for other and larger calibers, it was easy for the AK manufacturers to venture into shotgun making. Izhmash was the first to develop an AK-based shotgun. It was named like the other hunting Izhmash rifles, the Saiga. Today, both main Russian arsenals Izhmash and Molot make their AK-based Saiga and Vepr shotguns, respectively.

## SAIGA SEMI-AUTOMATIC SHOTGUN

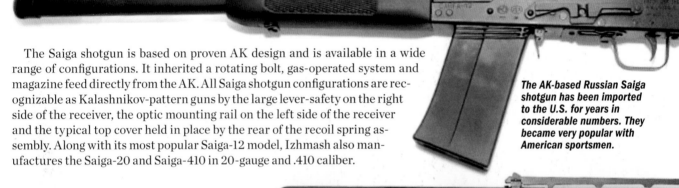

The Saiga shotgun is based on proven AK design and is available in a wide range of configurations. It inherited a rotating bolt, gas-operated system and magazine feed directly from the AK. All Saiga shotgun configurations are recognizable as Kalashnikov-pattern guns by the large lever-safety on the right side of the receiver, the optic mounting rail on the left side of the receiver and the typical top cover held in place by the rear of the recoil spring assembly. Along with its most popular Saiga-12 model, Izhmash also manufactures the Saiga-20 and Saiga-410 in 20-gauge and .410 caliber.

*The AK-based Russian Saiga shotgun has been imported to the U.S. for years in considerable numbers. They became very popular with American sportsmen.*

*The Saiga-12K is perhaps the most widespread sporting configuration of the shotgun.*

The Saiga semi-automatic shotguns have become very popular here in the U.S. Over the years, a great number have been imported by a number of importers. All early Saiga shotguns had a sporting "Monte Carlo" stock similar to that of the Saiga rifles. They came with standard five-round magazines. Just like the Saiga rifles, gunsmiths have converted these shotguns into the more desirable military configuration by installing a regular AK stock and pistol grip, provided state laws allowed the shotgun conversions.

Before too long these guns made their way into ever-growing 3-Gun competition where speed and precision is key. The competitors started to modify their Saigas for a high-speed competition. The otherwise inflexible Izhmash finally saw the writing on the wall and came up with their latest 12-gauge shotgun, offering the Saiga-12K-030. This particular gun was a departure from traditional hunter-configured Saigas. It was more

*The most desirable Saiga-12-030, with its "tactical" undertone, would have made it big if import from Kalashnikov Concern were allowed to continue.*

"tactical," featuring an extended magazine well, last round bolt hold open, hinged dust cover with Picatinny rail for mounting optics, Picatinny rail gas block, and a newly designed eight-round magazine. A limited number of these shotguns made it here before the U.S. sanctions were imposed on Kalashnikov Concern.

Prior to that, when the supply of Saiga shotguns was a constant stream, one could pick up a regular sporting Saiga for well under $1,000. Naturally, the tactical Saiga-12K-030 demanded a higher price. However, this is in the past now and it would be wise to expect prices for Saiga shotguns to rise dramatically. Will we see Saiga imports in our lifetime? Who knows? They, among many other things, got caught in the fecal world of politics.

## VEPR-12

The story of smoothbore Kalashnikovs does not end with Saiga shotguns. In fact, Molot also produced a smoothbore AK—the Vepr-12 shotgun. Like the Saiga-12, the Vepr-12 is a multipurpose shotgun patterned after the original AK rifle, built by Molot-Oruzhie Ltd. However, since the Molot arsenal is a builder of RPK machine guns, they had something to build on. It was natural to use a heavy RPK receiver in development of the new shotgun, whereas Saiga shotguns had to have purposely built heavy-duty receivers.

From the get-go, the Vepr-12 was built in the military or tactical configuration and resembled the Saiga-12K-030. To someone not closely familiar with the AK platform, both guns would appear identical. How did that happen? Easy. As a part of the government support for struggling manufacturers, the Izhmash arsenal was ordered to "share" their new Saiga drawings and production data with the floundering Molot. In the true spirit of friendly competition, not all drawings were shared and Molot was left to its own devices to finish the development of its Vepr shotgun. Molot managed to do just that and did it with poise and grace.

Out of the gate the new Vepr-12 was a very good gun, maybe even better than the Saiga-12K-30. Though there are many similarities between them, there were differences that made the Vepr slightly superior to the Saiga. Like the Saiga, the Vepr-12 was designed to be a versatile weapon platform, capable of being used by hunters and professional shooters alike. A great deal of attention was paid to the ergonomics of the new gun. Instead of the standard AK safety selector, the Vepr-12 has an ambidextrous safety that can be manipulated from either side of the rifle. The addition of a mag well, another unusual feature for an AK-type rifle, allows for "straight in" magazine insertion, as opposed to the "rock and lock" found on standard AK rifles. A side-folding stock is present on most models. However, Vepr-12 shotguns are offered with several stock options. The Vepr-12 is also chrome lined throughout, including the gas block, barrel and chamber, affording the rifle excellent cor-

Russia's Molot arsenal entry, the Vepr-12 shotgun, was configured in "tactical" guise from the factory.

*A considerable number of Vepr-12s made it here to the U.S. Due to new anti-Russian sanctions, there will be no more imports of these shotguns in the foreseeable future.*

rosion resistance. Unlike the Saiga-12, the gas system on the Vepr-12 is self-regulating, allowing it to shoot most commercially available 12-gauge loads without risking damage to the gun or hindering its operation. The Vepr-12 lacks the normal AK side-mounted accessory rail. Instead, there is a Picatinny rail mounted to the hinged top cover, allowing use of any modern aiming device.

The Vepr-12 shotgun was imported into the United States by SSI and several other importers. The pricing of the Vepr-12 was subject to dramatic rises and falls. It has settled at just under a thousand dollars. However, with Molot now included in anti-Russian sanctions for its proximity to the earlier-sanctioned Kalashnikov Concern, no further imports are feasible in the near future. I feel lucky to have one of these shotguns. I'm not sure how much of that feeling is for having it or shooting it, as it is an excellent shooter.

One may say that all is doom and gloom on the horizon of AK-based smoothbore guns. With Saigas and Veprs now gone, it's time for something else to take their place. Say "Hallo to my little Chinese friend."

Though this chapter deals with Russian arsenals that had to survive by learning to navigate the civilian firearms market, to paint a complete picture I have to tell about some non-Russian guns.

## CHINESE CATAMOUNT FURY

Nobody will outdo the Chinese. They wouldn't just stand aside and let others have all the fun. The new Chinese Catamount Fury AK-based semi-automatic 12-gauge shotgun is now here and gaining popularity. With major competition out of the way, the Catamount Fury has to bear the weight of being the representative of smoothbore AKs here in the States. The idea of the Chinese-built AK in the U.S. is absurd. After all, the import of Chinese AKs has been prohibited since 1993. However, the ban did not cover the import of sporting shotguns.

The Chinese gun makers and the Catamount Fury importer Century Arms have capitalized on the lack of import restrictions and brought to the U.S. this potentially popular firearm. Currently, two different models of the Catamount shotguns are offered by Century Arms, the Fury and the Fury II. The Fury II is slanted more toward 3-Gun competition, with an AR-style magazine well and SVD-type stock. The standard Fury is configured with a sporting "Monte Carlo"-style stock and conventional magazine well. Other than that, both guns are built on an AK-style receiver and use an AK-type gas operating system. They are fitted with a 20-inch barrel chambered for 3-inch magnums. The muzzle is threaded for choke tubes. The Catamount's gas block is approximately 1.2 inches farther forward than on a Russian Saiga and features two gas settings. The gas block also has a 2.3-inch modified Picatinny rail at the bottom. Unlike the Saiga, the Catamount Fury sports an upper handguard similar to a standard AK. The gun's furniture is made from a black polymer. The butt features a rubber recoil pad 3/4-inch thick, and it has a 14-inch length of pull.

Regarding the design itself, it is not simply a Saiga-12 copy, even though it is clear where Chinese designers drew their inspiration. One simply cannot miss the obvious similarities. However, the Chinese AK shotgun has some improvements and advantages. The best feature of the Catamount Fury is that it is here and available at a much lower price than the Saiga or Vepr. It also continues to be imported by Century Arms in good numbers and is distributed far and wide.

ONE OF THE AKs THAT IS ALLOWED TO BE IMPORTED FROM CHINA IS THE AK-BASED CATAMOUNT FURY SHOTGUN.

The catamount Fury shotgun may appear to look similar to the Russian Saiga-12, but there are many differences, cosmetic and functional.

I.O., Inc.'s IARMS EM12B AK-based Chinese shotgun comes impressively equipped. It has all the desirable features for this type of shotgun.

## I.O., INC., IARMS EM12B AK-BASED SHOTGUN

One more representative of Chinese AK-based shotguns is the IARMS EM12B 12-gauge imported by I.O., Inc.

The IARMS EM12B is an AK-based semi-automatic smoothbore with a 3-inch chamber and an 18.5-inch barrel. Although it is clearly based on the Russian Saiga-12 series of shotguns, unlike the Catamount Fury that used more of the sporting pattern, the EM12B went the tactical route. It comes from I.O., Inc., impressively equipped. It has a separate stock and pistol grip. The stock is similar to a typical AK stock, but slightly wider at the rubber butt plate with typical AK length of pull. The pistol grip is a copy of one of my favorite grips, the M249 SAW-type. I find it very comfortable. The EM12B sports a full-length aluminum M-LOK lower handguard and Picatinny-style top handguard. Unlike other AK-based 12-gauge shotguns,

The EM12B has similar AK-based shotgun controls. It comes with a separate stock and a very comfortable pistol grip.

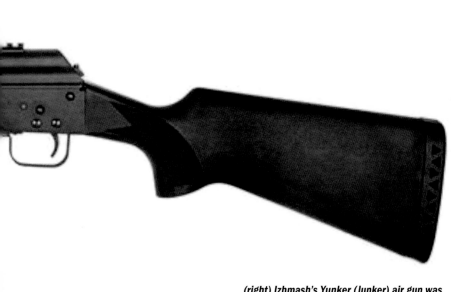

(right) Izhmash's Yunker (Junker) air gun was a standard gas-operated pistol enclosed in the AK-74M. It could be easily identified by the air pistol grip.

(below) Later models of Yunkers were identifiable by the receiver markings shown here.

the new EM12B has a four-position adjustable gas system that allows this gun to shoot any 12-gauge ammo. It comes with extended mag well similar to that of the Vepr-12 or Saiga-12-030. It comes with two five-round magazines that are a copy of Saiga mag, which means it would feed out of standard Saiga mags, whereas the magazines from Vepr, Saiga and Catamount are not interchangeable.

The gun's 18-inch barrel is not threaded for muzzle attachments. However, it is threaded for replaceable chokes and comes with all three. Following the standard theme for AK-based shotguns, the EM12B has a combination front sight/gas block that sports an adjustable front sight. The AK-type rear sight is also adjustable for range. It is on the heavy side, weighing 4.5 kg (~10 lbs.), warranting the use of a vertical front grip in my opinion. Luckily, the M-LOK slots allow installation of such accessories.

Cycling of the EM12B is on par with rest of the 12-gauge AK shotguns. It is not as smooth as the factory AK. The controls are identical to the standard AK rifle, except for the magazine release tang, which on the EM12B is longer and wider, reminding one of a butterfly. In theory, one can reach it with an index finger and the mag would drop out. However, I had to use my middle finger, as it is simply longer. For those who have long fingers this tang would work fine.

At the range, the EM12B proved to be a very good shooter. With all that weight up front it felt very smooth. It ate everything I tried to feed it. Good shooter, reasonably priced and available for immediate delivery. This gun's best feature is that one can modify it on the kitchen table with any stock grip combination. It accepts regular AK stock options and grips. I know I will be

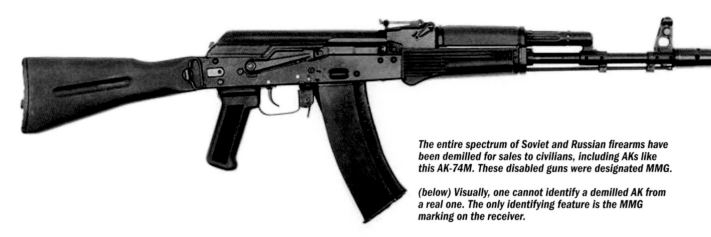

*The entire spectrum of Soviet and Russian firearms have been demilled for sales to civilians, including AKs like this AK-74M. These disabled guns were designated MMG.*

*(below) Visually, one cannot identify a demilled AK from a real one. The only identifying feature is the MMG marking on the receiver.*

putting a FAB Defense spring loaded buffer tube on mine, just to prolong my day at the range.

Hunting carbines and shotguns were not the only civilian AKs that Russians produced as a part of conversion to the free market. One of the early civilian AKs was the air rifle called Yunker (Junker, here in the U.S.). These were military AK-74Ms that were gutted out, with a gas-operated pellet pistol along with barrel liner installed into the receiver and barrel respectively. Several were imported into the U.S., but the ATF quickly prohibited any further imports of the Yunkers because of too many machine gun parts used in the construction of the pellet gun. It's hard to argue the point, since the air rifle was basically a gutted AK-74M Avtomat.

Nevertheless, the Russians did not give up and developed purposely-built gas-operated air rifles, the Yunker-2 and Yunker-3. None of them were imported into the U.S. However, these pellet AK guns were popular in Russia among a younger crowd.

Still, the Russians were not done. Next came

*Internally the MMG AK is easily identified as demilled. Numerous components of the gun have been permanently disabled, including barrel, front trunnion, bolt, bolt carrier and magazine.*

*A recent rise in popularity of historical reenactment spurred sales of tens of thousands of demilled firearms.*

demilled AKs of all models, from the first AK-47s to the latest AK-100 series the MMGs. These were fully functional non-firing replicas; except they were not made as replicas, these were real guns that went through a proscribed series of demilling to render them as non-firing replicas. One could cycle the gun, take it apart just like the real AK and put it together again, but it could never shoot. These became popular with collectors and re-enactors in Russia and Europe who wanted a real military Russian-built AK without the hassle that goes with owning a gun in those countries. To buy these MMGs, one did not need a license or any other special permit. Again, the MMG AK could not be imported into the U.S. because these guns are converted machine guns according to the ATF.

However, I do not think that Russian arsenals are complaining about lack of demand for the demilled AK. They sell a good number of them in Russia, at premium prices.

In response to the recent law permitting blank-firing devices, the latest offerings from Russian gun manufacturers are blank-firing guns, including a wide variety of AKs. Riding a wave of recently found patriotism, as a counterbalance to attempts by the West to re-write history, war re-enactment took on a different spin in Russia. It became a national pastime. Luckily, Russian history provides plenty of material for such activity. Again, the gun makers were happy to oblige. Hundreds of guns have been converted into blank-firing devices. Obviously, the majority of these guns are used in WWII battle re-enactments and have to be period guns, like Mosin 91/30 rifle or PPSh-41 machine pistols. However, the AK manufacturers saw their opportunity to take a bite from the newly opened market. Several models are available for sale at any gun shop in Russia.

These AKs do not represent any particular branch in AK evolution. They were part of the gradual AK transformation as part of the regular mass production run. I have included them here as an illustration of how the Russian arsenals have navigated the complicated terrain of commerce-driven markets and its ability to adapt.

*Though WWII reenactments are the most popular, Afghan war reenactment is gaining in popularity. Hence, the rise in demand for demilled AKs.*

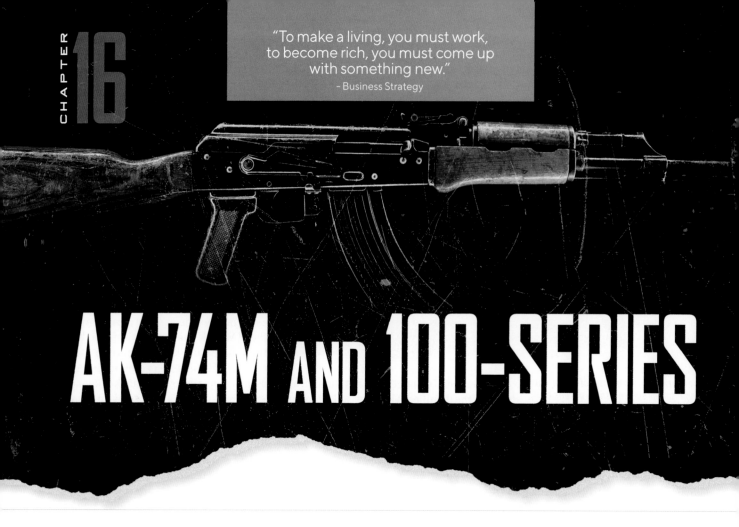

# AK-74M AND 100-SERIES

With the socioeconomic situations out of the way, let us continue with our AK evolution story. This chapter will tell the story of the last Soviet stage in the evolution of the Motherland rifle, which culminated in the appearance of the "black AK."

Positive experiences using the AK-74 in combat proved the viability of the platform. However, apart from the RPK-74 light machine gun and specialty AKSU shorty, the AK-74 family included four variants of full-length Avtomat. These varied by the fixed versus folding stocks and presence or lack of the accessory side rail. This

*Since the early 1990s, the AK-74M has become the standard-issue main battle Avtomat for Russia's armed forces.*

caused a great deal of confusion about what branch of military and what type of units would be issued a particular version. Even worse was the situation with production of these Avtomats. It was becoming unnecessarily expensive to maintain control over four different production runs. Citing these problems, the Soviets came up with a solution by the late 1980s: the AK-74M. As with the AKM, the "M" in the AK-74M model designation stands for "modernized." That's what the new variant was, a modernized AK-74, but with one caveat. Actually, the AK-74 modernization started in the mid-1980s with introduction of glass-filled polyamide composite furniture as a direct replacement for the laminate wood. However, the slight reduction in weight of the AK-74 was not enough and, at the same time, Izhmash engineers started to work on modernizing the platform.

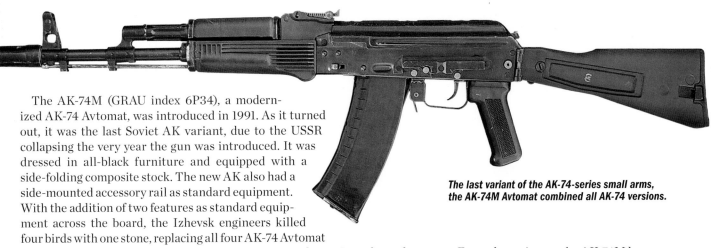

The AK-74M (GRAU index 6P34), a modernized AK-74 Avtomat, was introduced in 1991. As it turned out, it was the last Soviet AK variant, due to the USSR collapsing the very year the gun was introduced. It was dressed in all-black furniture and equipped with a side-folding composite stock. The new AK also had a side-mounted accessory rail as standard equipment. With the addition of two features as standard equipment across the board, the Izhevsk engineers killed four birds with one stone, replacing all four AK-74 Avtomat

*The last variant of the AK-74-series small arms, the AK-74M Avtomat combined all AK-74 versions.*

versions—AK-74, AKS-74, AK-74N and AKS-74N—with one. It made perfect sense. From that point on, the AK-74M became the main battle rifle for all of Russia's armed forces.

But, was it all that different from its predecessors? It is, after all, just a modification of the older AK-74. Or is it?

The AK-74M is what Russians call a deep modernization of the AK-74 Avtomat. The new modernized AK had several changes that made it slightly superior to its original predecessor. One of the most noticeable features is its polymer folding stock. Apart from being lighter than its metal counterpart, it is by far more comfortable. It doesn't snag on clothing, as the skeletonized metal stock did. I didn't realize that was a problem until I saw attempts by Soviet engineers to fix it by redesigning the metal stock with rolled edges.

It was a pain to clean the "moon" dust that accumulated in the metal stock grooves. Most soldiers who, like me, carried the AKS-74 or AKS-74N in Afghanistan, would stuff the individual trauma pack into the stock opening and wrap a rubber tourniquet around it. This played several roles: it freed space in our load bearing equipment, made the supplies ready and available, and provided some cushion for a good cheek weld.

The next improvement was more about aesthetics. The AK-74M was a true "black" gun, sporting black polyamide furniture all around. It did provide for better adhesion and improved the shooter's grip on the gun. Such a small detail did help to improve accuracy by facilitating a firmer grip on the gun. For the first time, a special anti-corrosion coating was used in conjunction with hard enamel. Both coatings played an important role. One reduced potential corrosion and made the gun more corrosion resistant, especially when firing corrosive ammunition. The second protected the gun's external components from abrasive elements.

Just like its predecessors, the AK-74M was equipped with a bayonet lug and additional accessories—one for mounting under-barrel grenade launchers. In addition, all of the new AK Avtomats came with a re-enforcement plate under the pistol grip to alleviate excessive dynamic loads when firing grenades. All AK-74Ms were now universally equipped with a side rail for mounting aiming devices. This eliminated the need to swap guns for a particular mission, which was especially problematic with reconnaissance and special operations units early on. Now everyone had the same gun and any of the guns in the unit could be equipped with night or optical sights.

The new muzzle brake saw a small but effective design change. Although it looks almost identical to the original AK-74 version, the new AK-74M muzzle brake is different in its construction. Instead of a one-piece device with two laser cut "zigzag" side ports, the new version had a baffle welded into it, creating two round slits on its sides. The muzzle brake now had a slightly larger burn chamber. All of these minute details contributed to it being a more effective device. When compared side by side with an older model AK-74, the AK-74M does display better characteristics. It is slightly more accurate and has softer recoil.

## TACTICAL-TECHNICAL CHARACTERISTICS OF THE AK-74M AVTOMAT

When in combat, not only the tactical parameters of the weapon such as weight, length and design features are important, but also its technical features that determine the convenience of using the Avtomat in combat conditions. When talking about the AK-74M, its combat characteristics speak for themselves:

- Caliber—5.45x39mm
- Muzzle velocity—900 m/s (2,953 fps)
- Aiming range—1,000m (1,094 yards)
- Rate of fire—650 rounds per minute
- Practical combat rate of fire—40 rpm single shot, 100 rpm short bursts
- Fire modes—select fire (semi-auto, full- auto)
- Weight—3.9 kg (8.6 lbs.) with a loaded magazine and 3.6 kg (7.9 lbs.) empty
- Range of a direct shot at 50cm (~20-inch) target—440 m (481 yards)

**I THINK THAT THE AK-74M IS AS CLOSE TO A PERFECT FIGHTING CARBINE AS IT GETS.**

AK-101 (5.56mm NATO)

AK-102 (5.56mm NATO)

AK-103 (7.62x39mm)

AK-104 (7.62x39mm)

AK-105 (5.45x39mm)

AK-107 (5.45x39mm)

AK-108 (5.56mm NATO)

*Following closely behind the AK-74M, Izhmash released the AK-100 series that included five new Avtomats in three most popular calibers, two full length and three shortened variants. Later, the balanced automatics AK-107 (second from bottom) and AK-108 (bottom) were added to the series.*

I think that the AK-74M is as close to a perfect fighting carbine as it gets. I'm talking about a gun that is issued *en masse*, of course.

Apart from becoming the Russian armed forces' main Avtomat, the AK-74M also played a very important role in the AK's evolution.

The late 1980s, flamed by the Perestroika, saw cracks in the Soviet Union foundation and the demise of the Warsaw Treaty organization a.k.a., the Warsaw Pact. The newly independent East European countries slowly but surely started to re-orient, turning to the West, toward NATO. Unable to do anything about it, the Soviets just stood and watched the collapse of their once powerful military block in Europe. However, the largest AK maker, Izhmash, saw an opportunity. By that time, the premier Soviet arsenal had tasted the fruit of the free market economy and had considerable export ambitions. Having already produced a proven, modern infantry small arms platform, the AK-74M, Izhevsk plant engineers and designers released a new line of AK-74M-based guns in two basic configurations and in three main battlefield calibers: the AK-100 series.

The AK-100 series was developed at the Izhmash plant, where most Kalashnikov Avtomats were manufactured, and was based on models already mastered in production. The base for all 100-series AKs was the AK-74M. In fact, the developers of the 100 series simply took the AK-74M Avtomat chambered for the 5.45x39mm cartridge and adapted it for two calibers—5.56mm NATO (5.56mm or .223 Rem.) and 7.62x39mm. Apart from the full-length Avtomats in all three calibers, the Izhevsk gun makers also released compact or shortened versions in the same three calibers—5.45mm, 5.56mm and 7.62mm. From their "parent," all 100-series AKs inherited the black glass-filled impact-resistant composite furniture, which included the folding stock, the side accessory rail for mounting optics and standard bayonet and accessory lugs for the full-length models.

Most of the AK-100 models are produced for export, except for the AK-103 full length and AK-104 short, both in 7.62x39mm caliber, and the AK-105 shortened Avtomat in 5.45x39. These guns were adopted for service by Russian security forces in 1993 and found popularity with anti-terrorism units. Today, AK-103s can be seen in the hands of Russia's Special Operations (SSO (CCO—Rus.)) troops fighting terrorists in Syria.

## AK-101

The AK-101 differs from the AK-74M only in the cartridge used—it fires the 5.56x45mm caliber ammunition used in the small arms of NATO. The ammunition drove most of the other changes in the design of the AK-101. The barrel and the chamber had to be redesigned to fit the 5.56mm cartridge. Also, considering the 5.56mm round ballistics, the twist rate and number of grooves had to change in the barrel rifling. The bolt, or rather bolt face, had to be redesigned to accommodate the cartridge casing. Additionally, the barrel's gas port along with the gas block/gas tube ports had to be changed to not over-gas the operating system, as the 5.56x45mm cartridge produces more powder gases. This way, the recoil impulse is comparable to that of the AK-74M chambered in 5.45x39mm caliber. The accuracy in semi-automatic fire of the AK-101 is noticeably higher than that of the AK-74M, thanks to the 5.56x45 ammunition.

Most of the AK-101 parameters are very similar to if not the same as those of the AK-74M. The total length of the Avtomat with stock unfolded is 934mm (~33.77 inches), and with the stock folded 705mm (~27.78 inches). The weight of the AK-101 with an empty magazine is 3.6 kg (~7.9 lbs.), and with loaded mag is 4 kg (~8.82 lbs.). The length of the AK-101's barrel is the same as the AK-74M, 415mm (~16.34 inches).

The muzzle velocity of the 5.56mm-chambered AK-101 is 910 m/s (~2986 fps), which is slightly higher than that of the AK-74M. The retarder is installed to limit the rate of fire to no more than 600 rounds per minute, slightly lower than that of the AK-74M.

The front and rear sights are identical in design to the AK-74M sights, except for the rear sight that is adjustable for elevation with built-in 5.56mm round ballistics. Just like on the AK-74M, it has 10 positions marked from 1 to 10. Each position corresponds with ranges from 100 to 1,000 meters in 100-meter increments. The AK-101 sports the infamous and highly effective AK-74M improved muzzle device.

The main visual difference of the AK-101 from the AK-74M is the shape of its magazine. The curve of the AK-101 magazine is much shallower and less pronounced than that of the AK-74M. I like to say the AK-101 version is less curvy than the AK-74M mag, which is clearly evident to those of us who have spent considerable time around AKs of different calibers. For most people, the two magazines can appear identical.

Unfortunately for Izhmash, the AK-101 did not garner wide popularity with new NATO members. It did not fully meet the NATO standards for small arms. As a result, most of the export sales of the AK-101 occurred in Southeast Asia, where AK-101s can be spotted in the hands of Indonesian and Malayan security forces. Here in the U.S., the AK-101 clones are very popular. One can encounter them as conversions from Russian Saiga rifles or imported directly from Bulgaria by Arsenal USA. I'm talking strictly about the AK-101 clones. However, there are other .223 AKs out there built by numerous manufacturers and gunsmiths.

*Chambered in 5.56x45mm NATO caliber, the AK-101 has the same features as the AK-74M.*

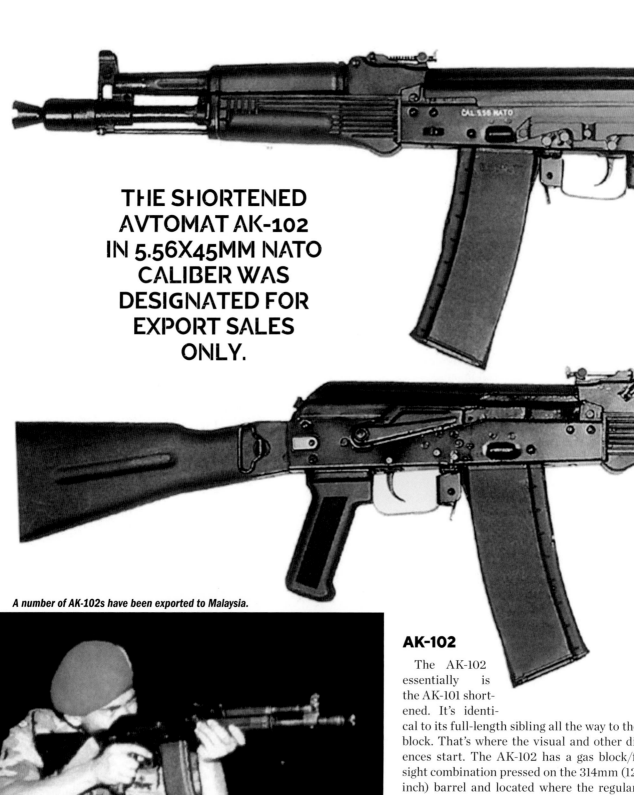

**THE SHORTENED AVTOMAT AK-102 IN 5.56X45MM NATO CALIBER WAS DESIGNATED FOR EXPORT SALES ONLY.**

*A number of AK-102s have been exported to Malaysia.*

## AK-102

The AK-102 essentially is the AK-101 shortened. It's identical to its full-length sibling all the way to the gas block. That's where the visual and other differences start. The AK-102 has a gas block/front sight combination pressed on the 314mm (12.36-inch) barrel and located where the regular gas block of the full-length Avtomat would sit. Unlike the AKS-74U, the compactness of the AK-102 is achieved by the 114mm (~4. 5-inch) barrel length reduction. However, because of the barrel's short length, the AK-102 has a muzzle brake similar though shorter than that of the AKSU. Due to the reduction in length of the barrel, the overall length of the gun was also reduced; with stock unfolded it is 824mm (32.44 inches), and with the stock folded 586mm (22.28 inches). Obviously, the weight of the AK-102 was somewhat lower

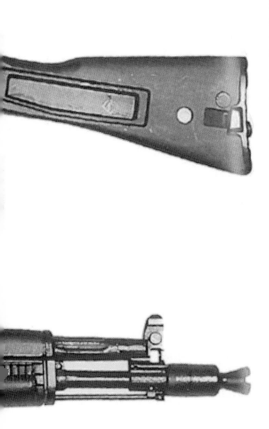

than that of the AK-101. The shorter gun weighs 400 grams (slightly over 14 oz.) less than the full-length version.

Other than that, visually and technically the guns are identical. However, the shortened AK-102 had different tactical or rather ballistic characteristics. The shorter barrel is responsible for a reduction in the muzzle velocity that was 820 m/s (2,690 fps) to the 910 m/s (~2,986 fps) of the AK-101. Based on the reduction of terminal velocity and effective range, the AK-102's rear sight is adjustable only to 500 meters, with markings that go from 1 to 5 in 100-meter increments. The automatic fire rate remained the same, at 600 rounds per minute.

## AK-103

The appearance of the AK-103 could confirm the proverb, "Everything new is a well-forgotten old." Be that as it may, the new 7.62mm Avtomat is not old, but rather a completely new animal. In its design, like other 100-series AKs, the AK-103 is fully based on the AK-74M Avtomat with the only difference being the 7.62x39mm a.k.a. M43 cartridge it fires.

*Based on the modernized AK-74M platform, the 7.62mm AK-103 Avtomat has all the features of its 5.45mm sibling. However, adaptation of the modern platform positively affected this gun's characteristics.*

The original Kalashnikov Avtomats, the AK-47 and AKM, fired this cartridge, as did many other weapons, like Simonov's SKS, the RPK machine gun, the hunting carbines of the Saiga family and other examples of military and civilian weapons. This cartridge was then and is now excellent ammunition for the mass-issued military weapons. Many would argue that the M43 cartridge is significantly better than the 5.45x39mm 7N6 that is used by almost all of today's Russian armed forces' small arms. I would argue this point on the cartridge as whole, but will concede and acknowledge that the M43, in some aspects, is better than 7N6 cartridge, but only in specific areas. The same group of people would also claim that, as main battle rifle ammunition, the 7.62x39mm M43 also surpasses the 5.56x45mm NATO cartridge. These "specialists" cite several factors as M43 advantages over its sub-caliber rivals. The bullet of the cartridge M43 is much more stable in flight, even after passing through minor obstacles stability is maintained, which cannot be said about bullets with a center of gravity shifted to the rear. The 7.62mm round would not be deflected by grass, twigs, bushes, small branches, thin doors and walls, car bodies, glass, etc. It will pass through all of this practically without changing the trajectory.

The 7.62mm-caliber bullet fired from an Avtomat, when it enters the human body, leaves an even wound channel and usually passes through. For combat, this is a plus, since the enemy soldier has many chances to survive, even with a chest cavity wound. This round does possess the overwhelming stopping power, deformation of the bullet in the body and the strong cavitation effect. These are traits of the 5.56mm and 5.45mm bullets. This is not required in war. After all, you just need to disable the enemy, it is not necessary to maim and kill.

In modern combat, fighters are usually protected by body armor. The 7.62mm-caliber bullet works better against the body armor than 5.45mm or 5.56mm rounds.

The bullet of 7.62x39mm cartridge keeps its momentum much longer than

*The AK-103 is the leading variant of the 100-series Avtomats in the export arena. The AK-103 is exported to many countries, and licenses for its manufacture have been sold to several clients abroad.*

bullets of 5.45mm and 5.56mm, because it has a larger mass. The M43 heavy bullet punches through enemy's parapets and breastwork, while small-caliber automatic bullets get stuck in the same parapet.

The myth about the instability of the 5.56mm or 5.45mm when compared to the 7.62 heavier slug is based on nothing but urban legend and comparison of mass and not on practical knowledge. Those who argue this point often forget basic ballistic principles of acceleration, speed, rotation, distance and transfer of energy. As described earlier, the 5.45mm 7N6 round that I have fired passed through everything just fine. In videos, one can see numerous penetration comparisons between the M43 and 7N6. After striking more formidable obstacles, the 5.45mm bullet would maintain its trajectory farther than the M43 round even at close ranges. But increase the distance and this gap widens. I would assume the same effect when the M43 is compared to the 5.56mm bullet, though it is perhaps not as dramatic.

How can a larger-diameter, slow-flying slug penetrate armor better than a high-speed, smaller-diameter bullet? Now, I am talking of direct comparison between the 7.62mm M43 and 5.45mm 7N6. Again, I have described earlier how the 7N6 bullet construction is conducive to body armor penetration, where the bullet's jacket transfers its energy causing the body armor to release the counteracting energy while the steel core that is suspended in softer lead travels forward practically unopposed.

Opposing arguments are based on mass of the bullets alone. It is true, if all things are equal, an object with greater mass will carry more energy and therefore have more energy to transfer. However, change the speed and range, what do you get?

The only disadvantage of the M43 bullet in their argument is attributed to the lesser ballistic performance of the 7.62mm round, its relatively short, flat trajectory and slow speed. Add low recoil impulse, better accuracy, high hit probability and reduced weight, and the arguments in favor of the 7.62x39mm cartridge will not stand.

Nevertheless, let us get back to the AK-103 and what a fine weapon it is.

In comparison to its folding predecessor the AKMS, the AK-103 is considerably better: it's more comfortable, it has better ergonomics and balance, the stock is made of composite material and of correct length, it's lighter, it has an effective AK-74-style muzzle brake (significantly improving accuracy), and it is equipped with a side accessory rail as standard equipment.

The technical characteristics of the AK-103 are almost identical to those of the AK-101 described earlier, the only difference being the cartridge it fires. The other differences include the weight of loaded magazine differential of 100 grams (~3.5 oz.) and muzzle velocity, which is 715 m/s (2,460 fps) to the AK-101's 910 m/s (~2,986 fps) due to a heavier bullet.

The AK-103 is adopted for service with Russian anti-terrorism and special purpose units. The gun is chosen for its caliber, where the heavier and slower slug is more conducive to the close quarter urban combat in environment in which these units often find themselves operating. The 7.62mm bullet has lesser penetration ability and is less likely to ricochet.

The 7.62mm-caliber AK-103 Avtomat is the most popular export Kalashnikov in recent years. This is attributed to the cartridge it fires, and a warm and fuzzy feeling other countries get from a familiar caliber and the fact that they don't have to re-tool their ammunition plants for other calibers. Russia has signed a contract with Venezuela for supplying a set number of the AK-103s, and for building and equipping a factory in Venezuela to make a licensed copy of the gun.

Before Gadhafi met his ultimate demise, Libya signed a similar deal with Izhmash to purchase and then produce the AK-103 Avtomat in Libya. Most recently, during his historic visit to Russia, the King of Saudi Arabia, King Salman, signed the same deal with Kalashnikov Concern for an unspecified number of AK-103s and a license to produce these in Saudi Arabia.

## AK-104

The shortened version of the AK-103, the AK-104 is similar in all respects to the AK-102, except for the 7.62x39mm-caliber cartridge it fires. With loaded magazine attached it weighs 100 grams (~3.5 oz.) less than its 5.56mm sibling.

Also, the muzzle velocity is 670 m/s (2,198 fps) as opposed to 820 m/s (2,690 fps) of the AK-102. Other than that, there are no differences. The AK-104 is adopted for service with Russian anti-terrorist and special forces units alongside full-length AKs.

## AK-105

Just as the AK-102 and AK-104 are the shortened version of full-length Avtomats in their respective calibers, the AK-105 is basically an AK-74M, but with a short 314mm barrel, a combination gas block and a buster muzzle brake. The gas/block

A SHORTENED VERSION OF THE AK-103, THE AK-104 IS GEARED TOWARD RUSSIAN ANTI-TERRORISM UNITS OPERATING WITHIN URBAN ENVIRONMENTS.

*The AK-104 found wide use with Russian anti-terrorism units. Its compact size is conducive to close quarter combat operations.*

combination and muzzle brake are similar to those of the AK-102 and AK-104. This Avtomat is produced mainly for the domestic market and is already supplied to some Russian units, as a replacement for the outdated AKS-74U.

## SPECIALTY MODELS

The AK-100 series introduced six new black rifles. Some were adopted for service with Russian forces and some were designated for export. All have been covered by numerous articles and books. However, there were a couple more specialty models that did not get wide press coverage.

There are three other versions of the basic variants of the "hundredth"-series AKs.

*The shortened AK-105 Avtomat is the compact version of the AK-74M.*

*The AK-105 sees service with Internal Ministry troops involved in anti-terrorism operations on regular basis.*

All versions that have the digit "1" at the end of their model designation (for example, AK-104-1) are semi-automatic carbines and are not capable of full-automatic fire. These were designed for police and security units, although it is unclear why. The police have regular Avtomats, and for guard duty, a shotgun would make more sense.

However, the AK-100 series modifications with the number "2" at the end of the model designation (like the AK-101-2) are a different story. These AK versions have three modes of fire. In addition to semi-auto and full-auto, the three-round burst capability was added. The distinct feature is that the safety/selector lever has four positions.

The last model of the special "hundredth"-series AKs is the AK-103-3. It stands out from the rest and marks a beginning of further AK development into a 200 series of Kalashnikovs. I will talk about this more a little later in this book.

AK-103-3 characteristics include a caliber of 7.62x39mm, with dimensions similar to the standard AK-103, and weight that is slightly higher. The shape of the pistol grip is changed to a more comfortable and ergonomic version, and an additional thumb-operated safety is installed at the top of the grip. The Picatinny rail section is mounted on top of the receiver cover. The cover itself is rigidly affixed to the receiver to avoid movement. The composite lower handguard is equipped with a section of Picatinny rail for mounting flashlights, laser designators and front grips. The AK-103-3 was supplied with a collapsible bipod attached to the lower handguard.

This was a short review of the most significant and somewhat recent stage in evolution of the AK rifle. This stage produced new black AK models in three popular calibers, shorties and full-length Avtomats, modernizing the AK platform and paving the way for the future development of modern Kalashnikovs.

*The AK-103-3 is a slightly "tacticooled" version of the AK-103.*

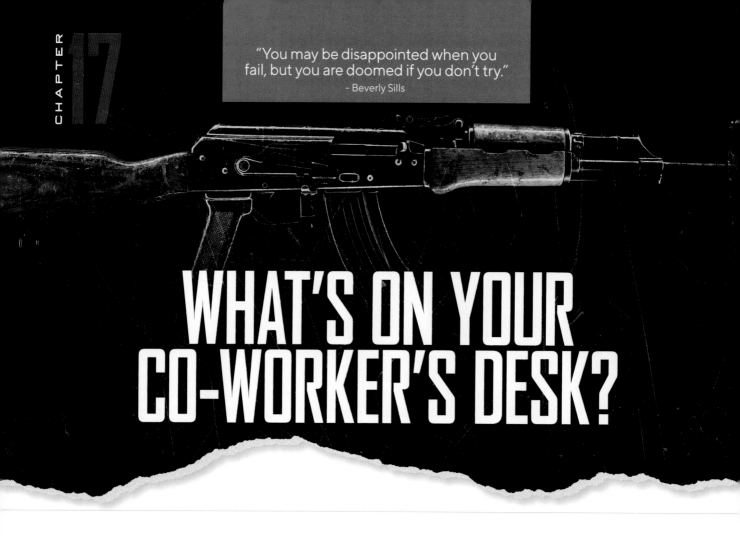

# WHAT'S ON YOUR CO-WORKER'S DESK?

I think I've shown in this book that it wasn't all smooth going for Mikhail Kalashnikov and his Avtomat. In fact, it's a miracle that the AK is still around as the Russian forces' main battle rifle. I say, what does not kill you makes you stronger. The AK Avtomat has taken the challenges head on and withstood the test of time and the numerous attempts to end its supremacy. Having said that, we have to consider the fact that, if not for those "attacks" by competitors, AK development may have been slower or even nonexistent. Out of competition comes the strongest.

Of the many attempts made by other Soviet firearm designers to dislodge the AK from its place by creating something better, some were brought on the designer's initiative and some dictated by military brass. In any case, every one of these attempts to replace existing Avtomats was spurred by the desire to improve the accuracy of full-automatic fire. The most recent such assault took root in 1981. Though unsuccessful, it produced some incredible weapons. It was called the "Abakan."

## AN-94

Despite advances in military equipment, precision weapons and robotic weapons systems, small arms remain the main battlefield implement of infantry units. The outcome of the battle and often the entire campaign depends on how well the soldier on the ground is armed.

The Kalashnikov Avtomat is undoubtedly a reliable and effective weapon, but does it meet all requirements of modern warfare?

Despite its legendary reliability, simplicity and ease of manufacturing, the AK is not without faults. It has some drawbacks, the main one being its so-called insufficient accuracy. The Kalashnikov was set up to arm a huge conscripted army in the face of a large-scale military conflict, while reducing the time it took to train an individual soldier.

However, today the situation has changed dramatically. The backbone of any modern military comprises well-trained professionals who need high precision, effective small arms. The standard, mass-produced Kalashnikov Avtomat may not fully meet these requirements.

*AN-94 designer Gennady Nikonov demonstrating his creation.*

The AN-94 Abakan automatic carbine in 5.45mm caliber, created by weapons designer Gennady Nikonov, was intended as an example of modern Russian small arms developed for, per the factory brochure, real professionals. Its designers claim the AN-94 possesses phenomenal accuracy, and at the same time, the gun does not require special training or maintenance.

The AK-74, developed for a 5.45mm cartridge, had high muzzle velocity and flat trajectory, but its characteristics did not fully satisfy the military. The main complaint pertained to the effectiveness of the gun's automatic fire, specifically the inability to strike a target with two- or three-round bursts.

I do not agree with this assertion. Multiple strikes on a single target with an AK-74 is not that uncommon. In fact, I have done it and can still do it with a high degree of consistency. It all depends on the distance to the target. The difficulty starts beyond 200 meters. Even at distance, the training manual has clear instructions on how to adjust your point of aim to maximize effectiveness of automatic fire. For example, aiming at the right knee of the front target would make the first round strike the target at the chest area and the second round go over the left shoulder with a high probability of striking a target behind. I personally have knocked down two staggered humanoid silhouette targets with two-round bursts many times. It's not rocket science, just following the instructions and practice.

However, the Soviet top brass thought that having recruits read manuals was a waste of time and that they are untrainable, so let's make a gun that will do everything for them.

In 1978, a tender was announced to create an Avtomat with fire efficiency twice as high as that of the AK-74. This tender did not produce the desired results, and two years later the Soviets announced a new contest with the codename Abakan.

Among the samples presented for the initial tests were models with a conventional automatic system, with balanced automatics, and samples with a delayed recoil impulse, among which were Nikonov's and Stechkin's Avtomats.

The samples with conventional automatic systems produced results far from desirable. Guns with the balanced automatics improved the accuracy of shooting, but it was still lower than the tender requirements. Only the Avtomats with the delayed

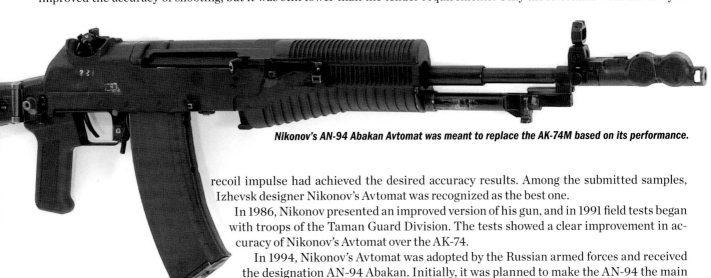

*Nikonov's AN-94 Abakan Avtomat was meant to replace the AK-74M based on its performance.*

recoil impulse had achieved the desired accuracy results. Among the submitted samples, Izhevsk designer Nikonov's Avtomat was recognized as the best one.

In 1986, Nikonov presented an improved version of his gun, and in 1991 field tests began with troops of the Taman Guard Division. The tests showed a clear improvement in accuracy of Nikonov's Avtomat over the AK-74.

In 1994, Nikonov's Avtomat was adopted by the Russian armed forces and received the designation AN-94 Abakan. Initially, it was planned to make the AN-94 the main battlefield weapon of the Russian army and replace obsolete AK-74s. However, this did

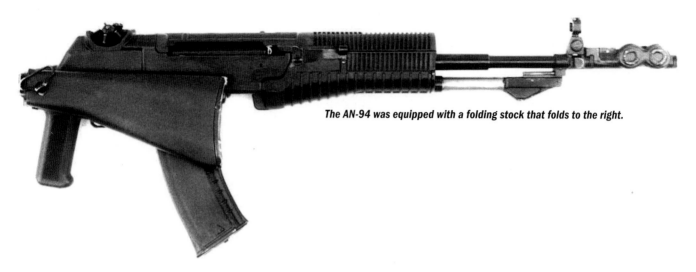

*The AN-94 was equipped with a folding stock that folds to the right.*

not happen. Abakan went into serial production, but that did not make it a mass-produced weapon. The reason was very simple: the Kalashnikov assault rifle was distinguished by its simplicity, reliability and low cost; even schoolchildren could shoot and maintain it during the beginner military preparation classes.

The design of the Abakan was much more complicated, and demanded from the operator a high degree of technical culture. Therefore, the AN-94 became the weapon of elite units of the Russian army and special units of the Ministry of Internal Affairs. At present, the prospects for this weapon are rather vague.

In appearance, the AN-94 Abakan is very similar to the Kalashnikov Avtomat. Its configuration is classic, with the magazine in front of the pistol grip. Instead of the conventional forend, the AN-94 sports the recoil carriage on which the barrel assembly travels during recoil and recycling. Automation works by free rollback of the shooting unit, consisting of a barrel and receiver. The chamber is locked by a rotating bolt.

The AN-94 is designed so that the recoil impact affects the gun after the bullets have left the barrel. The receiver contains a bolt carrier, a bolt and a hammer mechanism. The safety and selector levers are separate, and they are located on the left side of the receiver by the pistol grip. The Abakan's receiver is made of steel and high-impact plastic. The return spring is located at the bottom of the lower receiver, hence the offset of the magazine to the right.

Also in the lower receiver, directly under the barrel, a barrel guide rod serves as an upper carriage for the barrel as it slides back under recoil after each shot. This principle of operation is taken from much bigger guns—field cannons.

The Abakan has three modes of fire: single, automatic and two-shot burst. When the gun is fired in two-shot mode, the rate of fire is 1,800 rounds per minute. In full-auto mode, the first two rounds will go off at 1,800 rpm and automatically switch to 600 rounds per minute, which is the same as the rate of the Kalashnikov. The Abakan is fed from standard AK-74 and/or RPK-74 mags, with a capacity of 30 or 45 rounds. The buttstock is made of impact-resistant plastic and can be folded to the right.

A standard Russian GP-25 or GP-30 under-barrel grenade launcher can be attached to the Abakan. However, the grenade launcher sits lower than on the AK. The standard AK-74M bayonet can also be attached, but in a most unconventional way. It is attached to the side of the barrel, not the bottom like on most military guns in the world. The AN-94 is equipped with an unusual muzzle brake-compensator of a closed type, which resembles a figure eight. The accessory rail is mounted in the traditional space for the Soviet/Russian guns, on the left side of the receiver.

*The AN-94 with GP-30 under-barrel grenade launcher and bayonet.*

The main feature of the AN-94 Abakan Avtomat is its two-shot burst. After the first shot, the shooting unit rolls back and feeds the barrel from the special intermediate chamber. Almost immediately, there is a second shot. Only after that does the bolt carrier strike the rear of the receiver and the shooter feel recoil. This way the recoil does not affect the accuracy of the second shot.

The AN-94 is significantly more accurate in the two-shot mode than the AK-74 firing short, two- to three-round bursts. The accuracy of the new gun in this case is very impressive. At 100 meters a good shooter can put two bullets practically into one hole on the target. However, in the single- and automatic-fire modes, the Abakan has no practical advantage over the AK-74. The practice of shooting with fixed, two-round bursts significantly increases the effectiveness of the gun firing low-impulse high-velocity ammo.

However, the design and disassembly of the Abakan is much more complicated than that of the AK-74. When disassembling, the AN-94 is taken apart into 13 parts, including a cable, a roller and two springs. The muzzle brake-compensator is very effective, but at the same time, it is difficult to clean. Despite the complexity of this gun, the Abakan is reliable and in able hands is an effective and formidable weapon.

*Despite the designers' claims, the AN-94 was far more complicated than a standard AK Avtomat.*

When it came to the ergonomics of the AN-94 Abakan, it was in no way better than the AKs, and subject to the same criticism. Today, the AN-94 Abakan is produced in small batches in Izhevsk. In the end, despite early claims, designers of the AN-94 met only one of the original tender requirements—the automatic fire accuracy improvement. Even then, it was only true for the first two rounds that were fired at the rate of 1,800 rounds per minute before switching to a regular 600 rpm rate when fired continuously. The question of rearmament of the Russian armed forces with the Abakan is no longer on the agenda.

*Russian military conducted rigorous field tests with the AN-94 Abakan.*

## HANDS ON: PERSONAL EXPERIENCE WITH THE AN-94

In 2001, while visiting Izhmash with David Fortier and Marc Krebs, we had the privilege to test fire several new guns. Among those guns, Izhmash was gracious enough to let us handle the AN-94. In fact, this was the first time Izhmash allowed foreigners to handle the AN-94 Abakan . Today it is not such a big deal. Anyone can shoot the Abakan at the Park Patriot near Moscow. However, back then it was a big deal.

It was visibly bigger (longer) and more massive than the AK. Right away I could feel that it was also noticeably heavier. The ergonomics were identical to those of the AK-74. One detail stood out—the mag port. The magazine is inserted into the AN-94 at a slight angle. When inserted, the mag is slanted to the right. Being a right-handed shooter, I found this little detail pretty convenient for both holding the gun and for swapping the magazine. Later I found out that the mag's angle is a necessity rather than a feature. The whole thing became clear when the Izhmash engineer fieldstripped the gun for us. A system of cords and pulleys is so tightly packed into lower part of the receiver that every component is fighting for space.

I fired a series of single shots. I hit everything I aimed at. That was no big surprise, as we were shooting bricks at 100 meters. The recoil from a single shot was slightly softer than that of the AK-74. I switched to the two-shot mode using a thumb safety, which is a departure from the Soviet firearms norm. Another item uncharacteristic of Russian design was the diopter (peephole) rear sight that was set at the angle with only the top leaf on the aim line. You can adjust the elevation by rotating the sight on its axis, exposing other leafs. The two-round mode is where a surprise awaited me. When I pulled the trigger expecting two distinct shots, I heard only one. I also felt much harder recoil than with the 7.62x39mm M43 round.

What I saw was also different. When shooting bricks with single shots, the bricks would just break apart or fall to the ground. Now, they were exploding into a cloud of orange dust. It turns out the two rounds are fired at an extremely high rate of fire (1,800 rpm). The second round went off while the first one was still in the bore. Two spent casings flew out of the ejection port less than six inches apart. Next came full-auto mode. Again, I exploded the brick with my first shots striking it almost simultaneously and the rest of the bullets flying elsewhere as the AN-94 settled in to a regular 600 rpm rate of fire.

*In 2001, during his trip to Izhevsk, the author was the first non-Russian national to shoot the AN-94.*

After all three of us had a go at the Abakan, the time came to see what was inside this beast. The head engineer flipped the lever and the gun came apart into two parts, what we here in the U.S. call the upper and lower receivers. As I looked at the AN-94 innards, I could not help but wonder how this rifle met the reliability and simplicity requirements. Tightly packed cables, sheaves and pulleys suggested that one needed at least an associate's degree to operate this gun. At the same time, it was an

*The AN-94 was adopted for service with Russian armed forces. However, it is produced in very limited quantities and will not replace AKs anytime soon.*

amazing sight. All this complexity inside what appeared to be a combat-ready weapon, and it worked extremely well. Obviously, I could not determine how well the AN-94 Avtomat fared against others in the field, based on my limited experience. Ultimately, I was impressed by the engineering solutions employed in building the AH-94 Abakan, but underwhelmed by its prospects.

One more anecdote: Marc Krebs is somewhat of a mad genius when it comes to understanding even very complicated mechanics on the fly. The Izhmash engineers were very careful not to let us "play" with disassembly of their tightly guarded new gun. Therefore, if there was any disassembly to be done, it was done by the Izhmash personnel. However vigilant they were, it was not vigilant enough. Before anyone could say anything, Marc had removed the gun's unique muzzle brake and was examining it in his hands. When the minders realized what happened, it was too late. They were uncomfortably polite trying to retrieve the component from the clutches of the imperialist. Meanwhile, Krebs proceeded to tell them how the thing worked and what principles were employed. All the Russians had left was to bob their heads in agreement.

Currently, the AN-94 Abakan is in service with special units of the armed forces and the Ministry of Internal Affairs of Russia. A full transition of the army to these weapons is not planned.

## AEK-971, AEK-972 AND AEK-973

Nikonov's AN-94 was not the only impressive gun that came out of the Abakan tender. It was the only gun with delayed recoil impulse, but there were other guns no less impressive and with no less interesting designs. Two others employed the principle of balanced automatics. These were the Garev-Koksharov AEK-971 and Izhevsk AK-107 Avtomats.

As described earlier, in August 1981 the Soviet designers-gunsmiths, within the framework of the experimental design project to "create an automatic rifle that exceeds the effectiveness of the AK-74 by 1.5-2 times," more commonly known by its code name Abakan, began to actively develop advanced models of automatic weapons. When creating a new Avtomat, the main task was to improve the grouping from the continuous automatic fire by 5-10 times, even for inexperienced young soldiers. The new weapon developed under the Abakan project was supposed to preserve all the combat qualities of its predecessors, including reliability and the ability to accept all existing military equipment, and allow attachment of all the standard components (bayonet, grenade launcher and optical devices).

In 1984, twelve Avtomats from leading gunsmiths and designers of the USSR were submitted for the competition. Of the submitted samples, nine projects made it to the test stage, including the 5.45mm Garev-Koksharov Avtomat AEK-971, which was designed with no-recoil, impulse-balanced automatics.

A balanced automatics system is the distinguishing feature of the AEK-971 design. This system incorporates the additional gas piston connected to the counterweight that moves in synch with, but in the opposite direction of, the moving bolt carrier, compensating for the impulses that occur when the bolt group moves and when it strikes in the rear and forward positions. As a result of this balance, the gun designed with this system does not jerk when fired in full-auto mode. Because of the lack of impulses from the bolt carrier strikes and the absence of gun movements when fired, the AEK-971 Avtomat's automatic fire accuracy is improved by 1.5 times when compared to the AK-74, and by two times compared to the AKM.

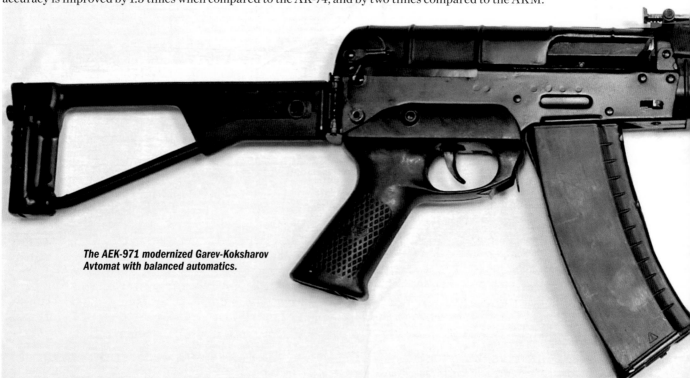

*The AEK-971 modernized Garev-Koksharov Avtomat with balanced automatics.*

The internal components of the AEK-971 include a counterweight (balancer) to counteract the movement of the gun's bolt group.

The AEK-971 is fed from standard AK-74 or RPK-74 magazines. The chamber is locked by the rotating bolt. The folding stock folds to the left. The safety/selector lever is ambidextrous. However, the lever on the left side does not activate the safety, which somewhat reduced its capabilities.

Another distinctive feature of the first model of the AEK-971 was an unusual muzzle device. The basis for the design of this muzzle brake/compensator was a completely new concept of gunfire from stable and unstable positions. In the course of automatic shooting, bursts from unstable positions (standing, on the move, from the knee) the operator used a special lever to reduce the diameter of gas ports on the muzzle brake. When firing from stable positions (prone with rest, sitting with rest, standing with rest) the ports could be open. Changing the diameter of the gas ports regulated gases flowing into the muzzle brake/compensator, which along with the balanced automatics provided for even better stabilization of the gun during automatic fire.

The AEK-971 trigger group mechanism allows single and automatic fire and fixed two-round bursts, which greatly increases the effectiveness the Avtomat's fire, with 1,500 rounds per minute automatic rate.

Subsequently, the construction of the AEK-971 was substantially simplified. At the insistence of representatives of the Ministry of Defense, the adjustable muzzle brake/compensator was replaced with a standard AK-74 muzzle brake that significantly reduced the rate of fire of the AEK-971. The stock and handguards were modified as well.

The upgraded Garev-Koksharov Avtomat showed 15-20 percent better results when firing in full-automatic mode than the AK-74. However, the AEK-971 was inferior to its main rival, Nikonov's AN-94, in accuracy of the second shot when firing in full-auto. However, the AEK-971 showed better accuracy than the AN-94 with long bursts or continuous fire. Nevertheless, the AN-94 was selected as the winner of the Abakan competition.

The AEK-971 story did not end there. In the late 1990s, the Ministry of Defense of the Russian Federation again demanded a weapon with balanced automatics.

In response to the new challenge, firearm designers and engineers at the Kovrov Plant revived and updated the AEK-971 to meet the new Defense Ministry requirements. The modernization included installation of the side mounted accessory rail for attaching optics and a new skeletonized metal stock that folded to the right. Additionally, the engineers did away with two-round fixed burst mode and replaced it with three-round instead. The gun went into serial production.

Based on the serial model of the AEK-971 Avtomat, the following variants were released:

- AEK-972 chambered for the 5.56mm NATO cartridge
- AEK-973 for 7.62x39mm ammunition
- AEK-973C same as the AEK-973 except for a telescopic metal stock

*The AEK was put through rigorous military field testing. The result was very positive.*

Other than the caliber of the ammunition these variants fire, and all the standard changes to the design stemming from it, all of the AEK Avtomats were identical.

The AEK-971 Avtomats were produced in small batches and placed into service with special purpose units of the Ministry of Internal Affairs and other law enforcement agencies. In 2006, the production of military products was completely discontinued at the Kovrov machinebuilding plant. All production was transferred to the Degtyarev Plant (ZiD) in the same city of Kovrov. However, the serial production of the AEK-971-series rifles in ZiD was suspended. The start of production of these guns at the new plant would require a major initial investment that could only be justified by large orders for a new Avtomat. In 2013, the Russian Ministry of Defense decided to develop a new generation of the soldier's individual battlefield equipment complex, the Ratnik (warrior), that included the uniform, individual scalable body armor, electronics and communications equipment and a new automatic rifle. The modernized AEK-971 Avtomat was selected as part of the Ratnik equipment complex, along with the newest AK-12.

*Based on field-test results, the AEK-971 was recommended as part of Russia's new individual soldier's kit, Ratnik, alongside the AK-12.*

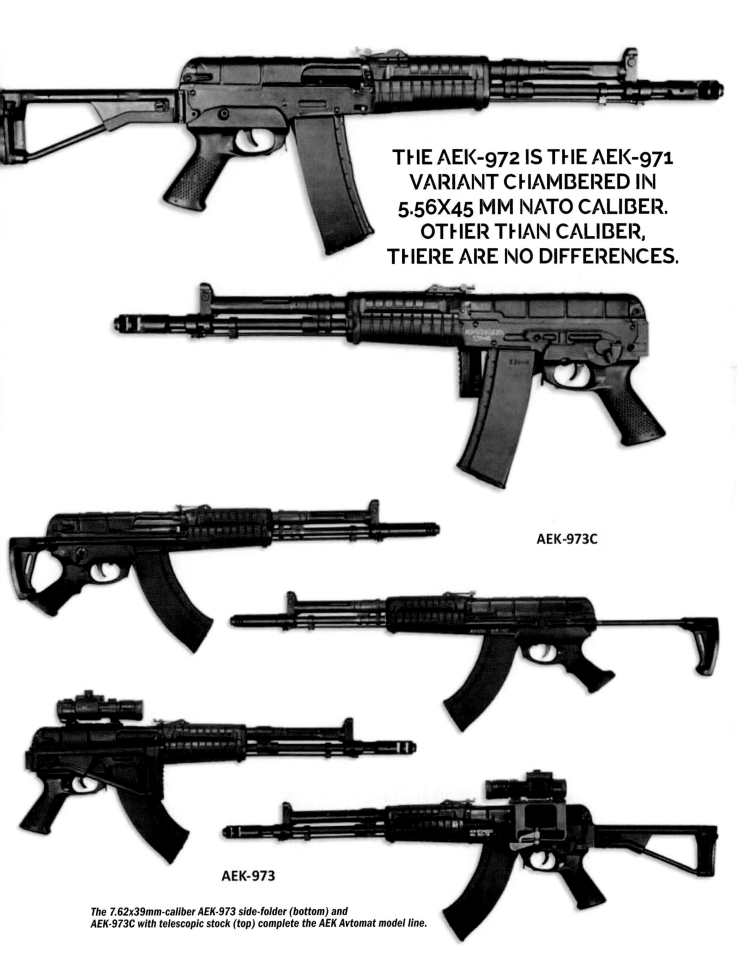

**THE AEK-972 IS THE AEK-971 VARIANT CHAMBERED IN 5.56X45 MM NATO CALIBER. OTHER THAN CALIBER, THERE ARE NO DIFFERENCES.**

AEK-973C

AEK-973

*The 7.62x39mm-caliber AEK-973 side-folder (bottom) and AEK-973C with telescopic stock (top) complete the AEK Avtomat model line.*

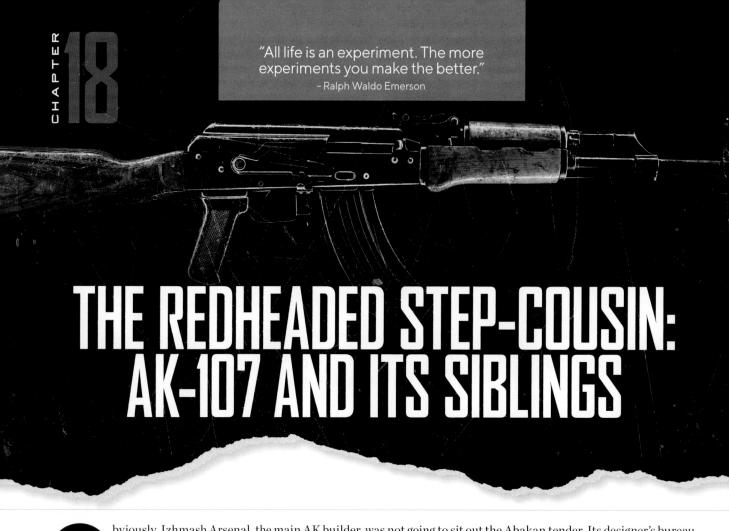

> "All life is an experiment. The more experiments you make the better."
> – Ralph Waldo Emerson

# THE REDHEADED STEP-COUSIN: AK-107 AND ITS SIBLINGS

O bviously, Izhmash Arsenal, the main AK builder, was not going to sit out the Abakan tender. Its designer's bureau, headed at that time by none other than Kalashnikov himself, submitted its own sample, the AK-107 Avtomat. Was it a serious attempt to dislodge the AK-74 from its dominance and, as such, was it the next step in the evolution of the AK?

*The Izhmash's balanced automatics, the AK-107 and AK-108 Avtomats, were added to the AK-100 Series. Despite the name, they are completely new animals.*

**THE AK-107 FOLLOWED THE AK-74M GENERAL CONFIGURATION, INCLUDING THE STOCK FOLDING TO THE LEFT.**

The AK-107, AK-108 and AK-109 Avtomats were developed by Izhmash designers Yuri Alexandrov and Valery Paranin and became part of the "100 series" of Kalashnikov rifles. They were based on the AK-74M (5.45x39mm), AK-101 (5.56x45mm NATO) and AK-103 (7.62x39mm) respectively, and differ from each other only in caliber. The main feature of the new Avtomats was the use of balanced automatics in their design.

The use of such a system provided a significant decrease in the recoil and vibration of the weapon when firing in full-auto mode, which significantly increased the accuracy of the gun. This solution had already been used by Izhmash designers in the experimental Avtomat AL-4 (7.62x39mm) and AL-7 (5.45x39mm), developed in the late 1960s and early 1970s and based on the AKM. However, these Avtomats did not go into production due to a number of serious deficiencies found during the tests. These shortcomings included heavy contamination (powder deposit) of the muzzle brake/compensator, low survivability of several parts and components, excessively loud sound of a shot and spontaneous opening of the top cover during firing.

A similar balanced automatic system was used in the AEK-971 Avtomat, developed at the Kovrov Mechanical Plant. The main feature of AK-107, AK-108 and AK-109 automatics that differentiated them from the earlier models was essentially a modernized design of automation, including an additional gas piston with a counterweight attached to its rod, a synchronizing device located between the balance bar and the bolt carrier, and a number of less significant differences, such as a modified top cover mount on the receiver.

The design of the AK-107 Avtomat is not that different from the conventional AK. It's not very complicated, especially in comparison with guns using the automatic system with movable shooting unit, such as the AN-94. Visually, the AK-107, 108 and 109 are distinguished by a considerably longer gas tube extending to the front, which has an integrated upper handguard and contains the balancing mechanism.

The principle of the balanced automatic system is in absorption of the recoil impulses. The recoil impulse of the gun consists of a combination of impacts that are produced by the firing of the cartridge and movement of components inside the gun. First, the weapon is affected by the shot impulse received with the bolt still locked. After that, the bolt group travels back and strikes the rear of the receiver, creating the next impulse. The last impulse, directly opposite the previous one, arises when the bolt group returns to the forward position and slams into battery.

From the start, the recoil of the AK-107, AK-108 and AK-109 Avtomats was reduced by use of an effective muzzle brake/compensator. Extinguishing the rest of the recoil impulses is a more complicated task. To accomplish that, the system has an additional balancer or counterweight that moves simultaneously with the bolt group in the opposite direction. The masses of the balance bar and the bolt group are equal in this case, and the speed of their movement (due to the synchronizer in the form of a simple gear) is equal but opposite in direction. Thus, the pulses of the balance bar and the bolt group are equal in absolute value, but are opposite in direction, which makes their total impulse equal to zero.

The elements of the moving group, reaching their extreme forward and rear positions during their movement, do not strike fixed elements of the weapon, which would cause the transfer of the impacts to the body of the shooter. The moving elements collide with each other, so that their impulses are mutually suppressed. As a result, when the gun is fired in full-auto mode, it is only a subject to impulse triggered by the shot itself, which in turn, is significantly reduced by the muzzle brake. The lack of recoil increases the accuracy of full-auto bursts and continuous fire. It shows considerable improvement over the conventional AK-74M of approximately 1.5-2 times. The length of cycle is also decreased compared to the "classic" Kalashnikov Avtomats, therefore increasing the rate of automatic fire from 600 rpm to 850–900.

In addition, the design has an original part that excludes the rebound of moving parts of the weapon when they come to the forward-most position. A rotating bolt, similar in construction to the AK-74 bolt, locks the chamber. The design of the AK-107, 108 and 109 Avtomats includes two return springs: the first is placed between the bolt carrier and the back of the receiver, and the second is located between the bolt carrier and the balance bar and is compressed when the bolt is open. The trigger group

The automatic system of the AK-107, 108 and 109 Avtomats is based on the principle of balanced automatics.

is similar to that of conventional AKs, but differs by the presence of an additional mode of firing with fixed 3-round bursts. The safety/selector lever remains unchanged, but has an additional position marked "3" for the 3-round burst mode.

Black plastic furniture with a side-folding stock and iron sights are identical to those on the AK-74M. The side rail for mounting a variety of aiming devices is standard.

Additionally, all the standard AK lugs are provided for attaching a bayonet or grenade launcher. However, there were some changes to the way the top cover installs on the receiver.

The adjustable rear sight is mounted on the top cover at the front. The top cover, in turn, is secured to the upper handguard. The ejection port has a different, smaller form. This is explained by the fact that the moving parts on the AK-107, AK-108 and AK-109 have shorter travel than the conventional AK. The shorter travel is the reason for the rate increase in automatic fire. The new balanced-automatics AKs are fed from the standard AK and/or RPK magazines.

Externally, the AK-107, AK-108 and AK-109 Avtomats are similar to the rest of the AK-100-series guns. However, in their design scheme the automatics principle is a new invention. At the same time, the AK-107, AK-108 and AK-109 are compatible with the conventional AK to the maximum.

Later, in 2011, Izhmash introduced an improved version of the AK-107, featuring a Picatinny rail section on the top cover, allowing quick and convenient installation of collimating, optical or night sights. The traditional open adjustable U-slot rear sight was

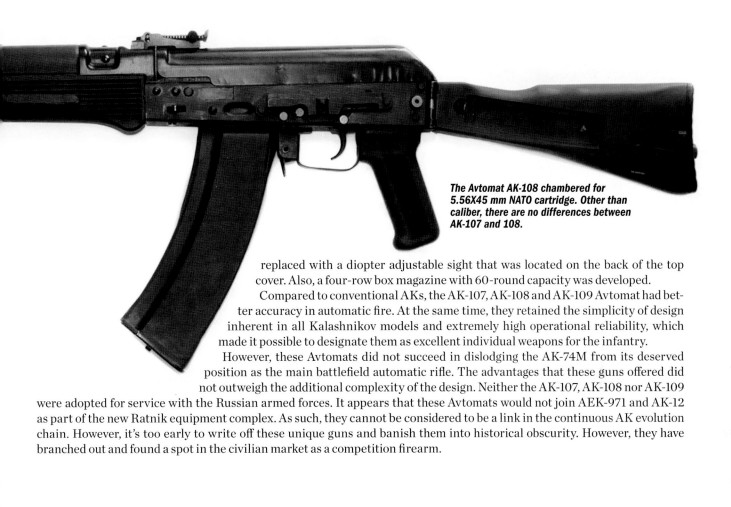

*The Avtomat AK-108 chambered for 5.56X45 mm NATO cartridge. Other than caliber, there are no differences between AK-107 and 108.*

replaced with a diopter adjustable sight that was located on the back of the top cover. Also, a four-row box magazine with 60-round capacity was developed.

Compared to conventional AKs, the AK-107, AK-108 and AK-109 Avtomat had better accuracy in automatic fire. At the same time, they retained the simplicity of design inherent in all Kalashnikov models and extremely high operational reliability, which made it possible to designate them as excellent individual weapons for the infantry.

However, these Avtomats did not succeed in dislodging the AK-74M from its deserved position as the main battlefield automatic rifle. The advantages that these guns offered did not outweigh the additional complexity of the design. Neither the AK-107, AK-108 nor AK-109 were adopted for service with the Russian armed forces. It appears that these Avtomats would not join AEK-971 and AK-12 as part of the new Ratnik equipment complex. As such, they cannot be considered to be a link in the continuous AK evolution chain. However, it's too early to write off these unique guns and banish them into historical obscurity. However, they have branched out and found a spot in the civilian market as a competition firearm.

# THE AK-109 AVTOMAT IS CHAMBERED FOR THE STANDARD 7.62X39MM M43 CARTRIDGE. I CONSIDER THIS MODEL TO BE THE MOST INTRIGUING.

### SAIGA 107: ULTIMATE PRACTICAL SHOOTER'S GUN?

Based on the AK-107, the Saiga MK-107 self-loading carbine developed at the Izhevsk machinebuilding plant (Izhmash, now the Kalashnikov Concern) is a civilian weapon designed primarily for shooters participating in IPSC, IDPA and 3-Gun practical shooting events. This outstanding competition rifle was developed at the request of leading Russian practical shooters. The design of the Saiga carbine MK-107 and its serial version the AK-15 is based on the AK-107 and AK-108 Avtomats with balanced automatic system, respectively.

With the introduction of the balancing mechanism, the recoil felt by the shooter, the vibration of the weapon and the barrel climb are reduced. This is especially important in high-speed shooting. Serial production started at the end of 2015. The serial version, which received the factory index AK-

The new and upgraded version of the AK-107 was introduced in 2011. It had several Picatinny rail sections, better ergonomics and diopter (peephole) rear sight.

15, will differ from the Saiga MK-107 by the choice of calibers (5.56x45 instead of 5.45x39mm), as well as a number of other improvements.

The Saiga self-loading carbines MK-107 and AK-15 use gas-powered automatics, with two gas pistons traveling toward each other into a common chamber located approximately in the middle of the gas tube. The rear gas piston is connected by a rod with the bolt carrier and moves back after the shot, cycling the weapon. The front piston is connected to a long balancer located on the top of the gas chamber above the bolt group, and moves forward.

Synchronization of the opposite movement of the bolt carrier and the balance bar is achieved with a pair of gears located in a special carriage that stays in place. The return spring of the bolt carrier is off center. The receiver is made of stamped steel. The chamber is locked by the rotating bolt with two lugs, which is typical for all AKs.

The sporting carbines have two reciprocating charging handles, one on each side. The top cover has an integrated Picatinny rail section. The cover is integrated with the upper handguard that covers the gas piston and balancer rods. It is completely removable and secured in place with a pin when on the gun, providing a rigid base for mounting optics. The gun's safety is made in the form of a transverse button located above the trigger guard. The design also has

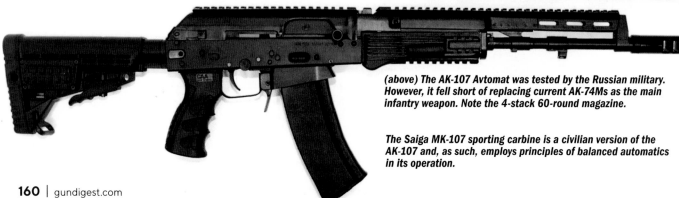

(above) The AK-107 Avtomat was tested by the Russian military. However, it fell short of replacing current AK-74Ms as the main infantry weapon. Note the 4-stack 60-round magazine.

The Saiga MK-107 sporting carbine is a civilian version of the AK-107 and, as such, employs principles of balanced automatics in its operation.

a bolt-hold-open and an extended magazine well, designed to speed up reloading. The carbine's stock is non-foldable and telescopic, similar to the AR-15.

Shooters who recently had a chance to shoot the Saiga MK-107 or AK-15 carbine remark that the rifle lies comfortably in the hands, the kickback is minimal and the barrel climb is almost undetectable. No malfunctions were reported and all targets at ranges up to 200 meters were hit consistently even when firing rapidly.

Of course, the disassembly of sporting carbines is somewhat more complicated than the traditional Kalashnikov Avtomat, but not by much. Anyone familiar with an AK should be able to disassemble the Saiga-107 or AK-15 and put it back together without additional help.

With development of these sporting Kalashnikovs, the AK evolution now has branched into the gun competition circuit with this impressive subspecies. I'm sure these rifles would gain popularity with U.S. shooters, but U.S. sanctions imposed on their maker have made it impossible any time soon.

*The Saiga MK-107 was primarily designed for use by practical shooters. As such, it sports many features popular among competitors.*

*There is no mistake about this gun's intended use when looking at the newest version of the Saiga MK-107.*

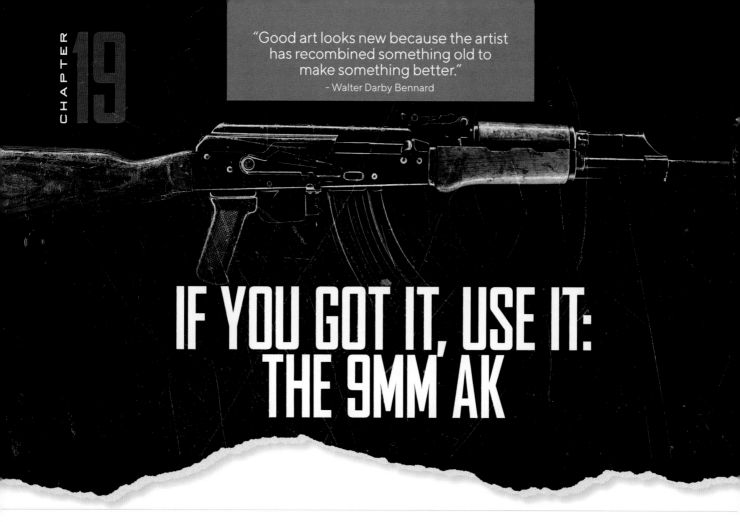

# IF YOU GOT IT, USE IT: THE 9MM AK

It was only natural that the AK Avtomat transcend into the realm of the 9mm subguns. One may say that AK family already had a small Avtomat, the AKSU. However, the AKSU fired the 5.45x39mm, regular AK-74 ammunition that, though being low-impulse ammo, still affected the gun's handling when firing in full-auto mode. Compactness of the AKSU made it suitable for police work, but the ammunition it fired had excessive penetration and bad ricochet characteristics.

In the urban environment, the fire from the Kalashnikov rifle, even from the shortened one, is hazardous to say the least. Nevertheless, the AKS-74U can often be seen carried by the police in Russia. In addition to the fact that the 5.45x39mm bullet retains its energy at sufficiently longer distances and can strike an object or a person far beyond the intended target, this ammunition has several other drawbacks that make the 5.45mm round less than perfect for police operations.

A perpetrator often cannot be neutralized with a single shot. In addition, the bullet,

*Russia produced two 9mm AKs. Both are designated for use with Russian police.*

passing through the criminal's body, can hit an unintended target behind him. Another drawback, as mentioned earlier, is that bullets from the 5.45x39mm cartridges are very susceptible to ricochets, which makes the use of such weapons in confined spaces dangerous. Ammunition loaded with a projectile designed to reduce ricochet did not solve the problems. The only option that would eliminate all these problems was a submachine gun firing a pistol round. In the West, most police units are armored with the H&K MP5 subgun, firing a 9mm pistol round that is more conducive to police action in an urban environment. Today in Russia, we can see that Kalashnikov Avtomats are being gradually replaced by machine pistols or subguns chambered in calibers more suitable for police work.

## BIZON

The fall of the Soviet Union and the onset of a free market economy allowed Russian firearms designers to develop weapons that complied with the requirements of a modern police force, producing many interesting police-specific subguns for pistol ammunition. In Russia, the prevalent pistol cartridge was the 9mm Makarov. Izhevsk Arsenal would not be out-designed. It, too, developed and introduced its own 9mm submachine gun, the Bizon machine pistol, designed by Victor Kalashnikov (son of the AK creator Mikhail Kalashnikov), along with Dmitry Dolganov, Alexey Dragunov (son of the SVD creator Evgeni Dragunov) and S.D. Gorbunov.

This subgun stands out among peers for two reasons. Without a magazine, it is unmistakably an AK. With the magazine, it is not like anything out there. The Bizon's 64-round capacity auger-type magazine separates it from the field.

The submachine gun or machine pistol PP-19 Bizon was designed in the early 1990s at the Izhevsk machine-building plant with the aim of arming the Russian police force with modern, small-sized automatic small arms to replace the AKS-74U.

The emphases in the design of the Bizon subgun were placed on maximum interchangeability of components and assemblies with the AK. Even if the gun from the beginning was a different type of weapon entirely, this was achieved. The PP-19, from its magazine well to the buttstock, is basically the AKSU.

The main visual differences start from the mag well forward. Perhaps the most noticeable feature of the Bizon is its 64-round capacity auger tube-type magazine. It was partially

THE MA-
CHINE PISTOL
PP-19 BIZON
WAS THE
FIRST 9MM
SUBGUN
BASED ON
THE AK.

based on the American Calico pistol magazine. Visually strange, the Bizon's tube magazine is conveniently attached and replaced. The magazine is located under and parallel to the barrel. It makes the gun less bulky and more conducive to concealed carry for secret service and undercover personnel. At the same time, the magazine serves as a handguard, and a comfortable one at that. For convenience of carrying and transportation, the Bizon has a folding stock. The design of the submachine gun allows firing with stock folded. The Bizon is perfectly adapted for use with suppressors. Just like on most modern AKs, there is a side accessory rail for mounting collimator, optical and night sights.

Automation of the PP-19 Bizon sub-machine gun works by a free bolt roll-back. Unlike many other subguns, the Bizon fires from the closed bolt, which improves single-shot accuracy. It has a hammer-type trigger group directly borrowed from the AK-74, along with a safety/selector lever.

*One of the distinct features of the Bizon is the cylindrical auger magazine. Its large capacity compensates for the extra time it takes to load.*

The Bizon is fed from its unique large-capacity auger magazine, which looks like a long cylinder with spiral guides for cartridges inside. The cartridges are placed into the magazine parallel to the gun's axis, with bullets facing forward. The cartridges are fed by a spring that is wound separately. This allows for storage of loaded magazines without winding the spring. When ready for use, the magazine spring is wound using a "butterfly" lever at the front of the magazine. To load the magazine, Cartridges must be fed in one by one. This takes a long time. However, the high capacity and shape allow carrying several of them easily and compensates for the minor inconvenience.

The front sight rests on the gas block/sight block combination. The rear leaf sight is similar to the regular AK sight. It is adjustable and designed for three positions, marked as such, for ranges from 50–150 meters in 50-meter increments.

The PP-19 Bizon definitely has several important advantages for this type of weapon. It has a relatively small length and height, extra-high-capacity magazine, a full-length comfortable folding stock, high firepower, reliable operation in adverse conditions, high accuracy with instinctive shooting, stability when fired with one and two hands in short bursts, above average retention and good controllability, as well as the ability to accept suppressors and aiming devices.

*Author (far left) and Marc Krebs (far right), with Victor Kalashnikov Jr. (second from the right) and his personal photographer, in 2001 during a visit to Izhmash.*

Among its shortcomings, the Bizon has rather considerable weight with loaded magazine, and the balance of the gun shifts as the ammunition is consumed. In general, the PP-19 is an effective and convenient weapon for close quarter combat. It's even more lethal if used with such loads as the 7N31 PBP for 9x19mm Parabellum (Luger) or the 7N25 PBM for 9x18mm Makarov, both armor-piercing projectiles with hardened core.

The following variants exist for the PP-19 Bizon:

• Bizon-1 has a front sight from the SVD rifle, a sectoral rear sight with three positions for 50/100/150 meters, the charging handle on the right and the left-folding stock and a standard brown plastic AKSU pistol grip.

• Bizon-2 is set up for 9x18mm Makarov caliber cartridges. It has an AKSU front sight and AK-100-series black plastic pistol grip. The rest is the same as the Bizon-1.

• Bizon-2B comes equipped with sound suppressor.

• Bizon-2-01 is chambered for the 9x19mm Parabellum (Luger) and has 53-round magazine capacity.

• Bizon-2-02 is chambered for the 9x17mm (Parabellum Kurtz or .380 Auto).

• Bizon-2-03 comes with an integrated silencer and uses the 9x18mm Makarov.

• Bizon-2-04 is a semi-auto-only version for 9x18mm Makarov.

• Bizon-2-05 is a semi-auto-only version in 9x19mm Parabellum (Luger).

• Bizon-2-06 is a semi-auto-only version in 9x17mm (Parabellum Kurtz or .380 Auto).

• Bizon-2-07 is chambered for the 7.62x25mm Tokarev with box-type 32-round capacity magazines.

• Bizon-3 has a diopter (peephole) rear sight, a stock that folds up and over the top cover and the ability to accept a suppressor. The charging handle is located on top of the receiver.

The weight of different variants ranges from 2.7 to 2.9 kgs (from just under 6 up to 6.4 lbs.) without loaded magazine; the loaded mag weighs just over 1 kg (2.2 lbs.). Combined, this makes the Bizon very heavy for a submachine gun by modern standards. The length of the barrel is 225mm to 230mm (8.9-9 inches) depending on the model. The rate of fire is 680 to 750 rounds per minute. Length with the stock unfolded is 690mm (27.2 inches), and with stock folded 460mm (18 inches). The capacity of an auger magazine for the 9x18mm Makarov is 64 rounds, and for 9x19mm Parabellum (Luger) it is 53 cartridges.

Unfortunately, even with all of its advantages, the PP-19 Bizon was shoved to the side. Despite the large capacity magazine, the gun had rather significant weight for the type of weapon it was, so it's not surprising that, based on the Bizon, the PP-19-01 Vityaz (knight) submachine gun became more popular. And, it is the Vityaz to which the Russian police force has pinned its hopes. However, the Vityaz is merely a further development of its ancestor, the Bizon.

**During my trip to Izhevsk in 2001,** along with the AN-94 Abakan Avtomat described earlier, Izhmash personnel allowed us to test the PP-19 Bizon. After fellow gun writer David Fortier had a turn, I had my chance behind the Bizon's trigger. I immediately liked the way the gun felt in my hands. When shouldered, I appreciated the round magazine/handguard. Being thicker than the standard AK lower handguard, it made the gun feel very comfortable in my meaty paws. Also, it provided plenty of options for a grip along its length. I could grip the Bizon close to the mag well, or all the way forward toward the front sight, or anywhere in between. With the stock folded, it presented a compact package without a "banana clip" magazine protruding. However, I could not help but notice the considerable weight of the Bizon fully loaded with 64 rounds of 9mm Makarov ammo. Shooting it was a blast. Lack of appreciable recoil made it almost unfair to hit suspended steel plates at 50 meters. After firing a few rounds in single-shot mode, I lifted the selector lever one notch up and went to town firing short bursts at the targets. The Bizon shot very well without any malfunctions. It behaved as a 9mm subgun should and it was easy to handle. We finished our Bizon testing with Marc Krebs blasting steel plates with a hail of bullets from long bursts, ultimately knocking one of the targets down from the cables from which it was suspended.

*A suppressed Bizon-2B in the hands of a police officer. The PP-19 Bizon was destined to replace the AKSU in service with Russian police.*

## VITYAZ

Though I may have come off as somewhat sentimental about the fate of the PP-19 Bizon subgun, I did it simply out of respect for the gun I once shot and liked. The truth is, the Bizon does deserve admiration from AK enthusiasts and gun lovers at large. In the true spirit of its evolution as an AK subspecies, it evolved into something better and more exciting—the PP-19-01 Vityaz. Let's meet the main contender to replace the AKS-74U for the Russian National Police.

As we can clearly see from the model designation PP-19-01, the Vityaz submachine gun is the further development of the PP-19 Bizon subgun, famous only due to its unusual magazine. In order to minimize the cost of production, both guns were based on a shorter version of the Kalashnikov Avtomat, the AKS-74U. According to the manufacturer, the interchangeability of parts between these machine pistols and the AK is approximately 70 percent. Truthfully, 70 percent is farfetched. Nevertheless, there are many common parts and assemblies. This becomes obvious when looking at the Vityaz.

Immediately conspicuous are the receiver, the folding stock and the fire controls that are similar or identical to those of the AK. In addition, the trigger group is borrowed directly from the AKS-74U. This shows that the designers worked hard on the interchangeability between the subguns and the conventional AK. Naturally, it was impossible to leave everything unchanged, due to the use of a pistol cartridge, which has less energy than a 5.45x39 round.

The PP-19-01 Vityaz submachine gun externally looks a lot like the AKSU, with the same controls layout, same or similar furniture, even the sights are similar to those of the AK-100 series. Visually, perhaps the only thing that stands out is the gun's magazine and the mag well. This standard-configuration Vityaz received the designation of Version 10. In addition to the stan-

THE MACHINE PISTOL
PP-19-01 VITYAZ IS
THE FURTHER DEVELOP-
MENT OF THE PP-19 BIZON.
IT HAS A MORE TRADITION-
AL CONFIGURATION.

The Vityaz is in service with Russian anti-terrorism units that operate in the urban environment.

Originally, the Vityaz had a side rail for mounting optics that was typical for the AK. The newer model sports a full-length Picatinny rail on top and smaller rail sections on the handguards, for mounting flashlights and laser designators.

735mm

705mm

*It is clearly evident that the PP-19-01 Vityaz is based on the gun it is replacing, the AKSU.*

dard version, there is an improved, more advanced Version 20. This version of Vityaz has several modern features that make it more convenient to operate. The Version 20 has a charging handle on the left, which is more convenient for the machine pistol. The new and improved version of the Vityaz has an ambidextrous safety/selector lever. And, of course, there is a section of Picatinny rail mounted on the hinged top cover. The cost to produce the improved Version 20 is only marginally higher than the standard Version 10. Both versions use black plastic handguards, standard for the AK-100 series. This allows Vityaz shooters to use standard AK handguard replacement accessories for additional mounting options.

The PP-19-01 Vityaz submachine gun is chambered in 9x19mm Parabellum (Luger). It's not very finicky when it comes to ammunition and eats everything it is fed no matter the manufacturer, load, material or type of ammo. Unlike the Bizon, with its unique auger cylindrical magazine, the Vityaz is fed from the conventional, proprietary two-row box-type 30-round magazine. The aftermarket mags are already available from the Russian maker PufGun. The gun comes from the manufacturer with two magazines and a mag clip that allows the magazines to be coupled together. It's an interesting accessory, but it allows a rapid switch between different types of ammo if the situation requires it.

The weight of the Vityaz without magazine is just about 3 kg (6.6 lbs.). The length is 460mm (18 inches) with stock folded and 698mm (27 inches) with stock deployed. The weight and the length are considerable for the type of weapon the Vityaz represents. We have the AK heritage to blame for that. The length of the barrel is 230mm (9 inches). Effective range of fire is up to 200 meters, but the greatest efficiency is achieved within 100 meters. The rate of full-auto fire of the Vityaz subgun is 750 rounds per minute.

As mentioned, the PP-19-01 Vityaz submachine gun is based on the AKSU, with supposedly 70 percent interchangeability of parts, components and assemblies. However, the most important thing that cannot be directly borrowed from the AK design is the automatic system of operation, due to the weaker pistol cartridge used in the Vityaz. The Vityaz has an automatic system that employs a free bolt travel principle. At the same time, it fires from the closed bolt. The rate of fire is relatively even; if delays occur, it's only due to substandard quality of the ammunition. In the end, the PP-19-01 Vityaz is a solid and reliable weapon. The overall quality of the gun itself is on the level with other Russian-made firearms, which is very good, but not perfect. In my opinion, to expect perfection from a workhorse gun is unrealistic. There is always something that can be improved.

The Vityaz has been in serial production for some time now and is already adopted for service and being used by Interior Ministry units. It appears that it became what its designers intended it to be—the main firearm for urban policing. However, despite the fact that the weapon is already in use, there is no guarantee that tomorrow something better will not come along and police agencies will decide to replace the PP-19-01 Vityaz with something else.

As I look at the Vityaz, I can't help but think what a great semi-automatic civilian shooter this gun would make.

## SAIGA-9

Apparently, I was not the only one daydreaming about a civilian version of the Vityaz subgun. Kalashnikov Concern engineers had the same idea, and they turned it into reality by way of the Saiga-9 carbine.

The semi-automatic Saiga-9 is based on the PP-19-01 Vityaz submachine gun, which in turn was based on the design of the AK family of Avtomats. And as such, the Saiga-9 had to be included in this book. The Saiga-9 carbine in 9x19mm caliber is produced by the Izhevsk machine-building plant (Izhmash), currently part of the Kalashnikov Concern. It was designed for the civilian commercial weapon market as a hunting and sporting gun. In Russia, the Saiga-9 with its 16-inch barrel falls into long-barreled hunting rifles and is sold under the appropriate license for this type of gun. It does not preclude the Saiga-9 from being used as a self-defense weapon or a rifle for practical shooting competition.

Just like the Vityaz, the Saiga operates on the principle of a free traveling bolt and fires from the closed bolt. The fire controls permit only semi-automatic fire. A special mechanism is installed that prohibits firing the gun with stock folded. The presence of the AK-style "gas tube" serves two functions. It's a guide for the bolt group and a support for the upper handguard. The front and rear sights are similar to those of the AK-100-series shortened rifles. At the top of the receiver, there is a Picatinny rail section for mounting various collimator or optical sights. The Saiga-9 comes with an AK-74 metal skeletonized folding stock as standard equipment. Its 16-inch barrel is topped with a removable flash hider. The Saiga-9 carbine is fed from the standard two-row box-type detachable Vityaz magazine. And, just like the Vityaz submachine gun, the Saiga is equipped with a mag well.

*The PP-19-01 Vityaz is becoming the main weapon for police operations in Russia.*

*The semi-automatic 9x19mm Saiga-9 carbine is a civilian version of the PP-19-01 Vityaz.*

JUST LIKE THE VITYAZ, THE SAIGA OPERATES ON THE PRINCIPLE OF A FREE-TRAVELING BOLT, AND IT FIRES FROM THE CLOSED BOLT. THE FIRE CONTROLS PERMIT ONLY SEMI-AUTO FIRE. A SPECIAL MECHANISM IS INSTALLED THAT PROHIBITS FIRING THE GUN WITH THE STOCK FOLDED.

The Saiga's plastic lower handguard has three Picatinny rail sections for installing accessories. The gun's pistol grip is more ergonomic than standard AK grips. The safety/selector lever is a direct transfer from the AK design. The charging handle is also on the right side, just like the AK handle that we all know and love. The ergonomics of the Saiga-9 carbine are similar to those of the AK Avtomat and leave much to be desired. Sometimes, good ergonomics and convenience in handling, with regard to a self-protection or competition carbine, take precedence over the AK's infamous super reliability. In this case, Saiga-9 civilian owners have complete and total freedom to accessorize their carbines to their liking. The market is saturated with AK accessories. Luckily for them, the Saiga-9 can accept most of the AK accessories.

Had a civilian Saiga-9 variant made it stateside, it would have been a huge success for Izhmash and the Kalashnikov Concern. The U.S. market has been ready for a viable AK variant in 9x19mm caliber.

## AMERICAN KR-9

It was all set, the Kalashnikov Concern appointed CAA (Command Arms & Accessories) as its exclusive importer to the U.S. The announcement was made at SHOT Show 2014 in Las Vegas. Shortly after, it was announced that the Kalashnikov Concern and CAA would form a joint venture called Kalashnikov USA to make AKs and other firearms in the U.S. They did, and announced the move at SHOT Show 2015. The future for U.S. AK nuts was looking bright, until the Kalashnikov Concern, with all of its holdings including Izhmash, made the U.S. sanctioned entities list.

At that point, all of the Kalashnikov Concern's activities came to a screeching halt. Imports, investments, etc., were gone, along with orders for 140,000 Saiga rifles and shotguns annually and any hope of something new from Izhmash ever hitting our shores, including the Saiga-9.

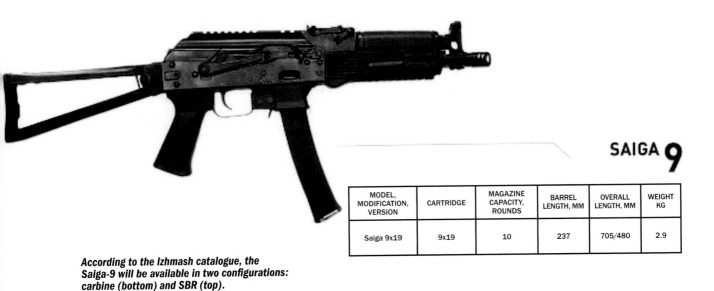

| MODEL, MODIFICATION, VERSION | CARTRIDGE | MAGAZINE CAPACITY, ROUNDS | BARREL LENGTH, MM | OVERALL LENGTH, MM | WEIGHT KG |
|---|---|---|---|---|---|
| Saiga 9x19 | 9x19 | 10 | 237 | 705/480 | 2.9 |

SAIGA 9

*According to the Izhmash catalogue, the Saiga-9 will be available in two configurations: carbine (bottom) and SBR (top).*

| MODEL, MODIFICATION, VERSION | CARTRIDGE | MAGAZINE CAPACITY, ROUNDS | BARREL LENGTH, MM | OVERALL LENGTH, MM | WEIGHT KG |
|---|---|---|---|---|---|
| Saiga 9x19 ver. 02 | 9x19 | 10 | 367 | 827/589 | 3.0 |

SAIGA 9 VER. 02

But just as it was all unfolding, a glimmer of hope manifested itself in the Kalashnikov USA American-built KR-9 9x19mm carbine. It was introduced to the American public at SHOT Show 2016. The Kalashnikov USA booth had three versions of the U.S.-built Saiga-9 clone, the KR-9. The gun came in three configurations: the exact copy of the Saiga-9 carbine with 16-inch barrel, the pistol with short barrel and no stock, and perhaps the most interesting—the short barrel rifle (SBR).

Despite all the excitement that the KR-9 created, it came short of everyone's expectations. At SHOT Show in 2017, Kalashnikov USA displayed the same three versions of the KR-9 gun in the same case, with no clear picture for the 9mm AK's prospects. The KR-9 had grown a single horn and, despite its black furniture, turned into a shiny white mystical creature. Everyone knows it's out there, but no one has ever seen one. Maybe the reasons that keep the KR-9 from hitting the market will be resolved sometime in the future and our hopes of owning an AK in 9mm will be realized.

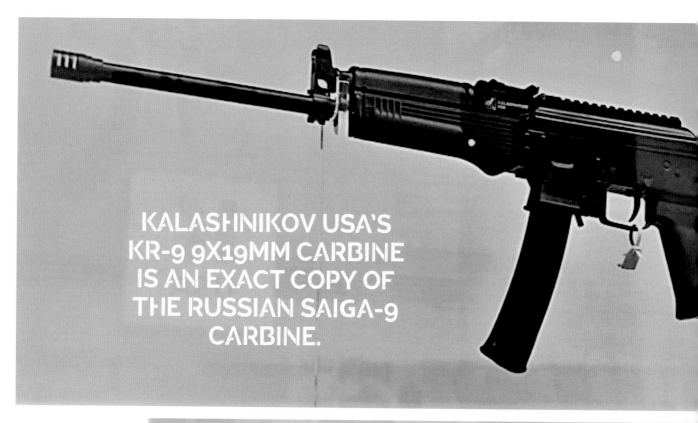

KALASHNIKOV USA'S
KR-9 9X19MM CARBINE
IS AN EXACT COPY OF
THE RUSSIAN SAIGA-9
CARBINE.

THE KR-9
COMES IN THREE
CONFIGURATIONS,
INCLUDING THIS
PISTOL.

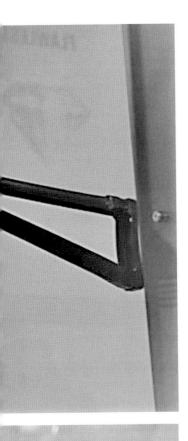

**THE MOST INTRIGUING CONFIGURATION OF THE U.S.-MADE KR-9 IS AN SBR.**

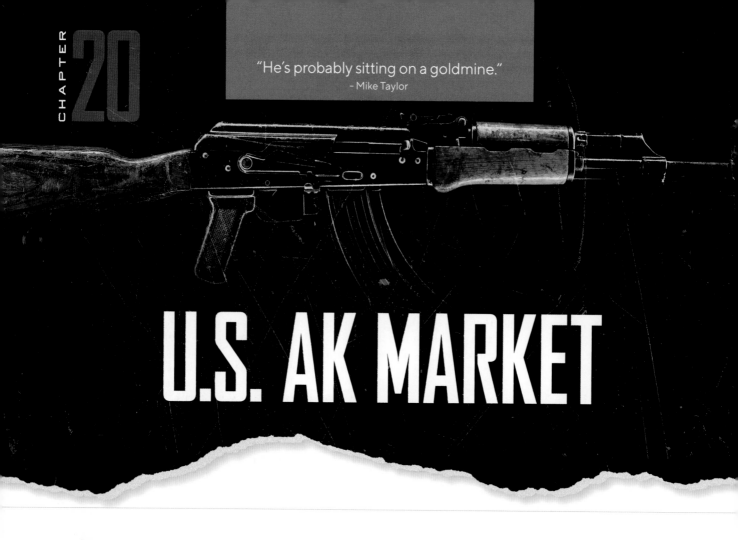

## CHAPTER 20

> "He's probably sitting on a goldmine."
> – Mike Taylor

# U.S. AK MARKET

**A**s we look at the AKs of old compared to what they are now, it is apparent that evolution is at work. Today's AKs are not what your father carried. Nevertheless, improvements have been applied to modern AK rifles. In all cases, these changes were driven by either the ambitions of arms designers or the end users. No matter how powerful the military or how ambitious the manufacturer may have been, nothing influenced the AK like the most powerful end user—the commercial civilian market. Not bound by bureaucratic restrictions, and with obligations to no one but themselves, private AK owners can do anything to their rifle to improve ergonomics and ultimately performance.

There is no doubt that the world's largest commercial AK market is the U.S. The AKs that one can find here are represented by a wide spectrum of variants, from the first obscure imports, like Galil, Valmet and the Chinese Type 56 variants, to today's

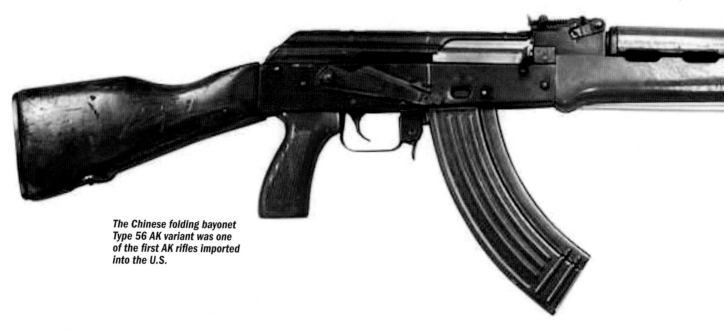

*The Chinese folding bayonet Type 56 AK variant was one of the first AK rifles imported into the U.S.*

modern versions, from Beryls to the U.S.-made tactical carbines. The U.S. AK market is ruled by a true free market economy and its basic principle of survival of the fittest. As such, it addresses the demand of a wide range of customers. Some prefer the classic AK design and layout, others want the modern rifle with all it has to offer.

What can one expect to encounter in the United States in the way of AKs? The answer is, just about anything. The U.S. AK explosion we experienced a few years back has subsided a bit due to the U.S. sanctions against Russia and a drop in imports from traditional AK suppliers like Romania and Bulgaria. However, U.S. manufacturers have stepped up to the plate and continue to produce Kalashnikov rifles for us, thus feeding the need.

There are AK enthusiasts, like myself, who have been at the AK game for a long time and accumulated large and historically correct collections. But, an overwhelming majority of AK shooters do not care about a correct number of rivets and dimples on their AK. They just want a gun that shoots every time they pull the trigger. Most of today's AK owners get their rifles from commercially available stock, imported or domestic. The modern AK ceased to be an exotic rifle that must be kept original and retain its distinct look. Today, to the modern shooter, the AK is a platform on which to build a functioning and modular rifle, pretty much the same as the AR. So, most of the AKs sold today wind up being built into something else, by the owners or by professional gunsmiths.

There are several categories of AK rifles available in the U.S. today: collector-grade AKs, imported AKs, domestically built AKs, domestically converted AKs from imported sporting rifles, and parts kit-built rifles.

The collector-grade AKs are the rifles that were imported into the United States years ago and have since been banned from importation. Some of the kit guns built by reputable gunsmiths are also collectable, based on the origin and value of the kit. This category would include the Chinese-made Norinco Type 56 (AKS47S) and its variants, the PolyTec Legend as the closest thing to the original Soviet milled receiver AK-47 model, and early import Egyptian MAADI as the closest copy to the original Soviet AKM rifle.

There are of course thousands of rifles that have been built by premier gunsmiths, like Marc Krebs, Richard Parker or Ted Marshall, to mimic the original Soviet rifle using Soviet parts kits that were available at one time from several distributors. Expect to drop close to a couple thousand dollars for one of these.

The imported AK category deals with complete AK rifles imported from various countries. The country of origin, model, configuration and quality of these rifles has fluctuated. One constant was the low price compared to specialty built rifles. These rifles have gained their immense popularity with shooters because of their availability and low price. One could walk into any sporting goods store and walk away with a Romanian WASR-10 or Egyptian MAADI. The quality of fit and finish of these guns was not on par with what you would expect from a new out-of-the-box gun. However, the $300-$500 price tag and ability to modify the AK rifle overcame the small imperfections.

Today, imported guns are of much better quality and finish. Most of the rifles that come in to the States have to comply with the firearms import regulations and in most cases have to be "finished" or turned into more sellable condition by an American importer here in compliance with the BATFE 922r regulation. Several rifles were imported at one time or other and/or are still being imported and available on the U.S. market today.

## CHINESE MAK-90

The Chinese MAK-90 is probably the first mass-imported, economically priced AK that hit this shore after the 1989 assault rifle import restrictions were introduced. Essentially, the MAK-90 was a civilian version of the famous Chinese Type 56 rifle with

*The commercial version of the Chinese Type 56, the MAK-90, equipped to comply with import restrictions, was one of the most popular imported AKs at one point.*

several "evil" features removed. The model designation MAK-90 stands for Modified AK-1990. This rifle lacked muzzle threads and bayonet lug, it was semi-automatic only and came with an elaborate thumbhole sporterized stock. Other than that, the MAK-90 was a Chinese factory-built AK exported from China in 1990-94 by Norinco and PolyTec. MAK-90s were mainly chambered in 7.62x39mm, with a fair number of rifles imported in .223. At that time, the MAK-90 rifle could be had for under $200. Since these rifles are no longer imported, if you are lucky enough to find a MAK-90 you should expect to pay several times that price.

## EGYPTIAN MAADI

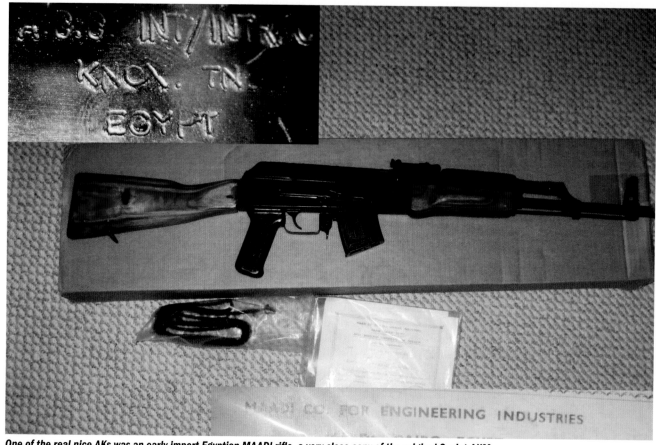

*One of the real nice AKs was an early import Egyptian MAADI rifle, a very close copy of the original Soviet AKM.*

The Egyptian MAADI should not be mistaken for early import rifles. These rifles came in sporting configuration with thumbhole stock, machined bayonet lug and non-threaded barrel. The overall quality of these rifles was not on par with their early import MAADI siblings. There are no more AK rifles imported from Egypt.

*The Romanian Romak 1 in 7.62x39mm and Romak 2 in 5.45x39mm calibers were widely available in just about every gun store.*

## ROMANIAN ROMAK

Romanian Romak 1 and 2 series rifles were imported during the Clinton-era Assault Rifle Ban of 1994. Like the MAK-90 and MAADI rifles, the Romak guns were based on Romanian military AKM-style stamped receiver rifles and were stripped of all the "evil" features, such as full automatic rate of fire and bayonet lug. Additionally, the muzzle nut was installed and welded in place to hide the threads, and it had an elaborate thumbhole sporting stock. Overall, the Romak-series rifles had nice finish and beautiful light laminate wood furniture. The sporting stock was reminiscent of the Soviet Dragunov sniper rifle, the infamous SVD. The same stocks were installed on the Romanian version of sniper rifles, the Romak 3 a.k.a. FPK or later PSL. The Romak rifles came chambered in two main AK calibers; the Romak 1 in 7.62x39mm, and Romak 2 or SAR-2 in 5.45x39mm.

There were a couple of subtle differences between the two guns. The Romak 2 had a distinct bulky front sight block and elongated bolt carrier charging handle. At that time, there was a plethora of Romak rifles in every sporting goods store and they could be had for under $300.

*(above) The Romak gave way to another Romanian mass import, the GP WASR-10 that is still a popular rifle today.*

*(left) The pre-ban FEG SA-85M was one of the nicest AK variants that was imported. It was distinguishable by its light color solid wood furniture.*

## HUNGARIAN FEG SA-85M

In 1986, Kassnar Imports in Harrisburg, PA, imported 7,000 AKM-type semi-automatic underfolding and fixed-stock Kalashnikovs from Hungary. The original pre–1994 ban Kassnar FEG (Femaru Fegyvar es Gepgyar in Budapest) SA-85M AKM is a civilian version of the Hungarian military AK63 AKM rifle.

*The other import from Hungary was the coveted and perhaps most unique AK variant, the AMD-65. It is easily recognized by its metal lower handguard, lack of upper and "crotch" folding stock.*

## HUNGARIAN AMD-65

Chambered in 7.62x39mm, this short, 12.6-inch-barrel rifle has the same front grip as the AKM-63. A side-folding wire stock is fitted to make it more maneuverable in confined spaces, such as armored vehicles and tanks. The shorter sight radius and barrel make this a less accurate rifle than the AKM-63, but the overall handiness offsets the loss in accuracy.

*Polish AKM (bottom) and AKMS (top) rifle are considered to be the closest copy of the original Soviet AKM rifle.*

*The Tantal rifle is Poland's take on the 5.45x39mm-chambered AK. The Tantal rifle is a departure from the traditional Soviet copies.*

## POLISH TANTAL

The Tantal is based on the Polish military Tantal WZ88 rifle chambered in 5.45x39mm. The commercial or civilian version of the Tantal rifle has been imported by Century Arms in the past. It is a slight departure from the traditional looks and function of the Soviet AK-74.

The military Tantal is distinctive in that it features three-round burst capability in addition to the usual semi-automatic, single-shot and full-auto capabilities. The commercial version that was imported into the U.S. obviously lacked the full-auto and three-round burst feature. The Tantal also had a unique selector switch on the left side of the receiver that could be operated by the shooter's thumb. Most of the U.S. models had a wire folding stock that bolted to the rear trunnion in place of the standard fixed one. It is fitted with a distinctive muzzle brake with grenade-launcher capability. The Tantal also came with a clip-on bipod. A specific saddle for it was pressed on the barrel. It also had Bakelite handguards. The supply of Tantals has gone dry, although there are some for sale in cyber space.

## ROMANIAN GP WASR-10

The Romanian WASR (Wassenaar Arrangement Semi-automatic Rifles) series consists of sporterized versions of the Romanian military PM model 1963 rifle that were built with export in mind. The PM model 63 itself is a close copy of Soviet AKM. These rifles have been imported into the U.S. for quite some time. The WASR series rifles can be easily differentiated from the earlier imported Romak or SAR guns by lack of "dimples" on the stamped receiver at the magazine well. They were dropped in favor of internal guides for ease and lower cost of production. The imported version of the WASR is intended to accept single-stack magazines. The rifles feature hard chrome-lined barrels,

*With significant reduction in imports of AKs to the U.S., the Serbian N-PAP rifle became a popular Kalashnikov variant.*

side-mount scope rail and non-laminate wood furniture with laminate wood stocks.

Before WASRs hit store shelves, Century at its factory modified these rifles to appeal to potential AK buyers. All of the modifications have to comply with Title 18, Chapter 44, Section 922(r) of the United States Code. The mods would include installation of U.S.-made gas pistons, fire control groups, pistol grips and stock.

## SERBIAN ZASTAVA N-PAP

The Serbian Zastava PAP rifle is based on the M70 Yugoslavian Kalashnikov variant. Today, Century Arms imports the sporterized version of the Serbian M70 rifle that has been reconfigured to comply with the U.S. firearms import laws. The new N-PAP M70 rifle sold by Century saw several shooter-friendly modifications compared to its military sibling. The new gun is built on a lighter, straight-cut 1mm receiver, double-stack bolt and AKM-type trunnion and side optic mounting rail. Although the gun retains the look of the Yugoslavian M70 rifle, at the same time it has been brought closer to the typical AKM variant.

The new N-PAP M70 is a much nicer rifle compared to the WASR guns. There is no all-around crudeness, the finish is smooth but not shiny coupled with light solid wood furniture. The PAP M70 can easily be differentiated from other AK rifles by the three cooling slots on the handguards, the light-colored teak furniture, different fixed stock attachment with black rubber butt plate and AK-47–style front sight. Likewise, the barrel is not chrome-lined, making it more accurate than a standard AKM, but at the cost of increased susceptibility to corrosion. Century Arms performs all the necessary modifications to the PAP rifles that are required by the U.S. government before rifles are sold. All of the N-PAPs are chambered in 7.62x39mm caliber. The underfolding stock model M70 AB is also offered by Century.

## POLISH RADOM 47

The Polish Radom 47 is a commercial version of the Polish military PMKM rifle, imported into the U.S. by I.O., Inc. It is chambered in 7.62x39mm and based on the gun that is the closest copy of the Soviet AKM rifle. It has a stamped-steel receiver and comes with either laminated wood or synthetic stock set and slanted compensator. It is the highest quality imported AK one can get today. Just like Century with GP WASRs and N-PAPs, to comply with 922r regulations I.O., Inc., converts the Radom 47s into military configuration at their factory in Palm Bay, FL.

*The most interesting AK variant imported today is the commercial version of the current Polish armed forces Beryl rifle, the Archer.*

## POLISH ARCHER (BERYL)

The Polish Beryl Archer is a commercial version of the current Polish military Beryl. This highly sought after rifle is now imported by I.O., Inc. It is made in Radom, Poland, featuring a hammer-forged barrel, and the integrated bolt hold-open thumb safety lever on the left side of the receiver. It's chambered in the 5.56 NATO round and comes with a fixed polymer stock that can be swapped for the original Polish telescopic stock that is included in the package. Also included is the removable top rail for installing optical sights.

Just like the Radom 47, I.O., Inc., converts these to be fully 922r compliant. It is fair to expect a much higher price compared to other mass-imported rifles. Ultimately, I believe the high price tag prevented these NATO-spec AKs from becoming a popular variant here in the U.S.

## BULGARIAN SAM7

Bulgarian SAM7-series rifles are built by the famed Arsenal factory in Bulgaria and imported into the U.S. by Arsenal USA, Las Vegas, NV. The SAM7 represents a merger between the milled-receiver AK-47 and the more modern AK-100–series of the guns. The robust milled receiver guaranties legendary AK-47 reliability, and the factory chrome-lined barrel assures the rifle's high pedigree. The rest of the components are directly borrowed from the Russian-designed AK-100 series, with 90-degree gas block and AK-74–style muzzle brake.

These rifles are finished at Arsenal USA's factory in Las Vegas and come in several configurations with fixed, side-folding and underfolding stocks. As a rule, SAM7 rifles come with polymer furniture in several colors, but customers can also get a quad rail handguard. All SAM7s come chambered in the original 7.62x39mm caliber.

## BULGARIAN SLR

Bulgarian SLR series rifles are based on the AK-74 family and AK-100–series rifles and may be the closest variant to the Russian military AK rifles. Built on stamped receivers, these rifles come with chrome-lined barrels. Once again, the finishing before the guns hit the stores is done at the Arsenal USA Las Vegas facility. The SLR rifles also come in a variety of configurations, with choice of furniture and stock options. They also come in all three calibers. The SLR-107 is chambered in 7.62x39mm, the SLR-104 in 5.45x39mm and SLR-106 in 5.56x45 mm NATO (.223 Remington). The finish of SLR rifles is the typical Russian modern military hard enamel. It gives the gun a smooth and finished look and feel.

Unlike the PAPs and WASRs, AK enthusiasts should expect to pay more for both the SAM7 and SLR rifles. However, considering the quality of these rifles and overall finish of the product, the higher price is justified.

## DOMESTICALLY CONVERTED AKs

This particular category of AKs has shrunk significantly lately, with both suppliers of sporting AKs on the U.S. sanctioned entities list. However, it is worth talking about these rifles, as considerable numbers were imported into the U.S. prior to the sanctions.

Until recently, Kalashnikov Concern, through its intermediary Kalashnikov USA, imported around 140,000–200,000 sporting/hunting Saiga carbines. The other Russian arsenal, Molot, produced its own line of sporting rifles based on the famed Kalashnikov RPK machine gun. These rifles are called Vepr and still are imported into the U.S. by Sporting Supply International (SSI) out of California, among others, and since 2016 by Arsenal USA of Las Vegas exclusively. Both the Kalashnikov Concern and Molot are now sanctioned by the U.S., and there are no imports from these companies coming in to the United States.

These rifles came into the U.S. in their sporting configuration with hunting "Monte Carlo" or thumbhole stocks and sporterized furniture. They lack any of the features that would categorize them under U.S. firearms laws as "assault rifles." Both Saiga and Vepr are semi-automatic rifles; they can only accept a special 5- or 10-round factory magazine due to the missing bullet ramp. One positive feature that the Saiga and Vepr rifles came in with is the military grade chrome-lined barrel, unlike the same model designated for Europe where the laws require the barrel of a hunting rifle to have a different twist rate to drastically reduce the gun's range.

Several companies in the past would convert these rifles to the military configuration. One of the first companies to do so was Krebs Custom. Krebs would take a stock Saiga sporting rifle and turn it into a close copy of original Russian AK-74 or AK-103. In fact, the model designation was the Krebs Custom AK-103, with the slightly shorter version called AK-103K. The quality of Krebs' AK rifles was impeccable. The finish was as close as you could get to the original factory finish. They look and work great. Krebs Custom has since stopped making these AK clone conversions in favor of more drastically modified rifles of their own design. I assume that there are some floating out there on the Internet and can be bought at a premium. I certainly will not sell mine any time soon.

The other company that was converting sporting Saiga rifles into military configuration was Arsenal USA. They'll continue to do so as long as the supply of Saiga rifles lasts. Arsenal made two main models, the SGL21 chambered in 7.62x39mm and the SGL31 in 5.45x39mm. Both models had several versions with side folding stocks and other-than-black furniture. The SGL gun was the closest thing one could get to the original Russian-built AK-74 or AK-74M and AK-103. All Arsenal SGL rifles came

*This early Krebs Custom Russian Saiga sporter was converted into an AK-103.*

out looking like the original Russian guns. The overall quality was better than just good. They were not quite as refined as the Krebs rifles, but certainly better than most. One can still order an SGL from Arsenal USA or its distributor K-Var Corp., but the supplies will not last for long, as the Kalashnikov Concern was barred from importing its products to the USA in 2014. As such, get them while they last or pay a premium later.

As a collector, I had to have these converted rifles for my collection. As a shooter, I also appreciate the smoothness of operation of these guns and the grace with which they fire every round.

## DOMESTICALLY BUILT AKs

Rising demand, constant disruption in supply of imported guns and simplicity of the AK design led to several companies launching domestic production of AKs here in the U.S. It was a baby-step process at first, with some locally built parts and some sourced from overseas, Romania mainly. Then, the appropriate investments were made in castings and the end result is the American-built AK.

Now there are many companies that build AKs here in the U.S. The introduction of a locally made stamped receiver, followed by a milled one as well, made it possible. NoDak Spud® is the company that took the lead in making AK receivers, putting many firearm manufacturers large and small in the AK-making business. Although many companies claim to be building American AK rifles, often the gun's receiver and the barrel are the only two American-built parts, the rest is from somewhere else. The availability of parts kits, spurred by significant influx of those a few years back, and AK parts in general, makes it possible to launch the AK assembling business. Therefore, there are many AKs out there that were built on the Bulgarian, Romanian, Polish, Hungarian and even Russian parts kits that were available one time or another.

Two companies that come to mind that build AKs "from scratch" are Century Arms and I.O., Inc., with Century being the larger of the two. Both companies are also importers of AKs and all things firearms-related. Hence, there is no shortage in parts supply from its partners overseas. However, both companies decided to go a different route and started building AKs in the USA.

Several years ago Century came up with its first all-American-built AK rifle, the Centurion C39. I had a chance to work with this gun. Unlike most domestic AK builders, Century chose to go with the milled receiver instead of the stamped one, for added feeling of robustness and supposed reliability. They made the rest of the components in-house, either directly copying the original 7.62x39mm AK-47 design or modifying it to improve it. As such, the Centurion C39 had several practical features added to it. The first was lightening cuts in the bolt carrier to soften the impact from recoil and, second, a proprietary chevron-style muzzle brake that also seemingly reduces recoil. A new set of polymer furniture with longer butt stock concluded the configuration of the new gun.

Since the initial success of the Centurion C39, Century came up with C39v2 and several variations of it. The company introduced its stamped-receiver RAS line of AKs. The Century Russian Army Standard (RAS) US-built AK is a slight departure from the C39 rifle. The idea remains to provide a U.S.-made AK with quality components and good fit and finish. From the front

*Century Arms' C39 Centurion (decked out with MagPul accessories, C39v2 is shown here at right) is an all-American-made milled receiver AK rifle. Century's stamped RAS rifle (left) is also entirely American-made.*

trunnion forward, it is identical to the milled-receiver Centurion rifle, with the exception of the C39 proprietary muzzle device that was replaced with standard AKM slanted muzzle compensator. The front sight block, gas block and gas tube stayed the same.

The main difference between the guns is the RAS's stamped receiver that falls in line with the majority of AK rifles in the U.S. I still wonder, why not follow suit and "modernize" the front end of the rifle—get rid of the AK-47 components, including the perforated gas tube, and make it more like the original AKM? Nevertheless, the new gun came with a set of beautiful wood furniture as standard. The overall fit and finish were a huge improvement over Century's earlier AKs, including the imported ones.

Right out of the box, the new RAS rifle looked and felt like a shiny new gun. It also did well at the range and is starting to build a reputation of a solid shooter. One negative aspect, along with the old gas system design I mentioned, is that the earlier RAS rifles came with a proprietary side mounted accessory rail. Only the original Century mounts would fit it. I see logic in it and, before long, the accessory manufacturers will make a mount to fit it, but using the standard design would have been much easier in my opinion. Be that as it may, the new Century RAS AK is here, available, reasonably priced and will provide its owners with plenty of AK fun at the range.

The RAS line also included rifles with other options and configurations, including a tactical model in MagPul furniture and a pistol. Overall, the RAS47 is an excellent representative of U.S.-made AKs, even if the name does not represent the reality.

Another one of the largest suppliers of U.S.-built AKs, I.O., Inc., started producing AK rifles at its facility in Charlotte, NC, in 1995. In the beginning, the guns built by the company were hybrid AKs with U.S. receivers and barrels and Romanian parts. This was reflected in the overall quality of the guns coming out of I.O.'s Charlotte facility: solid shooters with occasional malfunctions, and the fit and finish of a low-end AK. Luckily, one did not have to break the bank to buy one.

One benefit worth mentioning is that all of I.O.'s AKs were covered by the factory lifetime transferable warranty. The company would take the gun back and fix it or replace it at no additional cost to the customer. In an effort to improve the quality of their guns and change the production environment, in 2013 the company's owner decided to relocate his plant to a state-of-the-art facility in Palm Bay, FL. Hiring qualified personnel in NASA's back yard and investing in casting and CNC machines improved the quality of the company's products. The quality of I.O.'s all-American-built AKs improved significantly. It's still not perfect by some measures, but it's noticeably better. And, all the guns are still backed by the lifetime warranty.

In addition to its traditional product, I.O., Inc., has introduced a variety of other guns and models, illustrating that innovation is the other measure of success. All-American AK rifles that I.O. produces can be split in two categories: the classic and the modernized.

The classic category is represented by the AKM247, AKM247C, AKM247CUF and AKM247UF. The AKM247 is a very close copy of the fixed-stock Soviet AKM based on Polish drawings. It comes dressed in either the American-made black polymer, or laminate wood furniture mimicking original Soviet furniture by shape and color for C variant. The AKM247CUF and AKM247UF are the underfolding stock models. All the AKM247 rifles are chambered in the original 7.62x39mm caliber and have the slanted compensator on the threaded muzzle.

I.O., INC.'S LINE OF ALL-AMERICAN-MADE AK RIFLES IS BASED ON ORIGINAL POLISH DRAWINGS. NOT A PROM QUEEN, BUT A SOLID PERFORMER.

*Krebs Custom's drive to produce better AKs resulted in creation of the KTR series of rifles. Earlier KTR rifles like this one still looked like an AK.*

The company's modernized line of AKs is represented by the M214 and its several variants. The main difference between the AKM247 and M214 is that M214 has a gas block/front sight combination, as opposed to two separate components on the original AKs. Other differences include tactical full-length quad rail forend and polymer stock patterned after an East German design.

All of I.O., Inc.'s AKs come with nitrate-treated barrels and the ever-present lifetime transferable warranty. One more I.O., Inc., AK that enthusiasts may run into is the AK-74. This gun is the Bulgarian kit-built rifle that the company sells based on availability.

I've tested and worked with all of the American-built AK rifles covered in this section. They have worked for me as they should. I like some features on some rifles more than others, and I was able to work around the small things that I didn't like. All in all, having these American-built AKs available to American shooters at relatively low cost is a comforting thought. I'm a big fan of this category. You will clearly see why later in this book. For articles and reviews, I often work with accessories. These relatively inexpensive AKs provide a perfect platform for me to build and configure the rifle to test an accessory or the entire kit. I don't care how a gun or its furniture looks, and I don't care if the diameter of the rivet head is per spec. I do care if the gun shoots and functions reliably. The rest I can handle on my own and configure my AK the way I want. And for that, these guns are perfect.

## AK-BASED MODERN RIFLES

A separate category for AKs includes those specifically designed and developed by gunsmiths or gun manufacturers as tactical AK rifles. Often built on Russian sporting Saiga or Vepr rifles, these guns go beyond just changing the furniture and attaching a few accessories. They represent a complete redesign of the core gun to produce something that is modular, handy and corresponds with demands laid forth by modern gun operators. Russian hunting/sporting Saiga and Vepr rifles are often used as core guns because of their quality, military-grade barrels.

My introduction to specialty AKs by American companies came many years ago with the Krebs Custom KTR. Krebs has built a fair number of these with various modifications, all featuring accessories and improvements of their own design.

Krebs KTR rifles were built on the original Russian Saiga action, sporting original front sights and gas blocks with no bayonet or accessory lugs. The KTR usually was dressed in standard AK-100–series black plastic furniture, except for its ergonomic SAW-type pistol grip. Most of the Krebs rifles had the KCI enhanced safety lever that was much more comfortable and user friendly. KTR rifles could also have a variety of muzzle devices. Some rifles were equipped with a speed-loader device. No matter the modification, all KTR rifles were de-horned, with smooth finish and exceptional paint job. One can expect to pay extra for Krebs Custom rifles.

Today, Krebs Custom continues to build rifles of their own design based on the Saiga and Vepr. The two main production models Krebs builds are the AC-15 and its shortened version, the "Assneck." Both rifles use a folding telescopic MagPul MOE® stock and Krebs' own U.F.M. handguards, with the AC-15 using the full length and the Assneck using the shorter AK model. Both rifles are equipped with a bunch of Krebs improvements and carry renowned quality with price to match. Both AC-15 and Assneck guns are available now and can be ordered from the company directly or through its distributors.

Unlike the KTR series rifles that were converted from the Russian Saiga hunters, the KV guns, like this KV-13, are based on the heavier-duty RPK action.

## AK PISTOLS

Another category that is immensley popular is AK pistols. Ever since the short AKS-74U was introduced for service with Soviet armed forces in 1974 as a part of the AK-74 family of rifles, it instantly became popular on account of it being short, nifty and cool-looking.

The short AK was an enigma until the first parts kits started to arrive stateside in the 1990s. It seemed everybody had to have one. The only problem was and still is the 8-inch, short AKSU rifle was subject to the National Firearm Act as an SBR (short barrel rifle) and as such had a certain amount of hassle attached to it.

One of the most exciting and widely popular AKs in America is the AK pistol. These come in many forms and sizes, but all have the short barrel.

*With stock folded, the AKS-74U presents a small and compact package.*

Options for solutions included a permanent barrel extension in the form of a sound suppressor, a longer barrel protruding past the front sight/gas block combo, or configuring as a pistol. The first two options undermine the whole idea behind having a short AK. The pistol route appears more plausible for those who desire the compactness of the original AKSU shorty.

The AK pistol, as any rifle-based pistol, cannot have a shoulder stock, nor in any way can it facilitate stock installation, as it would immediately become an NFA-regulated SBR. Well, I should clarify the AK pistol can have a folding stock, but it has to be permanently pinned and welded in folded position. Most of the AK pistols simply do not have it. There are several manufacturers and importers offering these awesome guns.

## AK DRACO PISTOL

Century Arms' Romanian AK Draco pistol in 7.62x39mm caliber is only 21 inches long and comes with hardwood handguards and a polymer pistol grip. The 12.25-inch barrel has a combination of gas block and front sight and is tipped with a muzzle nut. In comes in a matte black parkerized finish.

## MINI DRACO AK PISTOL

The Romanian AK Mini Draco pistol is also chambered in 7.62x39mm. The Mini Draco features a 7.5-inch chrome-lined barrel, AR-style birdcage flash hider, synthetic pistol grip and hardwood handguards. Its overall length is only 18 3/8 inches, making it one of the smallest AKs one will encounter. Both the Draco and Mini Draco pistols are made for Century Arms by Romarm/Cugir.

**THE MINI DRACO FEATURES A 7.5-INCH CHROME-LINED BARREL, AR-STYLE BIRDCAGE FLASH HIDER, SYNTHETIC PISTOL GRIP AND HARDWOOD HANDGUARDS.**

*The Romanian Mini Draco takes the AK pistol idea a step further.*

## ZASTAVA PAP PISTOLS

Another Century Arms imported AK pistol is the Serbian Zastava N-PAP M85NP.

The M85NP takes its roots from the Yugoslavian M70 short rifle patterned after the Soviet AKS-74U. This pistol is chambered for the 5.56x45 mm cartridge and has an adapted mag well to accept AR-15 magazines. It has a 10.25-inch barrel and 21.5-inch overall length. It comes with the AKSU-style hinged top cover with flip-up rear sight, standard front sight with auxiliary flip-up white dot night front sight, black polymer Yugoslavian pistol grip, wood handguards and removable AKSU-pattern muzzle brake.

The Serbian M92PV AK PAP pistol, like the M85NP, is based on the Soviet AKSU, only it is chambered in 7.62x39mm caliber and accepts standard AK magazines. It has a 10.25-inch barrel and 19.75-inch overall length. It comes with the AKSU-style hinged top cover with flip-up rear sight, standard front sight with auxiliary flip-up white dot night front sight, black polymer Yugoslavian pistol grip, and wood handguards. The threaded muzzle is covered by a muzzle nut that is welded in place. The PAP M85NP, along with the M92PV AK pistols, are made for Century Arms in Serbia by Zastava.

## CENTURION C39 AK-STYLE PISTOL

Apart from the imports, Century Arms also makes AK pistols of its own. The American-made Centurion C39 Sporter pistol is based on the successful Centurion C39 rifle and, like the rifle, is chambered in 7.62x39mm caliber. The pistol is 100 percent American-made and features a milled receiver, adjustable post front sight integral to gas block, birdcage flash hider, black synthetic ergonomic pistol grip, and black synthetic upper and lower handguards with Picatinny-style rails.

Century Arms also offers a new U.S.-made AK pistol based on the RAS47 rifle. Inspired by Century's best seller, this pistol has modern upgrades in the form of MagPul furniture.

## SAM7K-01 AK PISTOL

Arsenal USA offers AK pistols based on its line of Bulgarian AKS-74U variants. Compared to Romanian and Serbian AK pistols, the Arsenal guns are more refined and may appeal more to the AK collector who is willing to spend a little more for the more authentic look.

Arsenal's SAM7K-01 AK pistol is based on one of the best-selling rifles that Arsenal USA imports from Bulgaria. The SAM7K-01 pistol is built on a milled receiver and chambered in 7.62x39mm caliber. It has a 10.5-inch chrome-lined hammer-forged barrel and scope mounting side rail. The AKSU-pattern hinged top cover is equipped with aperture sight. The SAM7 pistol has an ambidextrous safety lever that can be operated by a thumb. Total weight of this pistol is

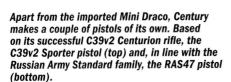

*Apart from the imported Mini Draco, Century makes a couple of pistols of its own. Based on its successful C39v2 Centurion rifle, the C39v2 Sporter pistol (top) and, in line with the Russian Army Standard family, the RAS47 pistol (bottom).*

*Arsenal's SAM7-01 AK pistol (top) is based on the milled receiver SAM7 rifle. The SLR106-58 AK pistol (bottom) is simply a copy of the Soviet AKSU chambered in .223 Rem.*

6.25 lbs. It is assembled and finished in Las Vegas at the Arsenal USA facility and contains U.S.-made and imported parts.

## SLR106-58 AK PISTOL

Arsenal's SLR106-58 AK pistol is based on another best-selling rifle, the Bulgarian-built SLR. The SLR106-58 pistol is built on a stamped receiver and chambered in the soft-shooting 5.56x45 mm (.223 Rem.) caliber. It comes with an 8.5-inch chrome-lined hammer-forged barrel that is tipped with a new-style muzzle brake. It comes with a scope mounting side rail. Its AKSU-pattern hinged top cover is equipped with an aperture sight. The SLR106-58 AK pistol from Arsenal USA is probably the closest thing to the AKSU rifle that has been produced by the factory. It closely follows the AKSU pattern. The only departure from the original is the two-chamber muzzle brake that really works. The SLR106-58 AK pistol only weighs 5.5 lbs. and is assembled and finished in Las Vegas at the Arsenal USA facility and contains U.S.-made and imported parts.

I.O., Inc., has manufactured and imported AK rifles for years. It was only natural for the company to jump into the AK pistol niche with a couple of offerings of its own.

Based on its M214 AK rifle, I.O., Inc., offers the M214 NANO pistol. One of the smallest AK pistols on the market, it comes with several cool features like quad rail short handguards and a Picatinny rail at the back of the receiver for attaching a sling of your choice.

## M214 NANO

I.O., Inc.'s M214 NANO is based on its all-American-made (in Florida) M214 Series AK rifles. It is chambered in the popular 7.62x39mm AK caliber. The NANO pistol comes with quad rail handguards and bolt hold-open safety lever, and accepts all standard AK high-capacity magazines. The M214 NANO has a 7-inch barrel that is tipped with a compensator. It's one of the smallest functioning AK pistols on the market today.

## HELLPUP

I.O., Inc., also imports the Hellpup pistol from Poland. The Hellpup is an intermediate-length AK pistol patterned closely after the Russian AK-105 intermediate-length rifle. This semi-auto, long-stroke piston-operated pistol is chambered in the traditional 7.62x39mm caliber. The barrel is 9.25 inches long, and the pistol weighs in at only 5 lbs. The Hellpup accepts all standard AK high-capacity magazines, has adjustable front and rear sights, and sports an AKSU-style muzzle device. Despite the Hellpup long-stroke piston, it's still only 21 inches long.

There are many other AK pistols made by smaller manufacturers or gunsmiths. Models covered here are readily available to anyone who would like to take their AK hobby up a notch and have a load of undersized and compact fun.

The Polish-built Hellpup is an AK pistol that is based on AKM-pattern rifle with an intermediate length barrel similar to that of Russian AK-104.

THE RECENT INTRODUCTION OF A STABILIZING ARM BRACE CAUSED A RISE IN AK PISTOL POPULARITY. IT IS EASY TO INSTALL ON JUST ABOUT ANY AK PISTOL.

## AVAILABLE ACCESSORIES

One of the best AK pistol accessories that came out recently is the stabilizing arm brace. It installs with a bracket that is held in place by the AK's pistol grip. It's designed to attach to the shooter's forearm to enable one-handed shooting of the heavy AK pistol by countering its weight. The brace looks like a shoulder stock but, make no mistake about it, the arm brace is just that, a brace.

When this accessory was introduced, the ATF issued a letter stating that the arm brace is not a shoulder stock and having it installed on the pistol does not turn that pistol into an NFA weapon (SBR). However, the ATF later followed up with an additional letter on the subject, stating that although having the arm brace installed on the pistol is not illegal, having to shoulder it is. So, make sure you are fully familiar with all federal, state and local laws before installing and/or using this and any accessory on your AK pistol.

Hopefully this chapter gives you a sense of the enormity of the U.S. AK market and the variety of the AK variants that are available here. It was also intended to illustrate the huge base of commercial AK shooters in the U.S. You know what they say, two heads are better than one. If there are millions of heads, something big may happen, something that can influence things even as big and as important as evolution. Read on, and you'll soon see what I mean.

*Though the arm brace looks like a shoulder stock, it is not.*

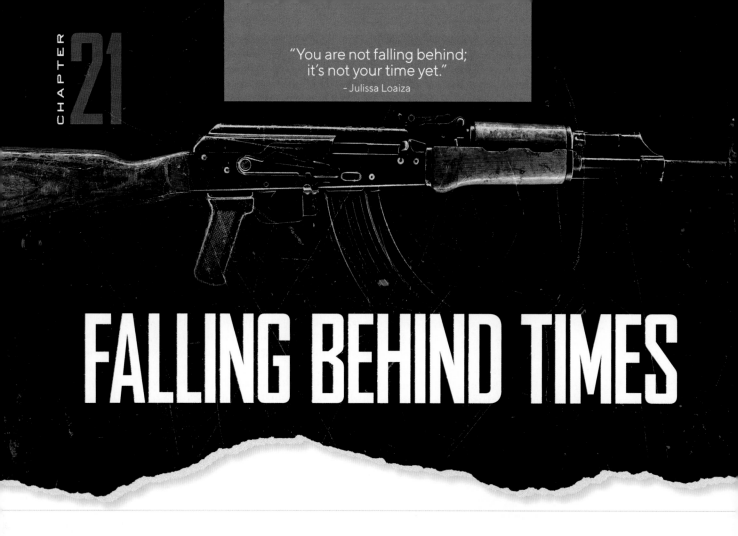

## CHAPTER 21

"You are not falling behind;
it's not your time yet."
- Julissa Loaiza

# FALLING BEHIND TIMES

**N**ow, back to our story of the AK transition from battle rifle born in the fires of WWII to what it is today. The sheer number of AKs in the U.S. gives fuel to the ancient AR-versus-AK argument. I'm sure that most firearm enthusiasts, like me, are tired of this "apples to oranges" comparison, but for the sake of this book allow me to elaborate on it once more.

What are the principal shortcomings that the AK is accused of having?

- Low accuracy (compared to the AR) of single-shot fire
- Significant recoil and muzzle climb, especially in 7.62mm caliber
- Difficulty installing optics and other accessories
- Non-ergonomic pistol grip
- Lack of magazine well
- No bolt hold-open
- Non-ergonomic, short stock
- Non-ergonomic safety/selector lever
- Old-style standard open sight

Let's take a closer look at each point.

The accuracy of single fire depends on several factors: the quality of the mass-produced guns and bulk ammunition, caliber, barrel length, range and shooter skill. The AK with 16-inch barrel and chambered in 7.62x39mm is often compared to the AR with 20-inch barrel chambered for the low-impulse 5.56x45 mm cartridge. You don't have to be a firearm specialist to understand that this comparison is not entirely valid. One can only compare the AK-47 or AKM to the M16 in the context of being two infantry rifles on opposing sides. In this case, comparing single-shot accuracy is futile.

However, a more correct accuracy comparison would be in full-auto with short or long bursts, where the AK with its predictable muzzle climb is on par with the sporadic M16, if not better. Again, the length of the barrel notwithstanding.

Nevertheless, comparing the accuracy of the two rifles should be done on more equal ground, like comparing the AK-74

**THE ACCURACY OF SINGLE FIRE DEPENDS ON SEVERAL FACTORS: THE QUALITY OF THE MASS-PRODUCED GUNS AND BULK AMMUNITION, CALIBER, BARREL LENGTH, RANGE AND SHOOTER SKILL.**

chambered for the low-impulse 5.45x39mm cartridge to the mass-issued M4 carbine with 16-inch barrel. In this case, the quality of the bulk ammo and experience of the shooter come into play. I concede that, at ranges of up to 100 meters, the M4 has a marginal advantage over the AK. At greater ranges, this advantage shrinks considerably, and it disappears entirely past 400 meters. In full-auto, there is no comparison at all, with the AK as a clear winner. To get valid results, always compare apples to apples.

The criticisms of the recoil and muzzle climb are subject to the same argument. One needs to compare the same type rifles. For example, a mass-produced military grade M16 or AR-15 with 20-inch barrel and firing the low impulse cartridge to an RPK-74 with longer barrel and chambered for the Russian equivalent of the low-impulse round, or an M4 with 16-inch barrel and the AK-74. One would agree that the M16 or full-length AR-15 recoil is negligible compared to the shorter M4. At the same time, the recoil of the RPK-74 is almost non-existent, compared to that of the AK-74. Granted, the AK-47 or AKM rifles have much more pronounced recoil that can't be compared to the M16's in any stretch of the imagination. However, the recoil of the AK-74 can be favorably compared to that of the M4. Its very effective muzzle device is to be "blamed" for this. Again, there is no comparison in muzzle climb between the AK-74 and M4 when both guns are fired in full-auto, the AK-74 would do significantly better.

The "difficulties" with installing optics on the AK appeared about 10 years ago, when ARs became more modular. Before that, there were no difficulties slapping scopes on an AK using the standard AK side rail. In fact, AKs had accessory rails before there was an AR-15. Granted, the variety of options for Soviet AKs was limited, but it expanded after the fall of the USSR. However, there was an option, while the AR had a hole in its carrying handle and a 3.2-power scope to go with it. Even before the AR-15A4 or the M4 carbine became a norm, AK owners had the option of using modern optics mounted on the aftermarket American-made mounts. This all changed when the AR lost its carrying handle in favor of the 1913 Picatinny rail followed by the quad rail handguard replacement. This took the AR from slightly behind to light-years ahead in the realm of optics mounts, but even more so with the ability to mount a variety of other accessories. The AK did find itself lagging behind, but not for long. It has caught up and today is on par with its adversary.

I personally like the standard AK pistol grip. I have big hands and it fits me just fine. There's a reason why the AK pistol grip is sized and shaped the way it is. You see, Russian soldiers have to fight six months in the winter wearing gloves. I also like the AR grip. It fits even better. This point is not worth arguing. The AK pistol grip is the easiest thing to replace. With the wide range of options available today, one can find the best fitting grip for him or her and install it themselves.

*The author believes the original AK stock length is not a problem. In fact, it is his preference.*

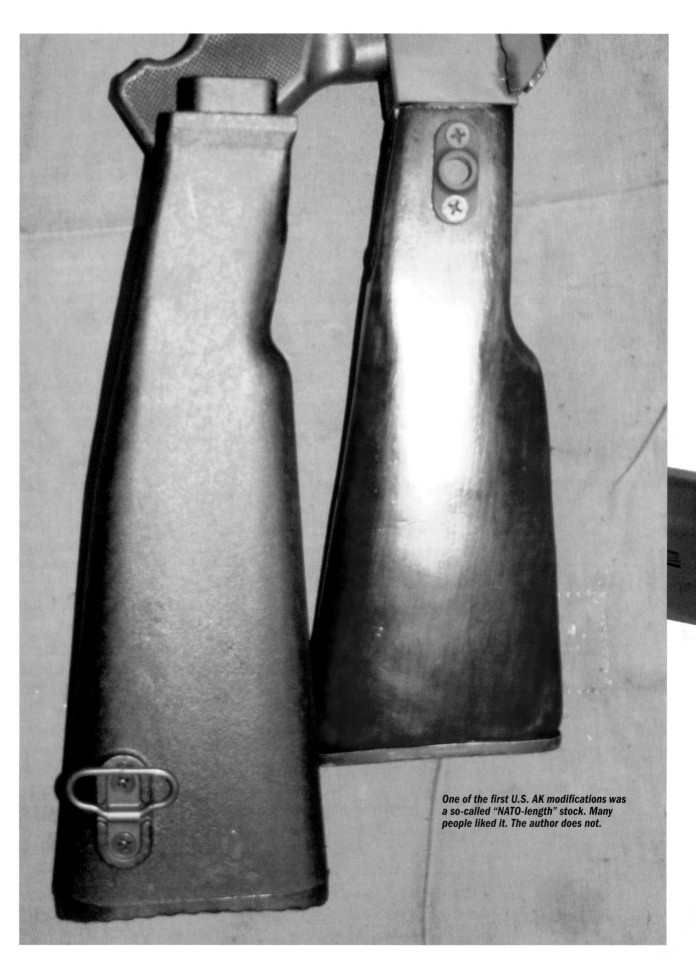

One of the first U.S. AK modifications was a so-called "NATO-length" stock. Many people liked it. The author does not.

The mag well, or rather the lack of one, is hardly a valid criticism, as it stems from design of the gun. Those who are trained on the AK and have experience with the platform do not have a problem with magazine swaps. After a while, the mag swap becomes intuitive. The problem arises when the AR shooter tries to master the AK platform. The funny thing is that the AK magazine retention system is not unique to the AK. The same mag retention was used on many other guns long before the AK was even conceived. From an engineering point of view, the mag retention used in the AK design is better than the pistol-type system used in the AR. It is more rigid and more secure, with positive fixation along the gun axis. The AR mag retention is achieved by applying pressure to the side of the magazine with a retaining lug located toward the back of the magazine, which causes the mag to skew. Also, once the AK mag "clicks" into place, there is no need to double tap it to make sure it is secured. It is. Those AR shooters who have had a mag drop from the gun as they're ready to shoot know what I'm talking about.

A bolt hold-open is not a divine miracle. It's a design feature that can be incorporated into any semi-automatic or automatic gun. It's not on the AK because it is not needed. What's the purpose of the bolt hold-open, and why is it so important? Time for a little excursion into firearm history.

After the inception of modern cartridge-firing guns, the issue of fast reloading arose once magazine-type rifles were invented. The important thing to remember is that the magazine-type rifle feeds from the magazine that is in the rifle itself and can accept and store number of rounds, just like most military rifles for the past 100+ years and any bolt, lever-action or semi-automatic hunting rifle today. All of these guns can be loaded with several rounds of ammunition. Once military rifles could be loaded with several cartridges, the question arose of how to quickly reload the magazine. That's where stripper clips came into play. Once the bolt was open and in the rearmost position, the shooter could insert the stripper clip into a receptacle and in one quick move send a number of cartridges into the rifle's magazine. This was the norm for all bolt guns. But, what to do with semi-automatic and automatic rifles?

If you pull a bolt handle back, the return spring pushes it forward. That's why the bolt hold-open device was engineered and incorporated into the gun's design. Since modern fighting rifles and carbines are fed from detachable magazines, the need for a bolt hold-open is greatly reduced, if not eliminated entirely. Again, it's a preference of the shooter and his or her training. Personally, I have no need for it, and not having it is one less thing to worry about. My AK will let me know it is out of ammo

*The less-than-ergonomic AK safety/selector lever can be easily replaced with the popular Krebs safety lever. It allows a shooter to operate it with the fire-control hand without removing that hand from the pistol grip. As a bonus, it also offers a manual bolt hold-open feature.*

by a distinct click or by three tracer rounds that I loaded first into each magazine. It would be naïve to think that the AR's bolt hold-open somehow automatically aids the shooter. You still have to train with it. There's no click after you fire the last round. Experienced shooters will glance at the ejection port to make sure it's an empty mag and not a malfunction that caused the gun to stop firing. Then you replace the mag and release the bolt by hitting the bolt release or pulling on the charging handle. It's a shooter's preference, training and experience that affect the gun's smooth operation. I see the bolt hold-open feature useful only when I go to ranges where it is necessary to show an empty chamber.

Stock length (length of pull) of the AK is often criticized for being too short. Again, I would suggest this is shooter preference. I like the AK length of pull. It's a lot easier to maintain a shoulder-stock weld (and thus control the gun) with the arm bent than with it extended. I can see the longer stock proponents' point, but it no longer stands when the shooter puts on body armor or a thick coat. Remember, Russians have to fight for half of the year in heavy clothing and sometimes with a combination of body armor and winter coats. However, I would concede the point that the ability to extend and collapse the stock at will is a useful feature.

The signature AK safety/selector lever is clumsy even for AK lovers like myself. I offer no argument there. Though it is also serves another important role of charging handle slot cover, it's neither convenient nor ergonomic. Those who have been running AKs for a while may have grown numb to the gun's safety lever or simply learned to live with it. One who has acquired an AK rifle should spend some time training on the lever operation. You can always adjust the tension on it by bending it slightly to achieve smooth operation. However, it's always a careful balance between the lever being too tight or too loose.

Last but not least, complaints are voiced about so-called deficiencies in the AK's iron sights. Yet again, I would cite preference or training of a shooter. I prefer the open U-slot of the AK's rear sight. It is open and away from the eye, allowing the gunfighter to observe and scan the engagement area without much obstruction. The U-slot sight's advantages come into play when, as often happens in a gunfight, the gun is dropped in or dragged through the snow, slush, mud or water. The U-slot rear sight rarely gets clogged and it's easy to brush off any obstruction. The same cannot be said for the diopter (peephole) sight. Another myth about the AK disadvantage in this area is the supposedly shorter sight line compared to an AR. It's true that having

## I PREFER THE OPEN U-SLOT OF THE AK'S REAR SIGHT. IT IS OPEN AND AWAY FROM THE EYE, ALLOWING THE GUN-FIGHTER TO OBSERVE AND SCAN THE ENGAGEMENT AREA WITHOUT MUCH OBSTRUCTION.

a longer distance between front and rear sights makes it more convenient to aim the rifle more accurately. It's also true that an AR-15 or M16A4 with a 20-inch barrel has a longer sight line. Again, I have to invoke the "apples to oranges" argument. The Russian RPK-74 machine gun is more suitable for comparison with the full-length AR. In this case, the RPK wins. Comparing the AK-74 with a 16-inch barrel to the standard battle rifle of the U.S. armed forces' M4 also does not favor the American gun. Nevertheless, it is what you are comfortable with that determines what sight works better for you.

Whatever position you take in the AK vs. AR argument, this chapter reflects my knowledge of the platform and experience with it. The fact remains that, in order to realize any gun's full potential, ultimately the shooter's training and experience must be employed. Another fact is that the modern war theater and battlefield conditions have changed and continue to evolve. No more bayonet charges across "no man's land." It is dynamic, with changing ranges and fire segments. The strategic mission may remain, but the tactics of achieving it may change several times throughout the firefight. This demands a certain degree of modularity from the fighter's weapon system, use of day or night optics, collimator sight with or without magnifier, flashlight, laser designator, etc. Although the AK-74M was a solid fighting carbine and could be equipped with optical and other sights, it fell short in modularity and ability to be used with other battlefield implements. As the modern firefight moved forward, the AK was left behind.

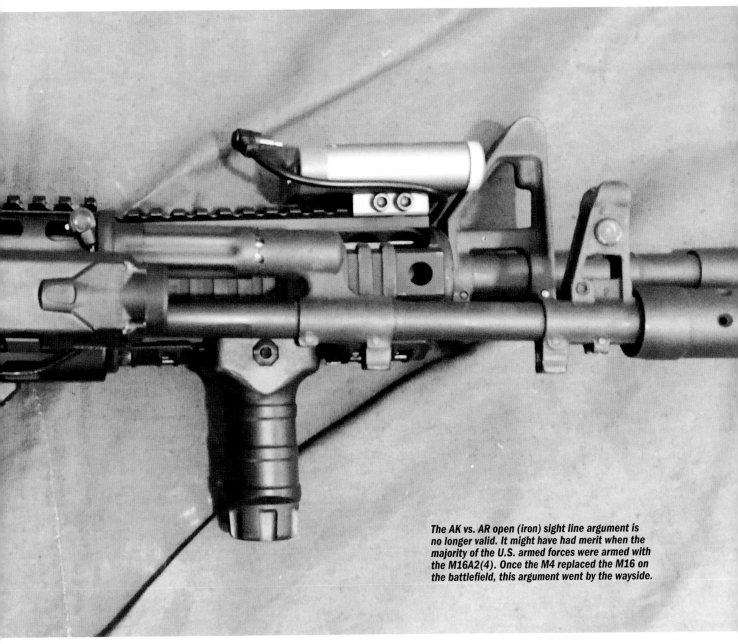

The AK vs. AR open (iron) sight line argument is no longer valid. It might have had merit when the majority of the U.S. armed forces were armed with the M16A2(4). Once the M4 replaced the M16 on the battlefield, this argument went by the wayside.

# ACCESSORIES: U.S. COMPANIES DRIVE THE AK EVOLUTION

'm sure I will catch all kinds of flak from Russian readers because of this chapter. But, it is my firm belief that the next stage of AK evolution, which paved the way for today's modernization of the Kalashnikov platform and ultimately led to the changing the appearance and functionality of modern AK Avtomats, was inspired and started not in the Russian designers' bureaus, but here in the U.S. And not by designers and engineers working for the government, but by firearm accessories manufacturers and gunsmiths serving the U.S. commercial civilian market, and by U.S. AK shooters and enthusiasts who sought to improve their guns' performance and handling.

Yes, for the first time the AK platform has fallen behind the times. The AK had to catch up with the AR platform that became very modular, affording its shooters unprecedented flexibility.

The AK was losing the modern platform battle and needed an upgrade. The accuracy of the gun has been at the base of all improvements. The ARs, having replaced the carrying

*The AK platform used its standard side accessory rail for mounting modern Russian or Belorussian optics like this AK-104 with "Cobra" collimator sight.*

handle with MIL-STD-1913 rail (Picatinny) section on top of the receiver, now could accept any aiming device on the market.

Don't get me wrong, the AK platform had several options of its own. After the fall of the Soviet Union and onset of a free market economy, the manufacturers of military hardware found themselves free from the grip of military bureaucracy and dictatorship. They took creative license. Using the knowledge and experience accumulated while producing products for the military, they could now employ their expertise to make something that corresponded with market demand. Optics manufacturers were not an exception. Former Soviet optics companies, namely NPZ in Novosibirsk and BeLomo in Balarus, released several collimator, block/red dot and optical sights for the AK platform. Several newcomers, like the Cobra sight maker Akciom Holding, entered the market with their products.

*Perhaps the most reliable mounting system for collimator and optical sights on the AK is the side rail mount, like this Picatinny mount from Russia.*

The AK had optics options, but they were all tied to the AK-specific side rail and in some cases used aging technology. This no longer satisfied the huge number of civilian AK owners in the U.S. and the world. Manufacturers of optics have made quantum leaps in development of sighting systems in recent years. Red-dots, reflex sights and collimators are more efficient and reliable since they started appearing in the 1970s. We all know of the battle-proven optics available on the American commercial market for many years — Aimpoint, EOTech, Leupold, Meprolight, Trijicon. Most of those brands will do the job required of them just fine and some do it perfectly. All are designed to help a shooter achieve quick and positive target acquisition. Unlike AK-specific sights and scopes, none of the modern Western optics come with side mounts to fit the AK mounting rail; they fit a MIL-STD-1913/Picatinny rail mounting system that is usually positioned on top of the gun. In order to use one of these sights on an AK, the transitional side or top mount had to be devised. Something had to be done and someone had to be first.

Luckily for AK enthusiasts, the spirit of innovation coupled with entrepreneurial drive spurred development and introduction of several viable mounting systems. There are really three types of new AK mounts to accommodate modern optics. The first is a front handguard replacement that offers a quad rail mounting solution. The second is a modification to the AK top cover by installation of the 1913 (Picatinny) rail, and the third is a separate side mount that is optics-specific or provides scope rings or Picatinny rail.

It's only natural that the AK upgrade trend started with trying to mount modern optics. Since there was no solid base directly on the top of the AK, like on the AR upper receiver, its side rail had to be utilized for mounting optics with use of the new side mounts. It was the easiest way to adapt the modern optic sight to the AK without reconfiguring the gun.

The side mount is still very popular. In fact, it is my favorite way to attach a scope on my guns.

To get the mount stable enough for an optical sight on the AK, one has to use the originally designed side rail and a good mount. Luckily for AK enthusiasts there are many options. I think that the side-mounting rail on the AK rifle is the best option, not because it was designed by a team of PhDs or tested by Soviet top military research specialists or because it has proven itself over and over in various conflicts, but because it offers an AK shooter options and flexibility without any modifications to the gun and by design any sighting system can be quickly removed from the rifle.

I prefer the AK's side rail also because the engineer in me sees that it is simply mounted on the most rigid part of the rifle. Thus, it will return to zero every time, as has been proven in the similar setup of the Dragunov sniper rifle or the SVD. Not all AKs come with a side rail, and installing it in the garage or basement is not easy unless you are a gunsmith. Nevertheless, the side rails are available from any company that specializes in AK parts and accessories and just about any AK gunsmith would be happy to install one. In any case, most of the guns sold today have the rails.

There are two types of side-mounted optics mounts for AKs. The optic-specific version with scope rings that are an integral part of the mount itself, and the side mount with universal 1913 rail that is positioned over the top cover of the AK when installed. The latter offers the flexibility to use different optics, but at same time tends to be a little heavier when compared to the optic-specific mounts.

## SIDE MOUNTS

There were some early examples of AK side mounts with Picatinny-style rails that came from Russia and Belarus back in the early 1990s. These early mounts had several flaws. They were heavy because of the heavy steel parts that were used and, generally, they were tall, placing any sight high over the top of the gun and making the use of a scope very awkward to say the least. The idea behind the high position of the side mount was that it would not obstruct removal of the AK's top cover. Not a valid reason in my opinion, one could simply remove the scope before gun maintenance. Most of the good Russian side rails had many shortcomings. They had too large of an offset toward the back, making a proper eye relief a problem; they were set too high, making a proper cheek rest impossible; and the Picatinny rail was too short, not allowing the flexibility to install

*I use this Midwest mount extensively on my work rifles with a variety of sights, including this ELCAN Specter DR. Note how low the rail sits over the gun.*

Midwest's 30mm scope mount allows a scope to sit low enough to co-witness with a gun's iron sights, as shown here in combination with Hi-Lux's CMR 1-4x24 carbine scope.

a variety of optical sights. The real breakthrough happened when American companies got involved. Based on years of research into successes and shortcomings of Russian or East European mounts, several companies came up with truly functional side mounts for side-rail-equipped AKs.

Over the years, I have possessed and/or tested several U.S.-made side mounts for AKs. By trial and error, I wound up using mounts from only two American manufacturers. Midwest Industries, Inc., (MI) makes AK mounts, along with its wide range of AK accessories, but also AR rifles and a full line of AR parts and accessories. RS Regulate is a much smaller company out of Chesterfield, MI, that concentrates on designing, developing and manufacturing AK mounts and other accessories.

Just like all of Midwest's AK side mounts, the 30mm Red-Dot Mount sits low enough for co-witnessing.

*RS Regulate's Universal 300 Series side mount base is truly unique. It is light, strong and truly a universal AK mounting solution for collimator sights.*

I currently own all three AK mounts made by Midwest Industries: the AK-47/AK-74 Side Rail Scope Mount with 7 inches of 1913 Picatinny rail; the AK-47/AK-74 30mm Side Scope Mount; and the AK-47/AK-74 30mm Red Dot Side Mount. All three are made of solid aluminum with lightening holes and cutouts, and they feature a proprietary locking mechanism. The company's most recent side mounts are optic-specific; a particular sight mounts directly to the side mount to achieve even closer positioning above the gun's bore.

*RS Regulate makes optic-specific upper mounts to accommodate most of the popular sights.*

Today, most modern carbine optics have 30mm tubes. The red-dot side mount has only one ring and fits most of the red-dot scopes on the market. The Midwest Industries side mount has two rings to allow use of most modern carbine telescopic sights on AKs.

When installed on any AK, both mounts sit low over the gun and do not require an additional cheek riser. The universal Picatinny rail mount from Midwest Industries is one of the lightest AK side mounts, but one of the most rigid ones as well. Once on the rifle, it locks solid and places the mounting rail right over the centerline of the gun, with less than a quarter of an inch clearance from the top cover. The newest offerings from Midwest Industries are lightweight optic-specific side mounts. Several designs to accommodate popular sights are available.

My other favorite AK side mount product comes from RS Regulate. RS Regulate is a much smaller company, dedicated to making high-quality AK mounts only. At least it started as such. Today, they offer many variations of AK mounts, along with other accessories. However, most of their mounts are based on several basic designs with unique scalability.

What sets RS Regulate apart from the rest of the field is its innovative approach to AK mounts. All of its mounts were designed to be the lightest and to provide the stability needed for rifle sights. The inherent flexibility was built into RS Regulate scope mounts by splitting them into two parts: the base and the upper mount. The base is basically a Picatinny rail cut in half with a series of threaded holes.

The upper mounts have a slotted bottom to match the base and mounting bolt-holes. This arrangement provides for unsurpassed flexibility to mount any kind of optical sight on the same base. RS Regulate offers a number of upper mounts to accommodate any modern optical or collimator sight that AK shooters choose to use on their rifles.

*Development of mounts at RS Regulate was driven by size and weight reduction. The result is a very small, flat and rigid mount.*

# HANDGUARD MOUNTS

The next step in the AK upgrade saga had to do with adding much needed modularity to the aging platform. The ARs offered the option of replacing original handguards with modern versions that had a permanent Picatinny rail or allowed rail section to be attached. With these rail sections, the shooter could use a variety of accessories that were previously difficult to install on the gun. The AK found itself at a disadvantage again, but not for long. Once again, American manufacturers stepped up to the plate with replacement handguards, this time for the AK. These new replacement handguards worked similarly to the AR guards and afforded AK shooters the opportunity to attach other accessories to their rifle.

The AK front handguard rail mounting solution comes in the form of total replacement of the original handguards. It can be made of plastic, aluminum or even steel. By the original design, the AK handguards are not positively retained. Because of this, the upper and lower handguards subject to movement. Therefore, the plastic replacement handguards with mounting rail cannot be considered for attaching optical sights, or any sights for that matter. The plastic rails on the handguards should only be used for mounting non-essential accessories, such as flashlights, vertical grips, etc.

There are other types of replacement handguards that are made of aluminum and secured in place with a series of positive mounts that prevent any movement. Midwest Industries, Inc., out of Waukesha, WI, makes several models of AK-47/AK-74 universal handguards in quad rail, SS, KeyMod or M-LOK™ versions. The Midwest Industries lower handguard hard-mounts on the barrel close to the front trunnion block with a couple of set screws, resting against the gas tube for positioning and additional rigidity. The upper handguard with rail bolts to the lower, independent of the gas tube. This mounting solution is rigid enough for collimator, red-dot or reflex type sights.

Midwest also makes optic-specific upper handguards to accommodate the most popular sights. This move was made to provide a low mount for co-witnessing in case of electronic sight failure and lack of QD mount.

Co-witnessing on a firearm is the ability to see both rear and front iron sights through the scope or any other optical or collimator sight. In case of electronic component failure, the shooter can still aim his or her rifle with iron or open sights that are visible through the scope or collimator sight.

Krebs Custom, Inc., from Wauconda, IL, offers its version of the AK handguards mounting solution. The quad rail forend for standard AK rifles is similar to the Midwest Industries version in that it has four permanent 1913 rails, but the retention of the handguard is differ-

*One of the details that separates Midwest Industries from the rest is the optic-specific upper handguard replacement. This allows co-witnessing with iron sights.*

*Trijicon RMR #MI-AKH-RMR*

*Leupold Delta Point #MI-AKH-LD*

*Burris Fast Fire II #MI-AKH-BF*

*Aimpoint #MI-AKH-T1/VS*

*Vortex Sparc #MI-AKH-T1/VS Will Not Co-Witness*

*Primary Arms Micro Dot #MI-AKH-T1/VS*

ent. Instead of mounting the lower handguard on the barrel, it is slotted into the receiver and retained with the original AK lower handguard retainer. To provide the necessary rigidity, the handguard is secured with an additional bolt through the cleaning rod hole in the retainer. The upper handguard with 4-inch rail mounts to the positively installed lower handguard. The latest introduction from Krebs is the AK-U.F.M. handguard with KeyMod mounting system on the side and bottom and 4-inch rail on the top. This handguard system is secured in place similarly to the quad rail handguard, but offers much smoother modern design with the option of mounting different length individual rails on an as-needed basis.

*Krebs Custom's aluminum quad rail forend also provides a solid top mount for any collimator sight of choice.*

The biggest issue to address with using Western-type sights on AK rifles was to ensure co-witnessing when the optical sights could not be detached quickly in case of failure.

## GAS TUBE MOUNTS

One solution to the co-witness issue was the gas tube replacement mount. This solution was unique to the AK, providing the ability to mount an optical sight low enough to co-witness with the open sights, and also providing more mounting options with additional length of Picatinny rail. I'm not a huge fan of the gas tube mount for optics. Having said that, I do use these on regular basis with mini–red-dot sights, and I do like them for mounting a PEQ-type laser designator device.

UltiMAK, Inc., of so-fitting Moscow, ID, was the first to come out with this AK-47 optics mount. The UltiMAK optics

The UltiMAK AK-47 optics mount allows you to mount a collimator sight low enough for co-witnessing.

mount is essentially a replacement for an original AK gas tube. It is installed in place of the gas tube and secured in place by two U-shaped yokes wrapped around the gun's barrel, providing a solid and secured mounting. This mount sits low enough to provide co-witnessing for just about any low-mounted modern sight.

This tube-type mounting system can be used with the rifle's original lower handguard. However, it also exposes the shooter's hand to the extremely hot metal

Just like the UltiMAK and Midwest Industries mounts, the Troy Industries AK-47 top rail can work with any AK lower handguard.

parts of the gun by removing the original upper handguard.

Similar gas tube mounts come from two other firearms accessory manufacturers: the AK railed gas tube from Midwest Industries and AK-47 top rail from Troy Industries. The idea is the same as UltiMAK's—to make a mount low enough for smaller collimator sights to be able to co-witness with iron sights.

However, that's where the similarities end. Whereas the UltiMAK AK-47 optics mount is shorter than the actual AK gas tube and is secured to the gun by U-shaped yokes, the Midwest Industries rail gas tube and Troy Industries top rail install into the gas tube slot in the rear sight block and fit over the gas block the same way the original tube would. Then, using a threaded bushing, the mount is torqued tight over the neck of the gas chamber. This takes out any possible movement from the mount. The MI mount also has an additional leveling seat that straddles the barrel, and two setscrews level the gas tube mount in relation to the barrel. Because of the "spreading" feature, both the Midwest Industries and Troy Industries gas tube mounts can fit most of the AK full-length variants. Also, because these mounts install into the original gas tube location, they can be removed for cleaning and reinstalled again without any special tools. However, the sight's (if one is installed) zero must be checked after cleaning.

This type of optics mounting system can be used on AK rifles if others are not available, and for mounting small red-dot sights only, as it would sit away from the shooter's eye. The idea of placing a sight near the gas exhaust system and on top of a heat-generating portion of the gun is not very attractive to me. Even though

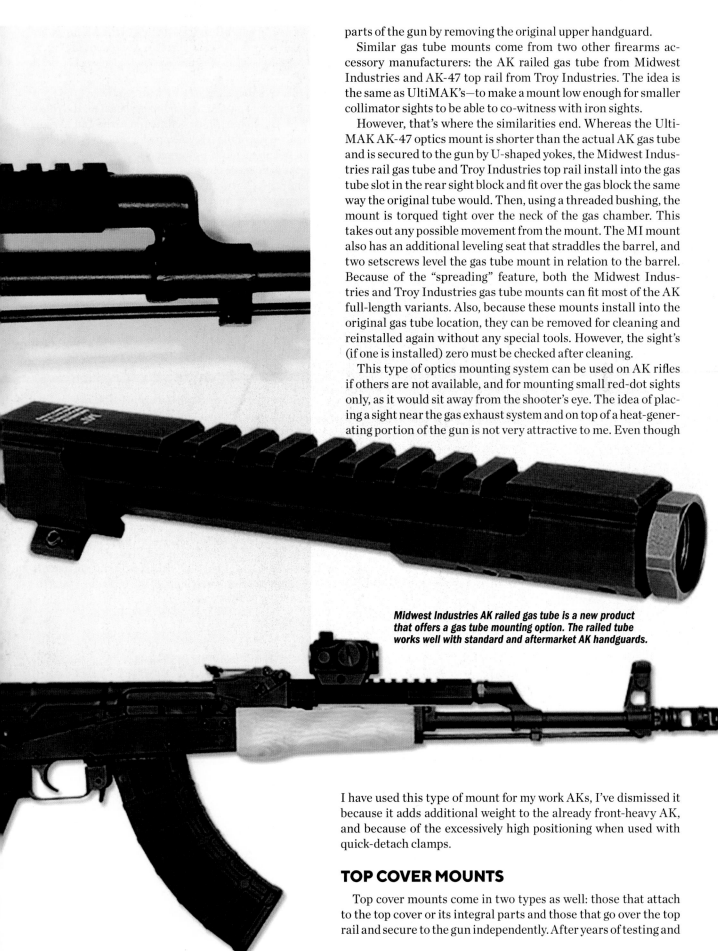

*Midwest Industries AK railed gas tube is a new product that offers a gas tube mounting option. The railed tube works well with standard and aftermarket AK handguards.*

I have used this type of mount for my work AKs, I've dismissed it because it adds additional weight to the already front-heavy AK, and because of the excessively high positioning when used with quick-detach clamps.

## TOP COVER MOUNTS

Top cover mounts come in two types as well: those that attach to the top cover or its integral parts and those that go over the top rail and secure to the gun independently. After years of testing and thousands of rounds fired, I've pretty much dismissed any attempts to rivet or bolt a Picatinny rail section to the AK top cover as impractical and a waste of time and money. This led me to select three mounts in this category that worked for me in the past: the Parabellum Armament Groups AKARS rail (AK Adaptive Rail System), Texas Weapon Systems Dog Leg scope rail mount and Krebs Custom's AK RSRS (Rear Sight Rail System).

All three "top cover" mounting systems employ a hinge attachment to the AK's rear sight mount, with removal of the sight itself. Two (the TWS Dogleg and Parabellum AKARS systems) are actually attached to, or are an integral part of, the rifle's top cover. Only one, the RSRS rail from Krebs, is independent of the top cover and mounted over the top of the gun to rigid mounting points. This type of mounting of the optics rail between two rigid points of the AK rifle provides the most rigidity, and is stable enough to reliably support not only collimator or reflex sights, but also a multi-power scope.

That is why I would start with the Krebs Custom RSRS, which is made of a solid piece of aluminum with an integral 9-inch Picatinny rail. The front part of the RSRS mount is attached to the mounting rail itself via a hinge, and is installed into the ears of the rear sight leaf on the rear block of the AK. It is secured in place with a setscrew and creates a positive and solid mount. The rail is placed over the top of the gun and attached to a "doll head" pin that replaces the original AK stock mounting screw.

Note that the RSRS rail will only work with fixed-stock AKs and those that have been converted to folders by replacing a fixed stock. Underfolding models and Russian or Bulgarian AKS-74,

The Krebs Custom RSRS rail is probably the most stable over-the-top optics mounting solution. It hinges up and away from the top cover and, because it is not attached to the top cover, it returns to zero every time.

AK-74M or 100-series rifles will not accept this rail, as they lack the stock mounting rear trunnion tang. The Krebs RSRS rail-mounting system is not attached to the parts of the AK that flex during firing, and is secured between the rear sight and rear trunnion block. The flexing of the receiver and top cover do not affect the position of the rail. Therefore, the RSRS ensures that scopes zero reliably. Since the RSRS rail sits over the top cover of the AK, it is in the way of access to the rifle's internal components, which is why the front hinge is provided. For cleaning or repair, the RSRS rail is detached from the rear trunnion by disengaging the pin, and then simply hinged away from the gun. After the gun is reassembled, the rail is hinged back and pinned in place.

Because the rail is returned to the same place every time by means of rigid mounting, it does not negatively impact the optical sight zero.

As mentioned previously, the original AK rear sight has to be removed to install this rail system. The Krebs RSRS rail comes with M16-style aperture sight with windage adjustment.

Another top cover optics mounting system is the Dog Leg scope rail mount from Texas Weapon Systems, Inc. (TWS) out of Austin, TX. The Dog Leg rail provides a full-length Picatinny rail on the top cover of the AK for a number of mounting options.

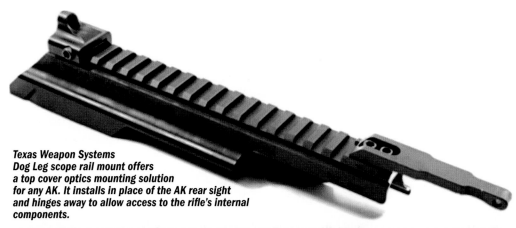

**Texas Weapon Systems**
*Dog Leg scope rail mount offers a top cover optics mounting solution for any AK. It installs in place of the AK rear sight and hinges away to allow access to the rifle's internal components.*

The Dog Leg scope rail mount is made out of a solid piece of aluminum with an integral top cover to replace the gun's original stamped steel one. It is hinged at the rear sight block, with a single finger-hinge placed between rear sight mounting ears, and attached with a provided hinge pin that is threaded through the mounting ears and the rail itself.

This allows the top cover to be lifted for cleaning and maintenance and returned to relative zero every time. Once on the gun, the mount sits pretty solidly, aided by the specifically designed tension

feature at the back of the cover and a return spring guide wedge-shaped spring retainer tang. This replacement spring guide is also provided with the Dog Leg installation kit. The TWS Dog Leg mount includes several design features that are supposed to make the mount more rigid when on the gun. And, it is, making it a good solution for collimator or reflex sights. Again, since the Dog Leg rail uses the mount for the rifle's original rear sight, it comes standard with nonadjustable aperture sight.

Just like the TWS Dogleg rail, the AKARS mounting system from Parabellum Armament Group of Columbus, OH, is installed into the rear sight mounting ears. The hinge part of the rail is placed into the rear sight block and threaded through with a hinge pin that is provided with the installation kit. The pin itself is secured with a setscrew in the rail.

The AKARS hinge is the three-finger type and thus more rigid when installed. The 7.5-inch 1913 rail is separate from the rifle's top cover. The AKARS top cover is the standard AK top cover with rail mounting block installed at the back. After the rail is installed on the rifle, it slides into guide pins of the top cover mounting block. The top cover is then installed very much the same way as a standard AK cover, i.e., placed into a top cover slot in the rear sight block and snapped in place over the main spring retainer tang.

The rail is designed so that it doesn't need to be affixed to the top cover, but instead remains loosely attached to allow the top cover to be installed. Once on the gun, it is locked to the rifle solidly. Again like the Dog Leg rail, it swings away from the gun for cleaning and maintenance. Unlike the TWS rail where the rear sight leaf spring must be removed for the Dog Leg installation, with the AKARS the spring remains in place and, by applying tension on the rail, provides additional stability.

The other difference from the TWS Dog Leg mounting rail, the AKARS has a machined U-type nonadjustable rear sight. The new Gen 3 AKARS comes with a standard aperture rear sight.

I've used both of these rails extensively. They work great. I would not hesitate to use them for 4–6 MOA red-dots. I will, however, remain skeptical about mounting a multi-power scope for precision shooting on either of them.

For this section of the book, I purposely selected mounting systems that do not require any permanent modifications to the AK. Some manufacturers mentioned here make products that offer more mounting options, but with "deeper" and more permanent modification to the rifle. These are covered in the Accessories section below.

## AK ACCESSORIES

The previous section dealt mainly with mounting modern optics on the AK. It was rightfully so, because modernization geared toward bringing the AK platform into the 21st century started with this important step. Now, thanks in part to American companies, AKs have sev-

*The Parabellum Armament Group AK Adaptive Rail System (AKARS) is similar to the Dog Leg, but it uses a modified original AK top cover married with a Picatinny rail section. Just like the Dog Leg, the AKARS installs in place of the AK rear sight and hinges away for maintenance and cleaning.*

eral viable options available to use for mounting any modern sight widely used on ARs. However, this was not enough to start claiming that AK modularity was on par with that of ARs. Further upgrades were needed. Yet again, the American commercial market led the way to AK upgrades. Most of these upgrades were to improve the modularity and ergonomics in the "Western" sense of the aging platform.

## BUTTSTOCKS

The main argument in the ancient battle of AR vs. AK lies with modularity of the rifle. Though AKs have been produced with side rail mounts since the 1950s, the main purpose of the side rail was to mount night vision units or a limited assortment of optical sights. The real breakthrough in accessorizing the battle rifle came with introduction of the flat-top AR model in the 1990s. The Picatinny rail (MIL-STD-1913 rail) is a variation of a Weaver rail mount that was adapted as a standard rifle mounting system for the U.S. armed forces. Adoption of the Picatinny rail led to a surge in development of mounting solutions, not only for optics or other sighting implements, but also for other rifle accessories, essentially making the battle rifle modular and ready to configure for each soldier depending on his or her mission requirements.

Converting the gun's forend or handguards into a quad rail system provided a very flexible mounting platform for a variety of combat accessories such as laser designators, infrared (IR) illuminators, flashlights, etc. In this regard, the AR took a giant lead over the AK in the battle of the black rifles. However, the gap was breached rather quickly with efforts from both sides of the pond. Before long, AK rifles, too, could be upgraded to compete with their American counterparts. The transition went slowly at first, with introduction of quad rail handguards followed by the Picatinny rail on the side mount, and spilling over to the fixed-stock AK conversions. Today, the selection of AK accessories is so diverse that one can take any model of AK with milled or stamped receiver and turn it into a modular fighting platform that accepts the same combat implements as an AR.

When talking about AK accessories, I didn't want to start in chronological order, but rather by ease of installation and greatest impact on the rifle's performance from the ergonomics point of view. The "hanging accessories" can come and go, depending on what the shooter is trying to do with the rifle, but some semi-permanent or permanent modifications to the rifle itself improve performance and operator expectations from the gun no matter what accessory is hung on it. I also decided to concentrate on improvements to the AK that can be reversed and would not require permanent modification of the gun. Nothing cut off, nothing milled or filed away. However, I will talk about the accessories that are available from several manufacturers that, when installed by modifying the AK rifle, would also offer additional benefits mainly associated with mounting solutions.

The original AK-47 was dressed in wood furniture designed to be mass-produced in a short time. Though not obvious, the ergonomics were actually considered during the design phase.

(below) The AK stock length is considered somewhat short by some American shooters. A longer stock is available as a replacement.

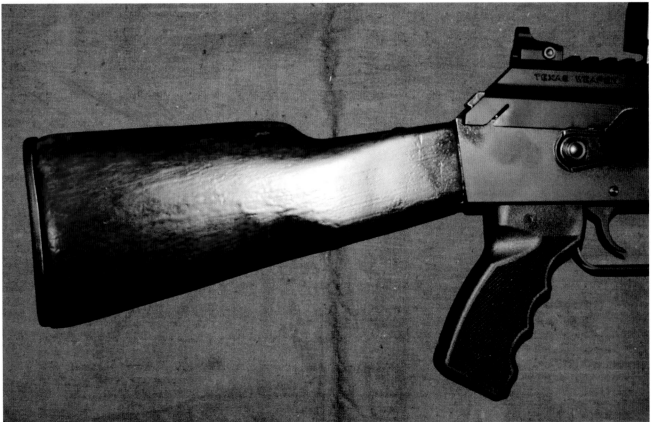

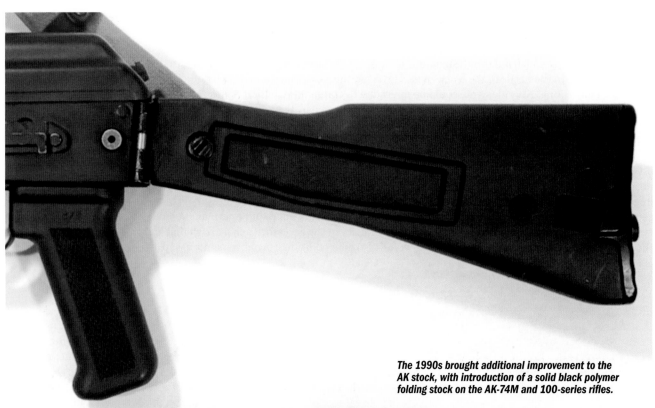

*The 1990s brought additional improvement to the AK stock, with introduction of a solid black polymer folding stock on the AK-74M and 100-series rifles.*

First on my list is the AK stock. I like the original AK-47 wood stock, though with its 6-degree downward slant it was not perfect. However, the later AKM and AK-74 straight stocks were pretty comfortable. Its length has come to be known as Warsaw Pact length in the U.S. AK world. Some may argue about the shortness, but as soon as a heavy winter coat, or body armor, or both are put on, the argument no longer stands. The Soviets came up with the buttstock length not out of economy of wood (there is certainly no shortage of that in Russia), but because of the six months of winter fighting they had to do in defense of their Motherland.

I still think that the AKS-74 side-folding stock is the best folding stock solution ever devised for a combat rifle. The only modification of this stock that actually improved it came with the introduction of plastic furniture in the early 1990s.

All of the new AK-100-series rifles were equipped with a solid polymer folding stock that used the AKS-74 folding mechanism, but by its shape resembled a conventional AK fixed stock. The new stock offered the better ergonomics needed for a modern rifle. I still think that the 100-series stock is very close to the ideal stock. One downside to the AK-74M or 100-series solid polymer folding stock is that it cannot be replaced for a better model. What I mean is, it can ultimately be replaced with some hard-to-get Russian stock that was made in some factory in very small batches, or via a custom job here. However, in all cases it would involve a fair amount of professional gunsmithing to further perfect the already good stock. This perfection is very subjective. What is perfect for one may not be for the other. Many AK shooters addressed the ergonomic shortfalls by simply replacing the fixed stock on their rifle with a longer plastic stock. It is still the simplest and cheapest way to improve the ergonomics for some shooters.

The real improvement comes by replacing a fixed AK stock with an AR-15/M4 tube to allow use of the telescopic AR-style stock. This modification is especially popular with American AK shooters who transitioned from the AR to the AK. With this modification, one can address the variable length of the rifle depending on seasonal clothing or personal protection requirements. In addition, it offers the flexibility of using any AR collapsible stock that a particular shooter knows and loves. There is no shortage of AR buffer tubes for AKs on the market today. One can choose based on simplicity or price. The same could be said about the AR stocks that can be installed on AKs using the AR-style buffer tube.

I have used many AR stocks on my AK rifles and, and based on years of experience with the buffer tube/stock combination, I certainly have my favorite. When dealing with non-folding telescopic stocks, I use the Vltor RE-47 AK Modstock adaptor because of its fit and overall quality and the fact that it also serves as a storage container in combination with a B5 or MagPul CTR or MOE stock. You just can't beat the quality and weight coupled with awesome value of these products. Some AK shooters using the AR buffer tube conversion may have their own tested and proven preferences.

The next step in AR buffer tube/stock combination modification for an AK rifle would be conversion of a fixed-stock model into a folder. There are options to convert an AK from fixed-stock to folder using either Romanian surplus folding "wire" stocks or newly manufactured stocks, like the Bonesteel AK/Saiga Folding Galil or the FAB Defense Tactical Side Folding Buttstock with Adjustable Cheek Rest, among others. These folding stocks bolt into the fixed stock position without any modifications to the gun. One particular stock in this category deserves separate mention, which I gladly do later in this chapter.

The other way to convert a stamped receiver AK to a folding-stock gun is to install the original Russian or Bulgarian AKS-74 or AK-74M folding mechanism and stock. This conversion would require a fair amount of gunsmith work, preferably by a qualified gunsmith. However, as mentioned, the most popular fixed-to-folding stock conversion is the installation of an AR buffer tube with folding mechanism. This modification allows use of the AR-style stock of the shooter's choice, and offers a telescopic feature and folding stock capability. There is a variety of folding AR-style buffer tubes on the market today, most using the Israeli Galil-style wedge lock folding mechanism.

AK enthusiasts can also choose what material the tube and mechanism is made of, steel or polymer, and to which side the stock folds. Again, I've used this folding stock system on numerous guns and have developed personal preferences. I like the stock to fold to the right side of the gun, so it doesn't interfere with a side-mounted optic. I also prefer a steel mechanism over plastic, due to rigidity and potential service life, even though I give up some weight advantages.

My personal favorites are the Bonesteel AK/Saiga folding stock or FAB Defense Folding Collapsible Buttstock Assembly with Metal Joint. I like to use these products in combination with MagPul CTR or MOE AR stocks due to their light weight and the dimensions. The MagPul stocks are slim and, as a result, fit nicely with this folding stock system on the AK rifle.

*The most popular stock replacement for an AK rifle is the AR-style buffer tube telescopic stock.*

## THE BEST AK STOCK

All of the buttstock options described above would work fine with pretty much any AK rifle. Some of the stocks are better than others, and all of the conversions have advantages and shortfalls. One, however, stands out as the best folding stock for a fixed-stock AK: the newest MagPul introduction, the ZHUKOV-S AK folding stock.

The ZHUKOV-S stock is made entirely of high-impact polymer, which MagPul has used for years on all its products. It's known for its durability and light weight. The stock has an integrated folding mechanism that is activated by pushing a button on the left side. The folding mechanism is not as bulky as some of its steel counterparts, and it folds the stock to the right of the gun and away from any interference with side-mounted optics. Even when folded, the position of the stock allows the rifle to be fired. It installs into the original fixed-stock slot at the back of the receiver and secures with a provided bolt and a bolt

driven wedge, which ensures the proper alignment of the stock assembly. Because the rear trunnion block tang is not used, it is cleverly hidden. The new stock is also telescopic, accommodating length-of-pull requirements for ergonomic reasons or for changes in seasonal clothing or body armor restrictions.

The ZHUKOV-S stock accepts standard MagPul cheek rest risers, depending on the type of sighting implement used. It also has several QD sling attachment ports, conducive to the use of a tactical sling.

When the newest Russian AK, the AK-12, came out in 2012, the biggest improvement over the standard AK-74M was not the abundance of Picatinny rails, but the ergonomic buttstock.

The new design addressed all the

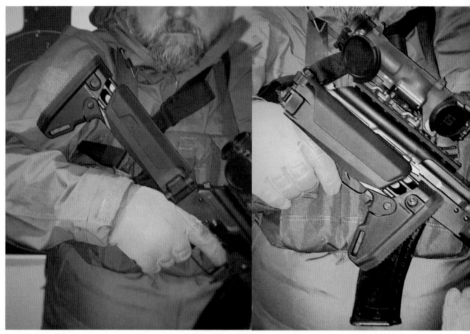

MagPul's ZHUKOV-S AK folding stock is simply the best AK replacement stock on the market today.

so-called shortcomings of the standard AK stock. The AK-12 stock is folding, it has an adjustable cheek riser and it is telescopic for adjustable length of pull. I attempted to build an AK-12 clone in my basement, and came close by adding accessories that mimic the AK-12 features to a standard I.O., Inc., AK-74. One major feature that I could not clone was the stock. MagPul did it for me with the new ZHUKOV-S. Light, functional, loaded with features, the ZHUKOV-S is one of the best stocks for an AK. But, its best feature is the $99 sticker.

Among its new AK accessories line, MagPul also released the MOE AK stock. Even lighter than the ZHUKOV, the MOE is a slim, fixed stock, and at $49 is a good option for AK enthusiasts who are not looking for a folder.

## PISTOL GRIPS

Just like the buttstock, the AK pistol grip can be easily replaced by anyone with a flathead screwdriver. The pistol grip is a feature that doesn't change the gun's performance, but could affect ergonomics and, as a result, the comfort level of the shooter. And, like a stock, it doesn't require irreversible modification to the gun.

In my opinion, there is nothing wrong with the AK original pistol grip. It fits my hand really well. Remembering that Soviet armed forces had to fight for six months in cold weather conditions wearing proper clothing, including heavy gloves, the original AK pistol grip was designed to be rather slim and does not have finger grooves. However, to address the differences in personal preference, options are available.

The original AK-47 pistol grip was a combination grip with steel frame and two Bakelite side plates. After switching to a milled receiver for the production model, the AK furniture received a face-lift and the pistol grip was replaced with a solid wood version secured to the gun with one long bolt and a T-nut. This simple pistol grip attachment survived numerous grip design changes and is the way the pistol grip is attached to most modern AK models. With introduction of laminate wood furniture, the pistol grip was made of laminate wood in line with the other parts.

Introduction of a lighter stamped receiver on the AKM saw a new Bakelite pistol grip as a cost- and weight-cutting measure. The switch to polyamide on the AK-74 in the 1970s resulted in the plum color and later black plastic grips. That's where development of the AK pistol grip in Russia stopped. The basic dimensions and form of the Bakelite grip survived until the recent introduction of Russia's new AK-12.

The lack of viable options for the AK in the pistol grip department spurred many accessories companies to develop an alternative to the original 60-year-old design. Today one can shop and choose a pistol grip to fit his or her ergonomic preferences.

While there are many options, replacing the AK pistol grip should not be for the sake of replacing and should have some substantiated reasoning behind it. In most cases, it would be to enhance comfort level for the shooter. Some of the replacement grips offer modularity and a nearly custom fit, with replaceable front and back straps, based on the size of the shooter's hand and length of fingers.

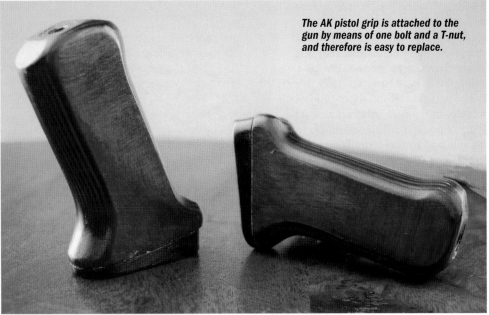

*The AK pistol grip is attached to the gun by means of one bolt and a T-nut, and therefore is easy to replace.*

*The Bakelite pistol grip replaced the laminate wood version and remained standard equipment into the 1980s on AKM, AK-74 and RPK-74 rifles.*

Most AK aftermarket grips are reasonably priced. A shooter may go through several options before settling on one particular model or design. Other than the AK's original polyamide grip, among my favorites are three models: the MagPul MOE AK grip and its rubberized mod the MOE AK+ grip; the U.S. Palm AK Battle grip; and the Tapco INTRAFUSE SAW-style pistol grip. All three are made of polymer and offer a great degree of comfort.

The U.S. Palm AK battle grip and the MagPul's MOE AK grip are modeled after these companies' successful AR grips. The Tapco INTRAFUSE SAW-style pistol grip follows the design of the M249 Squad Automatic Weapon pistol grip, as the name suggests.

All three of these grips are slim at the top, allowing for a comfortable grip and perfect trigger finger placement. All come with mounting hardware in place of an original AK grip bolt. The short mounting bolt allows use of the hollow space inside the grip for storage. In the case of the MagPul and Tapco grips, a trap door storage compartment is provided. These grips install in place of the original as a direct replacement.

The U.S. Palm Battle and MagPul MOE grips are priced at about $25, and the Tapco SAW-style pistol grip is under $20.

The pistol grips above are my favorite to use on my personal rifles. There are many other options when it comes to AK aftermarket pistol grips. Some of the standouts that I have tested in the past are the Hogue OverMolded (rubberized) AK pistol grip, the Command Arms (CAA) AK-47 pistol grip and the FAB Defense AK pistol grip, the latter two come from Israel and are based on the Israeli military design. All of these grips offer some advantage over the original factory grip, with more ergonomic contour, finger rests, and some even have replaceable back straps. There are many options and you should choose which you are more comfortable with. This quick and painless modification should add to the comfort level when shooting an AK rifle.

*One of the most comfortable and yet economically priced AK replacement grips is the Tapco INTRAFUSE SAW-style pistol grip.*

## HANDGUARDS

While I don't have a problem with original AK stocks and pistol grips to the point where I absolutely have to replace them to improve performance or comfort level, I cannot say the same for the handguards. Anyone who had to use an AK extensively has burned his or her hands once or twice. The size and design of the AK front handguards is good enough, and one can learn to work with them, but they're not ideal.

The evolution of the Kalashnikov rifle handguards is in line with the rest of the gun's furniture, from hardwood to laminate wood and on to polyamide. One point to notice is that AK handguards sit over the hottest part of the rifle. They wrap around the hottest part of the barrel and gas tube. As a result, the handguards get very hot if the rifle is being fired at an intense rate of fire. Wood is a poor heat conductor and works better than plastic.

Even then, the original AK-47 handguards had two heat-venting ports on each side to help with heat dissipation. These ports remained on the AK's wood handguards as the gun evolved into the AKM and later the AK-74.

However, later model AK-74 rifles' handguard design did away with the ports because of a larger gap between the upper and lower handguards. When the polyamide handguards were introduced on AK-74s, designers took the heat into consideration and installed a heat shield into the lower handguard.

The Soviet- and later Russian-made plastic lower handguards had a heat shield, polished almost to a mirror finish, that set them apart from Bulgarian or U.S.-made copies. The shield deflects heat upward where it escapes through the gap between the upper and lower handguards. This helped a bit, but still did little to help the gun move forward as a modern fighting carbine.

Even the first attempts by the Russians to add some sort of mounting rails on the lower handguard offered no adequate mounting solutions for modern combat implements demanded by the modern military. Again, the breach was filled by industrious American companies and later by Israeli manufacturers. The Russians followed suit. Today there are many options for aftermarket AK handguards ranging in material, functionality and even size.

AK handguards are easy to replace and usually do not require special tools, unless the new aftermarket handguards require different mounting to the rifle. In this case, most of the replacement handguards come with necessary tools. I've already touched on several handguard options in the optical sight mounting solutions section of this book. But, I'll repeat a bit here, as these products are also used to mount other accessories.

AK handguard solutions usually come in two types—aluminum and plastic. I use them both. The aluminum handguards require a specific attachment method, unlike the plastic ones, which use the original AK handguard retention system on the rifle.

## PLASTIC

Since the plastic handguards are basically a direct swap with original parts, I will cover them first. As with other AK accessories, I've had a chance to test and use a variety of polymer or composite handguards over the years. The obvious choice for direct replacement would be the newly produced Russian handguards that the Russian armed forces adopted for the AK-74M

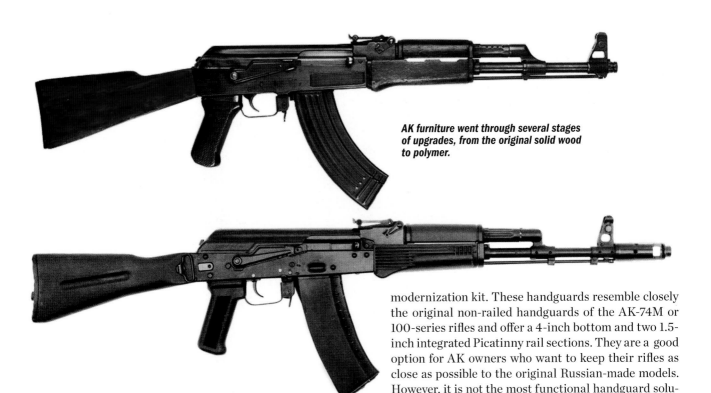

*AK furniture went through several stages of upgrades, from the original solid wood to polymer.*

modernization kit. These handguards resemble closely the original non-railed handguards of the AK-74M or 100-series rifles and offer a 4-inch bottom and two 1.5-inch integrated Picatinny rail sections. They are a good option for AK owners who want to keep their rifles as close as possible to the original Russian-made models. However, it is not the most functional handguard solution for a modern carbine.

Some other plastic handguards, like the CAA RS-47 and FAB Defense AK-47 polymer handguard with Picatinny rails, offer slightly better flexibility for mounting various accessories, coupled with ease of installation. The lower part of the handguards slides into the receiver of the rifle and is secured in place with the handguard retainer. The upper part is simply twisted into place like the original AK upper handguard. These handguards do not offer a rigid enough or reliable mount for optics or sights. They could, however, be used for mounting a variety of other implements, such as a vertical grip, a combat light or an IR illuminator. Mounting optics on the upper handguard would require a mechanical connection that some other handguard systems offer, such as the Mission First Tactical Tekko 2-piece AK-47 Polymer handguard with Integrated Rail System.

This set of upper and lower handguards, where the upper guard with mounting rail bolts to the lower, would provide a better mounting option for a collimator sight only and only for extreme close ranges. Just like the other plastic lower handguards, the Tekko guard installs directly as a replacement for the original AK part using the same retention. Again, it is not a solid or secure connection. Therefore, it is reasonable to expect significant deviation of POIs from POA. However, this option is good to go for mounting non-essential accessories from the marksmanship point of view.

Separately, I would like to mention the Hogue 2-piece AK-47/AK-74 Rubber Over-Molded handguard. It is for shooters who like the feel of a rubberized coating for extra grip. The Hogue handguards have a softer, smoother feel compared to other composite handguards. They're made of fiberglass with rubber overmold and install the same way as other composite handguards. As such, they are susceptible to the same mounting issues as the rest of the field. The lower guard is contoured to follow the original AK handguard design and therefore is very comfortable until one installs the removable optional rail. All of the mounting rails on the Hogue 2-piece AK-47/

*Attempts were made to add modularity to existing AK handguards.*

*I've worked with direct replacement plastic handguards and they usually work very well for mounting non-essential accessories, like vertical grips and flashlights.*

AK-74 Rubber OverMolded Handguard are removable and offer some mounting flexibility.

I'm not a fan of the plastic handguards, at least not until I find something that is practical and useful. With the obvious weight reduction benefit, most aftermarket AK composite handguards are suspect to me. Because they sit over the hottest part of the gun, they may be okay while at the range shooting at paper. But, when greater intensity of fire is called for, I would only trust the original factory composite guards with the factory heat shield.

There is, however, one newly introduced composite product (or rather products) that I will not hesitate to use on my "work" gun. In fact, I probably prefer it over the factory handguard: the MagPul MOE AK handguard, MOE AKM handguard and ZHUKOV handguard.

When I first saw the MagPul AK handguards, I knew that I would probably like them. First of all, they look like they belong with the rest of the MOE family of products. MagPul handguards for ARs have been proven many times over, even on the battlefield. They have earned the status of something to measure against when it comes to rifle composite handguards. Using the M-LOK rail mounting system, the MOE handguards offer vast mounting flexibility. The unmistakable MOE pedigree has been built into the new AK handguards. There are three MOE AK handguards, with two designed to fit two different modifications of the AK without any permanent modification to the gun itself. The third, the ZHUKOV, is the longer handguard that offers more mounting options and affords a shooter more gripping options for modern carbine handling or practical shooting. However, installation of the ZHUKOV requires simple but permanent modification to the rifle, i.e., removal of the front sling attachment from the handguard retainer. It can be done relatively simply with basic tools without help from a gunsmith. Some shooters would shy away from permanently modifying their rifle. It's certainly understandable, but the potential benefit that the extended handguard offers would most definitely outweigh any reason for keeping an ancient front sling attachment.

The MOE AKM handguard is the shortest of the three models and is a straightforward plastic handguard that replaces the AK's original parts without any modification to the gun. It utilizes the M-LOK mounting system for a variety of rails based on the shooter's requirements, and offers more ergonomic hand placement and grip compared to the standard AK handguard.

The MOE® AK handguard is designed to fit any stamped-receiver AK and installs in place of the original AK handguard with one small caveat. The MOE's lower guard is longer than the AKM model and, as such, would cover the front retainer with standard sling attachment on most newer AK rifles; that would interfere with its installation. Because of that, removal of the sling attachment is required.

When I got this handguard, I liked the length, which provided extra space for accessories. However, I was not keen on butchering my test rifle just yet. So, instead of modifying the handguard retainer on the rifle, I modified the lower handguard itself using a Dremel tool. I made two perpendicular cuts on the left side, removing the material slightly past the sling attachment, and the new lower handguard fit like a glove. The MOE was obviously designed to fit the Chinese Norinco Type 56 AK without any modifications. However, with a miniscule amount of elbow grease it could fit on any stamped-receiver AK.

All three models of MagPul AK handguards are made with proven high-impact composite material that is used on MagPul's other products, and all three have an integrated heat-deflecting shield. All three sets come with the same small and light upper guard that slides on the gas tube in place of the original. MagPul designers did not have any illusions of mounting optics on the flimsy AK gas tube, so they did not go for it. If there is a need for that mounting option, look into the UltiMAK or Troy Industries gas tube mounts that would work fine in combination with the MagPul handguards.

## ALUMINUM

Though plastic handguards with Picatinny rails would work fine on just about any AK, the thing to remember is that plastic, as any material, is subject to fatigue and stress when under load. It will break, crack, melt, chip or disintegrate at much less stress and load parameters than metal, including aluminum. The reason the original Russian polyamide handguards take more abuse is simply because they are steel reinforced. For AK shooters who would like a more rigid mounting option that involves the handguards, there are several products made of aluminum that offer just that.

Because of the lack of elasticity in metal compared to composite materials, almost all metal or aluminum AK handguards require mechanical mounting on the gun. Basically, they have to be securely bolted in place for rigid installation. The upper part of the set that replaces the original upper handguard is usually affixed to the lower handguard with bolts. Since the lower handguard is bolted to the gun, the aluminum handguard system as a rule offers a better platform for mounting optical sights on the upper rail.

I've already highlighted several aluminum handguard options in the "Mounts" section of this book, but I want to describe them here in detail to give you a better idea how to install them and how they would fit your AK.

The first is the Midwest Industries AK-47/AK-74 Universal handguard. I've been using this rail and its variations for years now. It's a solid piece of equipment that, once installed, should last for a long time. The lower portion is rigidly attached to the barrel of the rifle and the upper part is bolted to the lower.

The beauty of the Midwest Industries system is that shooters can choose an optic-specific upper instead of the 1913 rail. There are several variations to accommodate the most popular optical or collimator sights. The company has released several versions of the original quad rail handguards over the years. All had to do with different ways to install the "mission specific" 1913 rails instead of the integrated quad rail, thus reducing the weight and size of the handguards.

There is an SS model with a smaller 2-inch rail sections that can be attached using screws. The SS model was followed by the more advanced KeyMod handguard and later the M-LOK version. I've tested all of these and they are good-to-go no matter which one is chosen. They all attach the same way and accept the same top covers that are interchangeable.

The Midwest Industries AK-47/AK-74 Universal handguards do not require any irreversible modification to the gun and can be removed and replaced at will. The AK front sling ring stays untouched. However, most of the Midwest Industries AK handguards come with built-in QD sling attachment.

The Universal handguards offer pretty good flexibility for mounting accessories on an AK. However, the longer AK-47/AK-74 Extended handguard offers even more. Unlike the Universal handguards, the Extended version does require permanent modification to the lower handguard retainer. Again, it has to do with the front sling attachment that has to be removed. The benefits outweigh the small mod to remove the redundant part. Apart from the standard quad rail configuration, the extended handguards come in SS and KeyMod versions.

*The Midwest Industries AK-47/AK-74 Universal handguard is probably one of the first viable aluminum AK handguards that I encountered.*

Midwest Industries offers variations of handguards to fit just about any AK model that is available on the market today. Having worked with them, I consider them to be among the best AK accessories.

Krebs Custom offers two types of its own AK handguards. The quad rail forend for standard AK rifles is similar to aluminum handguards with integrated Picatinny rails from other manufacturers, with one exception. The company came up with solid attachment to the gun that does not involve the barrel. The Krebs quad rail handguard is a very good option for an AK.

However, for those who don't like the "cheese grater" effect of the quad rail handguard, Krebs released its latest AK-U.F.M. AK handguards. These are among the best aluminum AK aftermarket handguards available today. They install on the rifle similarly to the quad rail and sit solidly on the rifle. The accessory rails attach to the handguards with the KeyMod mounting system on the side and the bottom. The top part of the handguards has a 4-inch integrated 1913 rail.

The AK-U.F.M. handguards have rounded corners and feel just right in the shooter's hand. The smooth and slick forms make even an ancient AK rifle look like a modern fighting carbine. The KeyMod system offers necessary flexibility for mounting mission-specific accessories.

The last option for aftermarket AK aluminum handguards comes from Troy Industries in the form of its AK-47 Bottom Short Rail. Troy's rail is a one-piece replacement for a lower handguard and works with either the AK original upper handguard or an aftermarket replacement. I already described Troy Industries' AK-47 top rail as a replacement for the AK's gas tube in the "Mounts" section of this book. Together, the top and bottom rails make a complete and very flexible handguard mounting solution for any AK.

The Troy AK-47 bottom rail is made entirely from aluminum. It is long enough that, when installed on the gun, it extends from the front of the receiver all the way forward past the gas block. With the added length, this handguard not only provides adequate space to mount any combination of tactical implements, but it also gives the shooter more gripping surface—something AKs usually lack. The handguard itself is rounded in its cross section mimicking (to a point) the longer rounded AR handguards. The shape and length is conducive to improved handling by the shooter, resulting from a better grip. The necessary rail-mounting holes are provided along the entire length of the handguard. This allows any number of rail sections in different sizes to be installed if the need arises. Although this is a longer handguard, it does not require any permanent modification to the rifle. It installs in minutes in place of the original lower handguard using the same retention system. It comes with an Allen key wrench to tighten the tension on the handguard retaining bracket. No other tools are necessary.

There are other options from small and large manufacturers of AK accessories. The handguards described above are the ones with which I have personal experience. Whichever option is selected, make sure that practicality is driving your decision on what accessory to use on your AK rifle.

## MUZZLE DEVICES

With most of the important ergonomic and modularity-enabling accessories covered, the one other important accessory is the muzzle attachment. Though small, it can impact the accuracy, recoil and handling of the AK.

Originally, the AK-47 battle rifle adopted by the Soviet armed forces had a threaded barrel at the muzzle. However, no brake

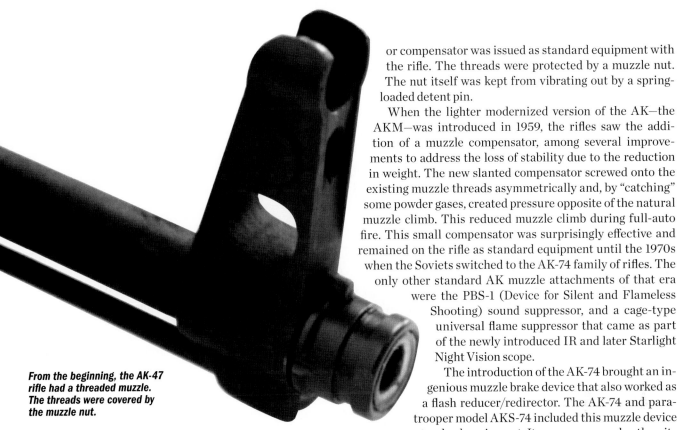

*From the beginning, the AK-47 rifle had a threaded muzzle. The threads were covered by the muzzle nut.*

or compensator was issued as standard equipment with the rifle. The threads were protected by a muzzle nut. The nut itself was kept from vibrating out by a spring-loaded detent pin.

When the lighter modernized version of the AK—the AKM—was introduced in 1959, the rifles saw the addition of a muzzle compensator, among several improvements to address the loss of stability due to the reduction in weight. The new slanted compensator screwed onto the existing muzzle threads asymmetrically and, by "catching" some powder gases, created pressure opposite of the natural muzzle climb. This reduced muzzle climb during full-auto fire. This small compensator was surprisingly effective and remained on the rifle as standard equipment until the 1970s when the Soviets switched to the AK-74 family of rifles. The only other standard AK muzzle attachments of that era were the PBS-1 (Device for Silent and Flameless Shooting) sound suppressor, and a cage-type universal flame suppressor that came as part of the newly introduced IR and later Starlight Night Vision scope.

The introduction of the AK-74 brought an ingenious muzzle brake device that also worked as a flash reducer/redirector. The AK-74 and para-trooper model AKS-74 included this muzzle device as standard equipment. It was more complex than its predecessor, the slanted compensator. It had an expansion chamber to allow more time and space for powder gases to burn and reduce muzzle flash, a "pancake" muzzle brake to reduce recoil, and a built-in compensator to reduce muzzle rise. It reduced muzzle flash significantly but it did not eliminate it entirely; that was evident when the rifle was fired in low-light conditions.

But it did redirect the flash blast to the sides. This helped the shooter to avoid temporarily blindness from the blast and continue shooting the rifle with good aim. It also allowed the newer Starlight NV scopes to be used without having to replace the muzzle attachment.

This AK-74 muzzle brake was so effective in reducing recoil and increasing the rifle's accuracy that all new Russian AK models no matter the caliber had one attached as standard equipment. Even the newest Izhmash offering—the AK-12—has a variation of this muzzle brake.

Other muzzle attachments came on the RPK-74 light machine gun and AKS-74U (the short version of the AK-74 rifle). The RPK-74 had a much longer and heavier barrel and bipod, and as such had no need for a recoil-reducing or stabilizing muzzle device. The longer barrel also offered more room and time for powder to burn, thus significantly reducing the muzzle flash. However, a small cage-type flash hider was installed on the gun as standard equipment. This small flash hider device worked like a charm and almost completely eliminated muzzle flash, eliminating the need to replace muzzle devices when using a NV scope.

The short AKS-74U device was an entirely different animal. The AKSU's 8-inch barrel provided no space for a finishing burn of the round's powder, with a 10-foot fireball making the short

*The 1959 AKM rifle came with a slanted muzzle compensator that was slightly offset to combat the rifle's muzzle rise.*

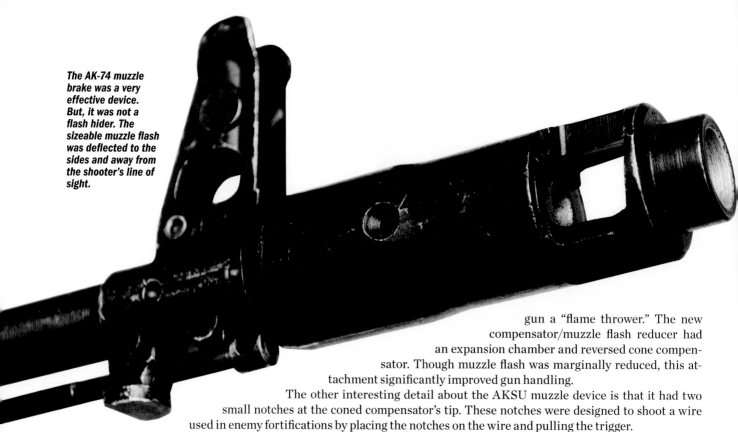

*The AK-74 muzzle brake was a very effective device. But, it was not a flash hider. The sizeable muzzle flash was deflected to the sides and away from the shooter's line of sight.*

gun a "flame thrower." The new compensator/muzzle flash reducer had an expansion chamber and reversed cone compensator. Though muzzle flash was marginally reduced, this attachment significantly improved gun handling.

The other interesting detail about the AKSU muzzle device is that it had two small notches at the coned compensator's tip. These notches were designed to shoot a wire used in enemy fortifications by placing the notches on the wire and pulling the trigger.

The original AK muzzle attachments can be classified as compensators, flash hiders, muzzle brakes and suppressors. There were attempts to make a combination muzzle brake/flash hider, but neither function worked perfectly.

There are many copies of the original AK muzzle attachments manufactured here in the U.S., mainly due to U.S. government actions. It's illegal to import any "assault rifle" with a muzzle attachment that is considered a flash hider. Flash hiders are deemed to be an "evil" feature and, as such, are banned from importation. At the same time, muzzle brakes are okay as long as they're permanently attached. This also gave a rise to the American-made AK muzzle devices as one of the six domestically produced parts to comply with BATFE 922r regulations when converting a sporting AK to more of the "military" configuration.

My philosophy on AK muzzle brakes is that they should only be replaced if the new device improves the rifle's performance. I like the original AK-74-style muzzle device. Therefore, I would not replace it on my AK-74 or AK-103 unless something better comes out. So far, I don't think there is such a thing. However, development is not standing still and we may see something better in the future.

Having said that about the AK-74 brake, I cannot say the same about the AKM slanted compensator. Although it works just fine, I think there's a lot of room for improvement in the muzzle brake and flash reducing categories. That's where the U.S. AK accessories manufacturers made huge strides. Today there is a plethora of AK muzzle devices, with the lion's share being muzzle attachments to fit the left-handed 14mm AK muzzle threads. As I've said before, the muzzle device should only be replaced if it will improve the performance and not just the looks of the gun. However, if the new device also looks good, then it is an instant winner. On my personal AKM rifles, I chose to go with muzzle flash reducing attachments versus the muzzle brakes. However, it's just a matter of personal preference. When choosing a muzzle device for an AK, consider what you are trying to achieve and go from there.

Most of the AK aftermarket muzzle attachments are reasonably priced. So, you might choose a couple for different shooting conditions. In any case, American AK enthusiasts are lucky that there is no shortage of muzzle devices to choose from.

## FRONT GRIPS

So far, I've covered the accessories that replace original AK equipment. But, what about the addition of non-standard accessories? One of the best additions to any AK is the front vertical grip, especially when the original handguards are replaced and some other accessories are installed.

The advantage of a front grip was recognized early on. Some of the Warsaw Pact countries, Hungary and Romania to be precise, even started equipping AKs with front grips. However, it wasn't until the wide use of front vertical grips by the U.S. Army on M4 carbines and the USMC M16A4 rifle that the front grip spread wholesale to the AK.

I have gone completely 180 degrees on the issue of a front grip on an AK. I trained with and used a rifle that didn't have one, so I thought there's no need for it. But, as soon as I installed a set of quad rail handguards with microdot sights on my AK, I realized the error of my ways. I couldn't handle the gun the same way I always had. The sheer size of the handguard setup prevented me from gripping the rifle by its handguards. Enter the front vertical grip. I quickly became a convert, and now I use them on most of my work rifles.

The advantages of a vertical front grip are obvious. It allows the operator to maintain a proper and positive grip on the front-heavy rifle. It makes the gun more maneuverable, especially in tight places. It provides support for additional weight of the handguard-mounted accessories, protects the shooter's hand from burns if the handguard gets too hot, and provides additional ways to carry an AK.

When choosing a front grip, consider the way the magazine is inserted into the rifle. The front upper tip of the magazine is inserted first, until it catches a trunnion block with its lip, then the magazine is rocked straight back until it locks into the gun. Because of the curvature of the AK magazine, a vertical front grip may interfere with insertion and removal of the magazine. So, the length and placement of the front grip must be considered. For example, a shorter grip can be installed closer to the receiver without interfering with the magazine change.

The curvature of the magazine itself, which is dictated by caliber, also impacts the location of the grip. The 7.62x39mm magazine has a smaller radius of curvature (it is more curved) and requires more clearance, forcing a shorter grip or farthest location. The 5.56 NATO (.223) magazine is the straightest of all AK mags, and would accept longer or closer-mounted front grip.

Krebs Custom went a different route and developed an offset front grip adapter that moves the front grip slightly off center, to the side of the gun and completely out of the way of the magazine. I've tried this setup and it works great. However, I prefer to have my grip directly under the centerline of the rifle.

Over the years, I've selected a couple of favorite grips. This is what I found to work for me and my meaty paws.

On my personal guns I use the MagPul RVG grip for Picatinny rails and the MVG grip for the M-LOK system or TangoDown Vertical Stubby foregrip QD or non-QD Stubby foregrip, with the MagPul being a better value and the TangoDown QD grip offering better flexibility.

There are a few things to remember when choosing a vertical front grip for an AK. There is no such a thing as an AK-specific front grip. Any vertical grip that works on an AR or any other rifle will work on an AK. Though some shooters prefer a longer grip, I found that the 3-3.5-inch grip works best for me. It can be installed closer to the receiver without interfering with magazine changes and still provide adequate grip. It also doesn't throw off the gun's geometry too much when shooting from a rest.

I prefer the grip mounted on a quick-detach mount, just in case I have to shoot off a sand bag or a pack for accuracy or for a long duration. I like to have the vertical grip installed as close to the receiver as possible, to better support the heaviest part of the gun and not have the support arm extended too far forward. But, my experience shows that the 3.5-inch vertical grip should be placed right at the middle of the AK regular-size lower handguard for a 5.45x39mm rifle and about one inch forward from the center of the handguard for a 7.62x39mm gun. As I've said, the location may vary depending on the length of the grip. In addition, the front grip should be located within the vicinity of other button-operated implements, such as a laser designators and/or tactical lights.

*The front-heavy AK is perhaps even more suitable for use with a front vertical grip than an AR.*

Some may ask about using angled foregrips instead of the full-blown vertical style. While it's a a solid product and a great fit for an AR carbine, the angled foregrip is not a good solution for the AK, mainly due to the possible interference with the magazine change. It can only be mounted toward the front of the handguard, forcing the support arm to extend too far.

## OTHER GREAT ACCESSORIES

Some smaller AK accessories are available that offer improvement of the gun's handling and performance.

Anyone who has handled an AK knows what the safety lever/fire mode selector looks like. It operates simply by sliding down from the safe position. One click for full-auto and two clicks for semi-automatic fire for select-fire rifles, and just one click all the way down for commercial sporting guns. Then back all the way up for safe.

The shape of the AK safety lever matches the cutout on the rifle's top cover and covers the opening for the bolt carrier handle, so the action is completely closed to protect it from the elements. The safety lever is operated with the right hand's thumb and index finger. This means you have to remove your hand from the pistol grip to manipulate the safety lever. I don't have any problem with that and can perform the task quickly and efficiently. However, for those who want to maintain a grip on the AK pistol grip there is a solution—the Krebs Custom Mk VI Enhanced Safety.

The lever on the Krebs safety has a small but important feature that significantly enhances its operation. Halfway down the bottom of the lever, there is an integrated lip that is within easy reach of the shooter's index finger. When properly installed, the Krebs safety lever can be operated by the trigger finger without releasing the pistol grip of the rifle.

The original AK safety lever is under tension to prevent accidental movement. Its tip has a small detent that is stamped into it, creating a small "bump" on the other side. The receiver has small dents corresponding with the "Safe" and "Fire" positions of the lever. The bump on the lever falls into the dent on the receiver, making a distinct click and securing the selector/safety lever in place. Because the lever is under tension, it rests in the chosen position rather reliably. However, too much tension on the lever makes it much harder to operate with the index finger alone. So, a careful balance of tension and movement has to be achieved when installing the Krebs safety by slowly and carefully bending it away from the receiver. Any bending should be done in small increments until the desired tension is reached.

The other small but important accessory is an ingenious replacement for the AK's original pin retaining clip, the infamous "paper clip." We already know that the AK is not the most sophisticated weapon. In fact, it is probably the simplest of all the rifles on the modern battlefield. However, there is a certain degree of sophistication in Kalashnikov's rifle. After all, modern operating and manufacturing principles had to be employed to make this gun function. Except when it comes to the axle pin retaining clip. The clip itself is nothing more than a piece of steel wire bent to fit around the grooves on the axle pins. The clip is under tension and rests flat against the inner left side of the receiver while it is jammed into the pins' grooves, preventing them from backing out of the gun.

It works just fine, but when the rifle is under maintenance and the fire control group has to be removed and then re-installed, it sometimes presents a challenge, especially for a less experienced shooter. Again, the solution is simple and practical—the Krebs Custom Trigger Pin Retaining Plate. The retaining plate simply drops in place and remains there secured by the safety/selector level. No tools of any kind are needed. Once installed, it can be removed and re-installed over and over again without worrying about losing tension. Both of these parts can be ordered from Krebs Custom, but I'm sure there are other manufacturers who make similar products. In any case, both are tested by me and are good to go.

Many AK shooters don't like to venture too far from keeping their rifles stock, but still want to modernize to what they are used to. Unlike the folding-stock AK rifles that have a rear sling attachment at the

*The MagPul RVG grip (left) and TangoDown Vertical Stubby foregrip (right) are the two grips the author uses on his rifles. Their size allows installation closer to the receiver for better stability.*

folding-stock hinge, allowing use of single-point sling, the fixed-stock models' sling attachment is at the back of the buttstock. One can certainly attach the sling to it, but it is cumbersome and not very practical.

The folks at Midwest Industries came up with a nice little solution, the Rear Single Point Sling Adaptor. This little gizmo is nothing more than a small base that attaches to the solid wood or plastic stock by two screws and a QD sling ring. This handy accessory modernizes the fixed-stock AK in minutes.

## ADVANCED AND HIGH PERFORMANCE UPGRADES

One more exciting AK accessory that I begged for from numerous manufacturers is finally here. The LINCH left-hand integrated non-reciprocating charging handle is designed as a drop-in application for the AK rifles offered by Davis Tactical Solutions, LLC.

The LINCH charging handle resides on the regular AK top cover. It requires no modifications to the weapon system and installs in seconds by simply swapping the rifle's top cover. The LINCH charging handle delivers a primary and alternate means of operating the bolt carrier. The charging handle is non-reciprocating during firing. The handle itself is a direct transfer from the FAL rifle. It can be folded out of the way when not in use. It rides on the guide rails that are welded to the standard AK top cover. The inner tab of the LINCH charging handle "hooks" to the bolt carrier on the left by the front trunnion block and pulls the bolt carrier back to recycle the rifle after a mag change.

With the LINCH, right-handed AK shooters can perform the entire reloading process with their left hand while maintaining the rifle in the line of fire.

As a complement to the LINCH left-hand charging handle, the FAB Defense magazine release accessory is easy to install right on the mag release tab and easy to use with a trigger finger.

I have known and used Geissele Automatics products for years. However, these were AR-15 components. Having extensively used their triggers, I've grown accustom to them and developed a kind of affinity for the feel and performance enhancement they provide. I can't say how many times squeezing the Geissele trigger I thought how nice it would be if they'd make one for an AK. They finally did. Since their release a couple of years back, I've installed ALG triggers in all of my work guns along with ALG return and hammer springs. To me this combination has become sort of standard for an AK upgrade. All of the Geissele ALG AK components are purposefully built to address certain deficiencies. Unlike most of the AK accessories that are geared toward cosmetic enhancement, these change the gun's performance.

All of the accessories described in this chapter are what I have tested and liked. I continue to use several of these implements on my rifles today. However, what works for me may not work for someone else and vice versa. The idea behind this chapter is to let AK enthusiasts know that there is a good supply of accessories to address any modification and/or improvements they may want to make to their rifles.

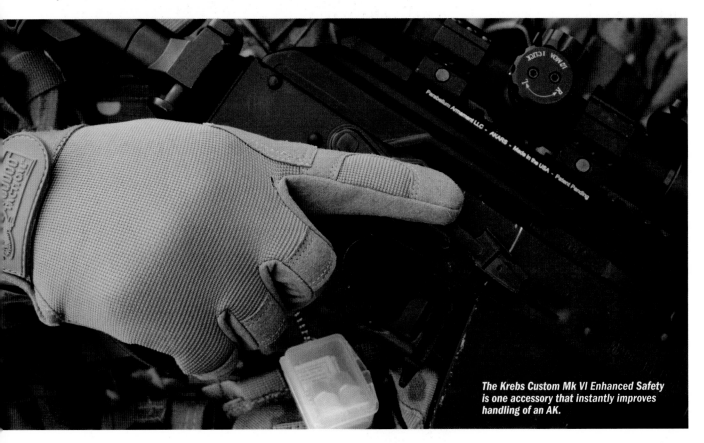

*The Krebs Custom Mk VI Enhanced Safety is one accessory that instantly improves handling of an AK.*

One of the most important things to keep in mind when modifying and accessorizing an AK is additional weight. The weight should be considered when choosing any accessory. Use plastic where possible, for example, when replacing the furniture. However, lightweight aluminum should be used for mounting critical attachments such as sights. The addition of weight to the gun not only increases the combat load (not as important in peace times), but it can also can throw off a gun's balance.

Another reason for this chapter was to show the depth of the field for American developed and built AK accessories and the fact that anyone with the desire and a little money can transform their "outdated" AK into something more modern. Here in the U.S. we have the luxury to pick and choose from the plethora of AK accessories.

*The LINCH left-hand integrated non-reciprocating charging handle is something the author has wanted for years.*

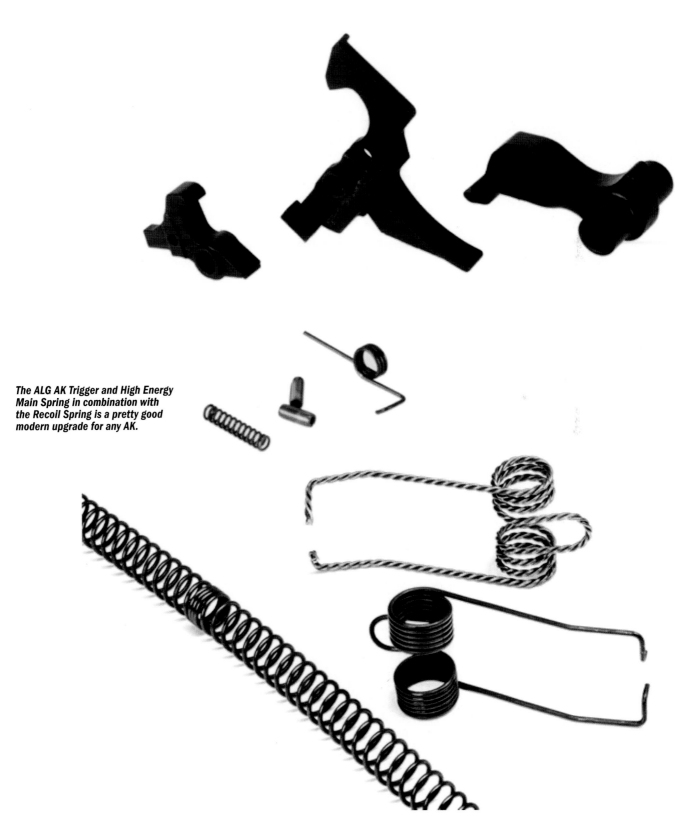

*The ALG AK Trigger and High Energy Main Spring in combination with the Recoil Spring is a pretty good modern upgrade for any AK.*

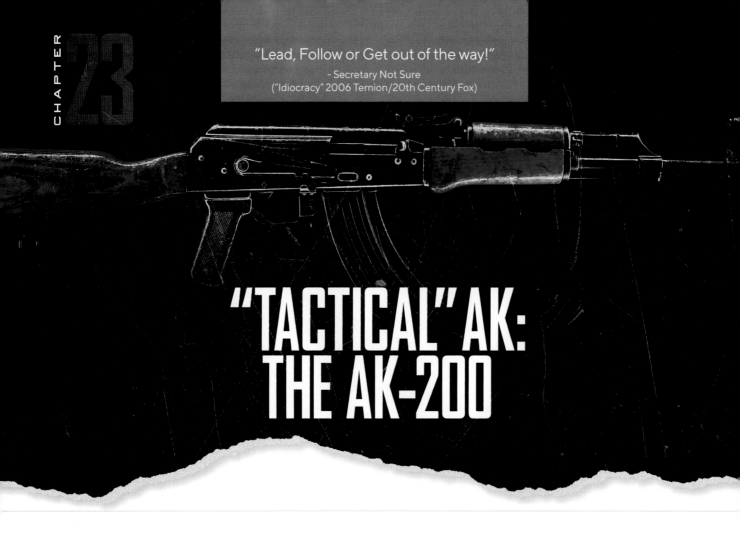

# "TACTICAL" AK: THE AK-200

I f I had to describe the Russian firearm industry in a few words, the words would be "old guard." The tradition of making military weapons for the Motherland has carried over to the way the Russian arsenals do business today, or at least until very recently. Aging personnel and management, who grew up on the fine Soviet bureaucratic system, continue to run the arms producing plants. One of their unmistakable traits is lack of flexibility when dealing with a constantly changing and demanding market. Their belief that they build the best guns in the world kills anything new and potentially good at its roots. That's why I was skeptical, to say the least, when Vladimir Gorodetsky, the Director General of Izhmash, announced the release of the AK-200 in 2010. Nevertheless, its release signaled the start of something that gun enthusiasts never expected: the beginning of the AK Avtomat's true modernization, or rather, the first attempt at trying to catch up with other, modern platforms.

*Director General of Izhmash Vladimir Gorodetsky demonstrates the AK-200 to the press in 2010.*

According to the Russian Defense Ministry, the AK-200 was to be delivered for full-scale testing in 2011. At the end of May 2010, the AK-200 was demonstrated to Vladimir Putin, Russia's Prime Minister at that time, during his visit to the Izhmash plant.

The distinctive features of the AK-200 were:

• Picatinny rail sections installed at the top, bottom and sides of the Avtomat.

• Increased magazine capacity to 60 rounds. Standard mags of 30- and 45-round capacity can also be used.

• Improved ergonomics.

• Quick caliber change with simple barrel replacement.

• Improved iron sights.

*On the surface, the AK-200 looks a lot like the standard AK-100-series Avtomats, with the addition of Picatinny rail sections that perhaps explain the weight increase.*

Unconfirmed yet claimed positive changes included greater reliability and accuracy of the new gun compared to previous models. Izhmash engineers claimed that the new AK-200 was on par with modern foreign Avtomats accuracy-wise.

The already identified negatives of the new AK-200 were:

• The new 60-round capacity magazine was not very reliable and wore out prematurely.
• Absence of a "modern" safety lever. The gun inherited the standard AK safety/selector level.
• Increased weight: 3.8 kg (8.4 lbs.) vs. 3.3 kg (7.3 lbs.) of its predecessor, the AK-74M.

The AK-200 was intended to have a clear advantage in combat efficiency over previous models—up to 40-50 percent.

*The new so-called safety lever is mounted on the pistol grip. It does not serve as a true safety or selector lever, but simply blocks the trigger from travel.*

According to the statement issued by Gorodetsky, the new Avtomat had a rail designed to facilitate attachment of additional equipment, such as laser target designators, sights and flashlights.

## LET'S SUMMARIZE

A number of Picatinny rail sections were added to the new Avtomat. Its new pistol grip was somewhat more ergonomic in comparison to the traditional one. The mechanical safety was added under the thumb of the right-hand side, which, unfortunately, was not connected in any way with the gun's traditional safety/selector lever, it simply blocked the trigger from moving back.

The AK-200 Avtomat was made simply and, probably, a bit crudely. As they like to say in Russia, it was assembled on the knee. The quality of such products is perhaps understandable for a small company that makes guns in a small shop and does not have competent staff. However, for an industrial plant with long manufacturing traditions this is simply unacceptable.

The top cover of the receiver, now hinged at the front, was fixed in place at the rear with use of a locking bar, somewhat reminiscent of the SVD or Valmet design, to ensure the uniformity with which the top cover sits on the receiver after each opening. This design eliminated the need to re-zero the sighting devices after each cleaning. Of all the AK-200 improvements, this particular modification would be employed by the Izhmash in making their newest AK-12 Avtomat and would be included in the new AK Modernization Program kit.

The top cover hinge was added to the redesigned rear sight block. The rear sight leaf hinge stayed unchanged. The leaf itself was shortened significantly, replacing the sliding range adjustment drum with rotating cam. The new model had a cleaning rod in a stock that retained the form and folding functionality of the gun's predecessors. Other than that, there were no changes to the design or functionality of the Avtomat.

It is necessary to distinguish between the desire to correct the shortcomings of the AK and the desire to make it look like

*The hinged top cover of the AK-200 was perhaps the best feature of the gun and was later used in the modernization kit for the existing Russian AKs.*

foreign counterparts. This difference should be the driving force behind designers' attempts to develop new weapons for the future. With the AK-200, they achieved neither. In the end, the AK-200 did not get the intended admiration or recognition in Russia. It was produced in a run of 5-6 units that were given away as gifts to "champions" of the project. I think that the AK-200 represents a clumsy attempt by the "Old Guard" to address modern requirements by adding accessories to the standard gun. Quite honestly, any AK shooter could have done it better here in the U.S. It was a useless variant any way you look at it, and cannot be viewed as a link in AK evolution, but rather as a subspecies that failed in its development. However, it was necessary. It had to happen to start looking at the aging AK platform from the point of view of a complete or significant redesign.

*Overall, the AK-200 received negative feedback from end users and was bound for obscurity. However, some of its features are employed today in the design of modern Russian firearms, like the hinged top cover with mounting rail and adjustable rear sight.*

# RUSSIANS ARE WATCHING AND ISRAELIS ARE HELPING

**H**umans are inherently lazy. If there is a way to cut a corner or two, the opportunity is almost always taken. In my experience, Russians are for the most part very practical people. Believe me, I would be the last person to belittle Russian inventions, innovations or discoverers. But, if you look at the Russian AK modernization program described later in this book, you can't help but notice a similarity in the plastic components in Russian modernization kits to those produced by the Israeli companies FAB Defense and Command Arms (CAA).

Why Israeli? If American AK accessory manufacturers led the way in this area, why did Russians ignore in some cases better U.S.-made components when they developed the modernization kit for their AKs? The answer is simple: marketing. If a customer doesn't know about your product or isn't able to get ahold of it, he will look elsewhere. The lack of flexibility in most U.S. small- and medium- size companies, that for many years relied on the domestic customer base, continues to hurt them. The U.S. market size would often accommodate the domestically oriented industries, but not always. Conversely, any size foreign manufacturer looks for export opportunities from the get-go.

Additionally, when it comes to firearms, U.S. manufacturers are subject to ITARs (International Traffic in Arms Regulations) restrictions that prohibit export of some things to some countries, with Russia at the top of the restricted list even before the sanctions. Foreign (especially Israeli) companies do not have similar restrictions pertaining to firearms accessories, including parts for AKs, hence the relatively easy entry of FAB Defense and CAA into the Russian AK market.

There's one more important factor. Historically, Russia is a multi-ethnic and multi-religious society. As such, it has a large Jewish population. Just like any other ethnic or religious group, representatives of the Russian Jewish diaspora contributed to the development and progress of Russia in many spheres of science and industry, from agriculture to space exploration and everything in between, including Russia's defense industry. There is an undeniable connection between Jewish Russians and Israel, where many have living relatives. Even so, the Soviet-Israeli relationship was a tumultuous one with no direct diplomatic relations. It really blossomed after the fall of the USSR. Israeli businesses did not waste any time taking advantage of the newly opened investment opportunities in Russia. Over the past 25 years, the business contacts between Russia and Israel have grown and expanded into many industrial areas covering interests of both countries. So, it should not be a surprise that it was the Israelis who occupied a leading role in the Russian AK accessory market.

Market penetration started in typical Russian style. When Russians adopt a hobby, it becomes more than just a hobby; it becomes a lifestyle. The same was true with paintball and later with airsoft. As the latter gained popularity in Russia, almost overnight the shops catering to the large body of airsoft enthusiasts became stuffed to the gills with all things tactical, including gun accessories that often can be used on real guns by real soldiers.

*This AK-74M, decked out in FAB Defense accessories, belongs to the Russian anti-terrorism unit "Alfa."*

Sometime in the early 2010s, Russian special operations troops started to carry upgraded AKs sporting Israeli-made plastic accessories. There was no uniformity in the way their Avtomats were upgraded. This would suggest that the modernization was initiated by the soldiers themselves and at their own expense. Luckily, they have a little more latitude in upgrading their weapons than the bulk of Russian troops. Since there was an abundance of Israeli products on the market, they were more widely used by the Russian Special Forces.

I can't argue with certainty that Israeli-made plastic AK accessories have been officially adopted by the Russian armed forces as the official replacement parts for military weapons. However, it's a fact that several Internal Ministry units have switched to FAB Defense AK upgrades across the board. The rest of the manufacturers had to catch up. Even today, one can enter a gun shop in Russia and find a full spectrum of AK accessories from FAB Defense and CAA. Some of the better AK products produced by U.S. companies rarely make it to consumers in Russia. Most of those that make it are imported through the grey market.

Dominance of Israeli AK accessories on the Russian firearms market determined the next chapter in the AK evolution.

*Given certain liberties, Russian Spetsnaz troops accessorize their AKs to fit the individual soldier. Here is a good mix of CAA and FAB Defense upgrades on the Alfa unit's AKs.*

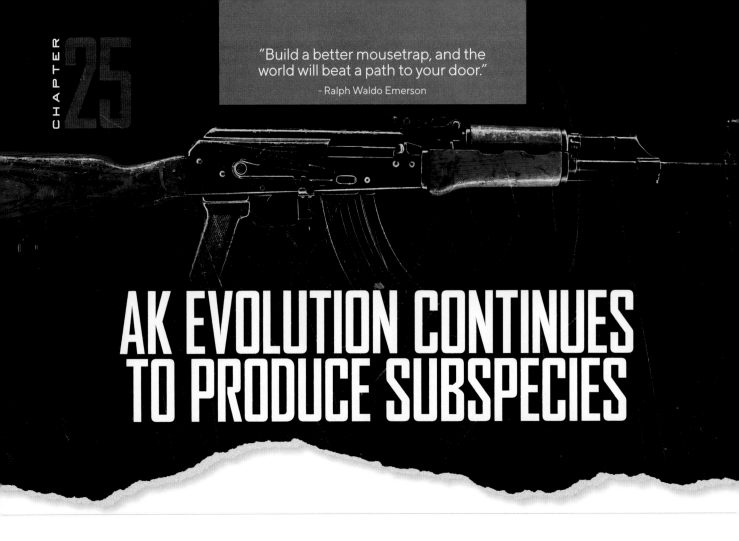

## CHAPTER 25

"Build a better mousetrap, and the world will beat a path to your door."
- Ralph Waldo Emerson

# AK EVOLUTION CONTINUES TO PRODUCE SUBSPECIES

I t's amazing how things work. Israeli companies influence Russian AK evolution and the AK inspires the Israelis to build something new. Well, new to us, not so much to them. Israelis are no strangers to the AK platform. Having captured a healthy number of new AKMs during the Sinai conflict with Egypt and producing the Galil in great numbers, the AK was hardly a foreign platform to them.

As described earlier, there was a strategic alliance made, between the Russian AK maker Kalashnikov Concern and Israeli firearm accessories manufacturer CAA, to create Kalashnikov USA and produce the legendary guns for the U.S. market.

However, as described, the alliance did not live long and succumbed to the pressures placed upon it by the U.S. economic sanctions. Nevertheless, Kalashnikov USA is alive and well and, in 2016 at SHOT Show in Las Vegas, presented something new—the AK-Alfa.

Does this new gun represent the next stage of the AK evolution? Will it replace all others or become another subspecies of the AK family?

"Russian tradition. Israeli innovation" was the slogan under which the new version of the Kalashnikov assault rifle—AK-Alpha—was presented to the U.S. public during the show.

The new AK variant was developed by Israeli designers. The official manufacturer of the new Avtomat will be the company "Kalashnikov Israel." This is a joint venture between the Kalashnikov Concern and the Israeli company CAA. Let's take a closer look at this venture.

*At SHOT Show in 2016, CAA under the Kalashnikov USA brand presented its take on the old Soviet platform, the AK-Alfa.*

The Israeli company CAA (Command Arms & Accessories) was established 12 years ago by brothers Moshe, Dudy and Eldad Oz. Before that, they all served in various Israeli army special operation and police units. Initially, CAA specialized in development of various attachments to popular types of weapons. The company's first product was an adapter for firing while standing (!) on the roof of the car. It was easily adapted to almost any type of weapon. The device quickly became popular, and has been adopted by special police units of several countries.

CAA's next product was a counter, showing how many rounds remained in the magazine of the rifle while shooting. Another well-known CAA product is a handgun attachment, Roni, that effectively turns a handgun into a carbine, sharply increasing the accuracy and efficiency of the gun, especially at distance.

*Fully modular, the AK-Alfa can be configured for an individual shooter and for any mission.*

CAA is based in Kiryat Gat, Israel, and has a branch in Florida. It is considered relatively small by Israeli standards, with annual revenue of approximately $50 million. However, the size does not stop CAA from constantly innovating and adding to its product portfolio. The development of the new version of the AK was started in 2011, after meeting with representatives of the Russian defense industry.

Having received a green light from the leadership of the Russian defense industry to modernize the AK and promote the new version on the world market, CAA created a new division, having recruited nearly 250 highly qualified designers, engineers and workers. Up to 90 percent of the employees were repatriates from the former USSR, so that some continuity in the development of the new version remained.

In the new rifle, the Israeli designers implemented an ambidextrous safety and charging handle, a telescopic stock, Picatinny rail on the entire length of receiver and handguards, removable Picatinny rail sections and index finger magazine release. As a result, an essentially new Avtomat was created with options to fit to any soldier, depending on his or her individual mission or preference. The new gun retained the original AK caliber of 7.62x39mm. I only wish that the designers would adopt the 74 platform and come up with 5.45mm and .223 variants in the near future.

The new Avtomat received the designation "AK-Alfa" after the famed Russian anti-terrorism unit. The years 2014–2016 brought further refinement of the new Avtomat. At the same time, the interest of the Russians to cooperate with CAA significantly increased as a result of the U.S. and European sections that affected Russia's defense industry.

As mentioned, developed in Israel by CAA, the AK-Alfa was first shown to the public in 2016. This weapon is being promoted in the world under two brands—Kalashnikov USA and Kalashnikov Israel—while the Russian Kalashnikov Concern has not officially commented on its attitude toward this model and its branding.

The AK-Alfa series is planned for production in four basic variants (two calibers and two barrel lengths). At the same time, we need to remember that the new gun is just a modernization of the classic Kalashnikov Avtomat. The existing prototypes are built on Russian-made Saiga carbines 5.56mm and 7.62mm barreled actions. It is assumed that the AK-Alpha series will be produced in both the semi-automatic carbine version for the civilian market and select-fire Avtomat for police and other government entities.

It's worth noting that there are no plans from the Israeli and Russian armed forces to adopt the AK-Alfa for service.

After all the excitement clears, the AK-Alfa is just another attempt to improve the ergonomics of the AK while maintaining its main advantages—high reliability and ease of maintenance. All of the main components that make the AK what it is are retained; the receiver, barrel, gas block, gas tube, bolt group and trigger group all come from the Saiga carbines manufactured in Russia. A plastic case with an integrated pistol grip, trigger guard and magazine shaft are installed over the receiver. The receiver itself was modified to fit a long aluminum top cover with an integrated Picatinny rail on top. The top cover is mounted on the "dovetail" in the front and is fixed with a transverse pin in the back. The AK-Alfa's plastic "exoskeleton" is equipped with a plastic collapsible adjustable folding stock. The 7.62x39mm version accepts standard AK magazines, whereas the .223 variant feeds from the standard Galil mags.

Like I said, the new AK-Alfa is an interesting gun. Its designers addressed most of the AK ergonomic problems. With the addition of one complete "kit" to the stripped down AK, they have turned the old platform into a modern rifle that is easy for Western shooters to comprehend. Such upgrades can affect the gun's performance by improving the handling of it. But, that is where they stop. The AK-Alfa rifle mechanically is identical to a regular AKM and, as such, it shoots about the same. Is it a link in the AK evolution chain? With its unclear prospects and lack of mass production or significant sales, it is most likely not. However, it is definitely a move in the right direction.

# AFTER ALL THE EXCITEMENT CLEARS, THE AK-ALFA IS JUST ANOTHER ATTEMPT TO IMPROVE THE ERGONOMICS OF THE AK WHILE MAINTAINING ITS MAIN ADVANTAGES—HIGH RELIABILITY AND EASE OF MAINTENANCE.

*Despite a solid marketing effort, the new Israeli AK is not being considered for service with Russian armed forces.*

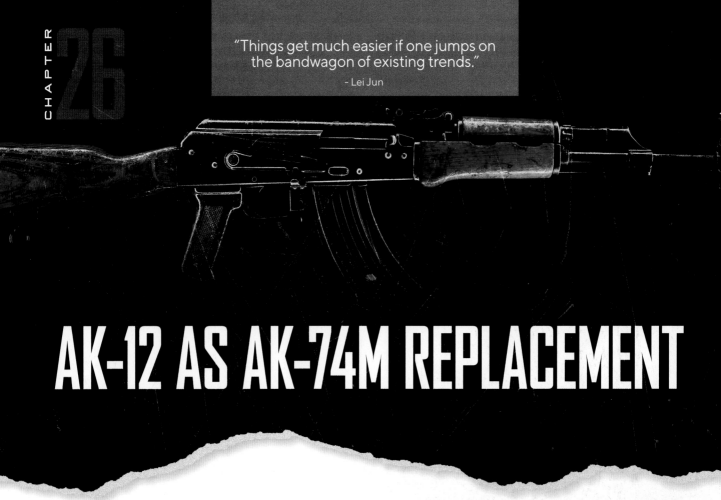

## CHAPTER 26

"Things get much easier if one jumps on the bandwagon of existing trends."

- Lei Jun

# AK-12 AS AK-74M REPLACEMENT

**M**eanwhile in Russia, with hands untied by the free market economy, the Russian Izhmash Arsenal finds itself in possession of creative license. Having realized some commercial success, the plant's designers now take it upon themselves to design and develop new firearms. Just as with the Israeli AK-Alfa, on their own initiative they took on the challenge of addressing all of the current AK's shortfalls in one big redesign. Except in this case, the Russians have also tried to address the performance of the gun.

By now, everyone knows about Russia's "new" AK-12 Avtomat released by the Kalashnikov Concern in 2012. The Izhevsk Arsenal placed a lot of stock in the development of this rifle for the Russian armed forces, whose main battle rifle was becoming rapidly outdated. Though it's a solid platform, the AK-74M does not fully satisfy the needs of today's gunfighter.

The new gun addressed the AK-74M's shortfalls in several areas. Ergonomically the AK-12 left the older AKs in the dust. The telescopic, folding stock

*The AK-12 was the first truly exciting Izhmash offering since the AK-74M was introduced in the late 1980s.*

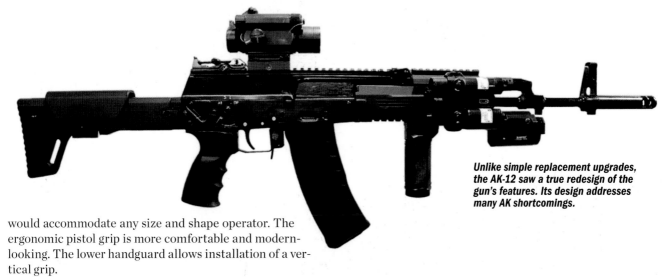

*Unlike simple replacement upgrades, the AK-12 saw a true redesign of the gun's features. Its design addresses many AK shortcomings.*

would accommodate any size and shape operator. The ergonomic pistol grip is more comfortable and modern-looking. The lower handguard allows installation of a vertical grip.

From the operational point of view, the new AK is now ambidextrous with thumb-operated selector/safety lever, push button magazine release and ability to have a charging handle on either side. Modularity of the rifle was increased dramatically. The AK-74M is equipped with a side mounting rail that was standard for the AK. It worked fine, but offered very limited space for mounting implements. There was no place to mount a combat light, laser designator or sight/night vision combination in tandem. In the U.S., we have a smorgasbord of commercially produced handguards with 1913 rails to address AK modularity. However, the Russian military did not have the same option. AK-12 designers corrected this deficiency with a full-length rail section running from the gas block to the back of the receiver, providing more adequate space for any accessory that one would want to slap on a rifle.

The biggest claim from the AK-12's creators, and what separates the new Russian gun from other upgraded AKs, came in the area of the rifle's functionality. Engineers claimed that the new gun had better firing efficiency, that it was 30-50 percent more accurate than its predecessor. The AK-74 is already a decent shooter. One can get pretty proficient with it. However, the new claim had to be considered and examined. The designers also claimed that they achieved better results, but kept the original Kalashnikov system. Visually one can notice a double-chambered elongated muzzle device. Adding a second "pancake" brake improved recoil slightly. The gun appeared to have the same barrel length and diameter as a standard AK-74. The other areas of improvement are the gas system, weight of a bolt carrier and recoil spring.

Having said that, is the new gun that much better? And, should the Russian military immediately re-arm? That's exactly what Russian top brass wanted to find out with tests. The results proved that the new AK-12 was, in fact, better than the standard-issue AK-74M, but only marginally, and did not warrant total re-armament of the entire Russian armed forces. Then there was also the question of 12 million existing AK-74 rifles in the hands of the soldiers and/or packed in military warehouses throughout the country. What did the top brass like and dislike in the new AK-12 Avtomat?

*Later modification of the AK-12 saw addition of front sight/gas block combination and new muzzle device.*

## BUILDING MY OWN

I immediately liked what the Izhmash engineers made and how they addressed some of the AK's issues. The new gun has everything that a modern AK shooter wants the rifle to have. But, how did it work? Would its upgrades improve the gun's performance? I wanted to find out for myself.

Before this radically redesigned AK appeared, AK enthusiasts could clone most of the Avtomat variants, as they were available in the U.S. However, with anti-Russian sanctions in place, I don't think we will see a commer-

*I took on the task of converting an I.O., Inc., standard AK-74 into a copy of the new Russian Avtomat.*

cial version of this gun stateside anytime soon. All we can do is build a standard off-the-shelf AK rifle into something that comes close to the new Russian gun ergonomically and functionally. I've built many rifles that I've used one time or the other for work. And as such, I've tested many configurations, employing numerous accessories from multiple manufacturers. I've rejected some and selected only the ones that worked perfectly for me based on functionality and practicality. I decided to embark on the great adventure of trying to clone the new Russian AK-12 Avtomat. I chose to build my AK-12 on a simple off-the-shelf I.O., Inc., fixed stock AK-74 built with Bulgarian parts.

I had to collect correct parts and accessories to match the new Russian gun. After closely examining the features of the AK-12 and analyzing their functionality, I came up with a short list of suppliers and their products. I planned to not only mimic the appearance of the gun but also replicate its performance.

## AK-12 MAIN FEATURES AND DIFFERENCES

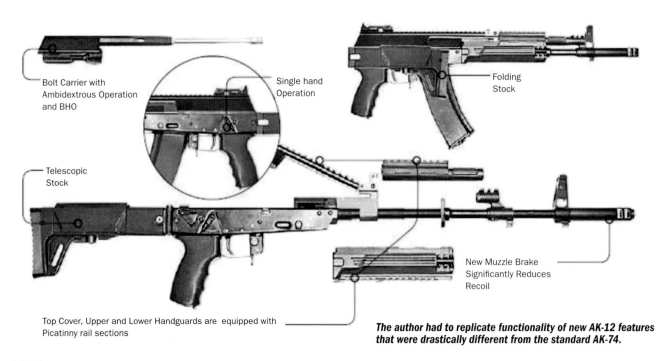

Bolt Carrier with Ambidextrous Operation and BHO

Single hand Operation

Folding Stock

Telescopic Stock

New Muzzle Brake Significantly Reduces Recoil

Top Cover, Upper and Lower Handguards are equipped with Picatinny rail sections

*The author had to replicate functionality of new AK-12 features that were drastically different from the standard AK-74.*

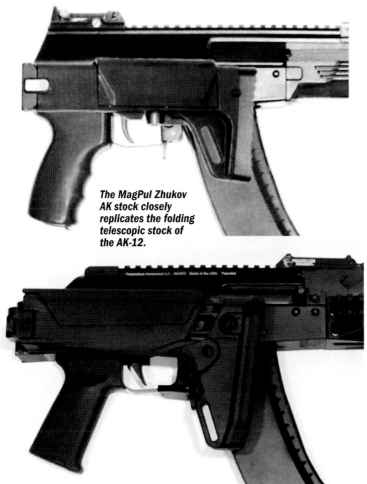

*The MagPul Zhukov AK stock closely replicates the folding telescopic stock of the AK-12.*

I have worked with MagPul, FAB Defense, Command Arms (CAA) and Brownells for years. The newcomers were CNC Warrior, Geissele Automatics and Legion USA for those hard-to-find Russian parts and accessories.

I started with appearance. First the stock. The AK-12's folding stock is a completely new design and had three main features: it is telescopic, it has an adjustable cheek piece and it folds to the right. Actually, the AK-12–style folding telescopic stock was easy to replicate with MagPul's ZHUKOV stock, in my opinion the best AK stock to come out of the commercial U.S. market. This stock has all the features of the AK-12's stock. It is telescopic and folds to the right. There is no built-in adjustable cheek riser, but one can order removable risers of different heights from MagPul. I've opted for a 1/4-inch riser.

It appeared the AK-12 had an ergonomic pistol grip similar to the one from CAA. There are many options for a similar modern Russian grip. Two obvious choices would be FAB Defense AG-47S or the G47 directly from CAA. However, I went with MagPul's AK grip for my AK-12 clone, simply because it is more comfortable for me and best fits my hand. Also, it is modern and, like the new Russian grip, has a storage compartment.

Next were the handguards. The AK-12 features front handguards specifically designed for it, with a full bottom and top 1913 (Picatinny) rail

as well as small rail sections on both sides. This presented a problem. None of the handguards I've worked with looked even remotely like the AK-12's. In my search for more solid and well-built AK handguards, I came across Legion USA and its line of Russian Zenitco products. I opted for the Zenitco B-10M lower guard and B-19 upper for my AK-12 clone because of solid mounting, smooth finish and light weight. Also, it looked good. However, the real reason was the upper guard/gas tube cover with low rail section that sits lower than HG retaining brackets. With basic appearance/ergonomics upgrades completed on my clone, I moved on to more serious upgrades, like additional 1913 rails on the receiver covers.

The new AK-12 had a full-length rail running on a top of the receiver cover. Here I had several options. The obvious one is the Texas Weapon Systems Dog Leg Rail, but I opted for AK Adaptive Rail System (AKARS) made by Parabellum Armament Group. I like the AKARS better because it has the three-finger hinge to TWS's one and it uses the original AK top cover without the return spring modification. I also like its built-in U-slot rear sight. Just like the Dog Leg, the AKARS installs into the original rear sight hinge. I had the AKARS rail to go on the gun, but it would only cover one feature. It would not replicate perhaps the most attractive feature of AK-12—the ability to charge the gun with the left hand. A search online produced an awesome find—the LINCH AK top cover with left-hand charging handle from Davis Tactical. A quick call revealed that they also make a LINCH/AKARS combi-

*It is impossible to find a close copy of the AK-12 handguards. the author chose the Russian Zenitco B-19 handguards for functionality and other positive attributes.*

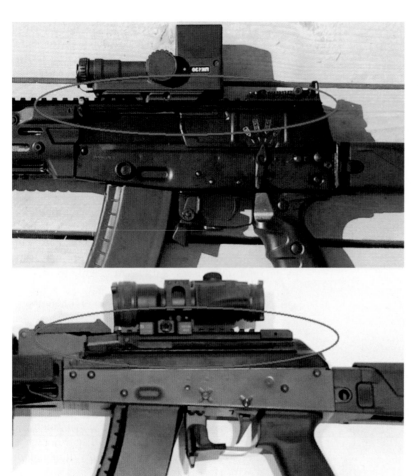

nation. That's what went on my AK-12 replica. With ergonomic and modularity enhancing upgrades out of the way, it was time for modifications that potentially would improve performance and operation.

AK-12 designers claim that the new rifle produces better results than the standard AK-74 when fired on full-auto. For obvious reasons, I could not easily replicate the improved full-auto performance on my clone guns. All I could do was try to improve rapid semi-automatic fire accuracy of the rifle. The standard AK trigger is not bad and allows a shooter to fire the rifle rapidly. However, I opted for a Geissele Automatics ALG Defense AKT AK trigger. The trigger group comes complete and drops in place of the original. It has a much smoother release and significantly shorter spring-assisted reset. I could feel significant improvement immediately after installing it. For additional improvement, I installed the ALG high-energy hammer spring. Now my AK-12 clone was more conducive to sustained rapid semi-automatic fire.

Recoil is usually blamed for less than perfect automatic rifle accuracy. There are three possible areas on the gas-operated rifle where

improvements can be made to lessen the recoil. The gas system I could do nothing about without serious modifications. However, I could do something with the muzzle brake and recoil spring.

First, I installed ALG AK recoil spring. The new spring is longer, has two compression zones and is somewhat more resistant compared to the original. In theory, the new spring should slow the traveling bolt carrier and soften the report while recycling quicker.

Next was the muzzle device. The AK-12 has a newly designed, longer double-chamber brake with expansion chamber similar to that of the AK-74. The additional "pancake" brake and elongated expansion chamber should soften recoil impulse. I was left with the prospect of finding a device that looks and functions the same or similarly to that of

the AK-12. Legion USA yet again had what I was looking for to create my AK-12 clone, its Russian-made Red Heat Storm muzzle brake. The Storm brake has a larger expansion chamber, a brake chamber and two additional sets of side baffles that assist with braking muzzle blast.

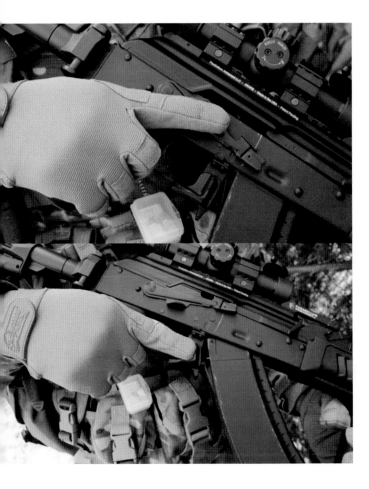

Obviously it is impossible to replicate the AK-12 controls exactly. The author was, however, able to achieve single-hand operation with use of a Krebs Safety and CAA extended magazine release lever.

A couple of other improvements had to be made to replicate the handling of the AK-12.

Since I was using a standard AK-74 and receiver and could not replicate the AK-12's thumb safety/selector and push button mag release, I did the next best thing by installing a Krebs Custom safety lever and CAA's AK-47/74 extended magazine release. Both can be operated by the shooter's index finger.

My AK-12 clone was done. It looked pretty close to the original Russian gun. Side-by-side comparison revealed very few differences from the original. But, would my newly upgraded rifle function like its Russian sibling? There was only one way to find out.

At the range, I set up at the 50-yard firing line. With red-dots installed on both rifles and a 21-inch steel humanoid target in place, I went to work with my AK-12 clone. After the first shot, I immediately noticed a difference in the recoil. Then I proceeded with a rapid-fire exercise with my 5.45, pulling the Geissele trigger as fast as my finger would move while keeping the dot on the target. This proved to be an easy chore. Only a couple of rounds missed the mark, the others were peppering the target, producing familiar pings.

I was ecstatic. First, the improvements to the standard AK-74 were immediately noticeable. Russian designers were right, the new AK-12 is not only more ergonomic and modular, but it also shoots very well. I'm not sure I'd go so far as to say it was 30-50 percent better than the AK-74M, but the difference was clear. Secondly, I built it with components readily available on the market today.

Now we just have to wait and see what fate befalls on the Russian AK-12. Will it become the next stage in evolution or remain the variant that influenced further development of the AK?

In the end, the author managed to put together a gun that not only resembles the AK-12, but also functions like one.

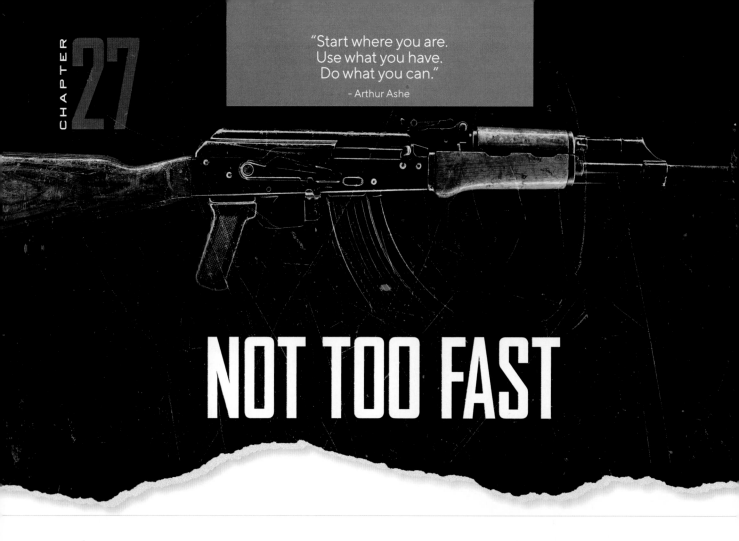

## CHAPTER 27

"Start where you are.
Use what you have.
Do what you can."
– Arthur Ashe

# NOT TOO FAST

**A**K-12 tests produced solid but marginal results. However, the idea of introducing the AK-12 to the Russian military was met with meager enthusiasm. The rifle's marginal performance improvements over its predecessor did not justify a huge and expensive re-armament program, especially considering the supposed 12 million AK-74 rifles still in the Russian armed forces possession, with the bulk of them still in factory grease packed away in warehouses throughout the land.

At the same time, the military officials understood the need for modernization of Russia's main battle rifle. The AK-74M was starting to show its age and no longer could fully satisfy the demands of modern combat.

The military opted for gradual rearmament. A relatively limited num-

*The Russian military brass made a prudent decision to upgrade existing AK-74s using a modernization kit. It was first shown to the public during the Victory Day Parade in 2015.*

ber of AK-12 Avtomats was ordered for advanced and special operations troops. The emphasis was placed on modernizing existing stockpiles of AK-74s.

This was a blow that could topple any manufacturer dependent on government orders to sustain its existence. Despite the disappointment of not receiving large orders for a new rifle, Izhevsk engineers accepted the challenge and came up with an upgrade kit. Unprecedented in its scope, the rifle modernization program was launched by Kalashnikov Concern and Russian

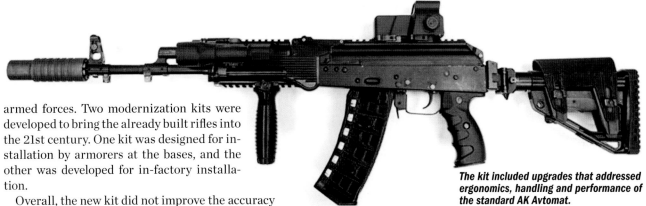

armed forces. Two modernization kits were developed to bring the already built rifles into the 21st century. One kit was designed for installation by armorers at the bases, and the other was developed for in-factory installation.

Overall, the new kit did not improve the accuracy of the AK-74 that much, as the rifle already had pretty good inherent performance well within the Russian military requirements. The only performance enhancement came in the way

*The kit included upgrades that addressed ergonomics, handling and performance of the standard AK Avtomat.*

of a muzzle brake "shroud" that installed over the standard AK-74 muzzle brake to reduce its blast signature. The other improvements addressed handling and modularity of the rifle. Now all the fixed stock rifles were fitted with AR-style telescopic folding stocks that can fold left or right. The AKS models' folding stocks were replaced with the new AR-style stock, with an additional hinge that would allow opposite side folding.

*The later version of the upgraded AK saw muzzle device replacement. Instead of a multi-piece baffle-type massive attachment, a simple cage type flash hider was installed.*

The lower handguard had a bottom rail, to which the front vertical grip (also part of the new upgrade kit) could be attached, and two smaller rail sections on both sides. The upper handguard was replaced with a 4.5-inch rail section that is in the same plane as the new hinged top cover with its own 7.5-inch Picatinny rail. The ergonomic pistol grip completed the upgrade kit.

Basically, the Russians arrived with their own modernized fighting carbine, only on mass production scale. Most of the components were based on American or Israeli designs. That was smart. By the time the kit arrived, all of the similar components had been tested and proven.

## BUILDING MY OWN

Looking at the newly upgraded Russian rifles, I can't help but think that anyone can upgrade their AK to the same level. U.S. AK shooters have been modernizing their rifles for years with accessories that are available on the commercial market. However, what makes the Russian kit different is that all of its components have been tested by the military and selected for mass issue to the troops in the field. If one of the world's most powerful armed forces adopted this kit as standard equipment, can we replicate it using products that are readily available?

Inspired by my AK-12 clone build and the results it produced, I decided to go a step further and chose the 7.62mm AKM-type rifle instead of the AK-74 platform. Why the AKM? The original modernization program was geared toward AK-74 rifles, but it also covered AKMs and AK-103s that are in service with Russian armed forces

*The author once again attempted to convert a standard AK (this time the I.O., Inc., AKM-247) into a Russian kit clone. He went with the .30 cal. version, thinking there would be a more dramatic performance change. Plus, the new kit was universal and would be used for AKM and AK-103 upgrades.*

## Universal Modernization Kit
### For Kalashnikov Avtomat

Hinged Top Cover with Picatinny Rail

Folding Telescopic Stock

**КАЛАШНИКОВ**
КОНЦЕРН

Ergonomic Pistol Grip

Handguards

Flash Hider

Tactical Flashlight

Front Vertical Grip

*(above) Looking at the factory poster, it seems pretty straight-forward. Most of the new components are direct replacements and are available on the market. The trick was to match them.*

*(right) The author was able to match the new Russian stock pretty closely in functionality and appearance.*

today due to the subsonic capabilities of the 7.62x39mm cartridge. Also, I suspected that all the enhancements I made to the AK-74 would dramatically improve the standard AKM's performance. I pulled I.O., Inc.'s best-selling standard AKM-247 from my gun safe to try and turn it into the Russian modernized AK Avtomat.

Once again, I had to examine the Russian kit closely to identify the components needed to turn my AKM into the Russian-style modern upgraded AK. Obviously, the cosmetic or external features were easy to see. However, apart from the modified muzzle device there was no information on any of the internal upgrades. Maybe they were not needed for the AK-74, but I thought I'd try to play with some components in an effort to improve the AKM's performance. My research identified required products. It turned out these components came from the same vendors that supplied the parts for my AK-12 build.

Again, I tapped into MagPul, FAB Defense, Command Arms (CAA), Brownells, CNC Warrior, Geissele Automatics, Legion USA and K-Var Corp. as sources for the components needed for my build.

I started with the buttstock. The Russian kit's stock was a telescopic AR-style folder. Telescopic and folding features for the modernized AKM were actually easier to replicate. The stock itself looked a lot like MagPul's CTR stock, making my choice very easy. A similar setup is the most popular modification for an AK rifle in the U.S. I went with the FAB Defense Galil-style M4AK folding tube and MagPul CTR stock provided by Brownells.

Next was the pistol grip. Again, the kit had essentially a copy of the Israeli design ergonomic pistol grip. Similar ones were readily available, the FAB Defense AG-47S or CAA's ergonomic pistol grip G47. Once again I opted for MagPul's AK grip as a matter of personal preference.

The handguards for my modernization kit were easier to find than those for my AK-12 clone project. The kit, unlike the AK-12 designed from scratch, had to have a set designed to replace standard-issue AK handguards. The result was a steel re-enforced plastic lower handguard with bottom rail and small sections on its sides. The new handguard slides in place of the standard one and attaches to a special mounting bracket that is bolted to the barrel. A replacement for the upper was more involved and saw a gas tube redesign. The new gas tube has no retaining brackets for the upper handguard and there is a slot cut into it for mounting a new aluminum one.

My parts bin produced a lower handguard from CAA's RS-47 AK-47 Picatinny handguard rail system. This lower guard was close in its appearance and function to the modernized Russian handguard. I used one of the removable rail sections that come with the CAA handguard set as a side rail. For the upper guard replacement, I wanted to use something stable and reliable. I decided on the UltiMAK AK-47 optics mount.

With my AKM starting to look more and more like the Russian kitted Avtomat, it was time to work on the more serious upgrades. Both new and modernized Russian guns have a full-length Picatinny rail section running on a top of the cover. Just like on my AK-12 clone, I decided to install the Parabellum Armament Group's AK Adaptive Rail System (AKARS). As I said earlier, I prefer the AKARS to similar accessories.

With appearance, ergonomics and modularity of the AKM sorted out, I could not wait to get into its innards to see if my Geissele ALG AK trigger upgrades would make a big difference in the gun's performance. I used the same set of high performance parts from Geissele ALG line: the AKT trigger group, the High Energy hammer spring and the two-zone compression return spring.

With all of the upgrades in the gun, the last upgrade was the muzzle device.

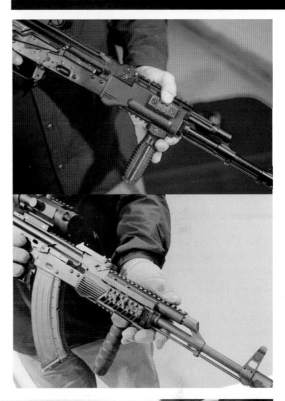

*Combination UltiMAK-CAA handguards were a good match to the new Russian kit handguards. Though the UltiMAK gas tube rail is lower than the original kit upper handguard, the author thought it would work better with non-essential accessories.*

**If you're** replacing your AK's trigger group, one worthwhile accessory that should be part of your kit is the Krebs Trigger Retainer Plate. This non-so-phisticated drop-in device replaces the standard AK "paper clip" retainer, which is not very user-friendly. All of I.O.'s AKs already come with its version of the retaining plate, making trigger group replacement much easier.

*The Russian AK modernization kit initially included a massive flame-suppressing device that was later replaced by a cage-type flash hider.*

*The first version of the kit's muzzle device consisted of a shroud with separate baffle that installed over the AK-74-type muzzle brake.*

The Russian AK modernization kit included a modification to the existing AK-74 brake, a shroud that screws on to external threads over the standard brake and secures a cone baffle on the tip of it. This was done to retain the effective muzzle brake and to reduce muzzle flash. Since I didn't want to start an engineering project and try to copy the original kit muzzle device, I was left with a prospect of finding a replacement that looked and functioned similarly.

CNC Warrior had something I thought would work for my modernized kit. I went with the AK-100-series 4-Piece Extended Brake and, since my donor gun was an AKM, a thread adapter. It worked very well. The reduction in recoil was apparent and there was significant muzzle flash reduction. However, it was very heavy. For that reason, I wound up looking for something a bit lighter but just as effective. The answer was a Russian-made Red Heat "Darkness" flash suppressor supplied by Legion USA. It was significantly lighter and worked just as well. It also looked more similar to the original.

*Both muzzle devices worked well. One was a better brake and the other a better flash hider.*

However, since the Russians changed the muzzle device that came with the kit, I had to do the same. After a quick search, I found a similar device online from K-Var Corp. A couple of days later I received a brand new FH AR-M1 Bulgarian flash hider. It lacked the external suppressor threads, but other than that it was identical to the original. It was also a very effective flash hider. I decided to keep both devices with the gun for future use.

In addition to those more complicated upgrades, I replaced the standard safety/selector lever with a Krebs Custom safety lever. I added CAA's AK-47/74 extended magazine release, and finished off my project with installation of the front vertical grip to mimic the one that was part of the Russian upgrade kit.

I compared my newly upgraded AKM to the Russian version. The result was similar to my AK-12 clone. Visually, the modernized AKM looked almost identical despite some subtle differences. The question was, would it perform better than it did as a stock AKM? I went to the range to find out.

I installed a red-dot sight on the top cover, bore-sighted the rifle using a LaserLyte bore sighting kit, and set up at the 50-yard firing line. At first I was more interested in functionality, to see if the changes in fact affected the gun's behavior and as consequence the accuracy. With my 21-inch steel humanoid targets in place, I squeezed the trigger.

I'm not a big fan of radical exclamations, but I was stunned by the drastic difference between the bare-boned AKM and my upgraded test subject. I repeated the exercise by pulling the trigger as fast as I could. The results were the same and the effect was more dramatic. The reduction in recoil was significant. While still noticeable, I could maintain a clear sight picture and re-acquire the target. With a great sense of satisfaction, I went home.

The original Russian kit included their version of the Krebs Safety to improve handling. The author went with the original Krebs product and topped off the upgrade with the CAA extended magazine release lever.

I had launched and successfully completed my very own AK modernization program to replicate the Russian version. I did it with products that are readily available and reasonable priced. Of course, I did not fully clone the Russian kit, but I came very close in appearance, functionality and especially in the spirit of this exercise.

Can the Russian modernization program be viewed as a stage in the evolution of the AK? It depends on how you look at it. This program consists of the installation of new components on existing barreled actions. Imagine for a moment that Russia did not have a stockpile of AKs in its possession and the barreled actions had to be built anew. Would it then be considered a link in the gun's evolution? I most certainly would think so. Just like the AKM or AK-74M were, years ago. This modernization program has put a huge number of Avtomats with modern features in the hands of Russian soldiers in a very short time. It also outlined the direction in which the Russian gun designers need to move when developing modern weapons.

Stepping back and looking at the modernized AKM, it appears very close to the Russian gun with their kit on it.

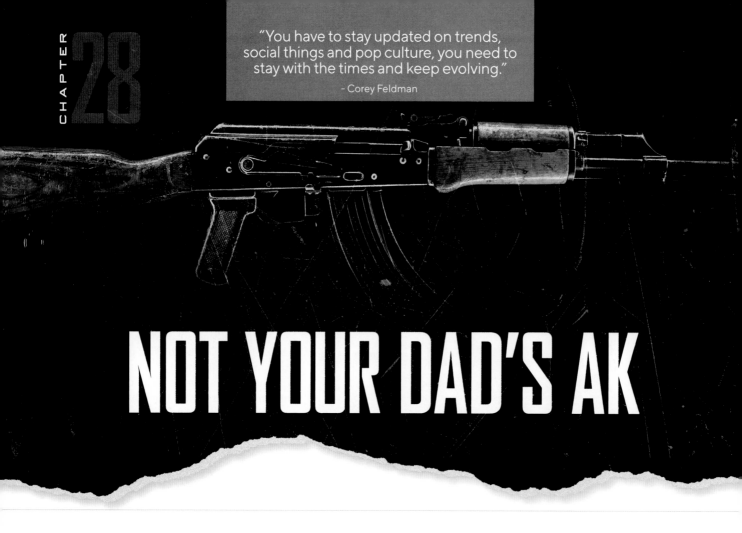

CHAPTER 28

> "You have to stay updated on trends, social things and pop culture, you need to stay with the times and keep evolving."
> - Corey Feldman

# NOT YOUR DAD'S AK

Parallel with the official AK modernization program, there was a small-scale "modernization program" going on within the ranks of the Russian special operations troops. These operatives are responsible for all of the anti-terrorism operations throughout Russia and must have guns that fully correspond to their requirements. With this in mind, the Russian top brass is pretty liberal when it comes to standard weapons upgrades by the special operations troops. Looking at numerous news reports in the media, one can see a drastic change in what the Russian troops carried decades ago and what they carry now.

In Crimea, during the developments there in 2014, the "polite green people" were mostly armed with small arms that are standard for the Russian infantry, the AK-74M with a variety of Russian AK sighting implements, RPK-74S, SVDs and Pecheneg machine guns. In stark contrast were the guns carried by Special Forces troops, who could be identified by different uniforms and equipment.

*When the armed "Green Men" or "Polite People" with no identifying features first showed up on the streets of Crimea during "Crimean Spring," for those familiar with military arms and equipment it was not a secret who these soldiers were. For the rest it was an enigma. The world saw for the first time the new Russian armed forces. Better armed and equipped, and very polite.*

It is worth noting that the special operations troops' guns, although AKs, were not similarly "dressed" and equipped, even within the same unit. Their Avtomats were accessorized reflecting their owners' preferences and the mission requirements of the individual operator. The same situation is now playing out in Syria. Russian special operations forces (CCO) troops have AKs dressed in a variety of configurations.

What did the special operations troops know when they installed a particular part or accessory on their guns? Why would they not wait for the official kit? The answer lies within the specifics of their work and their drive to do the work well with proper tools.

As a weapon platform ages, its shortcomings become increasingly evident, both those that were identified initially, and those that were identified in the course of time as the requirements for combat small arms and the nature of military operations changed. Today, the latest modification of the AK Avtomat, the AK-74M, is outdated from the professional operator's point of view.

A significant disadvantage is the AK's modularity, or rather the lack thereof. Its top cover cannot be used to mount modern types of sights (collimator, optical, night) using the Picatinny rails. Placing a heavy sight on the removable receiver cover is useless due to the fact that its fixation to the gun is not firm enough by design. The handguards do not offer options for mounting other attachments either. This puts the otherwise solid platform at a disadvantage.

However, given the freedom that we enjoy in the U.S. to accessorize our AKs, the aging but outstanding gun can be brought to the standards of today's demanding battlefield. Professional soldiers know best what type of tool to have in their bag for a particular job (read "mission"). Apparently, given the choice, they chose to upgrade their trusted AKs to some other weapons, just as was done in the U.S. for years, the term professional notwithstanding. Now the concept of AK upgrade to fit an individual and thus converting it to a viable and modern weapon has been proven by the Russian Special Forces fighting international terrorists in Syria. This is a fine example for

(top) *During the standoff with the Ukrainian military in Crimea, apart from the regular Russian troops, bystanders could see several groups of Russian special operations troops who were differently equipped and armed.*

(middle) *Having the liberty to modify their guns to suit their mission, Russian Special Forces can equip their AKs individually.*

(bottom) *Anti-terrorism units like FSB "Alfa" Group have been afforded liberties with gun modifications for a while now. Though the individual operator's expenses are compensated by the State, there is no government upgrade program for these guys.*

those who have been saying the AK hit the ceiling in its development. It can also be viewed as independent evolution of the AK as a platform.

If it's good for Russian SSO troops, it should be good for any AK shooter. As I have mentioned numerous times, I "build" or rather configure the guns I work with for me personally. It does not matter to me who the maker is of my AK, as long as it functions as it should and shoots straight. My interest is only in its barreled action and some internal components. Everything else I replace. I use the same principle as the "high speed" operators would, though I am not one. I build a mission-specific rifle that fits me as well as it can. In most cases, I would use an AK-74 rifle. Why? Personal preference. However, if you have not shot one, shoot it. No additional explanation would be necessary. No appreciable recoil is one argument, accuracy is another, light weight of ammo and gun itself, and outstanding 5.45x39mm cartridge

*(above) Today, newly established SSO (CCO, Rus. Special Operation Forces, MEV) forces in Syria sport upgraded AKs. It appears that these soldiers are upgrading their Avtomats similarly to the Alfa operators, using "what's best for the mission" principles. Though not shown here, the new "official" upgrade kit has been spotted in the hands of these soldiers.*

*(left) The author converts a standard AK-74 to resemble and function like this one, in the hands of a Russian SSO operator in Syria.*

*(below) The author will use the I.O., Inc., AK-74, which it seems is in abundant supply, and turn the Plain Jane rifle into an ISIS-killing weapon clone.*

performance should be enough for anyone to choose it as their favorite rifle.

I already described the accessories that I tested and prefer, and I used those to configure my perfect AK rifle.

First is the stock. There's no other choice for me than Mag-Pul's ZHUKOV stock. It just fits and feels right. I can install a cheek riser to accommodate optics, and it folds to the right so I can use side-mounted optics. Next is a pistol grip. Again, I went with MagPul's AK grip.

*MagPul's Zhukov stock and AK pistol grip combination is a no-brainer.*

For front handguards it was a toss-up between Midwest Industries and Krebs. I did not go with MagPul's plastic MOE guards because I wanted a top rail, just in case I use a night vision illuminator in tandem with a microdot sight or laser target designator. The aluminum handguards, with their mechanical attachment to the gun, provide enough stability for that. So, I went with Krebs' AK-U.F.M. handguards because they are smoother, smaller in circumference like original AK furniture, light and practical.

For the muzzle device, I wanted to replicate the flash hiders that are popular with the Russian Special Forces. The one I used came from Legion USA and is a flash hider with removable baffle. It worked like a charm at the range. Recoil was significantly reduced and typi-

*The Krebs Custom AK-U.F.M. handguards are smooth and light, like all Krebs products.*

cal "bowtie" AK-74 muzzle blast was gone. The flash, barely noticeable in a twilight session at the range, was a huge improvement. I kept the AK-74 muzzle device as a spare, just because it works great and there is no substitute for it yet. I also upgraded my work gun with Geissele ALG AK performance parts similar to those I used in the AK-12 clone and modernization kit builds.

That concluded a base for my perfect rifle. As for attachments, I had a few: MagPul RVG

(top) The author was pleased with the way the gun came out. He left it unpainted in case he had to use it or its accessories for other builds.

(above) This Ukrainian-made flash hider came from Legion USA. It is light, and reduces recoil and muzzle blast signature.

Author tried to upgrade a plain AK-74 to match the SSO operators' guns. It seems he succeeded.

Rail Vertical Grip because it is small, allowing me to place it closer to the receiver; a LaserLyte small center mass sight for quick target acquisition; and an L3 INSIGHT ML1-AA combat light. These last two were chosen due to their extremely light weight.

The crowning centerpiece of my perfect fighting carbine was the ELCAN Specter DR 1-4 scope. Some may say that this optics option is overkill for an AK, at more than four times the cost of the original rifle. There are more economical options, but the Specter DR is the perfect fighting carbine scope, especially for an AK-74. Its 5.56 NATO reticle with built-in BDC corresponds perfectly with 5.45x39mm cartridge trajectory out to 650 meters. You can't ask for a better match.

I mounted an ELCAN scope on the Midwest Industries' side rail scope mount, again, because it is

*(above) Though slightly on the heavy side, the ELCAN Specter DR scope works well in combination with the very light Midwest Industries mount. It also helps to distribute weight more evenly on the front-heavy AK.*

light, yet offers a solid platform for multi-power scopes. I decided to use my rifle's side mounting rail instead of top cover mounts because I wanted to retain the flexibility to switch between optical options if need arises. My newly dressed perfect rifle was complete and, after installing all the accessories excluding the Specter DR scope, I only added 0.7 lb. over the stock gun.

The reason I described my own builds is to demonstrate the point that I'm trying to drive home. Most of the AK upgrade components used in official modernization kits or on the individual weapons of Special Forces operatives are either directly from, copied or inspired by the products developed by U.S. AK accessories manufacturers, with the occasional injection of an Israeli or Russian innovation.

*Though author's favorite optic for carbines is the ELCAN Specter DR, he does use other devices, including the EOTech XPS2 and magnifier combo mounted on Midwest Industries side mount, same as on the Russian SSO soldier's gun in Syria.*

## CHAPTER 29

"The idea of waiting for something
makes it more exciting."
– Andy Warhol

# WHAT WILL THE RUSSIANS DO NEXT?

Y es, really. What will they do next? They will replace the AK-74M, but with what? One thing we know is that, to date, the AK has gone through several stages of evolution and it wound up a better weapon every time. However, something had to happen to spur each stage in its evolution, some event. Thus far, the Soviet and Russian designers were able to respond.

Because of the objective obsolescence of the AK-74 Avtomat and increased demands from the military in terms of accuracy, there has been a constant effort to replace the aging gun. What we see now is an epic struggle between the AK-12, newly released by the Izhevsk Plant, and Kovrov Arsenal's A-545. The A-545 is the modernized name for the AEK-971 Avtomat with balanced automatics described earlier in the book.

As a result of constant striving by the Russian military to increase troops' effectiveness on the battlefield, on February 21, 2015, the Defense Ministry selected both rifles as potential weapons that would be

*In recent years during the V-Day parade in Russia, spectators could see units marching in unfamiliar uniforms and sporting totally new kit guns.*

*The newly introduced Individual combat kit "Ratnik" is a fully modular loadout kit that includes everything from armor to a load-bearing system to communications and electronic equipment. It can be configured for any individual trooper depending on mission and responsibilities.*

included in the new serviceman's equipment complex "Ratnik." This complex included the battle uniform made with shrapnel-resistant aramid fabric, individual armor scalable for the specific mission, scalable load-bearing equipment, individual scalable communications set, electronic data interface and an individual weapon.

Though both Avtomats were adopted, preference was given to the AK-12 due to lower production cost and lower weight compared to the A-545. But wait, didn't we discuss the AK-12 earlier, and wasn't it rejected in favor of the modernization kit? Well, we need to remember that the modernization kit program was geared toward upgrading the enormous number of existing guns in a very short time with minimal cost to put modern weapons into the hands of Russian troops. The Ratnik complex is something different. Although, it is no longer a futuristic concept and is being issued today, it is a part of a gradual but complete re-armament initiative that Russian forces launched in 2015.

*Apart from being a fully modular and integrated universal kit that will be issued to all Russian land forces, the new Ratnik kit also includes two new Avtomats, the AK-12 and A-545, as well as machine guns and sniper rifles.*

*The A-545 Avtomat with balanced automatics is the updated version of the AEK-971.*

Again, didn't I state earlier that the new AK-12 was put on the back burner and is no longer a part of the re-armament program? I did. I will explain this in the next chapter, but first let's see what led the Russians to seek a replacement for their otherwise excellent main battle Avtomat, the AK-74M.

The AK platform had fallen behind times, and now Russia's top brass finally realized it. The major problem was not the performance of the gun. The main shortfall was with its low efficiency caused by the gun's inability to be fitted with modern battlefield implements. The accuracy of the existing AKs was also a problem. However, it can be helped by use of modern aiming implements. So, the problem that the Russian firearm designers faced was a complex one—how to combine modern modularity with desired reliability and at minimal cost.

If we talk about the degree of AK modularity, the conversation would be very short. There is no modularity in the sense of modern small arms systems, compared to the AR. Even the latest official AK modernization kit is not a permanent solution.

The high reliability of the AK family, or more precisely the methods used to achieve it, is at the same time the reason for its inherent flaws. The high momentum from the gas mechanism, in combination with the long stroke gas piston that is attached to the bolt carrier, and large gaps between all the components, lead to reliable operation even in very contaminated conditions. Most of the contaminants are literally "blown out" of the gun. On the other hand, large gaps in the bolt group mechanism are conducive to the appearance of opposing lateral impulses that move the weapon from the sighting line.

One of the disadvantages of AK is its safety/selector lever. In most modern foreign guns, the safety lever is conveniently located on the left by the pistol grip, which greatly improves handling of the gun. The Kovrovs A-545 has a similar arrangement for its safety lever.

Located on the right side, the charging handle is often seen as a disadvantage of the AK family of guns. This arrange-

*The AK-12 Kalashnikov Avtomat is the latest "simplified" version of the new gun. In its final design the AK-12 was brought back closer to the standard AK-74M.*

This latest version of the AK-12, after field-testing by the Russian military, is most likely the gun that will slowly but surely push older AKs (including the modernized ones) out of service sometime in the future.

ment was at one time adopted on the basis of very practical considerations. The left-handed charging handle would "dig" into soldier's chest when the gun was slung in front, it would snag on things when crawling and, finally, it would make it impossible to charge the gun when it was slung across the chest. Interesting note: The original Kalashnikov design had the charging handle on the left, but that was later rejected for the reasons above. However, other solutions could be considered.

Ergonomics of all AK variants is often criticized. The AK stock is considered unnecessarily short, and the handguards are not very practical. However, this weapon was created taking into account its use while wearing winter clothes and gloves.

Factory AK sights are considered rather coarse from the modern point of view, and a short sighting line does not contribute to high accuracy of the gun.

Most AK variants significantly upgraded by foreign shooters are equipped with more modern aiming devices, in most cases installing a collimator, reflex or optical sight.

In general, the AK certainly has many positive qualities and will continue to be suitable for combat in the future. At the same time, it's obvious that it needs to be replaced by more modern models, with radical design differences that would not encompass the shortcomings from the obsolete system.

American AK enthusiasts have been modernizing their AKs for many years now, bringing them closer to the modern counterparts. The Russian special operations troops followed suit with their battlefield hardware. Now it is the turn of the Russian armed forces to arm troops with something that has all the features of the modern weapon system, retains the positives and lacks the shortfalls of the previous gun.

This is the puzzle that the AK designers have to solve.

Based on its performance and accuracy, the A-545 (AEK-971) most likely will see plenty of action with Russia's armed forces in the years to come.

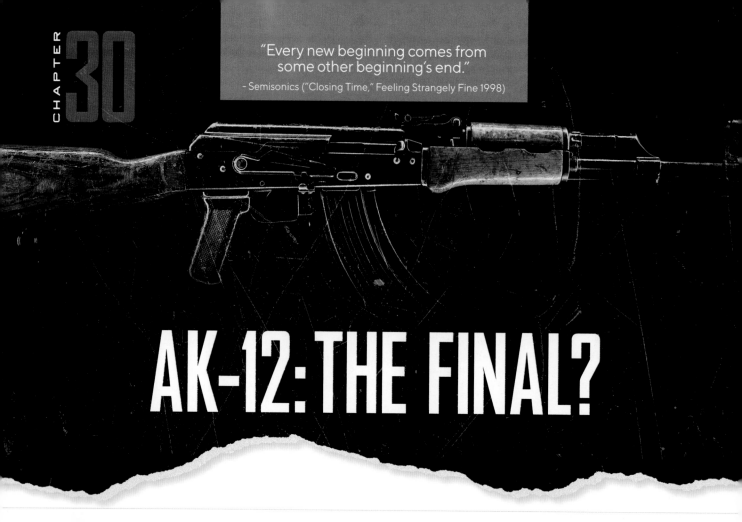

## CHAPTER 30

"Every new beginning comes from
some other beginning's end."

– Semisonics ("Closing Time," Feeling Strangely Fine 1998)

# AK-12: THE FINAL?

**A**s the AK evolution continues, it will reach critical mass when drastic gun re-design must occur to guide further development of the AK. The AK-12 Avtomat is the newest version of the Kalashnikov-designed rifle, created in 2012. It is a promising product developed by the Kalashnikov Concern at its Izhevsk Plant. The main feature of the AK-12 is improved ergonomics and modularity in comparison with its predecessors, the AKM, AK-74 and AK-74M. According to the gun designers, they improved the service life, reliability and accuracy of the gun. The AK-12 demonstrates excellent characteristics during initial testing. It has less recoil, better cooling, is lighter and shorter, and can be reloaded with one hand. That's why in 2015 the AK-12 Kalashnikov Avtomat was adopted and will be used as the main personal weapon for the Russian individual soldier equipment complex Ratnik.

Is it the same AK-12 they demonstrated in 2012? Not really. In fact, not at all.

The development of the new machine started in June 2011 under the leadership of the well-known chief designer of Izhmash, Vladimir Viktorovich Zlobin. It was entirely an Izhmash initiative. The new AK was based on the work and experience accumulated over the last 10 years. In 2011, the prototype was completed and testing of the fifth-generation Avtomat with the name AK-12 began. The AK-12 is designed to replace the previous versions of the AK-103, AK-74M, AK-74 and early AKM, AKMS and all other AKs still in service.

For the first time, the AK-12 was shown to the public in January 2012, hence its index "12." The main goals in the development of the AK-12 were to:

• Increase the universality of the gun.

• Improve the ergonomic characteristics.

• Preserve and possibly improve the gun's main performance characteristics (accuracy of fire, survivability, reliability in different modes).

The Russian government was not eager to provide any support to development of the new Avtomat, citing the success of old AKs. So, they didn't. During the period of 2013 and 2014, the AK-

*The new and perhaps final version of the AK-12 is very different from the gun the Russians unveiled in 2012.*

12 encountered some opposition from the Russian military under the pretext of many shortcomings, so state financing of the trials was denied. Nevertheless, on February 21, 2015, the Ministry of Defense evaluated the characteristics of the newly upgraded AK-12. As a result, it was adopted as the main weapon for the Ratnik individual equipment complex, alongside its more expensive and heavier competitor , the A-545. It also received a preferential role over the balanced automatics Avtomat.

*The newer version of the AK-12 in its design was brought back to the original Kalashnikov system. However, it now also included most of the ergonomic, handling and modular features of the previous model.*

In 2015, after preliminary tests, the fifth-generation Avtomat, already adopted for service, got a number of upgrades. The highlighted deficiencies were not critical to the design and would be corrected within a year. After the new Avtomat was tested again and passed the government tests with flying colors, its arrival in the Russian armed forces was slotted for 2016.

The AK-12 has the following tactical and technical characteristics:

- Caliber: 5.45x39mm
- Length: 730/940 mm (29.75/37 inches) with stock folded/unfolded
- Weight (without cartridges): 3.2 kg (7.1 lbs.)
- Barrel length: 415mm (16.3 inches)
- Bullet velocity: 900m/s (2,952 fps)
- Rate of fire: 650 rds/min.
- Max. aiming range: 1,000 m.
- Max. effective range: 600 m.
- Magazine capacity: 95 rounds for drum magazine, 30 or 60 rounds for box-type mags
- Firing modes: automatic, fixed 3-shot burst and single shot

All of this is in line with its previous model. You do not have to be an experienced firearms designer or famous gunsmith to see that the new AK-12, though it is a clearly a new weapon type, is still an AK. In fact, it appears to be a compromise between the original AK-12 and the modernization kit.

It appears to have the standard AK-74 stamped receiver, which encompasses the standard trigger and bolt groups. It takes a slight departure from the norm in a copy of the Krebs enhanced safety lever, which is not what the highly publicized original AK-12 had. There is no button mag release. Instead, the regular AK latch is used. The AR-style telescopic stock is installed instead of the multi-functional stock of the original gun. The stock-folding mechanism is identical to the AK-74. My very own AKS had the same one 30 years ago. The pistol grip is more ergonomic, and similar to one from Israel's FAB Defense or CAA. The top cover is hinged, using completely new mounting and retention mechanisms, but similar to the modernization kit nonetheless. The rear sight block is modified and no longer supports the rear sight. Instead, it is now used for the top cover hinge and to retain the upper handguard more firmly. The rear sight block is now removable and can be installed anywhere along the Picatinny rail that runs the entire length of the top cover and aligns perfectly with the section atop the upper handguard. The upper handguard has two mounting spots for small Picatinny rail sections, one on each side. The matching lower handguard has the rail at the bottom. The length of the handguards is about the same of those on the AK-74 with exception of the upper.

The differences begin forward of the handguards. Although the gas tube appears to have the same length and similar design, minus the upper handguard brackets, the gas block is a different story. It is a gas/front sight block combination of new design. It is higher than the standard AK and has the gas chamber going all the way forward, where it is topped with a gas regulator. The accessory lug is at the bottom of the combination block for mounting a grenade launcher. The muzzle of the upgraded AK-12 is tipped with a threaded block that sports a detent pin and bayonet lug. The gun uses two different muzzle devices. One is a modified version of the AK-74 brake and the other is similar to that of the Polish Tantal rifle. It is slimmer than the original AK-74 brake and much longer. According to AK-12 designers, this was done for use with foreign rifle grenades. I like the idea. I also think that the Polish Tantal muzzle brake is very effective.

That's it. That's what the AK evolved into. I don't know why the Russians didn't go with the original AK-12 design and instead settled for this one. Most likely, it was a question of funds needed for retooling the plant and more complicated (read more expensive) manufacturing process. However, I rather like it. It is intimately familiar to AK fans, it has all the features that a modern gun should have, it's lightweight and looks like a comfortable rifle. In addition, if you believe the designers, it is a better shooting AK than its predecessors. I would not mind owning one.

However, since there is no possibility of the AK-12 in its Saiga livery ever making it here, I have to build one.

Choosing a gun for the AK-12 build was a challenge. Needing an AK-74 with front sight/gas block combination, the solution came in the form of I.O., Inc.'s hybrid of a Bulgarian kit-built AK-74 and the M214 rifle.

## BUILDING MY OWN

By now you know I had to see if the latest solutions employed by the Kalashnikov Concern's gun designers could be replicated. I had to build one of my own to find out if it handles or shoots as claimed.

I once more embarked on the exciting journey of replicating something I cannot have otherwise. My biggest challenge initially was to find a donor gun in the proper caliber. There were two ways to do this. One was to find a complete gun with gas/front sight combination in 5.45x39mm. The other was to get a standard AK-74 and press off the gas block and front sight and replace them with the combo. I spent a week looking around and considering my options. The solution was an I.O., Inc., prototype rifle. The new rifle the company was working on was a combination of its M214 rifle and the AK-74. The new rifle had a combination block and threaded barrel. Exactly what I needed.

Having obtained a donor rifle, it was time to collect the rest of the components. By analyzing images of the new Russian AK-12, I came up with a list. Yet again, I tapped into FAB Defense, Brownells, Geissele Automatics, Legion USA and K-Vary Corp. as sources for the needed components. Additionally, I anticipated some actual gunsmithing work would need to be done to finish this project.

*I.O. Inc.'s rifle had two very important features: the front sight/gas block combination and the 14mm left-hand thread at the muzzle.*

As always, I started with the buttstock because it is the easiest thing to replace. By looking at the new AK-12 stock, I could not help but notice that it bears an uncanny resemblance to MagPul's CTR model. Telescopic and folding features for the AK-12 were easier to copy. Out of consideration for weight, I went with the FAB Defense plastic joint M4-AK P folding tube and MagPul CTR stock, once more provided by Brownells.

Just like the earlier model AK-12 and the modernization kit, the new gun's pistol grip is essentially a copy of CAA's ergonomic grip, the G47. FAB Defense was gracious enough to provide its AG-47S grip for the project; it is similar in design and fits perfectly on the gun.

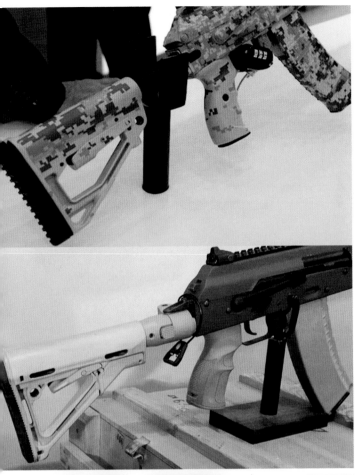

(above) The FAB Defense AKL-47/74 handguards proved to be a pretty good match for the AK-12 guards.

(top left) To match the look and most importantly the functionality of the AK-12 stock and pistol grip, the author used the FAB Defense M4-AK P folding plastic AR tube, MagPul's CTR stock and a FAB Defense AG-47S grip.

(bottom left) The Russian-made Red Heat AK dust cover provided by Legion USA with full-length Picatinny rail section in combination with original Russian safety/selector lever were a spot-on match.

I had to ponder which handguards to use on my AK-12 clone this time. The new Russian AK has handguards that are matching in length and parallel, with rails at the top and bottom. The clue came from the way the side rail sections mount the handguards. The AK-12's Picatinny side rails mount to the upper handguard, instead of the more traditional way to the lower. FAB Defense makes its AKL-47/74 guards with the same mounting option. After taking a closer look at these handguards I thought they were very similar to the originals. I got the FAB Defense handguards and installed them on my gun using standard AK brackets and hardware.

I chose the dark earth color for my accessories to most closely resemble the original.

The next step turning the I.O., Inc., gun into the newest Russian AK was the hinged top cover. As previously noted, I have considerable experience with these and used them on previous builds. My preferred railed top cover was the Parabellum AKARS. Except this time I wanted something else. My search revealed the Russian Red Heat AK dust cover with rail from Legion USA. It installed into the rear side leaf hinge and dropped into place as if it was an original part. Once on the gun, I noticed that it matched the upper handguard rail height perfectly. My rifle was starting to look like the original AK-12. Nevertheless, there was still plenty to do.

One more part that came from Legion USA was the Russian version of the Krebs Enhanced Safety lever. I thought I would stay as authentic as I could and used it on my clone along with the Geissele ALG AK High Energy Hammer Spring and the two-zone compression return spring.

I decided to try a different trigger group for the AK-12 this time. I opted for the FIME Group's (affiliated with K-Var Corp. and Arsenal USA) FM-922US trigger group. It was a drop-in replacement and had the look of the regular AK trigger, but with definite performance improvement.

The main body of the gun was done with the updates and, from the front sight/gas block back, it looked pretty close to the AK-12 Avtomat.

It was time for gunsmithing. I needed to find a block with detent pin and bayonet lug that would be pressed over the threaded barrel. Also, there was the matter of which muzzle brake to use. After a search, I decided to go with Polish Tantal parts. The Tantal's front sight had the bayonet lug and detent pin I needed. All I had to do was cut it, grind it and press it on. The Tantal muzzle device is highly effective as a brake and happens to be one of my favorite brakes.

Additionally, there was an issue with the gun's open sights. Since I had to remove the original rear sight, I had to find a substitute to go on top of the receiver cover with one caveat, it had to be very low. There was only one that I knew about, the TWS peephole sight, and I got it. The front sight also pre-

(above) The earlier version of the AK-12 muzzle device was a departure from the standard AK-74 type brake. It resembled the Polish Tantal device, affording the ability to launch rifle grenades.

(left) The later version of the AK-12 sported a familiar muzzle device, though slightly modified for flash and sound suppressor installation.

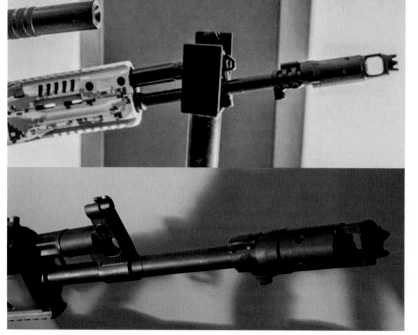

sented a problem that required some milling. The original I.O. front sight had a circle hood over the sight post. The higher-sitting handguards and a rail on the top of the receiver cover rendered the original sight useless. I needed to mill the top off the sight to provide more room for the post.

With my unfinished gun and with several parts in tow, I headed to the Erie Ordnance

In the end, the author was successful in cloning the newest Russian AK Avtomat. The clone gun appears to have a longer barrel. This was dictated by the location of the gas port on the original Bulgarian barrel.

It was not possible to match the new gun's entire list of features, like the adjustable gas system or additional accessory lug. However, the author came pretty darn close.

Depot (EOD) shop in Portage, Northern Ohio. Jim Weishuhn, owner of EOD, is a master gunsmith I often call upon when I reach the limits of my gunsmithing abilities. Having a full shop, he often helps me with my projects. This time was not different. We cut the Tantal front sight, creating a detent pin block, ground it into shape and pressed it on the barrel of my AK-12 clone, past the threaded tip exposing enough thread to install a muzzle brake. Jim pinned the block in place with a working detent pin. Next, he machined an opening in the enclosed front sight hood, making it more suitable for front sight adjustment and better looking. With the gun nearly complete, we moved on to the two muzzle brakes. All we had to do was modify the tips of both brakes to mimic the Russian parts. After Jim machined both muzzle brakes, all that was left was to refinish the modified parts of the gun.

It was done. Stepping back and looking at my creation, I was very satisfied with the way the AK-12 looked. It looked very close to the original.

*Not only did my AK-12 clone closely resemble the Russian Avtomat, it also shot exceptionally well.*

I did try to use most of the accessories in Dark Earth color to match the Russian AK-12, but stopped short of painting the whole gun, instead retaining the option of reconfiguring it later. Nevertheless, my AK-12 felt light and had an aura of "niftiness" about it. I have shouldered it several times and it felt almost intuitive. The ergonomics were improved and, at the same time, it retained the AK familiarity. Other than, it looked and felt like a foreign gun and it also looked and felt like an AK. It cycled very well with no hang-ups. All controls worked as they should, and the two-stage FIME Group trigger group felt very crisp. The only question was, would it shoot and would it shoot well?

At the range, I set up at 50 yards, as I was more interested in the gun's function than accuracy. I would check that later. For the first series of tests I installed the modified AK-74 brake to see if there was a difference between the standard AK-74 and my newly minted clone. First shots did not disappoint. The clone worked great and, in the best AK-74 tradition, was easy to shoot with no appreciable recoil.

I switched the muzzle devices, installing the modified Tantal brake. With the Polish-design brake, the next series of shots was surprising. The gun was noticeably smoother and its already almost negligible recoil was reduced even further. I was

impressed to say the least. So far, the gun was working well. Of course, I could not compare it the original. However, assumptions could be made. And, if the Russians did similar internal upgrades as I'd done, the new AK-12 is better than the AK-74M. I'm not putting myself in the same group with Russian firearm designers, engineers

*Here it is, my very own, the latest in the AK Evolution species, the AK-12 that I built mostly in my basement, with a little help from my friends.*

and gun makers. Even though I'm a mechanical engineer, I don't know the intricacies of the firearm design. All I can do is wrap my head around the mechanics of it, add some physics principles, and try to replicate a result, sort of a "proof of a concept," if you will. So, as far as I was concerned, it worked. My AK-12 clone looked very similar to the Russian AK-12 Avtomat and shot exceptionally well, enough for me to adopt it as one of my work rifles.

At the range, I continued to test my new gun. I used its open sights to see if it would produce a decent group and it did. All 30 rounds nestled in a tight group at the 1 o'clock spot, approximately 1 inch off the bull's eye of the target. At 100 yards, my group opened up some, but was still way within my expectations. In my hands, I had a gun that not only looked and felt great, but also worked well.

After installing a generic red-dot sight, I went to work on steel silhouette targets set up at 50 and 100 yards. It was a pleasure to put it mildly. The AK-12 clone's meager recoil allowed me to maintain a dot on the target while firing at all times and at both distances. Rapid semi-auto fire was an easy task. The gun felt like something you want to fire on the move during a carbine course or competition. I love the fact that I was able once more to build a gun that closely mimics the appearance and possibly the performance of the newest Russian Avtomat, and I did it with parts available in the U.S. at reasonable prices.

Is the AK-12 the last AK, the last link in its evolution? I don't know. In fact, no one does. As the "Old Guard" gun makers die off or retire, more and more voices in Russia today call for a completely new firearms system. It is time to replace the ancient technology, they say. I'm not sure I agree with them. One part of me, the engineering part, agrees. I would always love to see something new and different. But, would I stake my life on it? That's where my other side takes over, the practical side, the soldier side, the reasonable side. Why would anybody want to replace a gun platform that has been in service for 80 years? Maybe I let the Russian in me take over with its trademark conservatism. If it's not broke, don't fix it, I say.

# EPILOGUE

**A**fter researching the material for this book, writing it and then editing it, I could not help but notice that there was a "cosmic" event in the evolution of the AK that separated the process into two distinct parts. One was more of the natural and organic development of the AK "species" from inception to the last Soviet AK, the AK-74. The other resembled a collision of particles in the Large Hadron Collider. At the collision, particles explode into a wild array of trajectories and patterns. That's what happened after the fall of the Soviet Union and entry of the AK platform into the world of a free economy.

At this very point, the AK evolution took a radical, accelerated and random path, creating a variety of subspecies. Due to severed relationships, expired or ignored licenses, desire to capitalize on the established platform or drive to invent and innovate, we acquired the ability to possess an awesome array of Kalashnikov platform-based variants, everything from the tactical-looking WASR-10 to the purpose-built Krebs Custom Assneck SBR.

One might say that the evolution of the AK is winding down, and that the platform has lived to its full potential and should just move aside giving way to more modern firearms designs. I certainly do not share these views. We've heard all of this before, and look at AKs now. As a pragmatic, I cannot wait to see what the designers and engineers, no matter where—Russia, Europe, the U.S.—come up with next. I'm sure I won't be disappointed.

The reason I went through the trouble of building clone guns to match the functionality of "newly created" AKs was to see if I could put together something that is representative of the next stage of AK evolution. As you can see, I was able to do it with relative ease. Do the latest "tactical" models of the AK represent an evolution, or just an adaptation to the environment? It's not for me to decide. It seems that all I did to turn my standard model AKs into the modern Russian Avtomats was replace standard-issue components with aftermarket parts and accessories. The main and vital components, the barreled action, stayed intact. The gun has changed in appearance, but remained original inside. Does that make it an advanced species of evolution? Or was the platform, at the time of its inception, so ahead of its time that a few modern external accessories instantly bring it up to date? Though I have my personal opinion, I leave it for others to decide. It is for the historians to ponder, for fans to believe and for haters to hate.

When I started to work on this book, I planned to write something that was different from the field. I did not want to create another Wikipedia re-write. Everybody already knew the story of the Siberian tank mechanic and his gun. What is the point in repeating something that has been told by so many, and so many times? I wanted to discover and share something different. Something that was not readily available to AK enthusiasts at large. I dug deep and was rewarded with juicy tidbits of information. I made remarks on several subjects expressing my personal opinions based on the information I have or my personal beliefs. I also made some analysis of events. I hope you found something new and intriguing in these pages. If you did, then my job here is done.

Thank you for reading,
Marco

*P.S. As I was finishing this book, something happened that is worth mentioning, something without which this book would not be complete. In September of 2017, the Russians unveiled a monument to Mikhail Kalashnikov in the center of the Russian capitol, Moscow. It is an awesome composition, with St. George defeating the dragon, signifying victory and the strength of Russian arms. There is a statue of the man himself holding his creation. And, there is a panel featuring Kalashnikov's iconic guns. One can even trace AK evolution from the submachine gun to the AK-74M.*

*A truly fitting commemoration to the great designer, or is it? It would have been. Except for a small detail—the drawing of the Nazi Stg. 44 Sturmgewehr as a part of the gun panel in the memorial composition. I'm pretty sure that the sculptor simply made a mistake. Seeing how he was not a firearm specialist, when commissioned to do the work, he most likely searched* the web for suitable images for his models. And, since the name of Kalashnikov and his Avtomat is permanently attached to Schmeisser's gun because of a myth perpetrated by the less knowledgeable AK haters, the sculptor grabbed the drawing, not paying attention to what it actually was. The mistake was uncovered the day after unveiling and the panel section was promptly removed. However, the damage was done. A simple mistake by a "creative" type gave fuel to conspiracy theorists. The omen they say, the premonition... mistake! That's all it was, a small and insignificant mistake, however controversial. Even in death, Mikhail Timofeyevich Kalashnikov cannot escape controversy.

(above) Befitting a national hero, this monument, designed to commemorate a truly remarkable person—Mikhail Timofeyevich Kalashnikov—was recently unveiled in the center of Russia's capitol.

(left) Because of the ignorance of the sculptor and indifference of those who approved the project, the joyous occasion was marred by a stupid mistake, giving fuel to conspiracy mongers. The panel with Stg. 44 drawing has since been removed.